Lone Star Legacy II

A Texas Cookbook

LONE STAR LEGACY
AN OFFICIAL SESQUICENTENNIAL COOKBOOK
TEXAS
SESQUICENTENNIAL
1836–1986
© 1981 State of Texas

Austin Junior Forum

The objective of Austin Junior Forum is to create a greater interest among young women in civic, educational and philanthropic fields. All proceeds from the sale of *Lone Star Legacy II* will be returned to the community through Austin Junior Forum projects.

Library of Congress No. 85-72515
ISBN 0-9607152-1-5

Additional copies may be obtained at the cost of $14.95 per book, plus $2.00 postage and handling. Texas residents add $.77 sales tax. Send to:
Austin Junior Forum Publications
P.O. Box 26628
Austin, Texas 78755-0628

Photography by Mike Flahive
Austin, Texas
Cover Photo Courtesy of *Texas Highways*

First Printing October 1985, 30,000

Printed by Hart Graphics, Inc.
8000 Shoal Creek Blvd.
Austin, Texas 78767

Foreword

One hundred and fifty years have passed since the Lone Star banner of Texas first waved freely in the breeze. It seems appropriate that our second cookbook should be published as a Sesquicentennial gift to our state.

We are deeply grateful for the warm reception LONE STAR LEGACY has received in the homes and hearts of cookbook collectors everywhere. Its success has enabled us to realize a dream of our own — the restoration of a gracious historical home, the Daniel H. Caswell House, to its former elegance and grandeur. Now, as the home of Austin Junior Forum, we can open the doors of our "living legacy" to friends and neighbors throughout the community.

We are delighted to offer another collection of special recipes, shared with us by past and present friends. Our new collection has been selected to reflect the flavors and aromas that are uniquely Texas. These recipes, compiled and tested with the same painstaking care and dedication as those in our first book, will bring a bit of Texas into your kitchen.

With a deep sense of pride and gratitude, we present our contribution to the Texas Sesquicentennial Celebration, LONE STAR LEGACY II.

The Cookbook Committee sincerely appreciates the enthusiastic participation of the club membership in testing and compiling the recipes for this book.

Cookbook Committee

Sandra Smith, Chairman

Kathy Baker, Co-Chairman

Beverly Bone, Co-Chairman

Barbara Arndt

Mary Bowles

Melinda Bradford

Carol Bruney

Kathy Gordon

Mary Beth McMillon

Bonnie Moyer

Mary Kay Schultz

Diana Smith

Julie Sentell

Contents

Wine is a relatively new product for Texas, amazingly enough. Although the state has been touted for its rich soil and moderate climate, vineyards have only recently changed the landscape of the Texas Hill Country and points west. Fall Creek Vineyards, in Tow, Texas, was established in 1975. The primary grape varieties grown for their wines conjure up images of misty green valleys in Europe, with names like Sauvignon Blanc, Chardonnay, Chenin Blanc, Emerald Riesling, Cabernet Sauvignon, Carnelian and Zinfandel.

Appetizers and Beverages pictured: Stuffed Mushrooms, Stuffed Cherry Tomatoes, Ham Pinwheels, White Sangria, Escargot Monterey, Good Times Cheese Roll, Coconut Dip for Fruit, Frozen Strawberry Daiquiri, Ceviche and Pousse Cafe.

Appetizers and Beverages

Cold Artichoke Dip

1 package (0.8 ounces) buttermilk dressing mix
8 ounces cream cheese, softened

1 cup mayonnaise
1 can (14 ounces) artichoke hearts, drained and chopped
Crackers

Mix all dip ingredients together and chill. Yields 2½ cups. *This is a very easy and good dip. Serve with crackers.*

Mrs. John Perkins (Sandy)

Artichoke Bacon Dip

1 can (14 ounces) artichoke hearts, well drained
½ cup mayonnaise
1 tablespoon minced onion
1 teaspoon lemon juice
⅛ teaspoon salt

Dash of white pepper
Dash of cayenne pepper
4 slices of bacon, fried crisp, drained and crumbled
Chips or crackers

Coarsely chop artichoke hearts and put into a medium sized mixing bowl. Add mayonnaise, onion, lemon juice, salt and peppers. Mix on medium speed of electric mixer for about 1 minute. Refrigerate for several hours. Just prior to serving, stir in crumbled bacon. Yields 2½ cups. *Serve as a dip with corn chips or as a spread with crackers. This dip may also be served warm and is best made a day ahead.*

Mrs. Terry Arndt (Barbara)

Caviar Dip for Artichokes

½ cup mayonnaise
1 tablespoon lemon juice

1 jar (2 ounces) whitefish caviar
2 artichokes, cooked and chilled

Combine mayonnaise, lemon juice and caviar, mixing well. Dip with leaves and hearts of artichokes. Yields ¾ cup.

Mrs. Cecil Smith (Diana)

Fresh Artichokes with Lemon and Sour Cream

2 fresh artichokes	½ cup butter
Seasoned salt	Juice of 2 lemons
Garlic powder	3 tablespoons sour cream
Lemon pepper marinade	Salt and pepper to taste

Remove stems from artichokes with a sharp knife. Make an X at the base and run under cold water for 5 minutes; drain. Season with seasoned salt, garlic powder and lemon pepper marinade while damp. Place in a steamer basket over water. Cover and cook over medium heat 1 hour. Prior to serving, melt butter in small saucepan. Add lemon and sour cream to make a sauce. Salt and pepper to taste. Serve on a tray large enough to accommodate leaves after dipping. Serves 10.

Mrs. Steve McMillon (Mary Beth)

Avocado Dip

2 large avocados	½ cup mayonnaise
8 ounces cream cheese, softened	1 teaspoon lemon juice
	1 teaspoon garlic salt

Mash avocados and add softened cream cheese, mayonnaise, lemon juice and garlic salt. Beat with electric mixer until smooth. Serve at once. Yields approximately 2 cups.

Mrs. Glen Noble (Sharon)

Spicy Avocado Dip

1 can (10 ounces) tomatoes with green chilies	1 tablespoon minced onion
1 envelope (1.25 ounces) onion soup mix	2 teaspoons Worcestershire sauce
6 ounces cream cheese, softened	Juice of 1 lemon
3 avocados, mashed	Salt to taste
	Tostados

Drain tomatoes with green chilies and chop. Add remaining ingredients, and mix well. Serve with tostados. Yields 3½ cups.

Mrs. Marcus Bone (Beverly)

Blackeyed Pea Dip

½ green bell pepper, chopped
1 rib celery, chopped
1 tablespoon hot pepper sauce
½ cup catsup
3 chicken bouillon cubes
¼ teaspoon cinnamon
8 jalapeños, chopped
1 onion, chopped

1 teaspoon pepper
1 tablespoon salt
¼ teaspoon nutmeg
2 cans (16 ounces each) blackeyed peas
½ cup chopped tomatoes
1 teaspoon garlic powder
½ cup bacon drippings
3 tablespoons flour
Chips or crackers

In a large saucepan, combine bell pepper, celery, hot pepper sauce, catsup, bouillon cubes, cinnamon, jalapeños, onion, pepper, salt and nutmeg. Simmer for 20 minutes. Add blackeyed peas, tomatoes and garlic powder. Simmer 30 minutes. Blend flour with bacon drippings. Pour into cooked mixture and simmer 15 minutes. Serve with chips or crackers. Yields 1½ quarts. *This is powerfully hot, but wonderful! Adjust hot pepper sauce and jalapeños to taste.*

Mrs. Clay Wilkins (Marion)

Chutney Dip

16 ounces cream cheese, softened
¼ to ½ cup whipping cream

6 ounces chutney
Fresh fruit and crackers

Whip cheese with cream; then beat in the chutney. Serve with sliced apples, pears and sesame crackers. Serves 12 to 16.

Mrs. Greg Gordon (Kathy)

Cucumber and Bacon Dip

4 slices bacon
2 cups sour cream
½ cup grated cucumber
1 envelope (1.25 ounces) onion salad dressing mix

2 tablespoons chopped pimiento
2 tablespoons lemon juice
½ teaspoon Worcestershire sauce
Vegetable dippers

Cook bacon until crisp; drain and crumble; set aside. Mix sour cream, cucumber, dressing mix, pimiento, lemon juice and Worcestershire sauce. Chill at least 30 minutes. Before serving, stir in crumbled bacon. Serve with vegetable dippers. Yields 2 cups.

Mrs. Marcus Bone (Beverly)

Spicy Egg Dip

6 hard cooked eggs, finely chopped
1 tablespoon butter, softened
1¼ teaspoons imitation smoke flavor
2 teaspoons lemon juice
1 tablespoon prepared mustard

2 teaspoons Worcestershire sauce
1 drop hot pepper sauce
½ teaspoon salt
1 teaspoon minced onion
½ teaspoon pepper
¼ to ½ cup mayonnaise
Fresh vegetables or shrimp for dipping

Combine all dip ingredients and blend until smooth in blender. Chill 4 to 5 hours before serving. Thirty minutes before serving, whip to soften. Use as a dip for fresh veggies or shrimp. Yields 2 cups.

Mrs. Jim Schultz (Mary Kay)

Raw Vegetable Dip

1 cup mayonnaise
1 cup sour cream
2 tablespoons minced onion
1 large clove garlic, minced
1 teaspoon salt

½ teaspoon pepper
½ cup chopped fresh parsley
1 tablespoon Dijon mustard
Raw vegetable dippers

Blend all ingredients and refrigerate for 2 to 3 hours. Yields 2 cups. *Serve on a bed of iceburg lettuce as a dip for raw vegetables.*

Mrs. James C. Doss (Charlene)

Texas Garden Dip

1 package (10 ounces) frozen chopped spinach
1 can (14 ounces) artichoke hearts, drained
1 cup sour cream
1 teaspoon pepper

½ cup grated Parmesan cheese
3 tablespoons chopped green onion
Vegetable dippers or chips

Cook spinach according to package directions and drain well. Place all ingredients in blender. Blend at medium speed until well blended. Chill several hours or overnight. Serve with vegetables or chips. Yields 3 cups.

Mrs. B. Lynn Turlington (Jill)

Coconut Rum Dip

8   ounces cream cheese
1   carton (8 ounces) sour
    cream
¼   cup powdered sugar
¼   cup rum
¼   teaspoon nutmeg
½   cup coconut
½   cup coconut, toasted
Fresh fruit

Mix all ingredients except toasted coconut together in blender and blend until smooth. Chill; top with toasted coconut and serve with fresh fruit. Yields 2½ cups. *This dip is pretty when served in a coconut shell for a patio party.*

Mrs. Denman Smith (Sandra)

Sir Loin Dip

1½ pounds sirloin steak,
    uncooked
½   pound sliced cooked ham
1   apple, peeled and cored
4 to 5 slices sharp Cheddar
    cheese
4 to 5 sweet or dill pickles
1   cup fresh quartered
    tomatoes
¼ to ½ cup hot pepper sauce
¼ to ½ cup lemon juice
Assorted crackers or chips

Run everything through a grinder, 3 to 4 times, or until you get the taste you want. The more times ground, the hotter. Use as a dip with crackers, tostados, chips or flour tortillas. Serves 8 to 10.

S. D. Jackman

Crab Meat Dip

2   cups mayonnaise
1   cup small curd cottage
    cheese
¼ to ½ cup finely chopped
    onion
¼   teaspoon salt
¼   teaspoon hot pepper sauce
1½ tablespoons
    Worcestershire sauce
½   teaspoon celery seed
½   teaspoon caraway seed
¼   teaspoon garlic salt
½   tablespoon dry mustard
½   teaspoon pepper
1   cup crab meat
Potato chip dippers

Combine all ingredients together except crab meat and mix well. Set in refrigerator overnight. Just before serving add crab meat and mix well. Serve with potato chips. Yields 4 cups dip.

Mrs. Greg Gordon (Kathy)

Crab and Cheese Dip

1   stick (10 ounces) sharp
    Cheddar cheese
1   package (8 ounces) sliced
    American cheese
¼   cup butter

¼   cup sherry
¼   cup white wine
1   carton (16 ounces) crab
    meat
Wheat wafers or bread cubes

Cut cheese into small pieces and combine with butter, sherry and wine in saucepan. Stir over low heat until cheese melts. Stir in drained, shredded crab meat. Serves 8 to 12. *This may be served in a fondue pot or on a warming plate with wheat wafers or chunks of crusty bread.*

Mrs. Gary McKenzie (Claire)

Very Special Crab Fondue

8   ounces cream cheese
1   pound processed cheese
1   cup white wine

1   package (6 ounces)
    Alaskan snow crab
Toasted French bread squares

Cube and slowly melt cheeses with wine; fold in thawed crab meat. Serve with toasted French bread squares for fondue. Serves 12 to 15.

Mrs. Robert David Stallings (Sheila)

Hot Crab Meat Dip

1   package (6 ounces) frozen
    crab meat
8   ounces cream cheese
¼   cup evaporated milk
3   tablespoons dry white
    wine
½   teaspoon lemon juice

1   teaspoon prepared
    mustard
⅛ to ¼ teaspoon garlic
    powder
¼ to ½ teaspoon curry
    powder
Potato chips

Combine crab meat, cream cheese, evaporated milk, wine, lemon juice, mustard and garlic powder. Place in a casserole dish. Sprinkle curry powder on top and bake at 350° for 20 minutes. Yields 2½ cups. *This is a great dip served with potato chips.*

Mrs. Larry Strickland (Linda)

Exotic Dip

¼ cup finely chopped pecans
   or walnuts
4 strips bacon, cooked and
   crumbled, divided
6 ounces cream cheese,
   softened

4 ounces Bleu cheese
½ cup mayonnaise
¼ teaspoon salt
¼ teaspoon white pepper
Crackers

Combine all ingredients, reserving one half of bacon to sprinkle on top. Serve with assorted crackers. Yields 2 cups.

Ada Smyth

Spinach Salmon Dip

1 can (7¾ ounces) salmon
1 package (10 ounces)
   chopped frozen spinach,
   thawed and squeezed dry
1 cup mayonnaise
1 cup sour cream

½ cup chopped fresh parsley
1 tablespoon lemon juice
1 teaspoon grated onion
½ teaspoon dried dill weed
Chips or vegetable dippers

Drain and flake salmon. Combine with remaining ingredients. Chill for several hours and serve with chips or crisp vegetables. Yields 5 cups of dip.

Mrs. Jim Rado (Vicki)

Asparagus Dip

1 package (10 ounces)
   frozen chopped asparagus,
   cooked and drained
1 green onion, finely minced
8 ounces cream cheese,
   softened
8 ounces sour cream

½ teaspoon salt
¼ teaspoon white pepper
⅛ teaspoon garlic salt
⅛ teaspoon celery salt
½ teaspoon dill weed
Vegetable dippers

Combine all ingredients in a food processor and blend until smooth. Chill and serve with your favorite vegetable dippers. Yields 2½ cups.

Ada Smyth

Shrimp Dip

½ teaspoon celery salt
1 carton (16 ounces) sour
  cream
2 green onions, chopped
½ cup pecans, chopped
1 clove garlic, minced

Salt and pepper to taste
3 ounces cream cheese with
  chives, softened
¼ cup mayonnaise
1 package (16 ounces)
  frozen shrimp
Paprika

Mix together all ingredients except shrimp and paprika. Boil shrimp
for 2 minutes; drain and mix in. Sprinkle with paprika and chill.
Serves 10 to 12.

Mrs. Charlie Tupa (Sidney)

Sis's Hot Shrimp Dip

16 ounces cream cheese
1 red onion, chopped
2 torrido or banana peppers,
  chopped
1 fresh tomato, chopped

Garlic powder
2 cans (4¼ ounces each)
  small shrimp
Chips

Heat cream cheese in a double boiler, stirring until smooth. Add
onion, peppers, tomato, garlic powder to taste and shrimp. Heat until
all ingredients are bubbly. Serve with potato chips. Yields 4 cups.

Mrs. Greg Gordon (Kathy)

Hot Sherry Shrimp Dip

¼ cup chopped onion
1 clove garlic, minced
2 tablespoons butter
1½ tablespoons flour
½ teaspoon dry mustard
½ teaspoon salt
½ teaspoon pepper

¾ cup sour cream
½ cup milk
½ pound American cheese,
  grated
2 tablespoons sherry
1 pound shrimp, cooked
Chips

Sauté onion and garlic in butter until tender. Blend in flour and all
other seasonings. Add sour cream and milk gradually, stirring constantly until thick. Add grated cheese and when melted, add sherry
and shrimp. Serve in chafing dish with assorted chips. Yields 4 cups.

Mrs. Ronnie Kallman (Judy)

Quick Tuna Dip

1   can (6½ ounces) tuna,
    drained
½ to 1 envelope (1.25 ounces)
    onion soup mix

8   ounces sour cream

Combine all ingredients and mix well. Chill several hours before serving. Yields 2 cups.

Mrs. Gary Grissom (Janan)

Spicy Shrimp Dip

2   pounds fresh shrimp
8   ounces cream cheese,
    softened
½ cup Thousand Island
    dressing
½ cup mayonnaise

¼ cup chopped green onions
1   small onion, grated
1   tablespoon seasoned salt
1   tablespoon horseradish
Dash of hot pepper sauce
Chips or crackers

Boil shrimp. When cool enough to handle, peel, devein and coarsely chop. Mix together all ingredients except shrimp. When thoroughly combined, add shrimp. Chill and serve with chips or crackers. Serves 8 to 10.

Mrs. Jerry Holder (Pat)

Mushroom Dip

1   pound fresh mushrooms,
    sliced
4   tablespoons butter
1   tablespoon grated onion
1   tablespoon Dijon mustard
½ teaspoon salt

1   clove garlic, minced
2   tablespoons minced
    parsley
¼ teaspoon hot pepper sauce
8   ounces sour cream
Melba toast or crackers

Combine all ingredients except sour cream in a skillet and sauté 7 to 10 minutes. Stir in sour cream and heat thoroughly. Serve warm with Melba toast rounds or your favorite crackers.

Mrs. Jack Dempsey (Estelle)

"Scheffe's" Dip

2 cups mayonnaise
2 teaspoons garlic salt
2 teaspoons chopped onion
2 teaspoons horseradish

2 teaspoons wine vinegar
2 teaspoons curry powder
Vegetable dippers

Combine all ingredients and mix well. Chill several hours, then serve with your favorite vegetable dippers. Yields 2 cups.

Mrs. Stephen Scheffe (Betsy)

Dried Beef Spread

8 ounces cream cheese, softened
2 tablespoons milk
1 jar (2½ ounces) dried beef
2 tablespoons chopped onion
¼ cup chopped green bell pepper

⅛ teaspoon garlic powder
¼ teaspoon pepper
½ cup sour cream
½ cup chopped pecans
2 tablespoons butter
Dash of salt
Melba toast

Beat together cream cheese and milk. Stir in beef, onion, bell pepper, garlic powder, pepper and sour cream. In a saucepan heat pecans, butter and salt until toasted. Place cream mixture into a 6 inch quiche dish and top with pecan mixture. Bake at 350° for 20 minutes. Serves 6 to 8. *Spread on crackers or Melba toast.*

Mrs. Stephen Scheffe (Betsy)

Caviar Spread

¼ cup mayonnaise
8 ounces cream cheese, softened
1 teaspoon grated onion
Salt to taste

White pepper to taste
1 jar (2 ounces) black caviar
½ bunch parsley, minced, without stems
Wheat wafers or potato chips

Cream mayonnaise and cream cheese to spreading consistency. Mix in onion. Season with salt and white pepper. Spread into a flat container, *rounded plate or a glass pie pan.* Carefully spread caviar evenly over cream cheese mixture. Generously layer parsley on top of this, covering the entire dish. Refrigerate. Allow to warm to room temperature shortly before serving. This can be served accompanied by thin wheat wafers or potato chips. Yields 1½ cups. *This is a very pretty and elegant dish to serve before dinner. It is delicious and colorful. Someone once suggested to use red caviar at Christmas time. With the red and green, it would make a festive holiday dish.*

Mrs. Dudley Baker (Kathy)

Herbed Cheese Spread

8 ounces cream cheese, softened
8 ounces whipped cream cheese
6 tablespoons butter
1 clove garlic, minced
½ teaspoon oregano leaves
¼ teaspoon basil
¼ teaspoon dill weed
¼ teaspoon marjoram
¼ teaspoon thyme
¼ teaspoon celery salt
¼ teaspoon onion powder
¼ to ½ teaspoon black pepper
Assorted crackers

Blend cream cheeses and butter. Add garlic and mix well. Put all dry spices in mortar and grind with pestle. Add spices to cheese mixture and mix thoroughly. Refrigerate overnight to blend all flavors. Let warm slightly before serving. Serve as a spread with assorted crackers. Yields 2½ cups. *Keeps well and can be done ahead of time, as it gives flavors time to enhance each other. Can be frozen.*

Mrs. Dudley Baker (Kathy)

Sweet Brie

24 ounces Brie cheese
1 cup chopped pecans
2 cups firmly packed brown sugar
Crackers or ginger snaps

Remove top rind from cheese. Preheat broiler and place Brie in a 10 inch quiche dish or pie plate, and sprinkle with pecans. Cover the top and sides of the cheese with sugar, patting gently with fingertips. Do not worry if the sides are not completely covered. Broil on lowest rack until sugar bubbles and melts, about 5 minutes. Serve immediately with crackers or ginger snaps. Serves 10 to 12.

Mrs. Jim Rado (Vicki)

Curried Chicken Balls

8 ounces cream cheese, softened
4 tablespoons mayonnaise
1½ cups chopped almonds
1 tablespoon butter
2 cups cooked, chopped chicken
3 tablespoons chutney
1 teaspoon salt
2 teaspoons curry powder
1 cup grated coconut, toasted, optional

Blend cream cheese and mayonnaise. Sauté almonds in the butter until lightly browned. Add the almonds, chicken, chutney, salt and curry powder to the cream cheese mixture. Shape into walnut sized balls and roll in the coconut, if desired. Chill until ready to serve. Yields 5 dozen balls.

Mrs. Greg Gordon (Kathy)

Deviled Cheese Ball

16 ounces cream cheese
8 ounces grated Cheddar
    cheese
2 teaspoons grated onion
2 teaspoons Worcestershire
    sauce
1 teaspoon lemon juice
1 teaspoon dry mustard
½ teaspoon paprika
½ teaspoon seasoned salt

¼ teaspoon salt
1 can (2¼ ounces) deviled
    ham
⅔ cup finely chopped pecans
2 tablespoons chopped
    parsley
2 tablespoons chopped
    pimiento
Crackers

Soften the cream cheese in a small bowl, beating with an electric mixer. Beat in Cheddar cheese and add onion, Worcestershire sauce, lemon juice, mustard, paprika, seasoned salt, salt and ham. Beat until mixture is creamy. Stir in parsley and pimiento. Cover and refrigerate several hours, until mixture is firm enough to handle. Shape into ball and coat evenly with chopped pecans. Wrap in plastic wrap and refrigerate until ready to use. Serves 12. *If desired, sprinkle paprika and/or chopped parsley over top before serving. Serve with crackers. This cheese ball can be frozen.*

Mrs. John Wilbur (Nancy)

Good Times Cheese Roll

16 ounces processed cheese,
    softened
8 ounces cream cheese,
    softened
1 can (4 ounces) chopped
    green chilies, drained

1 jar (2 ounces) diced
    pimientos
3 green onions, chopped
1 teaspoon chopped
    jalapeños
½ cup chopped pecans
Crackers

Carefully roll out processed cheese between 2 pieces of waxed paper into a rectangle approximately 11x17 inches; remove top layer of waxed paper. Beat cream cheese until spreading consistency. Spread cream cheese evenly on top of processed cheese like a frosting. Sprinkle green chilies, pimientos, green onions, jalapeños and pecans evenly over cream cheese. Roll jelly roll style, removing wax paper with each quarter turn, until mixture is enclosed. Place seam side down in dish. Refrigerate until ready to serve. Serves 24. *This makes a very festive and delicious holiday appetizer.*

Mrs. Charley Batey (Gail)

Party Cracker Spread

8   ounces cream cheese
1   package (0.6 ounces)
    Italian salad dressing

1   teaspoon dill weed
Crackers or chips

Soften cream cheese to room temperature. Mix with salad dressing and dill weed. Serve with crackers or chips. Yields 1 cup spread.

Mrs. Rick Denbow (Susan)

Patty's Cheese Soufflé Spread

1   cup grated sharp Cheddar
    cheese
¾   cup mayonnaise
¼   cup prepared mustard
¼   teaspoon grated onion
    with juice
Dash of Worcestershire sauce

Dash of hot pepper sauce
1   teaspoon chopped parsley
1   teaspoon chopped chives
2   egg whites, beaten until
    stiff
Crackers

Mix all ingredients except egg whites and crackers. Gently fold in egg whites. Pour into a 4 or 5 inch round baking dish. Bake at 350° for 30 to 35 minutes, until brown on top. Cool a few minutes before serving with crackers. Serves 15 to 20 as an appetizer.

Mrs. Greg Gordon (Kathy)

Shrimp Butter

¾   cup butter, softened
8   ounces cream cheese
1   pound tiny fresh shrimp,
    cooked

2   tablespoons minced onion
Juice of 1 lemon
Salt to taste
Crackers

Whip butter and cheese with mixer until fluffy. Add remaining ingredients and beat until mixed. Put into serving dish and serve with crackers. Try not to refrigerate; but if you do, take out about 2 hours ahead of time to soften. Yields 3 cups.

Joan Winkelman

Chicken Liver Mousse

1 pound chicken livers
2 tablespoons butter
2 tablespoons minced green onions
⅓ cup cognac
¼ cup whipping cream
½ teaspoon salt
⅛ teaspoon allspice
⅛ teaspoon black pepper
Dash of thyme
½ cup butter, melted
Salt and black pepper to taste
Vegetable dippers or French bread

Cut livers into ½ inch pieces. Sauté with butter and green onions in a saucepan until livers are just stiffened but still rosy inside. Place in blender. Pour cognac into saucepan and boil rapidly until liquid is reduced to 3 tablespoons. Pour into blender. Add cream and seasonings to blender. Cover and blend at top speed until liver is smooth. Add melted butter and blend several seconds more. Force mixture through a fine-meshed sieve with a wooden spoon and taste carefully for seasonings. Add salt and pepper to taste. Pack into a 2 cup decorative bowl or mold and chill at least 3 hours. Use as a spread for appetizers. Yields 1¾ cups. *This is very good served with celery sticks or cucumber rounds, crackers or French bread.*

Mrs. Marcus Bone (Beverly)

Chicken Liver Paté

1 pound chicken livers
¼ cup margarine
2 hard cooked eggs
¼ cup minced onion
1 teaspoon dry mustard
Dash of ground cloves
Salt and pepper to taste
Sliced onion for garnish
Grated egg yolk for garnish
Crackers

Clean chicken livers and cut each in half. Sauté chicken livers in margarine until no longer pink. Drain, reserving drippings. Put chicken livers and eggs through a meat grinder. Add most of drippings, depending on consistency, and all remaining ingredients except garnishes, stirring well. Put mixture into a small mold sprayed with nonstick cooking spray. Chill well. Yields 2 cups. *Garnish with thin slices of onion and grated egg yolk, if desired. Serve with crackers. Best if made a day ahead.*

Ann Wurzelbacher

Sam Houston, David Burnet, Mirabeau Lamar and Anson Jones were all elected presidents of the Republic of Texas.

Corned Beef Paté

2 teaspoons instant minced onion	8 ounces braunschweiger roll
⅔ cup water	½ cup mayonnaise
1 can (12 ounces) corned beef	1 tablespoon vinegar
	½ teaspoon dry mustard
	Crackers

Soften onion in water for 5 minutes and then drain. Flake corned beef with fork and add braunschweiger, mayonnaise, vinegar, mustard and onion. Place ½ cup of the mixture in blender and cover. Using medium speed, mix until smooth. Remove and repeat until all mixture is blended. Turn into a 3½ cup mold or bowl and chill. Unmold onto serving plate and serve with crackers. Serves 8 to 10.

B. F. Wright, Jr.

Salmon Paté

1 small onion, chopped	2 teaspoons dill weed
1 can (15½ ounces) salmon	1 teaspoon Worcestershire sauce
8 ounces cream cheese, softened	Hot pepper sauce to taste
3 tablespoons lemon juice	Salt and pepper to taste
1 heaping tablespoon horseradish	Rye crackers or bread

Combine all ingredients except crackers or bread in blender or food processor and blend until smooth. Yields 3⅓ cups. *This is best made a day in advance. Serve with rye crackers or bread of your choice.*

Mrs. Denman Smith (Sandra)

Tuna Paté

1 can (6½ ounces) tuna, drained	¼ teaspoon cayenne pepper
½ cup butter, softened	¼ cup Madeira
¼ cup half and half cream	Salt and pepper to taste
½ teaspoon dry mustard	Crackers or French bread dippers

Combine all ingredients in blender until smooth. Pour into a lightly greased mold. Chill 2 to 3 hours or overnight. Remove from mold onto plate garnished with parsley or other greens. Serve with bland crackers or French bread. Yields 12 servings.

Mrs. Denman Smith (Sandra)

Microwave Artichoke Bottom Appetizers

4   ounces cream cheese,
    cubed
2   ounces Bleu cheese, cubed
¼   cup butter
2   tablespoons minced chives
¼   teaspoon salt

⅛   teaspoon pepper
2   cans (14 ounces each)
    artichoke bottoms,
    drained
Ripe olive slices for garnish
Parsley for garnish

Combine cheeses, butter, chives, salt and pepper in blender or food processor. Blend until smooth and fluffy, about 20 seconds. Mound cheese mixture in center of each artichoke bottom. Arrange in a 10 inch glass pie plate. Microwave on HIGH 2 minutes; turn dish one quarter and cook on HIGH another 2 minutes. Check to be sure they are heated through. Transfer to a serving tray and garnish. Serves 8.

Mrs. Greg Gordon (Kathy)

Scrumptious Hors D'oeuvres

2   cans (14 ounces each)
    artichokes hearts, drained
    and quartered
2   cans (14 ounces) hearts of
    palm, drained and sliced

2   cans (4.5 ounces) button
    mushrooms, drained
12 to 15 cherry tomatoes,
    sliced in half
1   package (0.7 ounces)
    garlic cheese dressing mix

In a large bowl combine artichoke hearts, hearts of palm, mushrooms and cherry tomatoes. Mix the dressing according to package directions and pour over vegetables. Marinate for several hours before serving. Drain before serving. Serves 8.

Mrs. John Perkins (Sandy)

Kibbie

1½ cups bulgar wheat
1   pound ground sirloin
1   small onion, finely
    chopped

2   fresh jalapeños, finely
    chopped
Salt and pepper to taste
Oil

Rinse bulgar wheat 2 or 3 times to remove flour taste. Soak bulgar for 20 to 30 minutes; drain and squeeze gently. Mix all ingredients together and knead to form a tight mixture. Form into small fingerlike balls, using a heaping tablespoon of the mixture. Fry until medium brown. Kibbie may also be baked at 375° for 30 to 40 minutes. Serve at room temperature. Yields 4 to 6 dozen.

Nora Joseph

Artichoke Hearts Supreme

5   tablespoons butter, divided
2½ tablespoons flour
1   cup whipping cream
½   teaspoon salt
Dash of cayenne pepper
1   tablespoon Worcestershire sauce
1   cup sherry

2   cans (14 ounces each) whole artichoke hearts, well drained
½   pound fresh mushrooms
2   tablespoons butter, melted
1   cup crab meat, drained
Parmesan cheese, grated
Paprika
Parsley

Melt 2½ tablespoons butter and add flour to make a roux. Add whipping cream, salt and pepper. When thick and smooth, add Worcestershire sauce. Remove from heat and add sherry. Place artichoke hearts in a shallow buttered baking dish and set aside. Sauté mushrooms in 2½ tablespoons melted butter; add crab meat and stir. Spread crab and mushroom mixture over artichoke hearts; cover with cream sauce. Top with Parmesan cheese and sprinkle generously with paprika and parsley. Bake at 375° for 20 minutes. Serves 10 to 12.

Mrs. Jim Nunnelly (Sandy)

Italian Fried Cheese

16 ounces Mozzarella cheese
3   eggs, beaten
¼   cup flour
⅔   cup seasoned bread crumbs
1   clove garlic, minced
1   tablespoon olive oil

1   can (28 ounces) chopped tomatoes
¼   teaspoon salt
Dash of pepper
1   teaspoon dried oregano
½   teaspoon sugar
¼   teaspoon basil
¼   cup oil

Cut cheese into 1½ inch pieces. Dip in egg, flour, then in egg, and finally in bread crumbs. Place on waxed paper-lined cookie sheet and refrigerate at least 1 hour. Meanwhile, in a heavy 2 quart saucepan cook garlic in olive oil. Add tomatoes, salt, pepper, oregano, sugar and basil; mix well. Simmer for 45 minutes, or until thick. In skillet, fry cheese in ¼ cup oil until browned, turning once. Entire cooking takes 2 to 2½ minutes. Drain on paper towels and serve with sauce. Serves 4.

Mrs. Marcus Bone (Beverly)

Crab Puffs

Puffs:

1   cup water
½   cup butter
½   teaspoon salt
⅛   teaspoon white pepper

1¼ cups flour
5 to 6 eggs, divided
1   teaspoon water

Combine water, butter, salt and pepper in a large saucepan and bring to a boil. Remove from heat and stir in flour all at once. Beat to blend thoroughly. Return to low heat and stir with a wooden spoon until flour is absorbed. Mash dough against bottom and sides of pan with spoon for 1 to 2 minutes. Remove from heat and let stand for 5 minutes. With metal blade in place, add dough to food processor bowl. Process for 5 to 10 seconds. Add 4 eggs and process until smooth and shiny, scraping down side of bowl as necessary. The dough should be thick and flow very slowly when lifted with a spoon. If it does not flow at all, add another egg. Spoon half-walnut sized gobs of dough onto a greased baking sheet, allowing room between for puffs to double in size. Brush tops of puffs with 1 egg beaten with 1 teaspoon water. Bake at 425° for 20 minutes or until puffs have risen and are brown and crispy. Remove from oven. Pierce each on one side with a knife so that the moist center can dry out. Return them to the turned off oven for 5 minutes.

Filling:

1   can (7½ ounces) crab
    meat, drained
⅓   cup chopped ripe olives
¼   cup chopped celery

⅓   cup minced green bell
    pepper
1   tablespoon minced green
    onion
Mayonnaise

Combine all filling ingredients using just enough mayonnaise to moisten. Do not use too much. Fill puffs shortly before serving. Bake at 350° for 10 minutes before serving. Yields 4 to 5 dozen puffs. *The unfilled puffs can be made ahead. They freeze beautifully. If frozen, remove from package to defrost and crisp in 350° oven for 5 minutes before filling. Do not fill puffs ahead of time, or they will get soggy.*

Mrs. Sid Mann (Kathi)

Some nuts are not really nuts. The macadamia nut and the cashew nut are actually seeds. Peanuts are legumes.

Crab Meat Bacon Rolls

½ cup tomato juice
1 egg, well beaten
1 cup dry bread crumbs
⅛ teaspoon salt
Dash of pepper
½ teaspoon chopped parsley

½ teaspoon chopped celery leaves
1 can (6½ ounces) crab meat
½ onion, chopped
12 slices bacon, cut in half crosswise

Mix tomato juice and egg together. Add bread crumbs, seasonings, parsley, celery leaves and crab meat. Mix thoroughly; roll into finger lengths. Wrap each roll with a half slice of bacon and fasten with a toothpick. Broil, turning frequently to brown evenly. Yields 24 rolls.

Mrs. Bernard Vise (Marion)

Crab Delights

1 can (6 ounces) crab meat, drained
6 tablespoons mayonnaise
½ teaspoon salt
1 tablespoon grated onion

1 tablespoon lemon juice
½ cup grated Parmesan cheese
7 slices of bread
Paprika

Mix together the crab meat, mayonnaise, salt, onion, lemon juice and Parmesan cheese. Spread on bread which has been trimmed and quartered. Sprinkle with paprika. Cook at 400° until bubbly brown. Yields 28. *This spread may be mixed early in the day and refrigerated. Spread on bread and brown just before servings.*

Mrs. Lorne Parks (Dephanie)

Deviled Eggs

6 hard cooked eggs
2 tablespoons salad dressing
1 teaspoon prepared mustard
¼ teaspoon parsley flakes

Pinch of celery seed, crushed
⅛ teaspoon chives
Dash of cayenne pepper
Salt and pepper to taste
Paprika to garnish

Cut eggs in half lengthwise and remove yolks. Place yolks in bowl. Mix remaining ingredients with yolks and stir well. Spoon yolks into egg whites and sprinkle with paprika. Yields 12.

Mrs. Dan O'Donnell (Sharon)

 Buy the expensive lump crab meat when it will be served alone; buy the less expensive flaked crab meat when it will be mixed with other ingredients.

Ham Pinwheels

1 package (8 ounces) Danish
  ham
8 ounces cream cheese,
  softened

1 can (16 ounces) asparagus
  spears, drained

Separate ham into individual slices and spread each slice with cream cheese. Place an asparagus spear on the edge of each slice and roll up jelly roll fashion. Chill and slice in ½ inch pinwheels. Yields 36 to 48.

Mrs. Denman Smith (Sandra)

Hot Clam Canapés

1 small onion, chopped
1 small green bell pepper,
  chopped
3 tablespoons butter
1 can (7½ ounces) minced
  clams, drained
¼ pound Cheddar cheese,
  grated

¼ cup catsup
1 tablespoon Worcestershire
  sauce
1 tablespoon sherry
⅛ teaspoon cayenne pepper
Rye rounds

Mix all ingredients together and cook until cheese melts, stirring constantly. Serve hot on rye rounds. Serves 8 to 10.

Mrs. Joe Bowles (Mary)

Bacon Wrapped Water Chestnuts

1 can (8 ounces) whole
  water chestnuts
¼ cup soy sauce
¼ cup oil
2 tablespoons catsup

1 tablespoon white vinegar
¼ teaspoon pepper
2 cloves garlic, minced
½ pound bacon, sliced in half
  crosswise

Drain water chestnuts and set aside. Combine soy sauce, oil, catsup, vinegar, pepper and garlic. Add water chestnuts and marinate in refrigerator for at least 4 hours. Drain and wrap each one with a half slice of bacon; broil until brown, about 10 minutes on each side. Serve immediately. Serves 6.

Mrs. David Hart (Sue)

Sausage Balls in Cranberry Sauce

1 pound bulk pork sausage
2 eggs
1 cup fresh bread crumbs
1 teaspooon salt
½ teaspoon poultry
  seasoning

1 can (16 ounces) jellied
  cranberry sauce
1 tablespoon prepared
  mustard
½ cup water

Mix sausage, eggs, bread crumbs, salt and poultry seasoning in a large bowl. Shape into 24 small meatballs. In a large skillet over medium high heat, brown meatballs well. Drain on paper towel. Pour all fat from skillet and wipe skillet clean. In same skillet over low heat, melt cranberry sauce, stirring occasionally. Stir in mustard, meatballs and ½ cup water. Cover and simmer 20 minutes or until meatballs are tender. Yields 24 meatballs. *This is a great appetizer for the holiday season.*

Mrs. J. Edward Reed (Marian)

Barbecued Meatballs

Meatballs:
1 cup milk
3 pounds ground beef
2 cups quick oats
2 eggs
1 onion, chopped

½ teaspoon garlic salt
½ teaspoon pepper
2 teaspoons chili powder
2 teaspoons salt

Combine all ingredients together and mix well. Shape into 1½ inch balls and place in a greased baking dish.

Sauce:
2 cups catsup
2 tablespoons imitation
  smoke flavor

1½ cups brown sugar
½ teaspoon garlic salt
½ cup chopped onion

Bring sauce ingredients to a boil. Pour over meatballs and bake at 350° for 1 hour. Yields 128 meatballs. *This recipe can be halved easily.*

Mrs. Robert Vossman (Nancy)

Saucy Meatballs

Meatballs:

2 pounds ground beef
1 large onion, grated
1 handful oatmeal

1 egg, slightly beaten
¾ teaspoon salt

Combine all ingredients and shape into 50 to 60 small balls. Brown well in a large skillet or broil on both sides.

Sauce:

1 bottle (12 ounces) chili sauce
1 jar (10 ounces) grape jelly

2 tablespoons fresh lemon juice

In a very large saucepan, combine all sauce ingredients. Drop meatballs into sauce. Simmer approximately 30 minutes. Serve from chafing dish with toothpicks. Yields 50 to 60 meatballs. *These freeze beautifully. When ready to use, defrost and reheat slowly.*

Mrs. Sid Mann (Kathi)

Cocktail Meatballs

2 pounds ground beef
1 teaspoon salt
½ teaspoon pepper
¼ teaspoon thyme

¼ teaspoon marjoram
2 onions, finely chopped
3 eggs
Bread crumbs

Mix all ingredients with enough bread crumbs to thicken. Roll into meatballs and bake on ungreased broiler pan at 400° for 10 minutes or until done. Serve with Sweet Mustard Sauce or Curry Sauce. Yields 48.

Sweet Mustard Sauce:

4 tablespoons prepared mustard

2 teaspoons horseradish
2 teaspoons sugar

Mix mustard, horseradish and sugar together. Stir well and serve with meatballs.

Curry Sauce:

½ cup mayonnaise

1 teaspoon curry powder

Thoroughly mix sauce ingredients.

Mrs. Robert Brown (Mary)

Meatballs in Mushroom Sherry Sauce

Meatballs:

2 pounds ground beef	2 eggs
1 cup seasoned bread crumbs	½ teaspoon oregano
	½ teaspoon garlic salt
½ cup catsup	Salt and pepper to taste
¼ cup finely chopped green bell pepper	

Combine all ingredients and mix well. Shape into cocktail sized balls. Place on lightly greased cookie sheet and bake at 350° for 30 minutes.

Sauce:

2 cans (10¾ ounces each) cream of mushroom soup	¼ cup minced onion
	1 tablespoon minced parsley
2½ cups sour cream	¼ teaspoon oregano
4 tablespoons sherry	½ teaspoon garlic salt

Combine all ingredients in a large bowl and microwave until warm, about 5 minutes, on MED-HIGH. Add cooked meatballs to sauce and warm in oven until ready to serve, 350° for 30 minutes or 250° to keep warm until ready to serve. Transfer to chafing dish to serve. Yields 60 meatballs.

Mrs. Jean-paul Budinger (Pat)

Egg 'N' Cheese Puffs

4 eggs	1 teaspoon baking powder
1 tablespoon chopped onion	½ pound sharp Cheddar cheese, cut into ¼" cubes
⅓ cup flour	
½ teaspoon salt	⅓ cup shortening

Beat eggs. Combine with onion, flour, salt and baking powder. Add cheese. Drop by spoonsful into hot fat. Fry until golden brown on both sides. Yields 12 puffs. Can be made the day before, refrigerated uncooked.

Mrs. Bernard Vise (Marion)

Ellen's Snow Peas

8 ounces snow peas
12 ounces crab meat
2 hard cooked eggs, finely
chopped
3 to 4 tablespoons
mayonnaise
1 to 2 tablespoons lemon
juice

4 dashes hot pepper sauce
1 to 2 teaspoons capers
3 tablespoons finely
chopped celery
1 to 2 tablespoons chopped
pimiento

Clean snow peas and split on top seam. Blanch for 10 to 15 seconds in boiling water until bright green. Immediately mix crab meat with remaining ingredients and use to fill snow peas. Serves 10 to 12.

Mrs. James Kimbell (Ellen)

Cheese Crisps

1 cup grated Cheddar
cheese
¼ cup butter
1 to 2 tablespoons milk

1 tablespoon spicy mustard
1 cup finely crushed potato
chips
¾ cup flour

Combine cheese, butter, milk and mustard. Toss chips and flour and add to cheese mixture. Form small round wafers and bake at 375° for 12 to 15 minutes. Yields 36 to 40. *You may vary the taste of these crisps by using different flavors of potato chips.*

Mrs. Dudley Baker (Kathy)

Shao-Pao

¼ pound ground pork
¼ pound ground sirloin
1 tablespoon soy sauce
1 teaspoon sugar
¼ teaspoon minced ginger
root

⅛ teaspoon black pepper
¼ teaspoon minced garlic
1 green onion, finely
chopped
1 tube (10 count)
refrigerated biscuits

Combine all ingredients except biscuits. Flatten each biscuit to form a circle 4 inches in diameter. Put 1 tablespoon of meat mixture in the center of the biscuit and fold up into a ball, pinching the top to seal. Place balls on a rack in a skillet with water at level below the rack and steam for 15 minutes. Serve hot. Yields 10.

Mrs. Ed Fomby (Beaty)

Broiled Stuffed Mushrooms

12 fresh medium mushrooms
¼ cup finely chopped celery
⅛ cup finely chopped onion
1 tablespoon butter
½ cup crab meat, drained
2 tablespoons mayonnaise

1 teaspoon lemon juice
Salt to taste
2 tablespoons bread crumbs
Parmesan cheese
Pimiento slices

Wash mushrooms and remove caps; set aside. Finely chop stems. Cook stems, celery and onion in the butter until tender; add crab meat, mayonnaise, lemon juice and salt. Stuff mixture into mushroom caps. Sprinkle with bread crumbs and Parmesan cheese. Top with a small pimiento slice. Broil 6 inches from heat for 8 minutes. Serve hot. Serves 4.

Mrs. Larry Strickland (Linda)

Sweet and Sour Chicken Wings

3 pounds chicken wings
Garlic salt
1 cup cornstarch

3 eggs, beaten
½ cup oil

Sprinkle chicken wings with garlic salt. Roll in cornstarch, dip in beaten eggs, and brown in hot oil. Drain well.

Sauce:
1½ cups sugar
2 tablespoons soy sauce
1 cup Chinese rice
  vinegar

½ cup catsup
½ cup chicken stock
2 teaspoons seasoned salt
1 teaspoon salt

Combine sauce ingredients and heat until sugar melts. Dip each wing in sauce, and place in a shallow baking dish. Pour the remaining sauce over the top. Bake uncovered at 350° for 30 minutes; turn and bake 30 minutes more. Serves 10.

Mrs. Ron Bruney (Carol)

Extra hard avocados will never ripen. They have been picked too early and will rot before they ripen.

Deviled Mushrooms

1 pound fresh mushrooms
3 ounces cream cheese, softened
1 can (4½ ounces) deviled ham

1 cup bread crumbs, divided
1 teaspoon onion powder
⅛ teaspoon black pepper
3 tablespoons butter, divided

Rinse, pat dry and remove stems from mushrooms. Set caps aside. Chop enough stems to make ½ cup. Reserve for later use. In medium bowl combine cream cheese, deviled ham, ½ cup bread crumbs, reserved chopped mushroom stems, onion powder and pepper. In a small saucepan melt 2 tablespoons of butter and brush outside of reserved caps with the melted butter. Mound stuffing mixture into each mushroom cap. Melt remaining 1 tablespoon butter and stir in remaining bread crumbs. Sprinkle over stuffed mushrooms. Place in a shallow baking dish and bake at 350° for 15 minutes. Yields 24 stuffed mushrooms.

Mrs. John Wilbur (Nancy)

Stuffed Cherry Tomatoes

12 to 16 cherry tomatoes, seeded
1 can (5 ounces) cocktail shrimp, drained and minced

1 green onion, minced
⅛ teaspoon minced garlic
2 tablespoons cream cheese
Salt and white pepper to taste

Mix all stuffing ingredients and use to fill cherry tomatoes. Yields 12 to 16.

Mrs. Denman Smith (Sandra)

Sausage Squares

3 cups biscuit mix
1 cup milk
⅓ cup mayonnaise
3 pounds bulk hot sausage
1 onion, chopped

2 eggs, beaten
½ cup grated Parmesan cheese
½ cup grated Cheddar or Swiss cheese

Combine biscuit mix, milk and mayonnaise to make a sticky dough. Sauté sausage and onion; drain. Add eggs and cheeses to cooked sausage. Place half of biscuit dough onto an ungreased cookie sheet and slightly flatten. Spread sausage mixture over it. Top with remaining biscuit mixture. Bake at 350° for 30 minutes. Serves 8.

Mrs. Ed Fomby (Beaty)

Cocktail Shrimp

1   pound medium shrimp
1   bottle (8 ounces) French
    dressing

½   pound sliced bacon, cut
    into thirds

Shell and devein shrimp. Place in bowl and add enough French dressing to cover. Marinate in refrigerator overnight. When ready to cook, wrap each shrimp with ⅓ piece of bacon and secure with toothpick. Arrange on broiler pan and bake at 400° for 20 minutes, turning once. Yields 35 to 50 pieces. *You can use Italian dressing instead of French and you can wrap with bacon and leave in the refrigerator to pop in oven shortly before guests come.*

Mrs. Joe Bowles (Mary)

Special Shrimp

8   slices bacon, halved
Hot mustard

16 large shrimp, shelled and
    deveined

Generously brush each strip of bacon with mustard. Wrap 1 bacon piece around each shrimp and secure with a toothpick. Broil on grill until crisp, turning once. Do not overcook shrimp. Yields 16 shrimp.

Mrs. Terry Arndt (Barbara)

Pickled Shrimp

2   tablespoons olive oil
1   pound shrimp, cooked,
    peeled and deveined
1   cup white vinegar
2   tablespoons water
¼   cup sliced onion

8   whole cloves
1   bay leaf
2   teaspoons salt
1   teaspoon sugar
Dash cayenne pepper

Pour oil over shrimp in a bowl. Combine the remaining ingredients in a saucepan and bring to a boil. Pour over shrimp while hot. Cool, then refrigerate 24 hours. Yields 40 to 50 pieces.

Mrs. Marcus Bone (Beverly)

To ripen an avocado, place it in a paper bag with a ripe apple. Poke small holes in the bag to allow the carbon dioxide to escape.

Curried Tuna Puffs

Pastry:

¼ cup water
¼ cup butter
¼ teaspoon salt

½ cup flour
2 eggs

Grease a large cookie sheet. Heat water, butter and salt until boiling in a 2 quart saucepan. Remove from heat and vigorously stir in flour with a wooden spoon until mixture forms a ball and leaves sides of pan. Beat eggs into mixture until blended. Spoon into a pastry bag with round tube. Makes 20 mounds. *A mound is about 2 teaspoons each set 1 inch apart on a cookie sheet.* Bake at 375° until puffy and light golden brown.

Filling:

1 can (6½ ounces) tuna,
   undrained
½ cup mayonnaise
¼ cup minced celery

2 hard cooked eggs, diced
1 tablespoon curry powder
1 teaspoon salt
⅔ cup chopped fresh parsley

Mix all filling ingredients except parsley; cover and refrigerate. When puffs are cool, cut horizontally to make 2 shells; spoon 1 teaspoon filling into each shell. Garnish with parsley. Yields 40 puffs.

Mrs. Dan O'Donnell (Sharon)

Cheese Puffs

1 loaf unsliced bread
3 ounces whipped cream
   cheese
1 cup grated sharp Cheddar
   cheese

½ cup margarine
2 egg whites, beaten

Remove crust and slice bread into 1 inch cubes. Melt cheeses and margarine in top of double broiler. Stir vigorously after melted to mix margarine and cheese completely. Remove from heat and fold in egg whites. Spear bread cubes with a two pronged fork and dip into mixture. Shake gently and place on a cookie sheet. Chill overnight or freeze. Defrost, if frozen and bake at 400° for 10 minutes or until lightly browned. Yields 50 puffs.

Mrs. Terry Steigelman (Kathleen)

Cheese Straws

1   pound sharp Cheddar
    cheese, finely grated
1   cup unsalted butter,
    softened
3   cups sifted flour

1   teaspoon salt
1½ teaspoons hot pepper
    sauce
2   teaspoons cayenne pepper

Combine all ingredients. Put through a cookie press in ¼ inch wide strips or roll out on a slightly floured board ⅛ inch thick and cut into ¼ inch strips 3 to 5 inches long. Place on an ungreased cookie sheet and bake at 375° for 10 to 15 minutes. Yields 36. *These can be stored in a sealed container for several weeks.*

S. D. Jackman

Cheese Crackers

1   jar (5 ounces) pasteurized
    processed cheese spread
¼   cup butter, softened

⅔   cup flour
3   tablespoons sesame seeds

Mix cheese, butter and flour together and form into a 12 inch log. Roll in sesame seed, wrap in plastic wrap and freeze until ready to bake. When ready to use, slice in ¼ inch slices and place on ungreased baking sheet. Bake at 375° for 12 minutes. Serve warm. Yields 4 dozen.

Mrs. Denman Smith (Sandra)

French Crescents

3   egg yolks, divided
3   ounces cream cheese
3   ounces Parmesan cheese

2   tubes (8 count) crescent
    rolls
Pinch of salt

Mix 1 egg yolk, cream cheese and Parmesan cheese. Halve each crescent roll to make 32 in all. In each piece of dough place 1 teaspoon of mixture and shape crescents. Place on a lightly greased baking sheet. Beat 2 egg yolks with a pinch of salt and brush the top of each crescent before baking. Bake at 350° for 15 to 20 minutes, or until lightly golden brown.

Mrs. Marcus Bone (Beverly)

Good Things

1 tube (8 count) crescent rolls	2 tablespoons minced dehydrated onions
3 ounces cream cheese	3 tablespoons water
1 can (2½ ounces) mushrooms, drained and chopped	1 teaspoon oregano
	½ teaspoon thyme
	¾ teaspoon seasoned salt
3 tablespoons water	Egg white, slightly beaten, Sesame seeds

Divide crescent rolls into 4 rectangles. Mix all remaining ingredients together except egg white and sesame seeds. Spread on rolls. Roll up lengthwise and cut into 8 pieces. Brush top with egg white and sprinkle with sesame seeds. Bake at 350° for 17 to 18 minutes. Yields 32.

Mrs. John Perkins (Sandy)

Pepper Jelly Turnovers

1 jar (5 ounces) pasteurized processed cheese spread	2 tablespoons water
½ cup butter	1 jar (4 ounces) jalapeño jelly
1 cup flour	

Cut cheese and butter into flour. Quickly stir in water and shape into a ball. Chill overnight. Roll dough very thin and cut with biscuit cutter into 5 inch circles. Fill half with jalapeño jelly. Fold over and crimp edges with fork. Bake at 375° for 8 to 10 minutes. Yields 24 to 36. *Turnovers are also good filled with orange marmalade. They may be frozen and reheated before serving.*

Mrs. Jim Rado (Vicki)

To help the bread rise faster, preheat the oven to 140° as you begin kneading the dough. After you have put the dough into the bread pans, turn off the oven and put the bread inside. It should be ready to bake in 20 minutes. Be sure not to get the oven too hot, and don't leave it on during the rising process or a crust will form as the bread rises, causing the bread to crack during baking.

Party Swirls

1 can (4 ounces) mushroom pieces and stems, drained and chopped
6 strips bacon, fried crisp and chopped
½ teaspoon garlic powder
4 tablespoons mayonnaise

1 tube (8 count) crescent rolls
6 ounces cream cheese, softened
1 egg white, slightly beaten
Poppy seeds

Heat oven to 375°. Mix mushrooms, bacon, garlic powder and mayonnaise. Remove 2 triangles of the crescent rolls without separating. Keep pieces connected in rectangular shape. Put remaining crescent dough in the refrigerator to keep it from getting sticky. Spread a layer of cream cheese over the dough. Then spread ¼ of the mushroom mixture over the cream cheese. Roll the dough lengthwise. Carefully slice the roll into ½ inch pieces. Place the slices on a greased cookie sheet. Repeat this procedure with the remaining crescent rolls. Brush each slice with egg white and sprinkle with poppy seeds. Bake for 8 to 10 minutes or until lightly browned. Serve warm. Yields 30 swirls. *You can keep leftovers in an airtight container in the refrigerator. Heat the swirls in the microwave for 1 minute before serving. These may be frozen.*

Mrs. Chris John (Anne)

Escargot Monterey

6 to 8 escargots
¼ cup butter
2 teaspoons minced garlic
2 to 4 tablespoons picante sauce

¼ cup grated Monterey Jack cheese
1 Mexican hard roll

Sauté escargots in butter with garlic and picante sauce for 5 to 8 minutes. Place in your favorite escargot dish or in small individual casseroles; top with Monterey Jack cheese and run under broiler for 1 minute to melt the cheese. Serve with a Mexican hard roll, so you can enjoy the sauce. Serves 1.

Mrs. Denman Smith (Sandra)

Never use a moist spoon to measure baking powder. The moisture from the spoon will affect the potency of the baking powder.

Roasted Pecans

2   tablespoons water
1   egg white, slightly beaten
½   cup sugar
½   teaspoon salt

¼   teaspoon cinnamon
¼   teaspoon ground cloves
¼   teaspoon allspice
2½ cups pecan halves

Add water to egg white. Mix sugar, salt and spices together and add to egg white mixture. Beat until sugar dissolves. Put pecan halves into mixture and stir until thoroughly coated. Place them flat side down on wire rack or greased cookie sheet. Bake at 250° for 1 hour. Yields 2½ cups. *These pecans were served at Christmas at Caswell House 1984.*

Susan Kingsbery

Beverages

White Sangria

1   gallon white wine
2   cups triple orange liqueur
    with cognac brandy
1   can (12 ounces) frozen
    orange juice concentrate

1   cup lemon juice
2   oranges, thinly sliced
2   lemons, thinly sliced
1 to 2 bottles champagne or
    club soda

Mix all ingredients except champagne or club soda and chill well. Add champagne just before serving. Yields 24 (6 ounces) servings.

Mrs. Denman Smith (Sandra)

Bloody Bull

1   can (46 ounces) tomato
    juice
1½ ounces steak sauce
1½ ounces Worcestershire
    sauce
1   teaspoon celery salt

½   teaspoon salt
½   teaspoon pepper
1   can (10½ ounces) beef
    bouillon
5   drops hot pepper sauce
1   ounce fresh lime juice

Mix all ingredients well and chill. Yields 2 quarts. *This is much better after several days; that is, if you can hide it. For a real eye opener the Bloody Bull base is good with vodka or tequila to taste.*

S. D. Jackman, Jr.

Belini

1 ripe fresh peach	Champagne
1 teaspoon powdered sugar	

Peel, cut in half and seed the peach. Place each half into your prettiest champagne glasses. Sprinkle with powdered sugar and fill with champagne and think of Venice, Italy, or Stonewall, Texas. Serves 2.

Mrs. Denman Smith (Sandra)

Brunch Fruit Pitcher

½ cup hot tea	1 cup orange juice
½ cup sugar	Juice of ½ lemon
1 can (12 ounces) apricot nectar	1 bottle (12 ounces) ginger ale

Combine hot tea and sugar in a pitcher and stir until sugar is dissolved. Add remaining ingredients. Stir and chill. Yields 10 (4 ounce) servings.

Mrs. Joe Bowles (Mary)

Bourbon Cooler

2 ounces bourbon	1 can (8 ounces) pineapple chunks, drained
2 ounces French sweet red aperitif wine	4 to 5 dashes of aromatic bitters
1 tablespoon curacao	12 ounces ginger ale, chilled
1 tablespoon anise liqueur	
½ orange, thinly sliced	

Put bourbon, aperitif wine, curacao and anise liqueur into a one quart pitcher and stir. Add oranges, pineapple chunks and bitters. Then add the ice and ginger ale and stir again. Yields 5 (4 ounce) servings. *This recipe can be made up 1 or 2 hours in advance. If made too far in advance, the fruit will look and taste mushy.*

Mrs. Marcus Bone (Beverly)

Candles will burn longer and slower if stored in the refrigerator before using.

Café Glacé

This recipe was stolen from J. Waddy Bullion from Dallas, Texas. Like kisses and watermelons, secret formulas and recipes that are stolen tend to taste better! J. Waddy is my father-in-law (I also have other names for him). He is an attorney specializing in corporate income tax work for oil companies. While on assignment in Venezuela, he chanced to sample this concoction (observing some ancient culture's fertility rites) in an obscure little Maracaibo (Hilton) Bar. It is so good, even those who don't like coffee will succumb. Collect 1 jigger day-old stale coffee, 1 jigger cheap brandy or expensive cognac (depending on whom you want to impress) and 1 pint vanilla ice cream. Chunk it all together in a blender and mix on high until smooth. Lock the door, close the drapes and serve in elegant clear glasses. Serves 2 to 4 adults.

Ed L. Mears III

Old Fashioned Cocoa

¼ cup water	¾ cup milk
2 tablespoons sugar	1 marshmallow, optional
1 tablespoon unsweetened cocoa powder	

Combine water, sugar and cocoa in a 2 cup glass measure. Cook in microwave on MEDIUM for 2 minutes. Add milk and continue cooking on MEDIUM until cocoa is hot, about 45 to 60 seconds. Pour into a mug and top with marshmallow. Serves 1.

Daryl Bone

French 75

2 bottles white champagne	1 bottle (33.8 ounces) club soda
½ to 1 bottle (25 ounces) cognac or brandy	1 bottle (6 ounces) maraschino cherries
1 bottle (33.8 ounces) lemon-lime carbonated drink	1 orange, sliced
	Ice

Mix all beverages and maraschino cherries in punch bowl. Add ice. Garnish with orange slices. Yields 25 (4 ounce) servings.

Mrs. Jim Rado (Vicki)

Grasshopper Supreme

1   pint vanilla ice cream,   ½   cup creme de menthe
    softened   ½   cup white creme de cacao

Combine all ingredients in a blender and blend for a few seconds.
Pour into small stemmed glasses. Serves 6.

Mrs. Lee Provinse (Dottie)

Orange Frost

1   can (6 ounces) frozen   ½   cup sugar
    orange juice concentrate   1   teaspoon vanilla extract
1   cup milk   8 to 10 ice cubes
1   cup water

Combine all ingredients in blender and blend until smooth. Serve
immediately. Serves 4.

Mrs. W. H. Heggen III (Mary Ellen)

Frozen Strawberry Daiquiri

1   can (6 ounces) frozen   Crushed ice
    lemonade concentrate   ½   package (10 ounces)
6   ounces rum   frozen strawberries
2   heaping tablespoons
    vanilla ice cream

Place frozen lemonade in blender. Use the same can to measure rum
and add to blender. Add ice cream and blend about 30 seconds. Add
crushed ice until the container is approximately ¾ full. Blend again for
30 seconds. Add strawberries and blend until smooth. Serves 4.

Mrs. James C. Doss (Charlene)

Creamy Piña Colada

1   can (12 ounces) cream of   1   cup vanilla ice cream
    coconut   Crushed ice
12 ounces rum   Cherries and orange slices for
24 ounces pineapple juice   garnish

Pour liquids into blender. Add ice cream and crushed ice to fill. Blend
until smooth and thick. Place 1 orange slice and 1 cherry in bottom of
a very tall glass. Pour blended mixture over and sip through a straw.
Serves 4.

Mrs. James C. Doss (Charlene)

Pousse Café

1 ounce creme de cassis (red, 18.1)
1 ounce creme de cacao (white, 14.2)
1 ounce creme de menthe (green, 12.0)
1 ounce curacao (blue, 10.9)

Liqueurs are listed above according to colors and weights. Using a very narrow, tall glass, carefully pour in the creme de cassis, *heaviest weight*. Continue carefully adding the creme de cacao, the creme de menthe or the curacao, *lightest weight*. This drink may be flamed for a few seconds and then drunk in one swallow, feeling it go from warm to cool and savoring each flavor. It can be made in many layers if you have a steady hand. Most liquor stores can furnish a chart of weights of liqueurs. Use red, white and blue for the 4th of July, or red, white and green for your Mexican fiesta. Serves 1.

Denman Smith

Red Riding Hood

3 cups tomato juice
1 cup plain yogurt
1 teaspoon Worcestershire sauce

1 teaspoon lemon juice
1 to 2 drops hot pepper sauce
Ice
4 ribs of celery for garnish

Put tomato juice, yogurt, Worcestershire sauce, lemon juice and hot pepper sauce in a blender. Cover and blend on medium speed about 2 minutes, until smooth. Pour into 4 tall ice-filled glasses and garnish with a rib of celery. Yields 4 (8 ounce) servings.

Mrs. Ernest Butler (Sarah)

Rum Refresher

½ cup dark rum
6 tablespoons pineapple juice
6 tablespoons orange juice
¼ cup coconut syrup

¼ cup fresh lemon juice
2 teaspoons sugar
4 fresh pineapple chunks
Dash of grenadine
Crushed ice

Combine all ingredients in blender and mix until smooth. Pour into tall, chilled glasses and serve. Serves 4.

Mrs. Tom Hollis (Doris)

Sullivan's Silver Fizz

1 ounce vodka
1 ounce sweet and sour mix
1 teaspoon curacao
2 ounces half and half
  cream

1 egg white
1½ teaspoons powdered sugar
Crushed ice

Combine all ingredients in a blender. Fill with 2 cups ice and blend until smooth and fluffy. Serves 2.

Mrs. Sid Mann (Kathi)

Singapore Sling

1⅓ jiggers dry gin
⅔ jigger cherry flavored
  brandy
2 teaspoons powdered sugar
Juice of ½ lemon

Dash of aromatic bitters
⅓ jigger brandy
1 teaspoon grenadine
Club soda

Mix gin, brandy, sugar, lemon juice, bitters, brandy and grenadine; shake well with ice and strain into tall glass. Add club soda and ice as desired. Garnish with a twist of lemon, cherry and orange slice. Serves 1.

Marcus R. Bone

Texas "Tea"

2 ounces vodka
2 ounces gin
2 ounces rum
2 ounces tequila

3 ounces triple sec
3 ounces sweet and sour
  syrup
3 ounces cola

Mix all beverages together and serve over ice in tall tea glasses. Serves 2. *This is the best tea in Texas.*

Mrs. Denman Smith (Sandra)

Boiled coffee becomes bitter.

Hot Fruited Tea

5 cups boiling water	¼ cup lemon juice
5 tea bags	⅓ cup orange juice
10 whole cloves	3 unpeeled oranges, sliced,
¼ teaspoon cinnamon	for garnish
½ cup sugar	

Pour boiling water over tea, cloves and cinnamon. Cover and let steep 5 minutes. Strain tea; stir in sugar and fruit juices. Heat to just below boiling. Serve hot with an orange slice in each cup. Serves 6.

Mrs. Marcus Bone (Beverly)

Traditional Eggnog

12 egg yolks	1 fifth rum
1 cup sugar	4 cups whipping cream
4 cups milk	Freshly grated nutmeg

Beat egg yolks until fluffy. Add sugar gradually, beating until very light and thick. Add milk and rum. Chill until very cold, at least 5 to 6 hours. Whip cream and fold in. Chill for 1 hour before serving. Sprinkle with grated nutmeg. Yields 20 servings.

Nancy Young Chandler

Orange Liqueur with Brandy Eggnog

8 cups dairy eggnog	1 cup triple orange liqueur
1 tablespoon grated orange	with cognac brandy
rind	2 cups whipping cream,
	whipped

Combine eggnog with orange rind; chill for 1 hour. Add orange liqueur with cognac brandy. Fold in whipped cream. Chill for 1 hour. Yields 12 (7 ounce) servings.

Nancy Young Chandler

Susan's Eggnog

12 eggs, separated	6 cups whipping cream
½ teaspoon salt	4 cups milk
2¼ cups sugar, divided	1 teaspoon vanilla extract
2 cups bourbon	1½ tablespoons milk
2 ounces rum	Nutmeg

Beat egg yolks with salt. Add 1½ cups sugar and beat until dissolved. Gradually add bourbon and rum, mixing constantly. Beat egg whites until stiff, slowly adding ½ cup sugar. Whip cream and stir in ¼ cup sugar. Add milk and vanilla to the yolk mixture, stirring constantly. Fold in egg whites. Taste. Add more whiskey if desired. It should taste strong at this point. Thin with milk. Fold in whipped cream and sprinkle with nutmeg. Yields 30 (4 ounce) servings.

Mrs. Jim Rado (Vicki)

Citrus Punch

2 cups cold water	⅓ cup sweetened lemonade mix
1 can (6 ounces) frozen grapefruit juice concentrate	2 tablespoons grenadine

Mix all ingredients together in a pitcher, stirring to dissolve drink mix. Serve over ice. Yields 3 cups.

Mrs. Steve McMillon (Mary Beth)

Nostalgia's Cranberry Punch

9 cups pineapple juice	2 tablespoons whole cloves
9 cups cranberry juice	½ teaspoon salt
4½ cups water	1 cup brown sugar
4 cinnamon sticks	

Use a large (30 cup) coffee pot. Put spices and sugar in basket and place juices and water into percolator. Perk 45 minutes. Yields 40 (4 ounce) servings.

Mrs. Craig Smith (Sherrie)

Peach Champagne Punch

1   can (32 ounces) peach
    nectar
1   can (12 ounces) frozen
    orange juice concentrate
1   can (6 ounces) frozen
    limeade concentrate

1   bottle (16 ounces) rum
2   bottles (33.8 ounces each)
    club soda
2   bottles champagne

Mix all ingredients together except champagne and refrigerate. At serving time, mix all ingredients in punch bowl and add champagne. Crushed ice or an ice ring may be used. Any remaining punch may be frozen for use later. Yields 50 (4 ounce) servings.

Mrs. Denman Smith (Sandra)

Peppermint Punch

¼   pound hard peppermint
    candy
1   can (46 ounces) fruit
    punch, divided

1   bottle (33.8 ounces) ginger
    ale

Melt candy in 1 cup of fruit punch over medium heat until dissolved. Cool. Mix with remaining fruit punch and chill. Add ginger ale just before serving. Yields 16 to 20 servings. *If an ice ring is desired, place 10 to 12 candies in a mold with water and freeze.*

Mrs. Tom Blair (Debbie)

Raspberry Punch

1   cup fresh or frozen
    raspberries
½   cup rosé wine

½   cup sour cream
Fifth of champagne

In a blender mix raspberries, wine and sour cream together and blend until smooth. Chill and add with champagne to punch bowl just before serving. Serves 8.

Mrs. Jim Rado (Vicki)

Ruby Punch

4   cups cranberry juice
    cocktail
1   cup pineapple juice

1   cup orange juice
Fruit for garnish

Combine ingredients in punch bowl. Garnish with orange slices, pineapple chunks and sliced strawberries. Add ice ring or Giant Ice Cubes. Yields 6 cups.

Mrs. Robert Vossman (Nancy)

Giant Ice Cubes

Water
Red food coloring
1   orange slice, quartered

1   lemon slice, quartered
2   pineapple chunks, sliced
1   large strawberry, sliced

Partially fill 7 or 9 ounce plastic cups with water. Add 2 drops red food coloring, 1 piece of orange, lemon, pineapple and strawberry. Freeze overnight. Place these in your punch to garnish the bowl and to keep it cold.

Mrs. Robert Vossman (Nancy)

Strawberry Citrus Punch

1   can (6 ounces) limeade
    concentrate, thawed
1   can (6 ounces) orange
    juice concentrate, thawed
1   can (6 ounces) lemonade
    concentrate, thawed
3   cups cold water

2   packages (10 ounces each)
    frozen strawberries in
    syrup
1   bottle (33.8 ounces) ginger
    ale, chilled
1   orange, sliced, optional

In a punch bowl combine juice concentrates. Add water and stir. Add thawed strawberries in syrup and stir gently. Just before serving, add ginger ale. Float orange slices on top. Yields 24 (4 ounce) servings.

Mrs. Greg Gordon (Kathy)

Coffee Pot Wassail

30 cup coffee percolator
1 cup brown sugar
4 cinnamon sticks, broken up
4 teaspoons whole cloves
Pinch of salt

9 cups cranberry juice
4½ cups water
9 cans (6 ounces each) apple juice
1 can (6 ounces) orange juice concentrate

In the top basket of a percolator place brown sugar, cinnamon sticks, cloves and salt. Put liquid ingredients in the pot and brew. Serves 30.

Mrs. Ron Bruney (Carol)

"Texas" Strawberry Wine Punch

1 pint strawberries
2 cups Texas rosé
½ cup sugar
1 can (6 ounces) pineapple juice concentrate

½ teaspoon almond extract
1 lemon
1 bottle (1½ liters) chilled Texas Burgundy

Wash and hull strawberries; crush coarsely. Combine with rosé, sugar, undiluted pineapple juice and almond extract. Grate rind from lemon; squeeze juice; add to rosé mixture along with empty lemon shell. Cover and refrigerate overnight. Strain liquid, discarding lemon pulp. Pour over ice and add Burgundy just before serving. *If you cannot find Texas wines, you may substitute wines of other origins, but Texas wines are the best.* Yields 16 (3 ounce) servings.

Mrs. John Perkins (Sandy)

Hot Bourbon Punch

3 oranges
Whole cloves
1 bottle (1 liter) bourbon
2 bottles (1 liter each) red wine

1 tablespoon maple syrup
1 teaspoon nutmeg
1 teaspoon ground ginger
1 teaspoon cinnamon
1 teaspoon aromatic bitters

Stud the oranges well with cloves and roast at 350° for about 20 minutes or until soft to the touch. Cut oranges into quarters; place in chafing dish. Cover with bourbon, wine and maple syrup. Add remaining seasonings. Heat until steam begins to rise from mixture, but do not boil. Keep hot and flame just before serving. Serves 30.

Dudley Baker

The exquisite fragility of a cactus bloom amidst the pristine radiance of a glistening snowfall — this scene is a study in contrasts, just as the state is itself. Mountains, plains, coastal regions, forests — Texas has some of everything! Succulents, like the prickly-pear cactus, are common to the temperate, almost tropical, climate in central Texas. More than one "greenhorn" in the past century had occasion to experience the life-giving sustenance of the juice and petals from these desert plants. The trick, they discovered, was getting past the prickly thorns!

Soups, Salads and Sandwiches pictured: Southern Railway Bean Soup, Avocado Soup with Cilantro, Fruit Salad, Super Salad with Shrimp, Meatball Sandwich and Classic Hero.

Soups, Salads and Sandwiches

Corn Chowder

2 cups water
2 cups diced potatoes
½ onion, chopped
4 ribs celery, diced
¾ teaspoon basil
1 bay leaf
1 can (17 ounces) cream style corn
2 cups skim milk
1 cup fresh tomatoes, chopped
Salt and white pepper to taste
2 ounces Cheddar cheese, grated

Combine water, potatoes, onion, celery, basil and bay leaf and bring to a boil. Simmer until potatoes are tender. Remove bay leaf and add corn, milk, tomatoes and heat thoroughly; do not boil. Add salt, pepper and cheese, stirring until cheese is melted and soup thickens. Serves 8. *This soup only has about 125 calories per serving.*

Mrs. Jim Schultz (Mary Kay)

Chinese Hot and Sour Soup

4 dried black oriental mushrooms
¼ pound ham, slivered
½ cup slivered bamboo shoots
1 tablespoon soy sauce
4 cups chicken stock
Salt and white pepper to taste
1 cup sliced bean curd
3 tablespoons red wine vinegar
3 tablespoons cornstarch
3 tablespoons cold water
2 tablespoons dried cloud ears
2 tablespoons dried lily pods
2 teaspoons hot oil
1 egg, slightly beaten
1 tablespoon sesame oil
3 green onions, finely chopped, for garnish

Soak mushrooms in warm water until softened. Drain; remove stems and slice caps. Combine mushrooms, ham, bamboo shoots, soy sauce and chicken stock in a large saucepan and bring to boil over high heat. Reduce heat and simmer 3 minutes. Taste and add salt and pepper if necessary. Add bean curd and vinegar and bring to a boil again. Dissolve cornstarch in 3 tablespoons cold water and add to mixture. Add cloud ears, lily pods and hot oil. Cook, stirring constantly, until soup is slightly thickened. Slowly add egg, stirring gently. Remove from heat and stir in sesame oil. Ladle into bowls and garnish with finely chopped green onion. Serves 8.

Cecil E. Smith

Texas Country Bean Soup Mix

1 pound dried yellow split peas	1 pound Great Northern beans
1 pound dried black beans	1 pound dried split peas
1 pound dried red beans	1 pound dried blackeyed peas
1 pound dried pinto beans	
1 pound dried navy beans	1 pound barley pearls
	1 pound dried kidney beans

Combine all of above beans. Mix well. Yields 20 cups. *Divide into 10 portions (2 cups each). This is wonderful included in a Christmas Gift Basket along with a recipe for Texas Country Bean Soup.*

Mrs. Steve McMillon (Mary Beth)

Texas Country Bean Soup

2 cups Texas Country Bean Soup Mix	1 can (16 ounces) tomatoes with juice, chopped
2 quarts water	1 can (10 ounces) tomatoes with green chilies and juice
2 pounds ham, diced and divided	
1 onion, chopped	4 carrots, diced
2 cloves garlic, minced	2 ribs celery, chopped
½ teaspoon salt	

Wash and soak beans overnight; drain. Put beans into 2 quarts fresh water with 1 pound diced ham, onion, garlic and salt. Bring to a boil; reduce heat and cover. Simmer for 2 to 2½ hours. Add remaining ingredients and simmer 30 more minutes. Yields 2 quarts. *For a change add diced chicken instead of ham and ½ cup red wine. This is good served with hot cornbread and a salad on a cold day.*

Mrs. Steve McMillon (Mary Beth)

Fort Davis in west Texas, with an elevation of 5,050 feet, is the highest town in Texas. The fort was established in 1854 to protect settlers from the Apaches. It was occupied briefly by Confederate forces in 1862 and was destroyed by the Indians after the soldiers abandoned it. In 1867 the Negro Cavalry built 50 new buildings, some of which were restored beginning in 1961.

Southern Railway Bean Soup

1 pound dried navy beans
1 ham shank
2 cans (16 ounces each)
   tomatoes
¾ cup chopped onion
1 cup chopped celery
1 teaspoon marjoram
1 bay leaf

Water or chicken broth
2 cups diced uncooked
   potatoes
1 to 2 pounds smoked
   venison sausage, optional
½ cup mashed potatoes
Salt and pepper to taste

Soak beans overnight. Drain beans, then add all ingredients except potatoes and sausage. Add water or chicken broth to cover by at least 4 to 5 inches. Simmer 2 hours until tender. Remove bay leaf and bone; cut ham off bone and return ham to pot. Skim fat and add diced potatoes and sausage. Cover and simmer 1 hour. Blend in mashed potatoes and heat. Add salt and pepper to taste. Serves 6 to 8.

Mrs. Jean Neal (Barbara)

Broccoli Soup

6 tablespoons butter
¼ cup chopped onion
¼ cup chopped celery
¼ cup flour
4½ cups milk, heated
1 package (10 ounces)
   frozen chopped broccoli,
   thawed
1 tablespoon chicken
   bouillon granules

1 teaspoon salt
½ teaspoon dried parsley
½ teaspoon thyme leaves
½ teaspoon crushed bay leaf
⅛ teaspoon pepper
½ teaspoon prepared
   mustard
⅛ teaspoon hot pepper sauce

In a heavy 3 quart saucepan melt butter and sauté onion and celery until tender. Stir in flour and cook on low heat for 5 minutes; do not brown. Add warm milk and remaining ingredients. Cook slowly until hot and thick. Serves 6 to 8. *This soup freezes beautifully.*

Mrs. Sid Mann (Kathi)

 Red chilies are green chilies that have ripened and dried. They are most commonly used ground or crushed.

Broccoli Cheese Noodle Soup

2 tablespoons oil	2 packages (10 ounces each) frozen chopped broccoli
¾ cup chopped onion	
6 cups water	⅛ teaspoon garlic powder
6 chicken bouillon cubes	6 cups milk
1 package (6 ounces) noodles	16 ounces American cheese, cubed
1 teaspoon salt	Pepper to taste

Heat oil in a large saucepan. Add onions and sauté over medium heat for 3 minutes. Add water and bouillon cubes. Heat to boiling, stirring occasionally, until cubes are dissolved. Gradually add noodles and salt and continue to boil. Cook uncovered for 3 minutes, stirring occasionally. Stir in broccoli and garlic powder. Cook 4 minutes more and add milk and cheese. Cook until cheese melts, stirring constantly. Season with pepper. Serves 8 to 10.

Mrs. Larry Morris (Diane)

Carrot Curry Soup

1 medium onion, chopped	2 teaspoons sugar
2 tablespoons butter	¾ teaspoon curry powder
5 to 6 carrots, peeled and chopped	½ teaspoon salt
	¼ teaspoon white pepper
4 to 5 cups chicken broth	¼ teaspoon dill weed
2 tablespoons lemon juice	3 tablespoons dry sherry

Sauté onion in butter in a large skillet. Add carrots, broth, lemon juice, sugar, curry powder, salt, pepper and dill weed. Reduce heat and cook until carrots are tender-crisp. Pour into blender and purée until smooth. Stir in sherry; cover and chill. Serves 8.

Mrs. Marvin Sentell (Julie)

C.J.'s Cauliflower Soup

2 tablespoons butter	1 Idaho potato, peeled and diced
1 onion, chopped	
½ teaspoon curry powder	½ cup whipping cream
5 cups chicken broth	Salt and pepper to taste
1 head cauliflower, cut up	

Sauté onions in butter. Stir in curry. Bring broth to a boil and add onions, cauliflower and potato. Cover, reduce heat and simmer for 30 minutes. Cool and purée in blender. Before serving, add cream; season to taste and heat to very hot, but do not boil. Serves 6.

Mrs. Sid Mann (Kathi)

Cold Cucumber Soup

4 cucumbers, peeled and
   chopped
2 to 3 leeks, chopped
4 tablespoons butter
¼ cup flour
8 cups chicken broth
2 bay leaves
3 cucumbers, seeded and
   finely chopped

1½ cups half and half cream
Juice of 1 lemon
½ to 1 teaspoon finely
   chopped fresh dill
1 teaspoon salt
¼ teaspoon white pepper
Sour cream to garnish

Sauté 4 chopped cucumbers and leeks in butter for 20 minutes or until tender but not browned. Stir in flour and add chicken broth and bay leaves. Simmer for 30 minutes. Remove bay leaves and place half of the mixture into a blender and blend until smooth. Repeat method with remaining half and chill. Add seeded and finely chopped cucumbers, cream, lemon juice, dill, salt and white pepper. Stir until well mixed. Adjust seasonings if necessary. Return to refrigerator and chill thoroughly. Serves 12 to 14. *This soup is best when served very cold. Serve in chilled cups with a dollop of sour cream and an additional sprinkle of dill weed.*

Mrs. Dudley Baker (Kathy)

Tim's Potato Soup

5 medium potatoes, peeled
   and cubed
3 medium onions, chopped
5 ribs celery with leaves,
   diced
1½ tablespoons butter

2 teaspoons salt
¼ teaspoon white pepper
1 cup chicken broth
1 can (10¾ ounces) cream of
   chicken soup
Chopped parsley to garnish

Boil potatoes until tender. In the meantime, sauté onions and celery in butter until tender; do not brown. Drain potatoes. Add remaining ingredients, except parsley, to potatoes and return to heat. Stir constantly until mixture comes to a boil. Reduce heat and simmer 2 minutes. Mash some of the potatoes in the soup to thicken the texture. Ladle into bowls and garnish with a pat of butter and chopped parsley. Serves 10 to 12.

Mrs. Tim Mizner (Carol)

 Fresh herbs are not as pungent as dry herbs, so you will have to use more of them.

Dave's Fabulous Garlic Soup

6 beef bouillon cubes
8 cups boiling water
20 fresh garlic cloves
2 tablespoons butter
1 bunch green onions, minced

1 tablespoon flour
½ teaspoon pepper
Pinch of salt
6 egg yolks, beaten

In a large bowl or saucepan, combine bouillon cubes and water, stirring until cubes are dissolved. Peel garlic and mince. In a heavy saucepan over low heat, lightly brown garlic in butter with minced green onions, stirring constantly so as not to burn. Add flour and stir until slightly browned. Add broth and pepper; simmer 30 minutes to an hour. Just before serving, slowly add egg yolks, stirring constantly. Serve with toasted French bread that has been topped with Monterey Jack cheese. Serves 6. *This is a wonderful cure for whatever ails you and a great substitute for chicken soup! The 20 garlic cloves make it so good.*

Mrs. David King (Priscilla)

Leek and Potato Soup

4 leeks (white part only), thinly sliced
2 onions, thinly sliced
¼ cup butter
8 medium potatoes, thinly sliced

4 cups chicken broth
4 cups whipping cream
Salt and pepper to taste
Chives for garnish

Put leeks, onions and butter into a kettle and cook 5 minutes over low heat. Add potatoes and broth. Cook until potatoes are very soft. Purée the mixture in a blender or food processor. Mix in cream, salt and pepper and garnish with chives. Serve hot or cold. Serves 6 to 8.

Mrs. Cecil Smith (Diana)

Cucumber Yogurt Soup

4 cups seeded and chopped cucumbers
2 cups water
2 cartons (8 ounces each) plain yogurt
2 tablespoons honey

1 clove garlic, crushed
3 fresh mint leaves
¼ teaspoon dried dill weed
Salt and white pepper to taste

Combine all ingredients in a large bowl and mix. Pour into a blender and blend until smooth. Cover and chill for several hours. Serves 8.

Mrs. Greg Gordon (Kathy)

Lentil and Brown Rice Soup

5 cups chicken broth
3 cups water
1½ cups lentils, rinsed
1 cup brown rice
1 can (32 ounces) tomatoes, undrained
3 carrots, cut into ¼ inch pieces
1 onion, chopped
1 rib celery, chopped
3 cloves garlic, minced
½ teaspoon basil
½ teaspoon oregano
¼ teaspoon thyme
1 bay leaf
½ cup minced fresh parsley
2 tablespoons cider vinegar
Salt and pepper to taste

In a heavy kettle combine the chicken broth, water, lentils, rice and coarsely chopped tomatoes and juice. Add carrots, onion, celery, garlic, basil, oregano, thyme and bay leaf. Bring liquid to a boil. Simmer covered, stirring occasionally, for 45 to 55 minutes, or until the lentils and rice are tender. Stir in parsley, vinegar, salt and pepper. Discard bay leaf. The soup will be thick and will thicken as it stands. Thin the soup, if desired, with additional hot chicken stock or water. Yields 14 cups, serving 6 to 8.

Mrs. Ernest Butler (Sarah)

Mushroom Soup

4 onions, chopped
2 cloves garlic, minced
¼ cup butter
2 pounds fresh mushrooms, sliced
2 cups whipping cream
2 cups beef broth
½ teaspoon salt
¼ teaspoon white pepper
1 cup grated Parmesan cheese

Sauté onions and garlic in butter, over medium heat until onions are tender-crisp. Add mushrooms and cook over low heat for 8 minutes until mushrooms are tender. Gradually add cream, broth, salt and pepper and continue to cook until heated. *Do not boil.* Sprinkle each bowl with Parmesan cheese before serving. Serves 12 to 16.

Mrs. Joe Bowles (Mary)

 Mushrooms absorb water, so do not wash them. Wipe gently with a damp paper towel.

German Potato Soup

6 to 8 large carrots, pared
and sliced
6 to 8 large potatoes,
quartered
2 large onions, diced
4 ribs celery, diced

6 green onions, chopped
2 tablespoons dried parsley
1 pound bacon, fried crisp
and crumbled
1 cup sour cream

In a large pan, just barely cover vegetables with water and boil until tender. Do not drain. Mash vegetables and add the bacon and sour cream. Mix well. Serves 8 to 10. *This soup tastes best if it sits several hours. Just reheat and serve.*

Mrs. Val Judd (Nancy)

Black Forest Potato Soup

4 cups pared and cubed
potatoes
2 cups peeled and chopped
tomatoes
1 cup chopped celery
1 cup cubed carrots

3 cans (10¾ ounces each)
condensed beef broth
1 bay leaf
1½ cups cubed pumpernickel
bread
1 cup sour cream, for
garnish

In a large saucepan combine potatoes, tomatoes, celery, carrots, beef broth and bay leaf. Bring to a boil then reduce heat and simmer covered for 20 minutes. Meanwhile, place bread cubes on baking sheet and toast in 350° oven for 10 minutes. Remove bay leaf from soup. Pour soup into 6 bowls and top with bread cubes and a dollop of sour cream. Serves 6.

Mrs. Thomas Price (Marie)

Saffron is the world's most expensive spice because it is so difficult to gather. Besides being known for its flavor, it also gives a yellow color to the dish to which it's added.

French Onion Soup

3 large white onions, sliced
2 tablespoons margarine
1 tablespoon flour
4 cloves garlic, minced
¼ teaspoon oregano
½ teaspoon thyme
½ teaspoon paprika

4 cups water
2 cups beef broth
1 cup chicken broth
4 slices French bread, optional
1 cup grated Swiss cheese

Brown onion in margarine. Add flour, garlic and spices. Sauté for 3 minutes. Add water, beef and chicken broth. Boil 20 minutes, stirring occasionally. To serve, place bread in bowls, ladle soup to cover, top with cheese and run under broiler till cheese is melted and bubbly. Serves 4.

Betsey Bishop

Fresh Italian Tomato Soupa

2 tablespoons butter
1 tablespoon olive oil
1 small bunch green onions, chopped
12 mushrooms, sliced
3 small yellow squash, thinly sliced
2 small carrots, julienne sliced
6 to 8 ripe tomatoes, peeled and chopped

2 cans (10¾ ounces each) chicken broth
2 tablespoons fresh basil
2 tablespoons parsley or cilantro
½ pound bulk Italian sausage
1 cup grated Mozzarella cheese
Sliced ripe olives
Parsley or cilantro for garnish

In a large soup pot heat butter and oil. Add onions, mushrooms, squash and carrots. Cook until done but still crisp. Add the tomatoes, stirring constantly. Add chicken broth, herbs and sausage. Cover and simmer 20 to 30 minutes. Serve the soup in individual bowls, adding grated Mozzarella cheese and sliced black olives on top. You may also add parsley or cilantro for garnish. Serves 10. *For a heartier winter soup, any variety of pre-cooked noodles may be added sparingly.*

Sharon Dolezal

The horse was introduced into Texas by the Spanish.

Hot Tomato Soup

¼ cup diced celery	½ teaspoon white pepper
¼ cup diced onions	⅛ teaspoon thyme
¼ cup diced carrots	3 to 6 whole cloves
2 tablespoons butter	1 teaspoon salt, optional
2 sprigs parsley, chopped	4 cups canned tomato juice
1 bay leaf	2 cups consommé, heated

In a large Dutch oven sauté all vegetables in butter for 5 minutes. Add remaining ingredients except consommé and bring to a boil. Cover and simmer over low heat for 1 hour. Strain and add heated consommé. Serve hot. Yields 6 cups. *This will keep in the refrigerator for about 2 weeks. Just reheat to serve.*

Mrs. Robert McGoldrick (Fran)

Cheesy Corn Soup

⅓ cup chopped green bell pepper	1 chicken bouillon cube
	1 cup boiling water
¼ cup chopped onion	1 can (8¾ ounces) cream style corn
2 tablespoons margarine	
8 ounces cream cheese, cubed	½ teaspoon salt
	Dash of pepper
1 cup milk	

Sauté bell pepper and onion in margarine. Add cream cheese and milk. Heat slowly stirring until smooth. Dissolve bouillon cube in water; stir into cream cheese mixture. Add remaining ingredients. Heat through. Serves 4.

Mrs. Ken McGinnis (Susan)

Vegetable Cheese Soup

3 tablespoons butter	2 cans (14½ ounces each) chicken broth
½ cup chopped onion	
½ cup chopped celery	1 cup diced potatoes
½ cup diced carrots	3 to 4 cups grated American cheese
½ cup finely diced cabbage	
2 to 3 tablespoons flour, optional	

Sauté all vegetables except potatoes in butter until tender. For a creamy soup, add flour to vegetables and stir for a minute or two. Add chicken broth and potatoes and simmer for 20 to 30 minutes. Add cheese, stirring to melt and blend. Serves 4.

Mrs. Phillip Hubnik (Lea)

Vegetable Beef Soup

2 to 3 pounds soup bones
2 large onions, quartered
Salt and pepper
¾ pound fresh green beans, snapped
1 pound carrots, peeled and sliced

1 stalk celery, sliced, and leaves
2 cans (14½ ounces each) tomatoes
1½ to 2 pounds round steak, cubed
1 to 1½ cups shell macaroni

Place soup bones, onions, salt and pepper into a large pan and cover with 3 to 4 quarts water. Cook slowly 4 to 6 hours. Refrigerate overnight. Add green beans, carrots, celery and tomatoes to broth and simmer 1½ to 2 hours. Add meat and simmer an additional 2 to 3 hours. Add macaroni and cook until done. Adjust seasonings to taste. Yields 4 to 5 quarts.

Mrs. Larry Crain (Pat)

Quick and Tasty Soup

2 cups water
2 teaspoons chicken bouillon granules
¼ cup chopped green onion
¼ cup chopped celery

¼ cup chopped broccoli
¼ pound tofu, cubed
2 tablespoons picante sauce
Dash of white vinegar
1 egg, beaten

Bring water to a boil and add chicken bouillon, onion, celery, broccoli, tofu, picante sauce and vinegar. Simmer until vegetables are crisp tender. Swirl in egg just before serving. Serves 2. *This soup is filling and low calorie. Any combination of vegetables you have on hand will work, such as cabbage, mushrooms, bean sprouts or snow peas.*

Mrs. Denman Smith (Sandra)

Hearty Hamburger Soup

1 pound ground chuck
2 cups canned tomatoes
2 cups diced potatoes
½ cup diced carrots
½ cup diced celery
½ cup diced onion

2 teaspoons salt
¼ teaspoon pepper
1 beef bouillon cube
¼ cup uncooked rice
6 cups water

Brown beef in heavy kettle; drain. Add vegetables, seasonings, bouillon cube, rice and water. Simmer slowly 45 minutes. Serves 6.

Mrs. John Bosch (Nancy)

Sausage Soup

1 pound bulk sausage
8 cups beef broth
1 can (28 ounces) whole
tomatoes, undrained
1 cup diced carrots
1 onion, finely diced
1½ cups sliced celery

2 tablespoons brown sugar
¾ teaspoon salt
½ teaspoon pepper
1 package (8 ounces) egg
noodles
1 cup shredded cabbage

Brown sausage in skillet and drain. Place sausage in a soup pot and add beef broth, tomatoes, carrots, onion, celery, brown sugar, salt and pepper. Simmer for 1 to 1½ hours. Add noodles to soup along with cabbage and simmer 15 minutes more or until noodles are done. Serves 12.

Mrs. David Armour (Betsy)

Bratten's Clam Chowder

2 cans (6 ounces each)
minced clams
1 cup diced onion
1 cup diced celery
2 cups diced potatoes
1½ teaspoons salt

1 tablespoon wine vinegar
¾ cup butter
Dash of white pepper
¾ cup flour
4 cups half and half cream

Drain clam juice over vegetables in a saucepan. Add enough water to barely cover vegetables with liquid; add salt and simmer, covered, over medium heat until tender. Stir in clams and vinegar. Melt butter, add flour and pepper and cook for a few minutes. Add cream, stirring constantly, until thick and smooth; do not boil. Combine *undrained* vegetables and clams and white sauce. Serves 8.

Mrs. Val Judd (Nancy)

Corn and Crab Meat Soup

¼ cup chopped onion
¼ cup butter
2 tablespoons flour
½ teaspoon curry powder
4 cups fresh or frozen corn

4 cups milk
1 cup half and half cream
Salt and pepper to taste
1 carton (16 ounces) crab
meat

Sauté onion in butter until soft. Add flour and curry powder and cook 1 minute. Add corn; cook 5 minutes. Stir in milk and cream, salt and pepper and bring to a boil. Stir in crab meat and serve. Serves 8 to 10.

Mrs. Marcus Bone (Beverly)

Clam Chowder

8 slices bacon	½ teaspoon white pepper
1 cup diced celery	1 cup diced potatoes
½ cup diced carrots	2 cups milk
1 cup diced onion	2 cups half and half cream
½ cup flour	1 can (24 ounces) minced
2 cups clam juice	clams
1 cup water	4 cups grated white Cheddar
1 teaspoon salt	cheese

Fry bacon until crisp. Remove and crumble. Sauté celery, carrots, and onion in bacon drippings until tender. Add flour and stir until lightly browned. Mix in clam juice, water, salt and pepper and stir until mixed. Add potatoes and simmer 30 minutes. Add remaining ingredients and stir until smooth. Simmer but do not boil. Top with crumbled bacon. Serves 10 to 12.

Mrs. Denman Smith (Sandra)

New England Clam Chowder

¼ cup diced bacon	2 cans (7 ounces each)
¼ cup minced onion	minced clams, undrained
1 can (10½ ounces) cream of	1 tablespoon lemon juice
potato soup	⅛ teaspoon pepper
¾ cup milk	

In a large saucepan sauté bacon and onions until bacon is crisp and onion tender. Drain bacon grease. Stir in soup and milk; heat thoroughly, stirring occasionally. Stir in undrained clams, lemon juice and pepper. Heat well. Serves 4.

Mrs. Marcus Bone (Beverly)

Cream of Scallop Soup

3 to 4 tablespoons butter	1 can (10 ounces) tomatoes
1 medium onion, chopped	and green chilies
1 clove garlic, minced	1 can (14½ ounces) chicken
1 pound bay scallops	broth
1 cup half and half cream	½ cup sour cream

Sauté onion and garlic in butter until tender. Add scallops and simmer until partially cooked; add cream and simmer on low for 20 to 30 minutes. Stir in tomatoes and green chilies and chicken broth and simmer an additional 15 minutes. Add sour cream and place in 2 batches into blender and blend until smooth. Serve hot or cold. Serves 8 to 10.

Mrs. Denman Smith (Sandra)

Corn Shrimp Soup

5 tablespoons oil
5 tablespoons flour
1 onion, chopped
1 cup shallots, chopped
3 cloves garlic, minced
1 green bell pepper, chopped
2 celery ribs, chopped
4 tablespoons chopped parsley
1 can (17 ounces) stewed tomatoes, chopped
1 can (10 ounces) tomatoes and green chilies
3 cans (17 ounces each) whole kernel corn
1 can (17 ounces) cream style corn
5 quarts water
Salt and pepper to taste
2 pounds shrimp, peeled and deveined

Heat oil in soup pot. Make a roux by adding flour and cooking until brown. Add onion, shallots, garlic, bell pepper, celery and parsley. Cook 10 minutes or until onion is tender. Add stewed tomatoes and tomatoes with chilies. Cook 10 minutes longer, stirring constantly. Add all corn and stir until well mixed with seasonings. Add water, salt and pepper. Simmer 1 hour, stirring occasionally. Add shrimp. Simmer 30 minutes longer. Serves 10 to 12.

Carolyn Moore

Susie's Fish Soup

2 tablespoons olive oil
3 cloves garlic, minced
1 medium onion, minced
2 ribs celery, chopped
1 can (28 ounces) tomato sauce
1 can (28 ounces) whole tomatoes
½ teaspoon marjoram
2 tablespoons chopped fresh basil
2 cups chicken stock or bouillon
2 pounds fresh white fish
¼ cup chopped fresh parsley
Grated rind of 1 lemon

In a 6 quart stainless steel soup pot, heat the oil and sauté garlic, onion and celery until wilted. Add tomato sauce, whole tomatoes, marjoram and basil. Cook for 5 minutes over medium heat. Add chicken stock and cook another 2 to 3 minutes. Reduce heat and partially cover. Simmer for 20 to 30 minutes. Add fish and simmer an additional 15 minutes. Just before serving, add the parsley and lemon rind. Serves 6 to 8. *I have searched for a good fish soup recipe for years, and this is it!*

Mrs. Dan S. Steakley (Susan)

Basic Gumbo

¾ cup oil
¾ cup flour
2 onions, chopped
3 tablespoons butter
4 cups sliced fresh okra
3 cups chopped fresh
   tomatoes
2 green bell peppers,
   chopped
3 ribs celery, chopped
4 cloves garlic, minced
2 tablespoons butter
¼ teaspoon dried thyme
2 quarts boiling water
2 chicken bouillon cubes

1 to 2 tablespoons crushed
   dried red pepper
4 tablespoons salt
2 bay leaves
2 teaspoons Worcestershire
   sauce, optional
1 teaspoon ground allspice
1 teaspoon ground black
   pepper
1 teaspoon hot pepper
   sauce, optional
Cooked meat of your choice
Filé powder
Hot cooked rice

Mix oil and flour in small heavy saucepan and cook over low heat 30 to 45 minutes, stirring frequently, until roux is the color of mahogany. In a large Dutch oven or kettle, sauté onion in butter until soft, about 5 minutes. Stir in okra and sauté 3 to 5 minutes. Stir in tomatoes, bell peppers and celery and simmer 20 to 30 minutes. Add remaining ingredients except filé powder and rice and simmer covered about 1½ hours, stirring frequently. At this point you may add cooked chicken, shrimp, crayfish, oysters, sausage or fish filets and simmer for 15 minutes more. Ladle into serving bowls and top each with a scoop of rice. Pass filé powder and hot pepper sauce. Serves 8.

Mrs. Don Bradford (Melinda)

Oyster Chowder

4 potatoes, peeled and diced
1 teaspoon salt
1 cup water
1 cup chopped celery
1 medium onion, chopped
1 cup corn, cut from 2 ears
   fresh corn

2 pints oysters
2 cups half and half cream
4 tablespoons butter
¼ teaspoon cayenne pepper
Salt and pepper to taste
½ pound bacon, crisply fried
   and crumbled

Cook potatoes in salted water about 8 minutes. Add celery, onion and corn. Cover and cook another 10 minutes. Add oysters, cream, butter and cayenne. Simmer for 30 minutes until oysters are cooked. Add salt and pepper to taste. Top with crumbled bacon. Serves 8.

Mrs. Denman Smith (Sandra)

Peach Soup

2   cups fresh peaches
½   cup sugar
1   cup white wine or
    champagne
1   teaspoon lemon juice

½   cup sour cream
1   carton (8 ounces) vanilla
    yogurt
Coriander for garnish

Place all ingredients in blender and blend until smooth. Refrigerate. Thirty minutes before serving, place soup in freezer. If champagne is used, you may wish to stir it in just prior to serving. Garnish with coriander if desired. Serves 6 to 8.

Mrs. Denman Smith (Sandra)

Raspberry Soup

1   cup fresh or frozen
    raspberries
½   cup rosé wine

½   cup sour cream
½   cup brown sugar (omit if
    raspberries are in syrup)

In a blender or food processor blend all ingredients until smooth. Serve cold. Serves 4 to 6.

Mrs. Jim Rado (Vicki)

Carrot Vichyssoise

3   tablespoons butter
⅔   cup chopped onion
1   pound carrots, sliced
1   pound potatoes, peeled
    and diced
6   cups chicken broth
½   teaspoon thyme

½   teaspoon salt
2   bay leaves
¼   teaspoon hot pepper sauce
2   cups half and half cream
¼   teaspoon white pepper
Nutmeg to garnish

Sauté onion in butter. Add carrots, potatoes and broth. Stir in thyme, salt, bay leaves and hot pepper sauce. After bringing to a boil, simmer until vegetables are very soft, about 30 to 40 minutes. Put a small amount into blender and blend until very smooth. Put into a glass bowl. Continue until all is blended, being careful not to burn yourself. Add cream and white pepper. Adjust seasonings. Chill until very cold. Serve in chilled bowls with nutmeg as a garnish on top. Serves 12. *You could use a dab of sour cream with a few shreds of freshly grated carrots and nutmeg for a pretty presentation. This can be served hot, but I prefer it served very well chilled.*

Mrs. Dudley Baker (Kathy)

Salads

Frozen Strawberry Salad

1 carton (8 ounces) whipped topping
1 can (16 ounces) strawberry pie filling

1 can (14 ounces) sweetened condensed milk
1 can (17 ounces) crushed pineapple, drained
¼ cup lemon juice

Mix all ingredients together. Put into a 9x13 inch pan and freeze. Serve frozen. Serves 10 to 12.

Mrs. Thomas Price (Marie)

Applesauce Salad

1 cup applesauce
1 package (3½ ounces) raspberry gelatin

1 cup lemon lime carbonated beverage

Bring applesauce to a boil. Let boil 1 minute. Mix gelatin into hot applesauce and add liquid. Mix well. Pour into mold and refrigerate until firm. Serves 4 to 6.

Mrs. Larry Morris (Diane)

24-Hour Fruit Salad

1 tablespoon lemon juice
1 can (26 ounces) pineapple chunks, drained, juice reserved
1 egg, well beaten
½ cup sugar
1 can (20 ounces) pear halves

1 bottle (4 ounces) maraschino cherries
1 pound marshmallows
Coconut, optional
Pecans, optional
1 cup whipping cream

Combine lemon juice and enough reserved pineapple juice to make ½ cup. In a saucepan cook egg, sugar, and pineapple juice mixture, stirring until thick. Set aside to cool. Drain the fruit and cut into bite sized pieces. Add marshmallows, coconut and pecans if desired, mixing well. Whip cream until thick and pour over the fruit and marshmallows. Pour the juice over mixture, stirring well and chill 24 hours. Serves 8 to 10.

Mrs. Cecil Smith (Diana)

Custard Fruit Salad

4   eggs, beaten
1   can (20 ounces) pineapple
    chunks, drained, reserving
    juice
½   cup sugar
1   teaspoon vinegar
2   tablespoons flour
Dash of salt

1   pound miniature
    marshmallows
1   cup whipping cream
1   teaspoon vanilla extract
½   cup sugar
2 to 3 bananas, sliced
1   cup chopped pecans,
    optional

Make a custard by cooking eggs, pineapple juice, sugar, vinegar, flour and salt over low heat until mixture coats a spoon. Remove from heat and cool. When almost cool, stir in marshmallows. Whip cream, adding vanilla and sugar. Lightly toss all ingredients together. If desired, add pecans. Chill overnight. Serves 8 to 10.

Mrs. Mark Veltri (Pam)

Marvelous Whole Apple Salad

9   Rome Beauty apples,
    peeled and cored
2   cups sugar
2   cups water

1   teaspoon red food coloring
3   cinnamon sticks
Chopped walnuts or pecans
8   ounces cream cheese

Bake apples in ¾ cup of water in a 9x9 inch pan at 375° for 45 minutes. Boil sugar, water, food coloring and cinnamon sticks together to a thick syrup, 15 to 20 minutes. Pour over cooked apples and simmer 10 minutes. Apples are hard to turn over so make 9 for 6 people. Take out of syrup. Cool on a plate. Chill. Put on lettuce leaf. Soften cream cheese with a little milk and place inside with a sprinkle of chopped nuts. Serves 6.

Mrs. Val Judd (Nancy)

Frozen Peach Salad

1   jar (28½ ounces) spiced
    peaches, reserve juice
1½ cups miniature
    marshmallows
2   tablespoons sugar

4   ounces cream cheese,
    softened
1   cup evaporated milk,
    chilled
1   cup chopped pecans
1   tablespoon lemon juice

Mash peaches and stir in marshmallows. Combine sugar, ¼ cup peach juice and cream cheese. Beat until fluffy. Add peaches and marshmallows. Whip milk and add to peach mixture. Add pecans and lemon juice. Freeze in individual molds or an 8x12 inch dish. Serves 8 to 10.

Mrs. Orland Patton (Alice)

Carmen's Blueberry Salad

2 packages (3 ounces each)
   grape gelatin
2 cups very hot water
1 can (21 ounces)
   blueberries, in heavy syrup
1 can (20 ounces) crushed
   pineapple, undrained

1 cup sour cream
8 ounces cream cheese,
   softened
1 teaspoon vanilla extract
½ cup sugar
Pecans

Mix gelatin and hot water in a 9x13 inch pan until gelatin dissolves. Add blueberries and pineapple. Mix well and chill until firm. Blend together sour cream, cream cheese, vanilla and sugar. Spread over top of gelatin mixture and top with chopped pecans. Chill until ready to serve. Serves 8 to 10.

Mrs. Thomas A. Bone (Carmen)

Cranberry Relish Mold

1 can (9 ounces) crushed
   pineapple
1 package (3 ounces) cherry
   gelatin
½ cup sugar
1 cup hot water
1 tablespoon lemon juice

1 cup ground fresh
   cranberries
1 small unpeeled orange,
   ground
1 cup chopped celery
½ cup pecans

Drain pineapple and reserve syrup. Add water to make 1 cup liquid. Dissolve gelatin and sugar in 1 cup hot water. Add syrup and lemon juice. Chill until partially set. Add remaining ingredients; stir and chill overnight. Serves 4 to 6.

Mrs. Tom Hutchison (Susan)

Cranberry Apple Salad

2 cans (16 ounces each)
   whole cranberry sauce
2 cups boiling water
2 packages (3 ounces each)
   strawberry gelatin

½ teaspoon salt
2 tablespoons lemon juice
1 cup mayonnaise
2 cups diced apples
½ cup chopped walnuts

Melt cranberry sauce over medium heat; drain, reserving liquid and berries separately. Mix together cranberry liquid, boiling water and gelatin. Stir until gelatin is dissolved. Add salt and lemon juice. Chill until mixture mounds slightly on spoon. Fold in cranberries, apples and walnuts. Pour into a 2 quart mold and chill overnight. Serves 10 to 12.

Mrs. Ron Bruney (Carol)

Bobbi's Grape Salad

2   pounds white seedless
    grapes
1   can (14 ounces) sweetened
    condensed milk, chilled
2   eggs
1   can (15¼ ounces)
    pineapple tidbits, drained

1   cup miniature
    marshmallows
¼   cup white vinegar
1   teaspoon dry mustard
8   ounces cream cheese,
    softened
1   carton (8 ounces) whipped
    topping

Cut grapes in half. Beat the condensed milk and eggs together and mix with grapes. Add pineapple and marshmallows. Combine vinegar, mustard, cream cheese and whipped topping. Add to fruit and pour into a 9x13 inch glass dish and chill for several hours. Cut into squares to serve. Serves 12.

Ruth Gardner

Holiday Salad Ring

2   packages (3 ounces each)
    lemon gelatin
1½ cups boiling water

2   cups orange juice
2   cups mincemeat
½   cup chopped nuts

Dissolve gelatin in hot water; add orange juice and chill until slightly thickened. Stir in mincemeat and chopped nuts. Pour into an 8 inch ring mold. Serves 12.

Mrs. Jack Frucella (Mary Nell)

Cider Mold Salad

3   packages (3 ounces each)
    orange gelatin
4½ cups apple cider, divided
½   cup seedless white raisins

2   large apples, cored and
    chopped
½   cup chopped walnuts

Dissolve gelatin in 2 cups boiling apple cider. Add 2¼ cups cold cider, mixing well. Chill until gelatin mixture is slightly congealed. Soak raisins in ¼ cup cider for 30 minutes. Add raisins, apples and walnuts to gelatin mixture, stirring lightly. Pour into a 2½ quart mold and chill until firm. Serves 10 to 12.

Barbara Beall Stanley

Avocado Gelatin Salad

1 package (3 ounces) lime gelatin	3 teaspoons lemon juice
1 cup boiling water	½ teaspoon salt
1 can (8 ounces) crushed pineapple, reserve juice	½ cup whipping cream
Water	½ cup mayonnaise
1 avocado, diced	Assorted fresh fruits for garnish

Dissolve gelatin in water and chill until partially set. Drain pineapple, and add enough water to pineapple juice to make ½ cup liquid. Add pineapple, pineapple juice, avocado, lemon juice and salt to gelatin mixture. Refrigerate until consistency is right for folding. Whip the cream; fold in along with mayonnaise into gelatin mixture, and pour into a mold. Chill. Serve with fruits around the mold. Serves 8.

Mrs. Thomas Price (Marie)

Pineapple Cheese Salad

2 envelopes plain gelatin	1 cup chopped pecans
½ cup cold water	½ cup salad dressing
1 can (20 ounces) crushed pineapple, reserve juice	1 tablespoon lemon juice
8 ounces American cheese, grated	1 cup whipping cream, whipped

Dissolve gelatin in cold water; mix with pineapple juice and heat; do not boil. In a large bowl mix pineapple, cheese, pecans, salad dressing and lemon juice. Let gelatin cool and combine with fruit mixture. Fold in whipped cream. Spoon into a 2 quart glass dish or mold and refrigerate until firm. Serves 10 to 12.

Clara Jo Huckaby

Dandelions get their name from the shape of the leaves. The leaves reminded people in ancient times of lion's teeth. Thus dent de lion is our dandelion. To use dandelion leaves in salad, harvest them from the young plants before the flowers appear.

Lemon Gelatin Salad

1 package (3 ounces) lemon gelatin
1 cup boiling water
1 can (8¼ ounces) crushed pineapple
1 tablespoon sugar
2 tablespoons fresh lemon juice
1 teaspoon grated lemon peel
¼ cup cold water
¼ cup sour cream
1 package (3 ounces) lime gelatin

Dissolve lemon gelatin in boiling water. Add undrained pineapple, sugar, lemon juice, lemon peel and cold water. Let cool in refrigerator a few minutes. Blend in sour cream. Chill in decorative 4 cup mold until congealed. Mix lime gelatin according to package directions and pour on top of congealed lemon mixture. Return to refrigerator until mixture is set, at least 4 hours. Serves 6.

Mrs. Lorne Parks (Dephanie)

Pineapple Party Salad

3½ cups crushed pineapple
1 package (3 ounces) lemon gelatin
1 package (3 ounces) lime gelatin
¼ teaspoon salt
1 cup cottage cheese
½ cup chopped pecans
1 cup mayonnaise
Mayonnaise to garnish

Drain pineapple. Add water to syrup to make 2 cups. Heat to boiling. Dissolve gelatin in boiling liquid and add salt. Cool until slightly thickened. Fold in pineapple, cottage cheese, pecans and mayonnaise. Pour into a 10x6 inch pan. Place in refrigerator until congealed. Cut into squares and serve on lettuce. Garnish with a dollop of mayonnaise. Serves 8.

Mrs. Thomas Price (Marie)

Kidney Bean Salad

1 can (14½ ounces) kidney beans, drained
½ cup finely chopped celery
½ cup finely chopped onion
¼ cup finely chopped dill pickle
1 hard cooked egg, finely chopped
1 heaping tablespoon salad dressing
½ teaspoon salt
¼ teaspoon cayenne pepper

Mix all ingredients together well. Cover and refrigerate until chilled. Serves 4.

Mrs. Ron Bruney (Carol)

Grandma's Tomato Aspic

3 envelopes unflavored
  gelatin
4 cups vegetable cocktail
  juice, divided
1 teaspoon salt
½ teaspoon onion powder
⅛ teaspoon garlic powder

1 teaspoon Worcestershire
  sauce
Dash hot pepper sauce
1 cup diced celery
1 cup sliced green olives
Lettuce
1 avocado, to garnish
  Juice of ½ lemon

Place gelatin in 2 cups vegetable cocktail juice. Heat remaining juice; add softened gelatin to dissolve. Add seasonings and allow to cool. Add celery and olives and pour into a ring mold. Refrigerate until set. At serving time, unmold on a bed of lettuce. Garnish with avocado slices dipped in lemon juice. Serves 10 to 12. *Marinated tiny shrimp also make a pretty and tasty accompaniment. I love this aspic! It is Dudley's grandmother's recipe, and it is not as sweet as most.*

Mrs. Dudley Baker (Kathy)

Artichoke Medley

2 cans (14 ounces each)
  artichoke hearts, drained
1 can (6 ounces) pitted ripe
  olives, drained
1 can (6 ounces) green
  olives, drained
1 cup celery, cut diagonally
1 onion, sliced in thin rings
2 teaspoons salt
1 teaspoon paprika

1 teaspoon pepper
½ teaspoon powdered sugar
½ teaspoon dry mustard
1 garlic clove, diced
Dash of cayenne pepper
¼ cup white vinegar
¼ cup olive oil
¾ cup oil
1 egg yolk, beaten

Place artichokes, olives, celery and onion into a bowl. Combine remaining ingredients and mix well; pour over artichoke mixture. Refrigerate at least half a day. Serves 8 to 10. *This dish keeps forever and is delicious.*

Barbara Beall Stanley

Fresh artichokes do not keep longer than a day or two. Keep them in a plastic bag stored in the refrigerator.

Bean 'N Bacon Salad

2   cans (16 ounces each)
    whole green beans,
    drained
½   cup chopped onion
⅓   cup salad oil
¼   cup white vinegar
½   teaspoon salt
¼   teaspoon pepper
4   hard cooked eggs, finely
    chopped

¼   cup mayonnaise or salad
    dressing
1   teaspoon prepared
    mustard
2   teaspoons white vinegar
¼   teaspoon salt
4   slices bacon, crisply fried
    and crumbled
Crisp salad greens
Paprika

Combine beans, onion, salad oil, vinegar, salt and pepper and toss lightly. Cover and marinate at least 4 hours in refrigerator. Combine eggs, mayonnaise, mustard, vinegar and salt; mix well and refrigerate. Just before serving, drain bean mixture and toss with bacon. Serve on crisp salad greens topped with a spoonful of egg mixture and a sprinkling of paprika. Serves 6.

Mrs. J. Edward Reed (Marian)

Salmon Mousse

2   envelopes unflavored
    gelatin
1   can (14½ ounces) chicken
    broth
¼   cup lemon juice
1   can (16 ounces) salmon
1   cup finely chopped celery
2   tablespoons grated onion

2   tablespoons chopped
    parsley
2   tablespoons fresh dill
½   teaspoon salt
½   teaspoon pepper
½   cup mayonnaise
½   cup sour cream
Lettuce leaves for garnish

Soften gelatin in chicken broth over low heat, stirring constantly until gelatin dissolves. Add the lemon juice. Flake the salmon and remove bones and skin. Add celery, onion, parsley, dill, salt, pepper, mayonnaise and sour cream to gelatin mixture. Spoon into mold and chill 4 to 6 hours. Serve on lettuce leaves. Serves 6 to 8.

Mrs. Denman Smith (Sandra)

Walnut and Green Bean Salad

Salad:

1½ pounds fresh green beans	Ice water
1 teaspoon salt	

Cook green beans in salted water until tender crisp, about 4 minutes. Cool in ice water immediately; drain and pat dry.

Dressing:

¾ cup oil	¼ teaspoon white pepper
½ cup fresh mint leaves	1 cup crumbled Feta cheese
¼ cup tarragon vinegar	1 cup diced red onion
¾ teaspoon salt	1 cup chopped, toasted
½ teaspoon minced garlic	walnuts

Combine oil, mint, vinegar, salt, garlic and pepper in food processor until smooth. Mix in crumbled Feta cheese. Toss green beans with dressing and onion. Top with toasted walnuts. Chill until serving time or overnight. Serves 6.

Mrs. Denman Smith (Sandra)

Sprouts 'N Bean Salad

½ cup sugar	1 can (16 ounces) bean sprouts
½ cup white vinegar	
½ cup oil	1 jar (2 ounces) pimiento slices
Garlic salt to taste	
Salt and pepper to taste	1 package (1½ ounces) slivered almonds
1 can (16 ounces) seasoned cut green beans	

Heat sugar, vinegar, oil, garlic salt, salt and pepper in a saucepan until sugar is dissolved. Mix green beans, bean sprouts, pimiento and slivered almonds in a bowl and cover with sauce. Marinate in the refrigerator for half a day or at least 2 hours. Serves 4 to 6.

Mrs. Bob Edgecomb (Mary)

Black Eyed Pea Salad

3   cans (15 ounces each)
    black eyed peas
1   can (15 ounces) carrots
1   cup chopped onion
1   clove garlic, crushed
1   jar (2 ounces) sliced
    pimiento

1   can (10¾ ounces) tomato
    soup
¾   cup sugar
¾   cup white vinegar
5   tablespoons
    Worcestershire sauce
⅓   cup oil

Drain, wash and dry black eyed peas. Add remaining ingredients. Mix well and chill until ready to serve. Serves 12 to 15.

Jerry A. Hunt

Three Bean Salad

2   cans (16 ounces each) cut
    green beans
1   can (16 ounces) wax beans
1   can (16 ounces) red kidney
    beans
½   purple onion, sliced
⅔   cup oil

⅔   cup cider vinegar
⅓   cup sugar
1   teaspoon salt
½   teaspoon pepper
2   dashes dry mustard
4   slices bacon, fried

The day before you plan to serve, drain beans and place in a glass bowl. Add onion. Mix oil, vinegar, sugar, salt, pepper and mustard together and pour over bean mixture. Cover and refrigerate. Just before serving, crumble bacon and toss. Serves 10.

Mrs. Sid Mann (Kathi)

Broccoli Cauliflower Salad

1   head broccoli, cut into
    flowerets
1   head cauliflower, broken
    into flowerets
1   onion, peeled and chopped
2   cups mayonnaise

1   cup sour cream
2   tablespoons white vinegar
2   tablespoons sugar
Dash of Worcestershire sauce
Dash of hot pepper sauce
Salt and pepper to taste

Mix broccoli, cauliflower and onion. Make a dressing out of remaining ingredients. Pour dressing over vegetables. Toss well and chill several hours or overnight. Toss again before serving. Serves 8.

Mrs. Terry Arndt (Barbara)

Broccoli Salad

1 pound broccoli	¼ cup sweet pickle relish
4 hard cooked eggs, chopped	1 can (8 ounces) sliced water chestnuts, drained
1 onion, chopped	⅔ cup mayonnaise
½ cup stuffed green olives, chopped	2 tablespoons lemon juice

Wash broccoli and cut into bite sized pieces. Add eggs, onion, green olives, pickle relish and water chestnuts to broccoli. Combine mayonnaise with lemon juice and toss with the vegetables. Chill. Serves 6 to 8. *This is a wonderful change from a lettuce based salad.*

Suzanne Sternen

Cabbage and Carrot Salad

Salad:

4 cups shredded cabbage	1 cup shredded carrots

Put cabbage and carrots into a large bowl and toss. Set aside.

Dressing:

1 cup whipping cream	1 teaspoon salt
1 egg yolk	½ teaspoon sugar
2 tablespoons lemon juice	¼ teaspoon paprika
2 teaspoons prepared mustard	

Whip cream and egg yolk until almost stiff. Stir in remaining ingredients. Chill until serving time. Just before serving, toss cabbage, carrots and dressing. Serves 8.

Mrs. Denman Smith (Sandra)

Cook cool in the summer! Combine chicken, ham or seafood with pasta, salad greens, cooked or raw vegetables; top with a favorite salad dressing and have a one dish meal.

Avocado Imperial

1½ cups crab claw meat
1   tablespoon grated onion
1   teaspoon chopped parsley
1   teaspoon chopped chives
Pinch of tarragon
2   tablespoons lime juice,
    divided

1   avocado, halved and
    seeded
½   cup mayonnaise
¼   cup whipping cream,
    whipped
⅓   cup chili sauce

Combine crab meat, onion, parsley, chives, tarragon and 1 tablespoon lime juice. Halve avocado, remove seed and sprinkle with remaining tablespoon of lime juice. For sauce combine mayonnaise, whipped cream and chili sauce. To serve spoon crab meat mixture into avocado halves and top with sauce. Serves 2.

Ada Smyth

Light and Tangy Coleslaw

Dressing:
⅓   cup mayonnaise
¾   cup plain lowfat yogurt
1   tablespoon honey

1   teaspoon mustard
¼   teaspoon fresh lemon
    juice

Mix mayonnaise, yogurt, honey, mustard and lemon juice and set aside.

Slaw:
½   cup minced parsley
1   green onion, minced
1   carrot, grated
1   rib celery, grated

½   head red cabbage,
    shredded
Sunflower seeds

Prepare vegetables for slaw and place in mixing bowl. Moisten slaw sparingly with dressing to taste. Sprinkle with sunflower seeds. Serves 6. *This is a great coleslaw and the dressing is only 14 calories per tablespoon. For a different, sweeter flavor substitute a grated apple for the sunflower seeds.*

Mrs. Dan S. Steakley (Susan)

Cucumber and Onion Salad

1   carton (8 ounces) sour
    cream
½ cup mayonnaise

3   tablespoons wine vinegar
2   cucumbers, sliced
2   onions, peeled and sliced

Mix sour cream, mayonnaise and wine vinegar. Place cucumbers and onions in a bowl and pour cream mixture over. Toss gently. Chill and serve. Serves 4 to 6.

Mrs. Jerry Holder (Pat)

Scandinavian Cucumbers

½ cup sour cream
1   tablespoon sugar
2   tablespoons minced
    parsley or cilantro
2   tablespoons tarragon
    vinegar

1   tablespoon chopped onion
¼ teaspoon dill weed
3   small unpared cucumbers,
    thinly sliced

Stir together sour cream, sugar, parsley or cilantro, vinegar, onion and dill weed. Fold in cucumbers and chill covered for 2 hours. Serves 6.

Mrs. W. H. Heggen III (Maryellen)

Quick and Easy Cucumber Salad

3   cucumbers
½ cup sliced green olives
½ green bell pepper, sliced
1   jar (5 ounces) whole
    mushrooms, drained

Italian salad dressing
Salt to taste
Garlic salt to taste

Peel and slice cucumbers as thinly as possible. Add olives, bell pepper and mushrooms. Pour Italian dressing over vegetables just to cover and add seasonings. Serve immediately or refrigerate. Serves 4.
Sometimes I add slices of avocado or artichoke hearts for a nice variety.
Mrs. Jim Helgren (Susan)

Marinated Mushroom Salad

1 **pound fresh mushrooms, cleaned**	6 **tablespoons fresh lemon juice**
8 **scallions, minced**	1 **teaspoon ground cumin**
3 **ribs celery, minced**	**Salt and pepper to taste**
	⅔ **cup olive oil**

Cut mushroom stems crosswise into thin slices until they are flush with the caps. Slice the caps thinly. In a salad bowl combine the mushrooms, scallions, and celery. In a small bowl, whisk together the lemon juice, cumin, salt and pepper. Add oil in a stream while whisking and continue until emulsified. Toss the salad with the dressing and season it with salt and pepper. Serve immediately. Serves 6.

Mrs. Ernest Butler (Sarah)

Mushroom Salad

½ **pound mushrooms, sliced**	1½ **tablespoons mayonnaise**
¼ **cup minced fresh parsley**	½ **teaspoon salt**
¼ **garlic clove, minced**	⅛ **teaspoon dry mustard**
⅓ **cup salad oil**	⅛ **teaspoon pepper**
2½ **tablespoons white wine vinegar**	**6 to 8 lettuce leaves, washed and chilled**

Wash mushrooms; trim off stems and slice fairly thick. Combine mushrooms and parsley. Chill. Combine garlic, salad oil, wine vinegar, mayonnaise, salt, mustard and pepper in a blender or food processor and blend well. Just before serving toss dressing with mushrooms and spoon salad onto lettuce leaves. Serves 4.

Mrs. Sid Mann (Kathi)

Oriental Pea Salad

1 **package (10 ounces) frozen English peas, thawed**	1 **tablespoon lemon juice**
	½ **teaspoon curry powder**
1 **can (6 ounces) shrimp**	1 **can (5½ ounces) chow mein noodles**
1 **cup chopped celery**	**Lettuce leaves**
¾ **cup mayonnaise**	**Tomato wedges**

Combine peas, shrimp, celery, mayonnaise, lemon juice and curry powder in a large bowl and mix well. Cover and refrigerate at least 30 minutes. Add noodles just before serving and toss well. Serve on lettuce surrounded by tomato wedges. Serves 4 to 6.

Mrs. Robert S. Brown (Mary)

Grandma's Hot German Potato Salad

3 pounds new potatoes
½ pound bacon, cooked and
  crumbled, reserving
  drippings
1 tablespoon flour
⅔ cup cider vinegar
⅓ cup water

3 to 4 tablespoons sugar
¾ cup chopped celery
¾ cup chopped onion
Salt and pepper to taste
3 hard cooked eggs
Paprika for garnish

Gently cook the potatoes in boiling water until just tender. Drain and set aside. Meanwhile, return ½ cup bacon drippings to the skillet over low heat and add 1 tablespoon flour, stirring until dissolved. Add vinegar and water, stirring gently for about 1 minute. Turn heat off and add sugar, stirring until dissolved. When the potatoes are just cool enough to handle, slice ⅓ of them into a large casserole; add ⅓ each of the celery, onion and bacon. Sprinkle lightly with salt and pepper and drizzle several spoonsful of dressing over the top. Repeat this process two more times, reserving 3 spoonsful of dressing. Slice the eggs over the top and drizzle the remaining dressing over the eggs. Sprinkle lightly with paprika for garnish. Serve warm. Serves 8 to 10.

Mrs. Terry Arndt (Barbara)

French Dijon Salad

Vegetable:
2 to 3 cups red potatoes,
  cooked and diced

½ pound fresh green beans,
  cooked

Mix potatoes with green beans. Chill.

Dressing:
2 to 3 tablespoons olive oil
3 ounces wine vinegar
1 teaspoon salt
¼ teaspoon white pepper
2 tablespoons Dijon
  mustard

Romaine lettuce
2 tomatoes, cut in wedges
12 ripe olives, pitted
Capers to taste

Mix olive oil, vinegar, salt, pepper and mustard. Pour over potatoes and beans and toss. Arrange romaine lettuce on a salad plate and mound salad in center. Surround with tomato wedges and top with olives and capers. Serves 4 to 6. *For a variety add tuna to potato mixture.*

Mrs. Randy Hagan (Robin Roberts)

Rice Salad

½ cup uncooked rice
1 cup water
1 bay leaf
1 teaspoon salt
1 pinch saffron
½ cup olive oil
3 tablespoons wine vinegar
¼ teaspoon white pepper

⅔ cup finely chopped onion
⅓ cup finely chopped tomato
½ cup finely chopped celery
½ cup finely chopped green
bell pepper
¼ cup raisins
⅓ cup chopped parsley
Salt and pepper to taste

Cook rice with bay leaf, salt and saffron. While still warm, stir in remaining ingredients. Toss well and adjust seasonings to taste. Chill 4 hours or overnight. Serves 6 to 8.

Mrs. Jack Frucella (Mary Nell)

Salad Nicoise

Salad:

6 cups cooked, peeled and
sliced potatoes
3 cups cooked green beans
1 red onion, sliced
1 green bell pepper, sliced
1 can (2¼ ounces) sliced
ripe olives

4 hard cooked eggs, sliced
2 cans (6½ ounces each)
tuna
1 jar (6 ounces) green olives
2 tomatoes, cut in wedges
1 head leaf lettuce

Toss potatoes with 1 cup of dressing mixture. Set aside to season. Toss green beans with remaining dressing. To serve, arrange lettuce on platter; layer with potatoes, green beans, onion, bell pepper, ripe olives, eggs, tuna, green olives and tomato wedges. Serves 8 to 10.

Dressing:

⅔ cup oil
½ cup tarragon vinegar
1 teaspoon minced garlic
1 teaspoon prepared
mustard

1 tablespoon chopped green
onion
1 teaspoon salt
½ teaspoon white pepper
¼ cup capers

Mix together all dressing ingredients.

Mrs. Denman Smith (Sandra)

 The outer leaves of lettuce and cabbage contain most of the nutrients so use as many of them as possible.

Furman's Sour Cream Potato Salad

½ cup Italian dressing
3 pounds new potatoes,
   cooked in jackets, diced
Salt and freshly ground
   pepper to taste
¾ cup diced celery
¾ cup minced green onions,
   including tops

¼ cup finely minced parsley
1 large kosher dill pickle,
   diced
1 cup mayonnaise
1 cup sour cream
1 heaping tablespoon Dijon
   mustard

In a mixing bowl pour dressing over diced, warm potatoes. Season with salt and pepper; stir well. Add celery, green onions, parsley and pickle to bowl and stir. In a separate bowl combine mayonnaise, sour cream and mustard. Blend and add to potato mixture. Cover and refrigerate 3 to 4 hours before serving. Serves 10. *For a variation, stir in crisp, crumbled bacon just prior to serving.*

William Furman

Old Fashioned Potato Salad

4 pounds red potatoes
1¾ cups diced celery
1 cup finely chopped green
   onion
1 cup salad dressing
1 cup mayonnaise

2 teaspoons prepared
   mustard
1 teaspoon cider vinegar
½ teaspoon salt
⅛ teaspoon pepper

Cook potatoes in salted water; peel and dice. Add celery and green onion to potatoes. Combine remaining ingredients and mix with vegetables. Refrigerate. Serves 8 to 10. *This potato salad is best made the day before serving.*

Mrs. Sid Mann (Kathi)

Shoestring Potato Salad

2 to 3 crisp sweet pickles,
   diced
2 eggs, hard cooked, cubed
½ cup grated processed
   cheese

1 onion, chopped
1 jar (4 ounces) pimientos
½ cup salad dressing
1 can (1¾ ounces)
   shoestring potatoes

Mix pickles, eggs, cheese, onion, pimientos and salad dressing. When ready to serve, add shoestring potatoes and toss. Serves 4 to 6.

Mrs. Jim Smith (Jare)

Tomatoes Rosé

4   large tomatoes
¼   cup finely chopped green
     onion
¼   cup finely chopped celery
1   package (1 ounce) Italian
     salad dressing mix
3   tablespoons wine vinegar

7   tablespoons salad oil
½   cup rosé wine
½   green bell pepper, finely
     chopped
Salt, optional
Lettuce

Cut tomatoes into thin slices. Arrange in a shallow serving bowl. Combine all remaining ingredients, adding salt if desired. Pour over tomatoes and chill at least 1 hour. Serve from bowl or arrange slices of tomatoes on crisp lettuce leaves and spoon dressing over the top. Serves 6.

Joan Winkelman

Moroccan Tomato Salad

3   tomatoes
3   ribs of celery
½   cup chopped parsley
⅓   cup capers
2   green bell peppers

6   hot cherry peppers
Salt to taste
¼   teaspoon cayenne pepper
1   teaspoon paprika
¼   cup olive oil

Core the tomatoes and cut into ½ inch cubes. Place in a salad bowl. Trim the celery and coarsely chop. Add to tomatoes along with parsley and capers. Trim bell peppers and cherry peppers; chop and add to salad bowl. Blend together salt, cayenne pepper, paprika and olive oil and pour over salad. Toss to blend well and serve at room temperature. Serves 6.

Mrs. Cecil Smith (Diana)

Americans should be eating the parsley they use on their plates as a garnish. Besides being a great source of Vitamin A and C and calcium, it is a breath freshener.

Fire and Ice Tomatoes

6 large tomatoes, skinned
   and quartered
1 large green bell pepper,
   cut into strips
1 large red onion, sliced
¾ cup cider vinegar
1½ teaspoons celery salt
1½ teaspoons mustard seed

1 teaspoon sugar
⅛ teaspoon red pepper
⅛ teaspoon black pepper
2 teaspoons salt
¼ cup water
1 cucumber, thinly sliced,
   optional

Toss tomatoes, green pepper and onion in a large glass bowl. Combine remaining ingredients except cucumber and bring to a boil for 1 minute. While still hot, pour over vegetables. Chill for several hours or overnight. At serving time the cucumber may be added if desired. Serves 12 to 14.

Mrs. Jack Frucella (Mary Nell)

Party Pasta Salad

1 package (12 ounces)
   macaroni shells
2 jars (6 ounces each)
   marinated artichoke
   hearts, drained and juice
   reserved
1 package (5 ounces)
   pepperoni, thinly sliced
1 onion, finely chopped

1 can (6 ounces) sliced ripe
   olives, drained
½ cup tarragon vinegar
½ cup artichoke liquid
1 to 1½ cups Caesar salad
   dressing
1 cup grated Parmesan
   cheese, divided
Salt and pepper to taste

Cook pasta per directions on package or until tender. Drain and put into a large bowl to cool. Cut artichokes into bite sized pieces. When pasta is cool, add pepperoni, artichoke pieces, onion and ripe olives. Combine tarragon vinegar and artichoke liquid with Caesar salad dressing. Mix well and pour over pasta mixture; add ¾ cup Parmesan cheese and stir well. Sprinkle remainder of Parmesan cheese on top. Serves 12 to 14. *This salad can be done a day ahead to allow flavors to mix.*

Mrs. Steve McMillon (Mary Beth)

Super Salad

1 package (8 ounces) shell pasta, whole wheat if possible
½ cup vinegar and oil dressing
¼ cup plain lowfat yogurt or sour cream
1 tablespoon picante sauce

1 cup fresh broccoli flowerets
2 avocados, cubed
1 red bell pepper, sliced
1 onion, sliced
3 ribs celery, sliced
2 carrots, sliced
Romaine lettuce

Boil pasta according to directions on package. Meanwhile, prepare the dressing by combining your favorite vinegar and oil dressing with the yogurt or sour cream and picante sauce. Drain pasta and transfer to a large bowl. Add half the dressing, then toss and refrigerate. Begin slicing vegetables for the salad. Place in bowl and toss gently. Make a bed of romaine lettuce on each plate; then add a generous layer of pasta on each one. Heap the vegetables on top and pour on the remaining dressing. Serves 4 to 6. *This salad is as beautiful as it is tasty and good for you. You can make this salad a complete meal by adding 1 cup cubed Cheddar cheese or 1 pound of cold shrimp.*

Mrs. Dan S. Steakley (Susan)

Vermicelli Salad

1 package (12 ounces) vermicelli
3 teaspoons lemon juice
3 teaspoons oil
½ cup chopped celery
½ cup chopped green bell pepper

½ cup chopped green onion
½ cup chopped pimiento
½ cup chopped ripe olives
Mayonnaise to moisten
Salt and pepper to taste

Cook pasta according to package directions. Drain, but do not rinse. When cool enough to handle, place in a bowl and add lemon juice and salad oil. Blend and cover tightly. Refrigerate overnight. Add vegetables the next day. Moisten with mayonnaise, and season with salt and pepper. Blend and refrigerate several hours or overnight. Serves 12. *This is a great change from potato salad.*

Mrs. Linden Welsch (Phyllis)

Iceberg lettuce is the favorite in American salads. However, other varieties of lettuce and salad greens such as romaine, bibb, endive, Boston, spinach and leaf have much more flavor.

Rice and Fresh Mushroom Salad

1   package (7 ounces) instant
    rice
5   chicken bouillon cubes
1   cup chopped onion
1   cup chopped green bell
    pepper

1   cup chopped celery
½   pound mushrooms, sliced
1   jar (4 ounces) diced
    pimiento, drained
1   bottle (8 ounces) creamy
    Italian dressing

Cook rice according to package directions, except omit the salt and add bouillon cubes. Let cool. Combine rice and remaining ingredients. Stir well and chill. Serves 8 to 10.

Barbara Beall Stanley

Zucchini Salad

4   small zucchini
Dash of salt
2   medium tomatoes, cut in
    eighths
1   small green bell pepper,
    chopped

4   green onions, chopped
½   cup French dressing
Dash of oregano
Dash of savory

Cook whole zucchini in boiling water 8 to 10 minutes. Drain; cut into ½ inch slices. Add to remaining vegetables and toss with salad dressing and seasonings. Allow to marinate several hours or overnight in refigerator. Serves 4.

Mrs. David Armour (Betsy)

Italian Salad

1   small head romaine
    lettuce, torn
1   small head iceberg
    lettuce, torn
1   can (14 ounces) artichoke
    hearts, drained and
    chopped
1   can (14 ounces) hearts of
    palm, drained and
    chopped

1   large red onion, chopped
1   jar (4 ounces) chopped
    pimientos, drained
½   cup grated Parmesan
    cheese
½   cup oil
⅓   cup tarragon vinegar
Salt and pepper to taste

In a large salad bowl combine lettuces, artichoke hearts, hearts of palm, red onion, pimientos and Parmesan cheese. Blend oil and vinegar and mix well. Pour over salad and toss gently. Add salt and pepper to taste. Serves 6 to 8. *Excellent with Italian food!*

Mrs. Mark Kiester (Jo Ellen)

Eastport Salad

Salad:

2 tablespoons olive oil
1 clove garlic, crushed
2 tomatoes, chopped
1 large head leafy lettuce

4 green onions, chopped
¼ cup Romano cheese, grated
8 slices bacon, cooked and crumbled

Put the oil in a large wooden bowl, add the crushed garlic and stir well. Add the tomatoes and stir. Do not stir again until serving time. Break the lettuce into the bowl. Add the onions, cheese and bacon, cover tightly and chill for 1 to 2 hours.

Dressing:

⅓ cup olive oil
Juice of 1 lemon

Freshly ground pepper
¼ teaspoon oregano

Make the dressing well ahead and chill. At serving time pour dressing over the greens and toss. Serves 6 to 8.

Mrs. David King (Priscilla)

Party Salad for a Crowd

2 to 3 heads Bibb lettuce
1 carton cherry tomatoes
2 green bell peppers, sliced in rings
1½ pounds fresh mushrooms
1 bunch fresh broccoli
1 pound fresh asparagus
1 can (6 ounces) whole ripe olives, drained

2 purple onions, sliced
1 cup vinegar
2 cups clear French dressing
1 clove garlic, minced
Salt and pepper to taste
Lettuce

Wash lettuce, separating leaves, and store with wet paper towels in plastic bags in refrigerator. Place cherry tomatoes, bell peppers and mushrooms in a large bowl. Cut broccoli into flowerets; cut off tough ends of asparagus and discard; add broccoli and asparagus spears to bowl. Add ripe olives and onions to the bowl of vegetables. Set aside. Mix vinegar, French dressing, garlic, salt and pepper and pour over vegetables; toss well. Marinate for 24 hours in a sealed container. When ready to serve, spread whole lettuce leaves on a huge tray and spoon vegetables over each leaf. Guests may easily scoop up a lettuce leaf and salad in one. Serves 12.

Mrs. Bill Hablinski (Sandy)

Greek Salad

1 cup olive oil	4 to 5 large tomatoes, chopped
¼ cup wine vinegar	1 cup Greek olives
Juice of 1 lemon	1 bunch green onions, chopped
2 cans (3 ounces each) anchovy fillets	2 cucumbers, peeled and thinly sliced
Reserved oil from anchovies	1 head romaine lettuce
½ teaspoon oregano	1 head red leaf lettuce
1 tablespoon basil, chopped	1 head iceberg lettuce
¼ teaspoon dill weed	1 head Boston lettuce
¼ teaspoon pepper	½ pound Feta cheese, cubed
½ teaspoon salt	1 cup walnuts, chopped
1 to 2 cloves garlic, minced	

Mix olive oil, vinegar, lemon juice, reserved anchovy oil, oregano, basil, dill weed, pepper, salt and garlic. Add tomatoes, olives, green onions, and cucumbers; refrigerate for several hours. Tear all lettuce into bite sized pieces. Take vegetables out of marinade and toss with lettuce. Add cheese and more dressing if needed. Toss lightly to coat all greens. Adjust seasonings. Lay anchovy fillets over all and sprinkle with walnuts. Serves 24.

Mrs. Dudley Baker (Kathy)

Wilted Watercress Salad

3 hard cooked eggs, sliced	¼ cup wine vinegar
2 pounds fresh watercress	Salt and pepper
½ pound bacon	

Wash watercress well; tear into large sprigs, drain and put into salad bowl. Cook bacon crisp; drain on paper towel and crumble; set aside. Reheat bacon drippings until very hot; pour over watercress and toss. Drain extra drippings back into skillet to heat and pour over cress again until cress begins to wilt. Add vinegar, bacon bits, salt and pepper and toss. Garnish with sliced hard cooked eggs. Serves 10 to 12.

Mrs. Don Bradford (Melinda)

For the most flavor, if you must buy dried herbs, never get the powdered type. Buy the leaves and crush them yourself.

Hot Chicken Salad

2 cups cooked chopped
 chicken
1 cup chopped celery
1 cup chopped onion
1 cup bread crumbs
1 cup mayonnaise

Salt and pepper
1 jar (8 ounces) pasteurized
 cheese spread
1 can (2.8 ounces) French
 fried onion rings

Combine chicken with celery, onion, bread crumbs, mayonnaise, salt and pepper. Bake at 350° for 15 minutes. Take out of oven and spread with cheese and bake 5 minutes more. Remove from oven and sprinkle onion rings on top; heat 1 to 2 minutes more. Serves 4 to 6.

Mrs. Thomas Price (Marie)

Hot Chicken Rice Salad

⅔ cup rice
1 can (14½ ounces) chicken
 broth
2 cups cooked chopped
 chicken
1 can (10¾ ounces) cream of
 chicken soup
1 tablespoon chopped onion
½ teaspoon salt

½ teaspoon pepper
½ cup mayonnaise
½ cup sliced almonds
1 can (14 ounces) water
 chestnuts, drained and
 sliced
2 teaspoons lemon juice
3 hard cooked eggs, diced
1 cup minced pimiento
Bread crumbs for garnish

Cook rice in chicken broth. Mix all ingredients together. Put salad into a 3 quart casserole or 2 small ones. Sprinkle with bread crumbs or cracker crumbs. Bake at 350° for 45 minutes. Serves 8.

Mrs. John Reesing (Hallie Jo)

Shrimp Salad a la Greek

1 to 2 pounds small salad
 shrimp
1 cup thinly sliced celery
4 to 6 green onions, sliced
1 can (14 ounces) artichoke
 hearts, chopped
1 can (4¼ ounces) sliced
 ripe olives

½ cup crumbled Feta cheese
1 to 1½ cups mayonnaise
¼ cup lemon juice
1 teaspoon salt
½ teaspoon white pepper
Leaf lettuce

Toss all ingredients except lettuce lightly together and refrigerate overnight. Adjust salt and pepper. Serve on leaf lettuce. Serves 6 to 8.

Mrs. Denman Smith (Sandra)

Shrimp Salad

½ head lettuce
½ cup mayonnaise
2 tablespoons chili sauce
1 pound shrimp, boiled, peeled and deveined
4 hard cooked eggs, chopped, divided
2 radishes, sliced

2 tablespoons chopped dill pickle
½ cup finely chopped celery
2 green onions, finely chopped
1 teaspoon horseradish, optional
Crackers or French bread

Line a large salad bowl or individual salad plates with lettuce torn into bite sized pieces. Combine all other ingredients and mix until well coated. Chill until serving. Serve with crackers or French bread. Serves 6. *This salad is wonderful for a ladies luncheon.*

Mrs. Joe Bowles (Mary)

Seafood Salad

1 pound loaf white bread, sliced
Butter
1 large onion, finely chopped
4 hard cooked eggs, diced

1 can (7½ ounces) crab meat
2 cans medium deveined shrimp
1 cup chopped celery
2½ cups mayonnaise
Salt and pepper to taste

Remove crusts from bread and butter one side of bread lightly. Cut into small cubes about ½ inch thick. Place in a bowl. Sprinkle with chopped onion and mix well. Cover bowl tightly and refrigerate overnight. Early the next day, add remaining ingredients. Mix well. Cover and refrigerate several hours before serving. Serve on a bed of lettuce. Also delicious served in avocado half. Serves 12 generously.

Mrs. Sid Mann (Kathi)

The smaller bay scallop is more desirable than the sea scallop. It does not have to be sliced to be added to recipes, and it is sweeter.

Sunny Salmon Salad

Salad:

6 broccoli flowerets
6 julienne strips carrot
1 can (7¾ ounces) salmon,
   liquid reserved
4 mushrooms, halved

4 slices cucumber
½ tomato, cut into 4 wedges
Lettuce
Lemon wedges for garnish

Steam broccoli and carrots for 5 minutes and cool. Drain salmon, reserving 2 tablespoons of liquid for marinade. Separate salmon into chunks and combine with broccoli, carrots, mushrooms, cucumber and tomato.

Lemon Marinade:

Juice of ½ lemon
2 tablespoons cider
   vinegar
2 tablespoons oil
2 tablespoons salmon
   liquid
2 teaspoons chopped
   onion
1 teaspoon chopped
   parsley

½ teaspoon grated lemon
   peel
½ teaspoon sugar
¼ teaspoon salt
¼ teaspoon crushed basil
   leaves
⅛ teaspoon garlic salt
⅛ teaspoon ground pepper

Combine all ingredients and mix well. Pour over vegetable-salmon mixture and chill 1 to 2 hours. Drain and arrange on a bed of lettuce and garnish with fresh lemon wedges. Serve with marinade as dressing. Serves 2.

Mrs. Randy Hagan (Robin Roberts)

Salmon Salad

2 cups uncooked shell
   macaroni
2 cups frozen English peas,
   thawed
1 can (16 ounces) pink
   salmon
2 tablespoons lemon juice

½ cup sour cream
½ cup mayonnaise
2 tablespoons fresh dill
   weed or 2 teaspoons dried
   dill
Salt and pepper to taste

Cook and drain macaroni. Mix macaroni with peas. Remove bone and skin from salmon and add to macaroni mixture. Combine remaining ingredients and toss well. Serves 4 to 6. *You may substitute 2 teaspoons curry powder for the dill.*

Mrs. Denman Smith (Sandra)

Chilled Tuna Rice

1 cup cooked rice, cooled
1 pound fresh mushrooms, sliced
1 can (6 ounces) tuna
¼ cup olive oil
2 ribs celery, chopped
1 teaspoon spicy mustard
½ teaspoon salt
½ teaspoon pepper
Lettuce
Tomato slices for garnish

Cook rice and cool. Steam mushrooms 1 minute. Combine all ingredients and mix well. Refrigerate overnight. Serve over lettuce with tomato garnish. Serves 4.

Mrs. Robert Brown (Mary)

Crunchy Tuna Salad

1 can (12½ ounces) tuna, drained
¼ cup chopped onion
3 tablespoons chopped green bell pepper
3 tablespoons chopped ripe olives
2 tablespoons chopped pimientos
½ cup mayonnaise
1 tablespoon cream
1 tablespoon wine vinegar
1 can (3 ounces) chow mein noodles

Combine all ingredients except noodles and chill. Just before serving, toss with chow mein noodles. Serves 3 to 4.

Mrs. Tony Macaluso (Suzy)

Salad Dressings

Bleu Cheese Salad Dressing

¼ pound Bleu cheese
¾ cup salad oil
¼ cup apple cider vinegar
1 cup sour cream
1 teaspoon salt
⅛ teaspoon lemon pepper
⅛ teaspoon garlic salt
⅛ teaspoon minced onion

Crumble Bleu cheese and mix with salad oil, vinegar, sour cream and seasonings. Chill. Yields 5 cups.

Mrs. Tom Hollis (Doris)

Buttermilk Cucumber Dressing

¾ cup buttermilk
½ cup peeled, seeded and
   finely chopped cucumber
1 teaspoon Dijon mustard

1 clove garlic, minced
¼ teaspoon salt
⅛ teaspoon white pepper

Mix all ingredients together. Cover and chill several hours. Shake well before serving. Yields 1 cup dressing.

Mrs. Terry Arndt (Barbara)

Delicious Green Salad Dressing

¼ teaspoon dry mustard
⅛ teaspoon pepper
½ teaspoon salt
¼ teaspoon celery salt
½ cup minced onion

½ cup olive oil
¼ cup cider vinegar
¼ cup sugar
½ teaspoon paprika

Mix all ingredients together. Blend well and chill. Yields 1½ cups dressing. *I like to use this dressing with spinach, fresh mushrooms and green onions. Mandarin orange sections are also a good addition.*

Mrs. Adrian Piperi (Carole)

French Dressing

1 cup olive oil
¼ cup tarragon vinegar
2 tablespoons chopped
   garlic
1 teaspoon salt

½ teaspoon white pepper
¼ teaspoon sugar
1 cup Roquefort cheese,
   optional

Combine all ingredients in a jar with a tight fitting lid. Shake well before serving. This is best made a day in advance and stored in refrigerator. If adding the Roquefort cheese, combine in blender. Yields 1½ cups.

Mrs. Denman Smith (Sandra)

Sweet Herb Dressing

½ cup white wine vinegar
1 cup sugar
1 cup oil

2 tablespoons poppy seeds
1 tablespoon celery seeds
1 tablespoon dill seeds

Mix vinegar, sugar and oil in a small pan. Heat and stir to melt sugar. Add remaining ingredients. Allow to cool. Chill and mix well prior to use. Yields 2 cups.

Dr. Gerald A. Beathard

Lemon Herb Dressing

⅔ cup vegetable oil
⅓ cup lemon juice
2 tablespoons red wine
    vinegar

2 teaspoons chopped parsley
1 teaspoon salt
½ teaspoon basil
½ teaspoon tarragon

Mix all ingredients together well. Serve over tossed green salad.
Yields 1¼ cups dressing.

Mrs. Jim Rado (Vicki)

Sid's Favorite Salad Dressing

2 eggs
Dash of garlic powder
Salt and pepper to taste
½ teaspoon dry mustard
1 tablespoon lemon juice
1 teaspoon Dijon mustard

3 tablespoons red vinegar
3 tablespoons dry tarragon
2 sprigs fresh parsley
½ cup olive oil
½ cup vegetable oil

Blend all ingredients briefly in blender or food processor and chill.
Yields 1½ cups.

Mrs. Sid Mann (Kathi)

Creamy Topping for Fruit

8 ounces cream cheese
2 tablespoons fresh lemon
    juice
1 teaspoon grated lemon
    rind

½ cup whipping cream
½ cup powdered sugar
Chopped pecans, optional

Combine cream cheese, juice and rind. Beat cream, gradually adding
sugar. Fold cream into cream cheese mixture. Pour over sliced fruit
and sprinkle with pecans if desired. Yields 1½ cups.

Mrs. Bob McGoldrick (Fran)

Fancy Dressing

1 can (14 ounces) artichoke
    hearts, drained and
    chopped
2 ribs celery, chopped
1 can (4¼ ounces) chopped
    ripe olives, drained

1 jar (8 ounces) whole
    mushrooms, drained
3 cups Italian dressing

Mix all ingredients together and blend well. Store in a covered jar in
refrigerator. Yields 4 cups.

Mrs. Larry Crain (Pat)

Dressing for Fruit Salad

1   cup sugar
2   tablespoons cornstarch
1   tablespoon flour
1¼ cups orange juice

¼ cup lemon juice
½ cup water
1   tablespoon butter
Salt to taste

Combine sugar, cornstarch, flour, orange juice, lemon juice and water in a saucepan; boil slowly for 3 minutes, stirring to custard stage. Stir in butter and salt, until butter melts. Chill; pour over fresh fruit. Pour over fresh fruit. Yields 3 cups dressing.

Mrs. Joe Bowles (Mary)

Green Pastures Strawberry Dressing

½ cup mayonnaise
½ cup sour cream
1   tablespoon fresh lemon
    juice

1   tablespoon powdered
    sugar
½ cup crushed fresh
    strawberries

Combine mayonnaise, sour cream and lemon juice; stir until well blended. Add powdered sugar and mix well. Stir in strawberries; chill several hours or overnight. Serve with fresh fruit salad, such as pineapple, melons, green grapes and strawberries. Yields 1½ cups.

Mary Faulk Koock

French Crème

1   cup whipping cream
½ cup sifted powdered sugar

½ cup sour cream
1   teaspoon grated orange
    peel

Beat whipping cream until foamy. Gradually add powdered sugar, beating until soft peaks form. Fold in sour cream and orange rind. Chill. Yields 2½ cups. *To serve, fill a glass bowl with melon balls, strawberries or blueberries and pour French crème over.*

Mrs. Bob McGoldrick (Fran)

Grandma's French Style Italian Dressing

1   cup oil
⅓ cup cider vinegar
1   teaspoon salt

1   teaspoon sugar
Several good shakes of
    paprika
Pepper to taste

Mix all ingredients together, shake well and refrigerate for several hours. Shake well again before adding to a salad. Yields 1⅓ cups.

Mrs. Terry Arndt (Barbara)

Sandwiches

Sandy's Pimiento Cheese

2 cups grated Cheddar
    cheese
2 cups grated processed
    cheese
1 jar (4 ounces) diced
    pimiento

½ cup chopped green bell
    pepper
½ cup chopped pecans
½ cup mayonnaise
2 loaves wheat bread

Mix together cheeses, pimiento, bell pepper, pecans and mayonnaise. Spread bread with pimiento cheese and you are ready to eat. Trim crust for party sandwiches. Yields 40 finger sandwiches.

Mrs. John Perkins (Sandy)

Jim's Pimiento Cheese

10 ounces Cheddar cheese,
     grated
1   jar (2 ounces) diced
     pimiento

3 or 4 heaping tablespoons
     mayonnaise
Salt and pepper to taste
Garlic powder to taste

In a large bowl mix Cheddar cheese, drained pimiento and mayonnaise by hand until the desired consistency is obtained. You may need to add more or less mayonnaise. Add salt, pepper and garlic powder sparingly. Yields 2 cups.

Jim Kimbell

Cheese and Olive Sandwiches

1 cup pimiento stuffed
    olives, chopped
¾ cup grated Monterey Jack
    cheese
½ cup mayonnaise
Salt to taste

3 green onions, finely
    chopped
¾ cup grated Cheddar
    cheese
½ teaspoon chili powder
6 English muffins

Combine all ingredients except muffins and mix well. Spread on muffins and bake at 400° until bubbly. Serve hot. *For a change of taste, you may substitute ripe olives and add a dash of curry powder.* Serves 6.

Mrs. Marcus Bone (Beverly)

Egg Salad Sandwiches

6 hard cooked eggs
2 tablespoons prepared
mustard
5 tablespoons mayonnaise
⅛ teaspoon crushed celery
seed

1 teaspoon dried parsley
⅛ teaspoon cayenne pepper
1 teaspoon chives
Salt and pepper to taste
12 slices bread

Grate the hard cooked eggs. Combine with other ingredients in a medium bowl. Spread on bread. Yields 6 sandwiches.

Patricia O'Donnell

Toasted Mushroom Sandwiches

½ cup butter, melted,
divided
1 small clove garlic, minced
1 tablespoon plus 1
teaspoon minced onion
1 pound mushrooms, finely
chopped

2 tablespoons whipping
cream
¼ teaspoon paprika
¼ teaspoon salt
Freshly ground pepper
12 slices bread

Combine 2 tablespoons butter with garlic and onion in a large skillet over medium-high heat, and sauté until onion is golden. Blend in mushrooms, cream, paprika, salt and pepper. Continue to cook, stirring frequently, about 2 minutes. Preheat broiler. Spread mushroom mixture evenly over 6 slices of bread. Top with remaining bread. Brush outside of each sandwich with remaining butter. Arrange on broiler pan. Broil on both sides until bread is toasted. Slice diagonally and serve hot. Serves 6.

Mrs. Lawrence Christian (Joyce)

Chicken Stuffed Pockets

4 chicken breasts, boned
2 avocados, sliced
4 pita pocket breads

Mayonnaise
Bean sprouts

Remove skin from breasts; separate into halves and grill until done. Halve the avocados, peel and slice. Cut pita bread in half and spread inside generously with mayonnaise. Put a half chicken breast in each half of pita bread; then add sliced avocado and top with bean sprouts. Yields 4 sandwiches. *This is great for a hot summer day's lunch.*

Mrs. Marcus Bone (Beverly)

Sloppy Joes

1½ pounds ground beef	1 teaspoon poultry
½ cup minced onion	seasoning
¼ cup diced green bell	1 teaspoon dry mustard
pepper	1 teaspoon salt
1½ teaspoons vinegar	¼ cup water
1 can (10¾ ounces) tomato	8 hamburger buns
soup	

In a large skillet, brown beef and drain any excess grease. Add onion and bell pepper and remaining ingredients. Simmer 30 minutes. Spoon mixture on hamburger buns and serve warm. Serves 8.

Mrs. Larry Deinlein (Betty)

Vegetarian Sandwich

1 medium eggplant	3 tablespoons cider vinegar
1 medium red bell pepper	Salt to taste
1 garlic clove, minced	½ teaspoon sugar
2 tablespoons chopped	Pepper to taste
onion	Pumpernickel bread
¼ cup oil	

Preheat oven to 400°. Prick eggplant and bell pepper with fork in several places. Arrange on a baking sheet. Bake pepper until tender, about 30 minutes. Let cool. Continue baking eggplant until tender, about 30 more minutes. Remove from oven and let cool. Peel pepper and eggplant and add to garlic in food processor. Add onion, oil, vinegar, salt, sugar and pepper and mix well. Serve on pumpernickel bread. Yields 6 sandwiches.

Mrs. Tom Hollis (Doris)

Corned Beef and Swiss Cheese Sandwiches

1 can (12 ounces) corned	¼ teaspoon horseradish
beef	2 sweet pickles, chopped
6 ounces Swiss cheese,	Rye bread
grated	Lettuce, optional
⅓ cup mayonnaise	Tomatoes, optional
1 teaspoon prepared	
mustard	

Cube the corned beef and place it in a blender with the cheese, mayonnaise, mustard, horseradish and pickles. Blend well. Spread on rye bread and add lettuce and tomato. This is a favorite with the men. Serves 6.

Mrs. Greg Gordon (Kathy)

Reuben Sandwich

1 jar (16 ounces) sauerkraut,
drained
16 slices dark rye bread
Horseradish sauce

1 pound cooked corned
beef, sliced very thin
8 ounces Swiss cheese,
sliced
Margarine

Squeeze excess moisture out of sauerkraut, then place it on paper towels to drain. Spread each slice of bread with horseradish sauce. Divide the corned beef evenly between 8 slices of bread. Top with sauerkraut, cheese and the remaining 8 slices of bread. Spread the outside of the sandwiches with margarine. Grill on a griddle or in a large skillet over moderate heat until nicely toasted and the cheese is melted. Serves 8.

Mrs. Terry Arndt (Barbara)

Greek Pocket

1 pound ground lamb
1 to 2 teaspoons thyme
½ teaspoon salt
½ teaspoon pepper
1 clove garlic, minced

4 to 6 pita pocket breads
Mayonnaise
4 to 6 ounces Feta cheese
Alfalfa sprouts
Spinach leaves

Mix lamb, thyme, salt, pepper and garlic; form into 4 to 6 burgers. Sauté until cooked to desired doneness. The size of the burger will depend on the size of pita bread. Split bread and spread with mayonnaise. Place a burger, slice of cheese, sprouts and a fresh spinach leaf on each pita. Warm in the oven or microwave for a few minutes. Serves 4 to 6. *Try substituting ground turkey for lamb.*

Mrs. Denman Smith (Sandra)

Curried Chicken Sandwiches

1 cup cooked chopped
chicken
½ cup diced celery
¼ cup diced onion
½ cup chopped salted
peanuts

½ cup mayonnaise
¾ teaspoon curry powder
1 tablespoon lemon juice
8 slices toast, buttered

Mix together all filling ingredients. Spread mixture on toast, being careful to cover it to the edges. Broil 3 inches from heat for 3 minutes, or until hot. Serves 8.

Mrs. Marcus Bone (Beverly)

Classic Hero

2 slices each of your 3
  favorite cold cuts
2 slices each of your 3
  favorite cheeses
¼ cup mustard

½ cup mayonnaise
½ cup chopped green olives
2 to 4 lettuce leaves
2 to 4 tomato slices
2 small French loaves

For a different and a pretty look, roll the meat and cheese. Mix the mustard, mayonnaise and olives together and spread on the bread; top with lettuce and tomatoes and then arrange. Meat and cheese may be held in place with a toothpick topped with an olive if desired. Serve with the top of the sandwich to the side for a pretty plate. Serves 2.

Mrs. Denman Smith (Sandra)

Italian Meatball Sandwiches

½ pound bulk Italian sausage
2 cups your favorite tomato
  spaghetti sauce
1 medium onion, sliced into
  rings
1 red bell pepper, sliced into
  rings

1 green bell pepper, sliced
  into rings
2 to 4 tablespoons olive oil
Dijon mustard
½ cup grated Parmesan
  cheese
2 small French loaves

Form sausage into 6 to 8 flatish meatballs and sauté for 3 to 5 minutes until browned. Cover with sauce and simmer until done. Sauté onion and peppers in olive oil until crisp tender, 3 to 5 minutes. Split bread and spread with mustard. Place meatballs on bread and spoon sauce over meat and arrange peppers and onions over top. Serve open faced, sprinkled with Parmesan cheese. Serves 2.

Mrs. Denman Smith (Sandra)

Ham and Chutney Sandwiches

2 cups ground cooked ham
¾ cup chopped chutney
½ cup mayonnaise

⅛ teaspoon curry powder
Rye bread

Mix all spread ingredients together and serve on thin slices of toasted rye bread. Serves 6 to 8.

Mrs. Joe Bowles (Mary)

Hot Chicken Salad Sandwiches

2   cups cooked and chopped
    chicken
½   cup chopped celery
4   tablespoons chopped
    green bell pepper
4   tablespoons chopped
    pimiento

3   green onions, minced
¼   cup mayonnaise
Salt and pepper to taste
8   hamburger buns
1½ cups grated sharp Cheddar
    cheese

Mix all ingredients together except cheese and buns. Spread chicken salad on one side of the bun, cheese on the other side. Wrap in foil. Bake at 450° for 10 minutes. These may be frozen. Defrost completely before cooking. Serves 8.

Mrs. Richard Riley (Joanne)

Chicago Style Deep Dish Pizza

Crust:

2   packages active dry yeast
1   cup warm water
1   tablespoon sugar
1½ teaspoons salt

1   teaspoon olive oil
2¾ cups flour
Oil
Cornmeal

Dissolve yeast in water. Add sugar, salt and olive oil. Stir in flour to make a soft dough. Knead 5 minutes on a floured surface, adding more flour until dough does not stick to your fingers. Put into a greased bowl; cover and let rise until double in bulk *about 1 hour in a 150° oven.* Punch dough down. Brush a 14 inch deep dish pizza pan with oil. Sprinkle lightly with cornmeal. Press dough in bottom and up sides of pan. Rim should be 1 inch. Let rise about 20 minutes.

Filling:

12 ounces grated
    Mozzarella cheese
1   pound pork sausage,
    cooked and drained
1   can (28 ounces) peeled
    tomatoes, drained and
    chopped

1 to 2 teaspoons dried
    oregano
1   teaspoon salt
1   teaspoon fennel seed
½   cup grated Parmesan
    cheese

Preheat oven to 500°. Sprinkle grated Mozzarella cheese on top of dough. Arrange sausage on top of cheese. Add tomatoes. Combine the seasonings and sprinkle over the tomatoes. Top with Parmesan cheese. Put pizza into oven and immediately reduce heat to 450°. Bake for 35 minutes or until cheese is melted. Let sit 5 minutes before cutting. Serves 4.

Mrs. Hal Williamson (Gayle)

"Nowhere but Texas!" It sounds like a boastful slogan, but most natives would agree it's the simple truth, especially in the spring. Wildflowers blanket the valleys and slopes like multi-colored squares in a patchwork quilt. Indian paintbrush, wild phlox and the state flower, bluebonnets, as well as a hundred other varieties, are vibrant harbingers of the season ahead, much as the ones pictured here outside Seguin.

Vegetables pictured: Pasta Prima Vera, Asparagus Francaise, Spaghetti Squash Picante, Brussels Sprouts with Hot Bacon Dressing and Acorn Squash.

Vegetables

Artichokes

6 medium artichokes
2 tablespoons olive oil
2 cloves garlic, crushed
1 teaspoon salt
2 tablespoons lemon juice

Wash artichokes and cut stem even with base. Peel off tough outside bottom leaves. Place in 3 quarts boiling water. Season with olive oil, garlic and salt. Boil 30 minutes or until tender. Drain well and remove center of artichoke with spoon. Be sure to remove all of the fuzzy part of the heart. Sprinkle inside with lemon juice. Serves 6.

Mrs. Larry Strickland (Linda)

Artichoke Stuffed Tomatoes

6 medium tomatoes
4 tablespoons butter
1 cup cooked rice
½ cup grated Mozzarella cheese
3 tablespoons grated Parmesan cheese
½ cup diced artichoke hearts, sautéed
1 tablespoon minced parsley
Salt and pepper to taste
Parmesan cheese for garnish

Cut a slice from the top of each tomato, remove pulp and seeds, then invert to drain. Melt butter and mix with the remaining ingredients. Season the inside of the drained tomatoes lightly. Stuff tomatoes with the rice mixture and sprinkle the remaining grated Parmesan cheese on the tops. Bake at 350° for 25 minutes. Serves 6.

Mrs. Lee Provinse (Dottie)

Asparagus Francaise

1 pound thin asparagus
2 tablespoons butter
2 to 3 tablespoons spicy Italian salad dressing
Lemon juice

Cook asparagus quickly in a skillet of boiling, salted water until they are a bright, rich green. Drain in a colander and refresh with cold water. Place skillet over medium heat to melt butter; add asparagus and coat with butter. Drizzle dressing over asparagus and add fresh lemon juice to taste. Toss and serve. Serves 4. *For a variation sprinkle with a scant amount of grated Parmesan cheese.*

William Furman

Sesame Asparagus

2   packages (8 ounces each)
    frozen asparagus
Salt and pepper to taste
1   jar (2½ ounces) sliced
    mushrooms, drained

2   tablespoons butter, melted
1   teaspoon lemon juice
1   teaspoon sesame seeds,
    toasted

Cook frozen asparagus according to the package directions. Drain well. Season to taste with salt and pepper. Gently stir in mushrooms, butter and lemon juice. Cook until heated through. Turn mixture into a serving bowl and sprinkle with sesame seeds. Serves 6. *I also use fresh steamed asparagus when in season.*

Mrs. J. Edward Reed (Marian)

Barley Casserole

½   cup butter
2   medium onions, chopped
¾   pound mushrooms,
    chopped
1¼ cups pearl barley
1   jar (2 ounces) sliced
    pimiento

½   teaspoon salt
¼   teaspoon pepper
2   cups chicken broth
4   ounces pine nuts or
    slivered almonds

Melt butter and sauté onions and mushrooms. Add barley and cook until barley is a delicate brown. Add pimiento, salt and pepper and mix. Place in a 2 quart casserole. Add chicken broth and sprinkle nuts on top. Cover and bake at 350° for 1½ hours. Serves 6. *This is a nice change from rice as a meat accompaniment.*

Mrs. Clark Rector (Sue)

Bacon Wrapped Beans

2   cans (16 ounces each)
    whole green beans
½   pound bacon strips, cut
    crosswise in half

¼   cup brown sugar
½   teaspoon allspice
Salt to taste

Drain beans, reserving 1 cup liquid. Wrap half slice of bacon around every 10 to 12 beans and fasten with a toothpick. Place in casserole dish. Mix bean liquid and brown sugar together and pour over beans. Sprinkle with allspice and salt. Bake at 400° for 25 minutes, or until bacon browns. Turn once during cooking and baste. Serves 8 to 10.

Mrs. Ronald B. Cass (Sherry)

German Style Wax Beans

8 slices bacon, diced	¼ cup wine vinegar
½ cup chopped green onions	2 tablespoons sugar
1 can (16 ounces) sliced wax beans, drained	2 tablespoons chopped pimiento

Fry bacon in medium skillet until almost crisp. Drain off all but 2 tablespoons drippings. Add onions and fry until bacon is crisp. Stir in remaining ingredients; heat through. Serves 4.

Mrs. Lee Provinse (Dottie)

Dill Pickle Baked Beans

2 tablespoons bacon drippings	1 large dill pickle, chopped
½ green bell pepper, finely chopped	2 cans (16 ounces each) pork and beans
2 onions, finely chopped	3 tablespoons brown sugar
1¾ cups catsup	1 cup water

Sauté bell pepper and onion in bacon drippings. Remove from skillet and place in a 2 quart dish. Add catsup, pickle, beans, brown sugar and water. Mix well. Bake at 300° for 1 hour. Serves 6 to 8.

Mrs. Ron Cass (Sherry)

Baked Beans

1 can (31 ounces) pork and beans, drained	1 cup chopped celery
2 tablespoons brown sugar	½ cup chopped green bell pepper
1 tablespoon sugar	1 tablespoon chili powder
4 tablespoons catsup	1 teaspoon hot pepper sauce
1 tablespoon prepared mustard	2 tablespoons Worcestershire sauce
1 cup chopped onion	3 strips bacon

In an 8x8x2 inch baking dish combine all ingredients except bacon. Mix thoroughly. Place bacon strips on top and bake covered at 250° for 2 hours. Uncover the last 15 minutes. Serves 4 to 6.

Mrs. Jerry Holder (Pat)

Do not store onions in the refrigerator. Keep them in a cool, dark place for best results. Allow air to circulate around them.

Smoky Baked Beans

2	cans (16 ounces each) pork and beans	2	tablespoons prepared mustard
⅓	cup brown sugar	1	tablespoon minced onion
¼	cup honey	½	teaspoon imitation smoke flavoring
3	tablespoons Worcestershire sauce	3	slices bacon

Combine all ingredients except bacon in a large mixing bowl and stir well. Pour into a 2 quart baking dish and top with bacon strips. Bake at 350° for 1 hour. Serves 6 to 8.

Mrs. Ron Bruney (Carol)

Worcestershire sauce contains soy sauce as an ingredient.

Harvard Beets

1	can (16 ounces) tiny whole beets	½	teaspoon salt
½	cup sugar	½	cup cider vinegar
1	tablespoon cornstarch	½	cup water

Drain beets and set aside. Combine sugar, cornstarch, salt, vinegar and water in a saucepan. Cook and stir until thickened. Add beets to saucepan and simmer until beets are heated through. Serves 4.

Mrs. Sid Mann (Kathi)

Broccoli California

2	packages (10 ounces each) frozen broccoli spears	¼	cup chopped almonds
⅓	cup olive oil	⅔	cup sliced ripe olives
1	clove garlic, crushed	2	teaspoons lemon juice

Cook broccoli until tender crisp. Drain well. Heat oil and garlic for 2 minutes. Add remaining ingredients and heat thoroughly. Pour over broccoli. Serves 4 to 6.

Mrs. Drue Denton (Jan)

Broccoli Casserole

2   packages (8 ounces each)
    frozen chopped broccoli
2   tablespoons chopped
    onion
1   can (10¾ ounces) cream of
    mushroom soup

1   cup mayonnaise
Salt and pepper to taste
1   cup grated Cheddar
    cheese

Cook and drain broccoli. Mix all ingredients except cheese with the broccoli. Place in a baking dish and top with cheese. Bake at 350° for 30 minutes. Serves 8 to 10.

Mrs. W. H. Heggen III (Maryellen)

Broccoli Elegance

1½ cups water
¼   cup butter
1   package (8 ounces)
    stuffing mix with
    seasoning packet
2   packages (10 ounces each)
    frozen broccoli spears,
    thawed
2   tablespoons butter
2   tablespoons flour

1   teaspoon chicken bouillon
    granules
¾   cup milk
3   ounces cream cheese,
    softened
¼   teaspoon salt
4   green onions, sliced
1   cup grated Cheddar
    cheese
Paprika

Combine water, ¼ cup of butter and seasoning mix; bring to a boil. Remove from heat and stir in stuffing crumbs; let stand 5 minutes. Spoon stuffing around the outside edge of lightly buttered 13x9x2 inch baking dish. Arrange broccoli on bottom of dish; set aside. Melt the remaining butter over low heat and add flour, stirring until smooth. Cook 1 minute, stirring. Stir in bouillon. Gradually add milk; cook over medium heat, stirring until thick and bubbly. Add cream cheese and salt; stir until smooth. Stir in onions. Spoon mixture over center of broccoli; sprinkle with cheese and paprika. Cover with foil and bake at 350° for 35 minutes. Remove foil and bake 10 minutes longer. Serves 8.

Mrs. Bob Smith (Martha)

Yellow on the tips of broccoli buds mean that the vegetable is past its prime. Buy only green, tightly closed, bunches of broccoli.

Broccoli Mornay

3 bunches broccoli, cut into
  flowerets
¼ cup butter
1 cup flour

4 cups milk
2 pounds American cheese
1 can (12 ounces) beer
Swiss cheese

Steam broccoli flowerets until crisp tender. Melt butter; add flour and cook until bubbly. Gradually add milk and stir until smooth. Boil 1 minute. Cut cheese into small pieces and beat into hot cream sauce. Add a little beer at a time to obtain the consistency desired. Pour over broccoli; sprinkle with Swiss cheese and run under broiler for browning. Serves 8 to 10.

Mrs. Joe Bowles (Mary)

Brussel Sprouts with Hot Bacon Dressing

Brussel Sprouts:
4 slices bacon
1 teaspoon salt

2 packages (10 ounces each)
  brussel sprouts, thawed

Fry bacon in skillet until crisp; drain on paper towels. Discard all but 2 tablespoons of bacon drippings. Fill a large pan with water to a 1 inch depth. Add 1 teaspoon salt and bring to boil. Add sprouts; cover and reduce heat. Cook about 8 minutes; drain.

Hot Bacon Dressing:
1 egg
2 tablespoons sugar
5 tablespoons white
  vinegar
3 tablespoons water

¼ teaspoon dry mustard
½ teaspoon salt
Dash of pepper
Crumbled bacon for garnish

Beat egg in a jar. Add remaining ingredients and shake well. Pour into skillet with bacon drippings. Cook over low heat for about 4 minutes, stirring constantly, until dressing is smooth and thickened. Remove from heat and cover. To serve, place sprouts in a bowl; pour warm dressing over, and garnish with crumbled bacon. Yields 6 to 8 servings.

Mrs. J. Edward Reed (Marian)

Red Cabbage

3 tablespoons butter
2 tablespoons minced onion
6 cups shredded red
   cabbage

6 tablespoons brown sugar
3 tablespoons cider vinegar
1 tablespoon caraway seeds

Melt butter and sauté onion until tender. Add the remaining ingredients; cover and cook over low heat until tender. Serves 6.

Betty M. Williams

Skillet Cabbage Plus

3 tablespoons butter
6 thin strips bacon
⅔ cup coarsely shredded
   carrots
1½ cups thinly sliced celery
4 cups finely grated
   cabbage, firmly packed

½ cup sliced green bell
   pepper
½ teaspoon sugar
1 teaspoon instant chicken
   broth granules
¼ cup water
1 teaspoon salt
⅛ teaspoon pepper

In a 12 inch skillet melt butter and slowly cook the bacon, carrots and celery until slightly softened, about 5 minutes. Add cabbage, bell pepper and a mixture of the sugar, chicken granules and water. Mix well. Cover tightly and simmer just until tender crisp, 8 to 10 minutes. Serve at once. Serves 6 to 8.

Betsey Bishop

What You Do with Cabbage

3 tablespoons margarine
1 medium head cabbage,
   finely shredded

½ cup milk
Salt and pepper to taste

Melt margarine in skillet. Add cabbage and stir. Cover and steam for 5 minutes. Stir again; cover and cook 5 more minutes. Add milk, salt and pepper. Cover and cook 3 minutes. Serves 4 to 6.

Mrs. K. L. McConchie (Katherine)

When frying vegetables, be sure all pieces are cut the same size. If not, pieces will not cook evenly.

Carrot Crunch

6 to 8 medium carrots
½ teaspoon salt
1½ tablespoons butter
1½ tablespoons brown sugar

1 teaspoon grated orange rind
¼ cup slivered almonds, toasted

Cut carrots into uniform sticks. Cook in a small amount of salted water until barely tender. Remove carrots and set aside. Pour out the water and in the same saucepan stir together the remaining ingredients. Return carrots to pan and simmer for 5 minutes, turning carrots to coat with the butter mixture. Serves 4 to 6.

Mrs. Lee Provinse (Dottie)

Cognac Carrots

2 cups slivered raw carrots
1 teaspoon sugar

½ cup butter
⅓ cup cognac

Place all ingredients in a covered baking dish and bake at 350° until tender, about 30 minutes. Serves 4.

Mrs. Marcus Bone (Beverly)

Peg Corn

¼ cup margarine
8 ounces cream cheese, softened
¼ cup milk

2 cans (12 ounces each) shoe peg corn, drained
1 can (4 ounces) diced green chilies, drained
Salt and pepper to taste

Melt margarine, cream cheese and milk together in a saucepan. Add corn and chilies to cheese mixture; salt and pepper to taste. Pour into a greased casserole dish and bake at 350° for 30 minutes. Serves 8 to 10.

Mrs. Jack Ford (Connie)

Corn that has been husked soon loses its flavor and dries out. Always buy corn with the husk still intact.

Jalapeño Corn Rice Casserole

1 cup uncooked rice
1 medium onion, chopped
1 medium green bell pepper,
   chopped
1 cup chopped celery
½ cup butter
1 tablespoon sugar

1 jalapeño pepper, seeded
   and finely chopped
2 cans (17 ounces each)
   cream style corn
1 cup grated mild Cheddar
   cheese

Cook rice according to the package directions; set aside. Sauté onion, bell pepper and celery in butter until tender. Combine with all other ingredients and pour into a greased 2 quart casserole. Bake at 325° for 30 minutes. Serves 6.   **Mrs. Andrew Tewell (Judy)**

Corn Pudding

2 tablespoons cornstarch
2 eggs
¾ cup sugar
1 can (13 ounces)
   evaporated milk

1 can (17 ounces) cream
   style corn
2 tablespoons butter

In a small casserole mix together cornstarch, eggs and sugar. Add milk and corn and mix well. Melt 2 tablespoons butter and pour over top. Bake at 325° for 1 hour and 15 minutes or until firm. The top should be slightly browned, and a knife inserted in the middle will come out clean. Serves 4 to 6.   **Mrs. Bill Wittenbrook (Linda)**

Celery Casserole

2 stalks of celery
1 green bell pepper,
   chopped
1 can (8 ounces) sliced
   water chestnuts, drained
1 tablespoon finely chopped
   onion

1 can (10¾ ounces) cream of
   mushroom soup
1 package (8 ounces)
   slivered almonds
Salt and pepper to taste
Butter

Cut celery into ½ inch pieces and boil in water for 5 to 8 minutes. Place in a casserole dish and mix with bell pepper, water chestnuts, onion and soup. Toast the almonds in the oven with salt, pepper and butter. Sprinkle almonds on top of casserole and bake at 350° for 30 minutes. Serves 6 to 8. *A stalk of celery consists of 6 to 8 ribs.*
        Mrs. Jean-paul Budinger (Pat)

Creamed Cauliflower and Peas

1 package (10 ounces)
   frozen English peas
Milk
¼ cup butter
¾ cup finely chopped onion
3 tablespoons flour
½ teaspoon salt
¼ teaspoon pepper

¼ teaspoon nutmeg
1 cup half and half cream
1 head cauliflower, cut into
   flowerets and cooked in
   salted water
1 tablespoon butter, melted
¼ cup dry bread crumbs

Bring peas to boiling in salted water for 5 minutes. Drain peas, reserving liquid. Add enough milk to liquid to make 2 cups; set aside. In ¼ cup butter in medium saucepan, sauté onion until golden; remove from heat. Stir in flour, ½ teaspoon salt, pepper and nutmeg until well blended. Gradually stir in reserved liquid and the cream. Bring to a boil stirring constantly. In a 2 quart casserole, gently combine peas, cauliflower and sauce. Combine melted butter with bread crumbs; sprinkle over vegetables. Refrigerate covered overnight. To serve, preheat oven to 400° and bake casserole, covered, 30 minutes. Uncover and bake 20 to 30 minutes, or until bubbly. Serves 6 to 8.

Mrs. James Eccles (Patricia)

Eggplant Parmesan

1 large onion, chopped
2 cloves garlic, chopped
1 tablespoon olive oil
10 medium tomatoes, peeled
   and chopped
½ teaspoon anise seed
1½ teaspoons basil
1½ teaspoons oregano
2 bay leaves
Salt and pepper
3 cups chicken stock

1 can (6 ounces) tomato
   paste
1 large eggplant, peeled and
   cut into ½ inch slices
2 cups flour
3 eggs, beaten
3 cups bread crumbs
Oil
1 pound Mozzarella cheese,
   sliced

Sauté onion and garlic in oil. Add tomatoes, spices and chicken stock. Simmer for 30 minutes. Mash tomatoes; add tomato paste and simmer for 1 hour. Remove bay leaves. Bread eggplant in flour, then egg and finally in bread crumbs. Sauté eggplant in oil until golden brown. Drain. Layer sauce, eggplant and cheese. Top with more sauce and eggplant. Bake at 325° for 35 to 45 minutes until bubbly. Serves 8 to 10.

Mike Stout

Scalloped Eggplant

1 eggplant
1 onion, chopped
2 tablespoons butter
1 egg, beaten
½ cup milk

1 cup dry bread crumbs
8 ounces Cheddar cheese, grated, divided
½ cup cracker crumbs

Peel and dice eggplant; cook in boiling water until tender. While eggplant cooks, sauté onion in the butter. Drain eggplant and combine with onion, egg, milk, bread crumbs and most of the grated cheese, mixing well. Place in a 2 quart casserole and sprinkle with cracker crumbs and remaining cheese. Bake at 350° for 30 minutes. Serves 4.

Mrs. Clark E. Rector (Sue)

Creamed Green Beans

½ cup margarine
½ cup flour
1¼ teaspoons salt
2 cups milk
½ cup dry white wine

2 teaspoons prepared mustard
4 cans (16 ounces each) green beans, drained
Bread crumbs

Melt margarine in a large saucepan and stir in flour and salt. Gradually stir in milk, wine and mustard. Cook, stirring constantly, until sauce is thick. Stir beans into sauce. Pour into a casserole dish and sprinkle the top with fine bread crumbs. Bake at 350° for 30 minutes. Serves 16.

Mrs. Joe Bowles (Mary)

Green Beans Italiano

3 cloves garlic
2 to 4 tablespoons olive oil
1 can (28 ounces) tomatoes
1 tablespoon oregano
Salt and pepper to taste

2 tablespoons chopped parsley
½ cup water
2 packages (10 ounces each) frozen cut green beans

Brown garlic in olive oil. Discard the garlic. Crush the tomatoes and add to pan along with the oregano, salt, pepper, parsley and water. Boil uncovered for 15 minutes, stirring occasionally. If mixture becomes too dry, add ¼ cup water. Lower heat and add beans. Cover and simmer long enough to thaw and cook beans, about 10 minutes. Serves 6. *You may also use fresh parboiled green beans.*

Mrs. Jim Rado (Vicki)

Green Beans and Tomatoes

2 tablespoons oil	1 teaspoon salt
2 tablespoons chopped onion	1½ pounds green beans, sliced and cooked
1 garlic clove, minced	2 tablespoons chopped fresh parsley
4 medium tomatoes, peeled and chopped	

Sauté onion and garlic in oil until tender. Add tomatoes and salt, and simmer covered for 10 minutes. Add the green beans. Cook until heated through. Add parsley before serving. Serves 4 to 6. *Two 9 ounce packages of frozen French style green beans may be substituted for fresh.*

Mrs. Jim Schultz (Mary Kay)

Baked Mushrooms

1 pound fresh mushrooms, stems removed, cleaned	¼ cup olive oil
2 cloves garlic, cut in half	¼ cup water
½ cup chopped parsley	Salt and pepper

Spread mushrooms in a 9 inch baking dish. Add garlic, parsley, olive oil, water and salt and pepper and bake uncovered at 350° for 15 minutes. Remove garlic and discard before serving. Serves 4.

Mrs. Jim Rado (Vicki)

Mushrooms a la Bordelaise

2 pounds fresh mushrooms, quartered	3 cloves garlic, minced
3 tablespoons oil	8 tablespoons fine bread crumbs
6 tablespoons butter	Salt and pepper to taste
1 bunch green onions, chopped	4 tablespoons chopped fresh parsley

Sauté mushrooms very quickly in hot oil and butter until no liquid remains and mushrooms are a little browned and crisp. Add onions, garlic and bread crumbs and sauté for just a minute after each addition. Remove from heat. Add salt, pepper and parsley. Serves 12. *Excellent as a side dish with steaks, also.*

Mrs. Sid Mann (Kathi)

Fried Okra

1 quart young okra	Salt and pepper
2 quarts boiling water	2 cups yellow cornmeal
2 teaspoons salt	2 cups cooking oil

Wash okra; discard stems; cut into ¼ inch pieces. Parboil in 2 quarts salted boiling water for 5 to 7 minutes. Drain in colander. Sprinkle with salt and pepper and roll in cornmeal. Let rest for 20 to 30 minutes so the cornmeal will stick to the okra when ready to fry. Fry in deep oil just a few minutes until golden. Drain on paper towels, and season with salt and pepper. Serves 4.

S. D. Jackman

Crusty Potato Pancakes

2 pounds potatoes	2 teaspoons salt
¼ cup grated white onion	Oil for frying
3 eggs	Applesauce
¾ cup flour	

Peel and coarsely grate potatoes into a bowl of cold water. This keeps them from turning dark and removes excess starch. Make a batter in a separate bowl of onion, eggs, flour and salt. Drain potatoes, pressing out all liquid. Beat potatoes into batter. Using a pancake griddle or cast iron skillet, heat oil. Spoon heaping tablespoons of batter into oil, spreading batter with back of spoon into 4 inch rounds. Brown on one side, turn and brown on the other side. Brown the pancakes slowly so potatoes will cook through properly. Drain on absorbent paper. Serve with applesauce. Serves 8 to 10.

S. D. Jackman

Chantilly Potatoes

12 large potatoes	1 cup whipping cream,
4 tablespoons butter	whipped
½ cup milk	8 tablespoons grated
Salt and pepper	Cheddar cheese

Peel and wash potatoes and cook in boiling salted water until done. Drain and mash with the butter and milk and beat until light and fluffy. Season with salt and pepper. Pour into a buttered casserole. Cover with whipped cream and sprinkle with cheese. Bake at 350° until browned on top. Serves 12.

Mrs. Stephen Scheffe (Betsy)

Potato Knishes

Knishes:

4 cups flour
½ teaspoon salt
½ teaspoon baking powder

2 eggs
½ cup oil
½ cup water

Mix all dry ingredients into a bowl. Make a well in the center; add eggs and oil and stir to combine. Add water and knead for about 3 minutes, adding a little more water and oil if dough is too stiff. Divide into 5 parts and set aside while preparing filling.

Filling:

2 pounds potatoes
2 large onions, minced

½ cup chicken fat
Salt and pepper

Boil potatoes in jackets, peel and mash. Sauté onions in chicken fat while potatoes are boiling and add to mashed potatoes. Season to taste. Roll out the dough on an unfloured surface, as thin as possible. Put filling in a line across one end of the dough. Roll as for jelly roll. Cut diagonally into pieces about 1½ inches thick. Brush top with beaten eggs. Bake on an ungreased cookie sheet in center of oven at 450° for 15 minutes. Yields 65 pieces.

Shirley Senior

Twice Baked Potatoes

6 medium potatoes, baked
½ cup butter
½ cup half and half cream
½ cup sour cream
12 slices bacon, cooked, crumbled and divided

½ cup chopped green onions
1 cup grated Cheddar cheese
1 cup finely chopped spinach, frozen or fresh, optional

Slice the top off the potatoes when they are cool enough to handle. Scoop potatoes from skins and put skins aside to refill. Whip potatoes, butter, cream and sour cream until fluffy. Stir in most of bacon and green onions. Stuff potato skins; top with remaining bacon and bake at 350° until heated through, about 20 to 30 minutes. If spinach is used, it should be squeezed as dry as possible and should be added with the bacon and green onions. Serves 6.

Cookbook Committee

Never store potatoes in the refrigerator. They take on a sweet taste if stored under cold temperatures.

Potato Kugel

3 eggs
3 cups grated potatoes
⅓ cup flour
½ teaspoon baking powder

1½ teaspoons salt
White pepper
4 tablespoons oil
3 tablespoons grated onion

Beat eggs well. Pat grated potatoes dry. Combine all ingredients. Spoon potato mixture into greased 1½ quart baking dish. Bake at 350° for 45 to 60 minutes, or until lightly browned. Serves 6.

Sarah Sutton

Scalloped Potatoes

1 can (10¾ ounces) cream of chicken soup
⅔ cup milk
1 teaspoon salt
¼ teaspoon pepper

6 potatoes, peeled and thinly sliced
1 cup grated Cheddar cheese

Combine soup and milk, mixing until smooth. Add salt and pepper. Place half of potato slices in a buttered 8x12 inch baking dish. Pour half the soup mixture over potatoes. Sprinkle with half the grated cheese. Repeat layers. Cover with foil and bake at 350° for 1 hour. Uncover and bake 30 minutes more or until golden brown and potatoes are tender. Serves 6. *You may also add 1 sliced onion or 1 cup boned chicken for a main dish.*

Mrs. Clark E. Rector (Sue)

Southern Potato Casserole

1 package (32 ounces) frozen hash brown potatoes, thawed
2 cups sour cream
½ cup butter, melted
1 can (10¾ ounces) cream of chicken soup

½ cup chopped onion
2 cups grated sharp Cheddar cheese
1 teaspoon salt
1 teaspoon pepper

Mix all ingredients together. Pour into a 9x13 inch glass dish and cook uncovered at 350° for 45 minutes. Serves 10 to 12. *This casserole freezes well. Bake about 10 to 15 minutes more if necessary to heat thoroughly.*

Barbara Beall Stanley

Green Rice

4   green onions, finely
    chopped
½   green bell pepper, finely
    chopped
¼   cup butter, melted

⅓   cup minced fresh parsley
3   cups chicken broth
1½ cups uncooked rice
¼   teaspoon salt
⅛   teaspoon pepper

Sauté onion and bell pepper in butter until tender. Stir in remaining ingredients and bring to a boil. Reduce heat and cover; simmer about 20 minutes or until rice is done. Serves 6.

Mrs. Bill Pohl (Kelly)

Rice and Sour Cream Casserole

¾   pound sharp Cheddar
    cheese
2   cups sour cream
1   can (4 ounces) chopped
    green chilies, drained

1   jar (2 ounces) pimiento,
    drained
4½ cups cooked rice, divided
Salt and pepper to taste

Cut cheese into strips and grate a little for topping. Combine sour cream, chilies and pimiento. In a buttered 1½ quart casserole dish, arrange layers of rice, sour cream mixture and then cheese strips, ending with rice. Sprinkle the top with grated cheese. Bake at 350° for 30 minutes. Serves 6 to 8.

Mrs. Joe Bowles (Mary)

Rice Pilaf

1½ cups rice
¼   cup finely chopped onion
3   tablespoons butter

1   can (13¾ ounces) chicken
    broth
1   cup water
½   teaspoon salt

In a large skillet sauté rice and onion in butter until rice is golden, stirring often. Add chicken broth, water and salt. Bring to a boil; reduce heat. Cover and simmer about 14 minutes, or until rice is tender. Fluff with a fork. Serves 8.

Mrs. Dudley Baker (Kathy)

Do not be satisfied with dried parsley as it is too readily available fresh in our markets.

Sherried Wild Rice

2 cups wild rice
2 teaspoons salt
Salt to taste
1 teaspoon celery salt

¼ cup butter
¼ cup sherry
½ pound mushrooms,
    sautéed in butter

Rinse and drain the rice 20 times. Leave it soaking in hot water overnight. Drain and refill with hot water in the morning, adding salt and celery salt. Simmer for 2 to 3 hours, until the kernels have popped. With a slotted spoon, draining well, transfer the rice to a buttered casserole dish. Add salt to taste, butter, sherry and sautéed mushrooms, plus the juice. Cover and bake at 300° for 30 minutes. Before serving add a little more sherry and continue baking uncovered to dry out a little. Serves 6 to 8.

Mrs. Bob Edgecomb (Mary)

Pecan Wild Rice Casserole

1 box (6 ounces) wild and
    long grain rice
½ cup butter
½ pound fresh mushrooms

1 cup chopped green onions
½ cup minced fresh parsley
1 cup pecan halves

Prepare rice according to package directions. Sauté mushrooms and onions in butter until tender. Mix rice, vegetables, parsley and pecans together in a 1 quart casserole dish. This may be refrigerated or held until ready to bake uncovered at 350° for 30 minutes. Serves 4 to 6. *If refrigerated, allow extra time for baking.*

Mrs. Chris John (Anne)

Chinese Spinach

1 pound fresh spinach
2 tablespoons oil
2 tablespoons soy sauce
½ teaspoon sugar

½ cup sliced water chestnuts
2 tablespoons chopped
    onion

Wash fresh spinach and tear leaves into bite sized pieces. In a large covered saucepan simmer spinach with small amount of water for 3 minutes; drain well. Heat oil, soy sauce and sugar in skillet. Add spinach, water chestnuts and onion. Toss until spinach is well coated and heat thoroughly, 2 to 3 minutes. Serves 4.

Mrs. J. Edward Reed (Marian)

Cream Cheese Spinach

2   packages (10 ounces each)   2   tablespoons butter
    frozen chopped spinach   ½   teaspoon instant dried
3   ounces cream cheese,   onion
    softened   Parmesan cheese

Cook spinach and drain well. Mix cream cheese, butter and onion together. Stir in spinach and mix well. Place in a casserole and sprinkle top with Parmesan cheese. Bake at 350° for 20 to 25 minutes. Serves 8.

Mrs. Bill Wittenbrook (Linda)

Stir Fry Spinach

3   teaspoons lemon juice   1   package (8 ounces) fresh
1½ tablespoons soy sauce   mushrooms, sliced
1½ teaspoons sugar   ½   cup thinly sliced onion
3   tablespoons oil   6   cups washed, torn spinach
1½ cups diagonally sliced   leaves
    celery

Mix lemon juice, soy sauce and sugar together and set aside. Heat oil in wok or heavy skillet over high heat about 1 minute. Add celery, mushrooms and onion. Stir 2 or 3 times, turning vegetables over with a long spoon. Add spinach and lemon juice mixture. Cook, stirring quickly, about 2 minutes or until vegetables are crisp-tender and spinach is just limp. Do not overcook. Serve immediately. Serves 4.

Mrs. David Armour (Betsy)

Sautéed Spinach with Pear

1   pound fresh spinach,   1   ripe pear, peeled, cored
    washed and trimmed   and finely chopped
1   teaspoon butter   Generous pinch of freshly
3   tablespoons minced   grated nutmeg
    shallots   Salt and pepper to taste

Cook spinach until just wilted; squeeze dry, and chop finely. Melt butter in large saucepan over medium-high heat. Add shallots and cook until golden. Blend in spinach, pear and nutmeg. Cook, stirring constantly, until heated through. Season with salt and pepper. Serve immediately. Serves 4.

Mrs. Lawrence Christian (Joyce)

Mom's Green Rice

1 medium onion, chopped
2 tablespoons butter
4 cups cooked rice
4 cups grated American
  cheese
1 can (5 ounces) evaporated
  milk

2 eggs, beaten
1 can (8 ounces) sliced
  water chestnuts, drained,
  optional
1 package (10 ounces)
  frozen chopped spinach,
  thawed

Sauté onion in butter until tender. Toss onion with remaining ingredients. Place into an 8x8 inch dish and bake at 350° for 30 to 45 minutes. Serves 6 to 8.

Mrs. Denman Smith (Sandra)

Acorn Squash Supreme

4 small acorn squash
½ cup boiling water
Salt to taste
¾ cup firmly packed brown
  sugar, divided

1 can (20 ounces) sliced
  apples, drained
Ground nutmeg

Wash squash and cut in half lengthwise; remove seeds and membrane. Place cut side down in shallow baking pan and add boiling water. Bake at 350° for 45 minutes or until tender. Remove from oven; turn cut side up and sprinkle with salt and 1 tablespoon brown sugar. Combine apples with remaining brown sugar. Spoon into squash cavities. Sprinkle with nutmeg. Bake at 425° for 10 minutes. Serves 4.

Mrs. Jim Rado (Vicki)

Zucchini with Sour Cream Topping

8 small zucchini
2 tablespoons butter, melted
Salt and pepper to taste

1 cup sour cream, room
  temperature
⅓ cup grated sharp Cheddar
  cheese

Wash and trim ends from zucchini. Drop in salted, boiling water and cook until tender, about 10 minutes. Brush with melted butter and place in a baking dish. Add salt and pepper to sour cream and spread over zucchini. Sprinkle with cheese. Broil just until cheese melts and begins to brown. Serves 4 to 6.

Mrs. Jim Kimbell (Ellen)

Spaghetti Squash Picante

1 medium spaghetti squash, halved lengthwise, seeds removed
1 medium onion, diced
1 teaspoon garlic powder
2 ribs celery, thinly sliced
3 tablespoons butter

½ cup tomatoes and green chilies
Salt and pepper
Black olives, garnish
½ cup grated Parmesan cheese, optional

Lay squash cut side down in skillet with 2 to 3 cups water. Cook at medium boil for 15 to 20 minutes. Sauté onion, garlic and celery in butter until tender crisp. Add tomatoes and green chilies and simmer 5 to 10 minutes. Remove pulp from squash by raking with a fork. Toss with onion mixture. Season with salt and pepper. Mound in one shell and garnish with olives or Parmesan cheese. Serves 6 to 8.

Mrs. Denman Smith (Sandra)

Garlic will sprout if kept in the refrigerator. It is best stored in an open container in a dry, dark place.

Cheese Stuffed Squash

1½ pounds yellow squash
1½ tablespoons butter
2 tablespoons flour
¼ teaspoon salt
⅛ teaspoon pepper
½ cup milk
1 tablespoon grated onion

4 slices bacon, cooked, crumbled and divided
1 cup grated Cheddar cheese, divided
Salt and pepper to taste
½ cup buttered bread crumbs
Paprika

Cook whole squash in boiling water until almost tender; drain well. Cut in half lengthwise; scoop out pulp, reserving all. Mash pulp. Melt butter in a saucepan over low heat; blend in flour, salt and pepper. Remove from heat and gradually stir in milk. Return to heat and cook while stirring constantly until sauce is thickened. Combine sauce, reserved pulp, onion, ¾ of the bacon and half the cheese. Mix well. Season with salt and pepper to taste; spoon into reserved shells. Sprinkle with remaining bacon and cheese. Garnish with buttered bread crumbs and paprika. Place in a shallow baking pan; add a small amount of water. Bake at 375° for 25 to 30 minutes or until browned. Serves 6.

S. D. Jackman

Cheesy Squash Casserole

1½ to 2 pounds yellow squash
2   medium onions, chopped
Pinch of sugar
1   teaspoon salt
6 to 8 saltine crackers,
      crumbled
½   cup butter

2   eggs, beaten
½   teaspoon pepper
1   jar (4 ounces) diced
      pimiento
1½ cups grated processed
      cheese
Fresh bread crumbs, optional

Slice unpeeled squash, cutting off the ends. Boil with the onion *as you would potatoes* in a covered pot with plenty of water. Add sugar and salt after squash gets tender. When soft, pour off water. Add crackers to absorb remaining liquid. Then mash squash with an electric mixer, adding butter. *Additional crackers may be added if mixture seems soupy.* Add eggs, pepper, pimiento and cheese. Turn into 2 small casseroles and bake at 325° until lightly browned, about 30 minutes. Fresh bread crumbs may be added as topping if desired. Serve 1 casserole; wrap the other in plastic and freeze. Each casserole serves 4 to 6.

Mrs. Ken Moyer (Bonnie)

Squash Casserole

2   pounds yellow squash
½   cup butter
½   cup flour
2   cups milk
Salt to taste
12 ounces processed cheese,
      cubed

½   cup slivered almonds,
      optional
4   hard cooked eggs, grated
1   small onion, grated
Bread crumbs

Wash, slice and cook squash in a small amount of water until tender; drain and mash. Make a cheese sauce by melting butter and blending in flour. Add milk and salt and stir over low heat until it begins to thicken; add cheese and cook until thick. Add almonds, squash and salt to taste. Add eggs and onion. Place in a buttered casserole and sprinkle with bread crumbs. Bake at 400° for 20 to 30 minutes. Serves 6 to 8.

Mrs. Richard Jones (Sherlyn)

To test an egg for freshness, put it in a bowl of water. If the egg floats, it is too old to use.

Stuffed Yellow Squash with Cheese Sauce

Squash:
2 pounds yellow squash	½ pound ground beef
2½ cups water, divided	½ cup raw long grain rice
2 teaspoons salt, divided	⅛ teaspoon pepper
1 tablespoon salad oil	1 can (16 ounces) stewed
1 clove garlic, crushed	tomatoes

Wash squash; cut off and discard stems; cut squash in half lengthwise. Scoop out and discard seeds. In medium skillet with tight fitting cover, bring 2 cups water and 1 teaspoon salt to a boil. Add squash, cut side down; cook, covered, over medium heat for 5 minutes, or until tender, not mushy. Drain well. In hot oil in a medium skillet, over medium heat, sauté garlic and beef, stirring until beef is no longer pink, about 10 minutes. Add rice, 1 teaspoon salt and the pepper; mix well. Cook and stir for 2 minutes. Stir in stewed tomatoes and ½ cup water. Cook tightly covered, over low heat for 20 minutes, or until rice is tender and liquid is absorbed. Fill squash halves with rice mixture, dividing evenly.

Cheese Sauce:
2 tablespoons butter	Dash of cayenne pepper
2 tablespoons flour	1 cup milk
½ teaspoon dry mustard	¼ cup grated Parmesan
¼ teaspoon salt	cheese
Dash of pepper	

Slowly melt butter; remove from heat. Stir in flour, mustard, salt, pepper, cayenne and milk until smooth. Return to heat and bring to a boil, stirring until thickened. Reduce heat. Add cheese and cook over low heat until melted. Arrange squash in bottom of baking dish. Pour a little cheese sauce over each. Cover tightly with foil. Bake at 375° for 15 minutes or until heated. Serve with remaining sauce. Serves 6.

Mrs. Andrew Tewell (Judy)

 The dark purple eggplant we buy in our markets is only one of a number of varieties. Eggplants can be round or pickle shaped and can be striped or any of a number of colors. The vegetable is much more popular in the Middle East than it is in America.

Yellow Squash Casserole

5 pounds yellow squash, sliced
1 large onion, chopped
1 teaspoon sugar
1 teaspoon salt
½ teaspoon pepper
1 cup water
24 ounces cream cheese, softened
4 tablespoons butter
½ cup buttered bread crumbs

Preheat oven to 350°. Combine squash, onion, sugar, salt, pepper and water in a large, covered saucepan and cook until tender. Drain, reserving liquid. Mash well and drain again. Cream cheese with a little reserved liquid until the consistency of whipped cream. Add butter to squash and stir until melted. Pour squash into a buttered casserole and cover with cream cheese mixture. Mix lightly with a fork. Cover with bread crumbs. Bake at 350° for 30 minutes or until bubbly. Serves 10 to 12. *This makes an elegant vegetable when squash mixture is stuffed inside hollowed out tomatoes.*

Mrs. Jim Rado (Vicki)

Sweet Noodle Kugel

1 package (8 ounces) wide noodles
3 eggs, beaten
½ cup plus 1 tablespoon sugar, divided
1½ teaspoons salt
1 cup raisins
2 apples, peeled, cored and chopped
2 tablespoons cinnamon, divided
6 tablespoons soft butter

Boil noodles about 6 to 8 minutes until done and then drain. Mix noodles, eggs, ½ cup of sugar, salt, raisins, apples, 1 tablespoon cinnamon and butter. Pour into an 8x8 inch buttered casserole dish. Mix 1 tablespoon sugar and 1 tablespoon cinnamon together and sprinkle on top. Bake at 350° for 45 minutes or until slightly browned. Serves 6 to 8. *Serve as an accompaniment with roast beef or chicken.*

Sarah Sutton

Use large eggs in recipes. Using too small or too large eggs could ruin your effort.

Sweet Potatoes Hawaii

4 tablespoons butter
1 cup brown sugar, divided
1 can (8¼ ounces) sliced
   pineapple, drained
3 cups mashed sweet
   potatoes

½ cup half and half cream
½ teaspoon salt
Marshmallows, coconut and
   pecan halves for garnish

Melt butter and ½ cup brown sugar in baking dish. Arrange pineapple slices in bottom of dish and top with sweet potatoes seasoned with cream, remainder of brown sugar and salt. Garnish top with marshmallows, coconut and pecan halves. Bake in 350° oven for 20 minutes. Serves 6 to 8.

Vera Milton

Sweet Potato Soufflé

Sweet Potatoes:
2 cans (29 ounces each)
   sweet potatoes
½ cup butter
¼ cup milk

3 eggs
2 teaspoons vanilla extract
2 cups sugar

Mash potatoes with fork until well blended. Add remaining ingredients and mix well. Place mixture in shallow 2 quart greased casserole.

Topping:
½ cup butter
½ cup sugar
¼ cup flour

1 can (8 ounces) crushed
   pineapple, drained
1 egg

Melt butter. Cream in sugar and flour. Add pineapple and egg and mix well. Pour over sweet potato mixture and bake at 350° for 20 minutes. Serves 10.

Mrs. David King (Priscilla)

Do not store onions in the refrigerator. Keep them in a cool, dark place for best results. Allow air to circulate around them.

Sweet Potato Supreme

Sweet Potato Layer:

4 to 5 sweet potatoes	1 cup brown sugar
½ cup butter	Salt to taste
1 teaspoon cinnamon	Milk
½ teaspoon nutmeg	

Peel and cube potatoes and boil until tender. Mash potatoes with butter, cinnamon, nutmeg, brown sugar and salt. Add enough milk to make mashed potato consistency. Pour into a 10 inch baking dish.

Topping:

4 tablespoons butter	¼ teaspoon salt
½ cup sugar	1 teaspoon vanilla extract
2 tablespoons milk	½ cup chopped pecans

Combine butter, sugar, milk and salt in a saucepan and cook over low heat, stirring until thick and bubbly. When cool, add vanilla. Sprinkle chopped pecans over sweet potatoes, then pour the topping over the pecans. Bake at 400° for 15 to 20 minutes. Serves 6.

Mrs. Bryan Wooten (Sherri)

Do not buy nuts (except peanuts) that rattle. The sound means it is old.

Stuffed Tomatoes

6 tomatoes	2 tablespoons chopped onion
Salt	
3 tablespoons brown sugar	2 tablespoons butter
Bread crumbs	Salt and pepper to taste

Cut tomatoes in half and remove and save the pulp. Salt the shells and invert for 15 minutes. Season shells with brown sugar. Chop tomato pulp and combine with an equal amount of bread crumbs. Lightly sauté onion in butter. Add onion to filling and season with salt and pepper. Fill tomato shells. Bake at 350° for 20 to 30 minutes. Serves 6. *This recipe can be made ahead of time and is especially good in cold weather.*

Mrs. Larry Strickland (Linda)

Baked Vegetables

1 pound fresh broccoli	½ pound carrots, peeled and
2 tablespoons butter	diced
1½ tablespoons soy sauce	1 onion, diced
1½ teaspoons minced garlic	7 eggs, slightly beaten
1 teaspoon celery seeds	1¼ cups milk
½ teaspoon dill	16 ounces Monterey Jack
½ teaspoon salt	cheese, grated
¼ teaspoon pepper	

Break broccoli into flowerets and sauté in melted butter in saucepan. Add soy sauce, garlic, celery seeds, dill, salt and pepper. Cook over low heat for 4 to 5 minutes, stirring occasionally. Add carrots and onion and cook until tender, about 8 to 10 minutes. Beat eggs and milk in a large bowl. Add cheese and vegetables. Turn into a lightly greased 3 quart baking dish. Place baking dish in a large shallow pan filled with 1 inch of hot water. Bake at 350° for 50 to 60 minutes or until a knife inserted in the center comes out clean. Serves 10 to 12.

Mrs. Marcus Bone (Beverly)

Vegetables Supreme

2 tablespoons butter	1 can (10¾ ounces) cream of
½ medium onion, chopped	mushroom soup
½ cup chopped celery	8 ounces processed cheese
½ cup slivered almonds	⅔ cup sour cream
1 package (20 ounces)	⅛ teaspoon garlic powder
frozen mixed vegetables	Salt and pepper to taste

Sauté onion, celery and almonds in butter until lightly browned. Cook frozen vegetables as directed on package; drain and set aside. Combine soup, cheese, sour cream and garlic powder. Heat slowly until cheese is melted. Add vegetables and almonds. Salt and pepper to desired taste. This 9x13 casserole can then be baked at 350° for 20 minutes if desired, but it is not necessary. *This recipe is also good using only a single vegetable, such as broccoli, cauliflower or asparagus.* Serves 8.

Mrs. Jim Carpenter (Holly)

 If boiling vegetables, always have the water already boiling before you put the vegetable in.

Zucchini Casserole

2 pounds zucchini, thinly sliced	2 cups sour cream
1 large onion, chopped	¾ teaspoon salt
6 tablespoons butter, divided	¼ teaspoon pepper
2 eggs	8 ounces Parmesan cheese, grated and divided

Cook squash in boiling water until tender. Drain well. Sauté onion in 4 tablespoons butter until tender. Combine with squash and place in a shallow 2 quart casserole. Beat together eggs, sour cream, salt, pepper and half the Parmesan cheese. Pour over squash; dot with remaining butter and sprinkle with remaining Parmesan cheese. Bake at 400° for 15 to 20 minutes. Serves 8.

Mrs. Jim Rado (Vicki)

Onions grown in warm climates (Hawaii or the southern states) are milder than those grown in colder climates.

Egg-Stuffed Zucchini

4 medium zucchini squash	3 eggs, beaten
½ cup water	¼ teaspoon salt
Dash of salt	Dash of black pepper
1 large tomato, chopped	¼ cup grated American cheese
2 tablespoons butter	

Halve zucchini lengthwise. Scoop out pulp, leaving a ¼ inch shell. Chop pulp to make 1 cup; set aside. Place zucchini shells cut side down in a large skillet. Add ½ cup water and simmer, covered, until just tender, about 5 to 6 minutes. Drain and turn cut side up in the same skillet. Sprinkle with a dash of salt. Meanwhile, in a medium skillet, cook zucchini pulp and the tomato in butter until squash is tender, about 3 minutes. Add the eggs, salt and pepper. Cook over low heat until eggs are just set, lifting with a spatula so the uncooked portion runs underneath. Spoon egg mixture into zucchini shells. Top with cheese; cover and heat until cheese melts. Serves 4. *This dish can definitely enliven an ordinary luncheon or supper.*

Mrs. J. Edward Reed (Marian)

Steaming vegetables preserves the nutrients that boiling removes.

Vegetable Fettuccine Carbonara

4 eggs
¼ cup whipping cream
8 slices bacon
½ cup sliced mushrooms
½ cup sliced carrots
½ cup sliced cauliflower
½ cup frozen English peas, thawed
½ cup sliced zucchini

½ red bell pepper, seeded and cut into strips
¼ cup sliced green onion
1 clove garlic, minced
1 package (16 ounces) fettuccine
¼ cup butter
1 cup grated Parmesan cheese
Salt and pepper to taste

Beat eggs with cream in a small bowl and set aside. Cook bacon in a heavy skillet until crisp. Remove with slotted spoon and set aside. Add mushrooms, carrots, cauliflower, peas, zucchini, red bell pepper, onion and garlic to skillet, and sauté until tender crisp. Meanwhile, cook fettucine according to package directions and drain well. Transfer to a large serving bowl. Add butter and toss through. Add egg mixture and toss lightly. Add vegetables, bacon and cheese and toss again. Serve immediately. Serves 6 to 8.

Mrs. Lawrence Christian (Joyce)

Mom's Cornbread Dressing

1 recipe of cornbread
1 package (8 ounces) herb seasoned stuffing
2 to 3 slices dry white bread, crumbled
1 teaspoon sage
½ teaspoon onion salt

1½ cups water
2½ cups turkey stock
3 eggs, well beaten
1 teaspoon salt
½ teaspoon pepper
½ cup chopped onion
2 teaspoons margarine

Crumble cooled cornbread into a large bowl. Add seasoned stuffing, bread, sage, onion salt and water. Mix well and refrigerate overnight. The next day, add turkey stock, eggs, salt and pepper to mixture; sauté onions in margarine and add. Mix thoroughly, adding water as needed, to make moist dressing. Do not use milk to thin. Pour into a greased oblong baking dish and bake at 325° for 1 hour or until lightly browned. Serves 8 to 10. *I make cornbread from a mix, adding 1 tablespoon sugar per recipe. The dressing can be made ahead and frozen either before or after baking. This was a requested Christmas present from my mother, Ruth Buckellew in 1971.*

Mrs. Ken Moyer (Bonnie)

"Remember the Alamo!" It's a battle cry which can still stir the hearts of native Texans well over a century after the final shot. The building itself stands as a symbol of the indomitable spirit and courage of the people who settled this land. Within the walls of this small mission, less than two hundred men, women and children held off the attack of Santa Ana's advancing army. For five grueling days — first with cannon, then rifles, then hand-to-hand — they fought fiercely to wrest Texas' independence from the tyrannical grasp of Mexico. They were victorious, even though the Alamo fell and none of the brave soldiers inside the compound lived to join in celebration. Ultimately, their sacrifice enabled Sam Houston's troops to assemble and crush the invasion at San Jacinto near Houston. When the final battle was over, Texas emerged as an independent nation, free at last from unjust domination.

Mexican Dishes pictured: Spanish Style Chicken, Border Buttermilk, Sangria Blanc, Pralines, Pumpkin Empanadas, Candied Mexican Orange Shell, Pan Dulce, Creamed Cornbread, Mexican Rice, Fajitas, Mexican Beans and Great Layered Taco Dip.

Mexican Dishes

Appetizers

Ceviche

1 pound raw, boneless cod
8 ounces lime juice
1 large onion, chopped
15 cherry tomatoes
1 small jalapeño pepper, chopped
30 pitted Spanish green olives, chopped

20 capers
1 tablespoon cumin
¼ cup olive oil
1 tablespoon parsley
1 teaspoon oregano
Salt and pepper to taste
Chips

Place fish in a glass container and cover with lime juice for 3 hours or until fish has a white, flaky, cooked appearance. Drain off lime juice. Cut fish into bite sized pieces and add remaining ingredients and marinate for 2 to 4 hours. Serve with chips. Serves 8.

Mrs. Tom Hollis (Doris)

Robin and Peggy's Favorite Ceviche

1½ to 2 pounds fresh white fish
10 to 12 fresh limes
1 teaspoon seasoned salt
1 onion, chopped
4 to 5 tomatoes, chopped
1 teaspoon olive oil
½ cup sliced black olives

4 jalapeños, sliced and seeded
Dash of hot pepper sauce
1 tablespoon chervil
Lettuce
Tortilla chips
Picante sauce

Cut fish into chunks and put in a deep covered glass dish. Squeeze limes and cover fish completely with juice. Add seasoned salt and chopped onions; leave to 'cook' in refrigerator overnight. The second day add chopped tomatoes, olive oil, olives and jalapeños. Add hot pepper sauce and mix well. Let 'cook' overnight again. Sprinkle with chervil. Serve ceviche over loose lettuce bed with tortilla chips and hot sauce. Serves 4. *This is the best diet food you can eat!*

Mrs. Randy Hagan (Robin Roberts)

Texans are familiar with a parsley-like fresh herb called cilantro. It is also known as coriander on the spice shelf.

"Hot" Guacamole Dip

1	cup mashed avocado	1	small clove garlic, crushed
2	teaspoons finely chopped onions	1	teaspoon vegetable oil
		1	teaspoon cider vinegar
2	teaspoons minced fresh jalapeños	¼	teaspoon salt
			Tortilla chips

Combine all ingredients well. Chill. Serve with tortilla chips. Yields 1 cup.

Matt Martinez, Jr.

Cheese Stuffed Tortillas

8	ounces cream cheese, softened	1	can (14 ounces) chopped green chilies, drained
1	carton (8 ounces) sour cream	1	tablespoon chopped pimiento
1½	cups grated sharp Cheddar cheese	1	teaspoon garlic salt
		1	tablespoon minced onion
1	cup chopped ripe olives	12	flour tortillas

Mix all ingredients together except tortillas. Spread on flour tortillas; roll up in jelly roll style. Chill several hours. Slice and serve. Yields 72 half inch slices.

Mrs. Reed McFadden (Penny)

Taco Dip

8	ounces sour cream	3	tablespoons dry taco seasoning
1	can (11½ ounces) bean with bacon soup	1 to 2	tablespoons minced onion
½	cup grated Cheddar cheese		

Combine all ingredients and mix well. Heat thoroughly and serve with tortilla chips. Yields approximately 2½ cups.

Mrs. Jack Dempsey (Estelle)

Hearty Queso

1 pound ground beef
1 pound bulk pork sausage
1 cup chopped onion
2 pounds processed cheese
1 can (10 ounces) tomatoes
  and chilies

1 can (10¾ ounces) cream of
  mushroom soup
½ teaspoon garlic powder
1 to 3 teaspoons hot pepper
  sauce
Tostado chips

Brown ground beef, sausage and onion; drain and set aside. Melt cheese with tomatoes and chilies and mushroom soup. Add spices and heat. Works well in a slow cooker for parties. Serve with chips of your choice. Serves 12 to 15.

Mrs. Randy Denbow (Virginia)

Great Layered Taco Dip

3 ripe avocados
1 tomato, chopped
Salt and pepper to taste
1½ teaspoons lemon juice
¼ teaspoon garlic powder
2 tablespoons minced onion
Hot pepper sauce to taste
1 cup mayonnaise
1 cup sour cream
1 package (1½ ounces) taco
  seasoning

1 can (32 ounces) refried
  beans
4 tomatoes, chopped
1 bunch green onions,
  chopped
8 ounces Cheddar cheese,
  grated
1 can (4¼ ounces) chopped
  ripe olives
Tostados

Peel and mash avocados. Add 1 chopped tomato, salt, pepper, lemon juice, garlic powder, minced onion and hot pepper sauce and set aside. Mix mayonnaise, sour cream and taco seasoning and set aside. On large platter spread refried beans as first layer of dip. Next, spread the avocado mixture. Cover with the sour cream and mayonnaise mixture. Sprinkle with 4 chopped tomatoes, green onions and cheese; top with black olives. Serve with tostados. Serves 10.

Mrs. James Hurlbut (Marsha)

Guacamole consists of mashed avocados with various seasonings. It is used either as a salad with lettuce or as a dip with tostado chips.

Nachos y Pollo

2 whole chicken breasts, boned and skinned
1½ teaspoons salt, divided
2½ teaspoons ground cumin, divided
1 onion, chopped
2 tablespoons butter
1 can (4 ounces) chopped green chilies
1 cup chopped tomatoes
¼ teaspoon pepper
Tortilla chips
8 ounces Monterey Jack cheese, grated
Jalapeño pepper slices
Sour cream, optional

Place chicken with 1 teaspoon salt in a saucepan; cover with water and bring to a boil. Cover and reduce heat; simmer 6 to 8 minutes. Drain chicken, reserving broth. Place chicken with 1½ teaspoons cumin in food processor and process until coarsely ground. Set aside. Sauté onion in butter until tender and add ¾ cup reserved chicken broth, green chilies, tomato, 1 teaspoon cumin, ½ teaspoon salt and pepper. Simmer uncovered for 20 minutes or until liquid evaporates. Place tortilla chips on a cookie sheet and spoon 2 tablespoons of chicken mixture on each chip. Top with cheese and a jalapeño slice. Broil until cheese melts. Yields 36 nachos. *You can also put a dollop of sour cream on these nachos after they come out of the oven to enhance the flavor.*

Mrs. Marcus Bone (Beverly)

Jolly Cholly Holly Peña Eggs

12 round flat tostado chips
4 jalapeños, sliced into thirds
12 slices Monterey Jack cheese
12 slices Cheddar or American cheese

Place chips on a cookie sheet; do not overlap. Place a jalapeño slice in the center of each chip. Place a round slice of Monterey Jack cheese on top, then center a smaller round slice of Cheddar cheese on top of the Monterey Jack cheese. Put under broiler just until cheese melts. Serve immediately as an appetizer or with Mexican beans. Serves 4 to 6. *Any size of round flat chip may be used, but adjust the cheese circles to fit. The nachos come out of the oven looking like an egg. You might warn your guests about the hidden firepower under the "yolk"!*

Charley Batey

Mexican Roulette

Water
Salt
¼ cup sliced celery
¼ cup sliced carrots
½ cup cauliflowerets
⅓ cup oil
½ onion, sliced
2 cloves garlic, diced

1 cup white vinegar
1 bay leaf
½ teaspoon dried oregano
¼ teaspoon dried thyme
8 peppercorns
½ teaspoon seasoned salt
1 can (6½ ounces) sliced jalapeños

Bring 2 cups salted water to a boil in a small saucepan. Drop in celery and immediately remove with a slotted spoon. Set aside. Drop in carrots and boil 4 minutes. Drain and rinse with cold water; set aside with celery. Bring another 2 cups salted water to boil. Add cauliflowerets. Boil for 4 minutes. Drain and rinse with cold water; set aside with carrots and celery. Heat oil in medium saucepan. Add onion and garlic. Cook until onion is crisp-tender but not browned. Add vinegar, bay leaf, oregano, thyme, peppercorns and seasoned salt. Simmer 5 minutes over low heat. Add jalapeños, celery, carrots and cauliflowerets. Bring to a boil and remove from heat. Spoon vegetables into a clean jar. Cover with the hot cooking liquid. Let cool; cover with a tight fitting lid. Let sit in refrigerator for 1 to 2 days to blend flavors. Oil in pickles will become cloudy in refrigerator, but if left to stand at room temperature for a few minutes before serving, the cloudiness will disappear. Yields 2 cups. *If a less potent pickle is desired, use whole jalapeños instead of sliced.*

Mrs. Don Bradford (Melinda)

Periche

3 pounds lean ground beef
1 pound Cheddar cheese, grated
1 bunch green onions, finely chopped
10 jalapeño peppers, finely chopped

5 tablespoons Worcestershire sauce
1 teaspoon garlic powder
6 lemons, juice and pulp
Tostados

Mix together meat, cheese, onion and peppers. Add Worcestershire sauce and garlic powder. Stir in lemon juice and mix well. Marinate overnight. Serve with tostados. Yields 4 pints. *This is the beef version of ceviche. It is quick and easy to make with a food processor and will keep in the refrigerator for about 3 weeks.*

Mrs. Paul Holcomb (Cindy)

Pico de Gallo con Aguacate

4   avocados, diced
Juice of 2 limes
2   large tomatoes, diced
1   bunch green onions,
     chopped
1   teaspoon onion powder
½   teaspoon salt

½   teaspoon garlic powder
1   cup parsley, finely minced
½   cup cilantro, finely minced
1   can (4 ounces) salsa
     casera
1½ cups picante sauce

Put diced avocado into a large bowl and sprinkle with lime juice and toss. Add remaining ingredients and stir. Yields 6 cups. *Excellent as a dip or an accompaniment for fajitas. May be halved or doubled.*

Mrs. Dudley Baker (Kathy)

Ken's Pico de Gallo

2   large tomatoes, diced
2   large onions, chopped
     finely
3   medium tomatillos,
     chopped
2   serrano peppers (1½
     inches each) finely
     chopped

1   tablespoon oil
½   teaspoon white vinegar
1   teaspoon salt
½   teaspoon pepper
⅓   cup cilantro leaves, finely
     chopped, optional

Mix all ingredients together. Can be served right away or chilled for several hours. It is best the same day because of the fresh tomatoes, but keeps well for several days. Cilantro is optional, and as a traditional herb of Mexico, is a delightfully authentic flavor, and a surprise as well. Yields 2 cups. *This recipe is wonderful with fajitas, but is also a tasty relish with any Mexican dish.*

Mrs. Ken Moyer (Bonnie)

Bert's Green Chile Sauce

4 to 5 green tomatoes
1 to 2 green chilies
½   clove garlic, minced

½   onion, chopped
Cilantro

Boil green tomatoes and green chilies for 10 minutes. Drain and combine in blender with garlic, onion and cilantro. Taste; if too hot, add more green tomatoes. Yields 2 cups. *This sauce can be frozen. To keep several days, put in a pan with a little oil and cook 30 minutes.*

Mrs. Reece Goodman (Leslie)

Picadillo

2 pounds ground beef	½ cup Worcestershire sauce
2 cups minced onion	1 cup beef bouillon
2 teaspoons minced garlic	2 cans (6 ounces each)
1 cup minced green bell	tomato paste
pepper	3 cups cubed raw potatoes
1 can (16 ounces) tomatoes,	1 jar (4 ounces) chopped
undrained	pimientos
2¼ teaspoons salt	1 can (4 ounces) chopped
¼ teaspoon pepper	ripe olives
¼ teaspoon cayenne pepper	1 jar (8 ounces) sliced
½ teaspoon paprika	mushrooms
1 tablespoon white vinegar	1 can (6 ounces) stuffed
1 cup slivered almonds	olives, sliced
1 cup golden raisins	Cooked rice, crackers or
1 teaspoon cumin	chips, optional
½ teaspoon oregano	

In a large skillet brown ground beef. Remove beef and sauté onion, garlic and bell pepper until translucent. Drain and return meat to skillet. Add tomatoes with liquid, breaking up tomatoes with fork. Add remaining ingredients and simmer 1 hour. Skim off excess fat. Serve with rice or as an appetizer with crackers or chips. Serves 12. *This may be frozen and reheated in the microwave.*

Mrs. Robert S. Brown (Mary)

Jim's Homemade Picante Sauce

2 cans (16 ounces each)	1 teaspoon garlic powder
tomatoes	1 teaspoon cayenne pepper
5 jalapeño peppers, chopped	¼ onion, chopped
1 teaspoon salt	2 tablespoons vinegar
1 teaspoon pepper	3 green onions, chopped

Place all ingredients in blender and blend slowly for 1 to 2 minutes. Pour into jars and refrigerate. Keeps for several weeks. Yields 5 cups.

Jim Stasswender

Jalapeño chilies probably have the hottest reputation. They may be bought fresh, canned or pickled and are the basic ingredient of many Mexican sauces.

Gazpacho Dip

1 pound tomatoes, peeled, seeded, and finely chopped	1 can (4 ounces) diced ripe olives
¼ pound mushrooms, finely chopped	1 can (8 ounces) tomato sauce
1 bunch green onions, green part only, finely chopped	½ teaspoon garlic salt
1 can (4 ounces) diced green chilies	3 tablespoons oil
	2 tablespoons vinegar

Combine all ingredients and mix well. Chill several hours or overnight. If desired, drain off excess liquid before serving with tortilla chips. Yields approximately 3 cups.

Mrs. James Schloss (Cindy)

Willie's Picante Sauce

4 to 5 tomatoes	1 tablespoon salt
2 onions	1 teaspoon crushed coriander seeds
3 to 4 cloves garlic	1 teaspoon crushed comino seeds
4 jalapeño peppers	
1 cayenne pepper	1 teaspoon paprika
5 dried chilepequin peppers	
1 tablespoon vinegar	

Core and quarter tomatoes. Quarter onions. Chop garlic and peppers. Put all ingredients into blender and blend until smooth. Pour into a large pot and bring to a boil. Reduce heat and simmer for 45 minutes, stirring every 5 minutes or so. *It will not look or smell like picante sauce until near the end of the cooking period.* Fill a sterilized quart jar to within ¼ inch from top. Store in refrigerator or process in a hot water bath for 35 minutes. Yields 1 quart. *For a mild sauce use 5 serrano peppers; for hot, use 6 jalapeño peppers.*

Mrs. Don Bradford (Melinda)

Viva La Dip

2 cans (15 ounces each) refried beans with jalapeños	2 cups sour cream
	2 cups grated Cheddar cheese
1 package (1.25 ounces) taco seasoning mix	Nacho type corn chips

Spread refried beans in an 8x11 inch glass dish. Mix taco seasoning and sour cream together. Spread over beans. Cover with grated cheese. Bake uncovered at 325° for 30 minutes. Serve warm with nacho chips. Serves 8 to 10.

Mrs. Jim Schultz (Mary Kay)

Stuffed Jalapeños

1 can (1 gallon) jalapeños
24 ounces cream cheese,
   softened

1 can (12½ ounces) tuna,
   drained
Mayonnaise

Do not handle jalapeños without rubber gloves! Clean jalapeños, remove stems and wash out all seeds. If peppers are whole, split down one side. Let soak in ice water in refrigerator overnight. In mixer blend cream cheese, tuna and enough mayonnaise to make a thick spreading consistency. Fill jalapeños with cream cheese mixture so that pepper closes into original position. Place toothpicks through pepper about every half inch. Place on waxed paper in a large pan. You may layer them. Refrigerate at least overnight. The peppers may be refrigerated for a couple of days. At serving time, cut between toothpicks. This will make a bite sized piece with a toothpick handle. Serves 24. *The jalapeño juice can be used as a marinade for scraped, cut carrots or mushrooms and keeps forever in refrigerator.*

Mrs. Bob Kelly (Margaret)

Mexican Beverages

Border Buttermilk

1 can (6 ounces) frozen
   limeade concentrate

6 ounces tequila
Ice to fill blender

Pour all ingredients into a blender and blend on high until ice is crushed and mixture is frothy. Serves 4. *This is famous in the valley to welcome newcomers.*

Mrs. Dudley Baker (Kathy)

El Matt's Frozen Margarita

1 cup white tequila
1 cup triple sec

1 cup fresh squeezed lime
   juice
Crushed ice

Pour tequila, triple sec and lime juice in a blender. Add ice and mix. Yields 5 cups.

Matt Martinez, Jr.

Frozen Margaritas

1 tablespoon orange extract	Juice of 3 limes
2 cans (12 ounces each)	1 quart tequila
frozen lemonade	Water
concentrate	

Mix all ingredients except water. Put into a gallon jar. Add enough water to make 1 gallon. Freeze. Mixture will be slushy. Serve from a punch bowl which has a rim of salt on it. Yields 32 (4 ounce) servings. *This is a quick and inexpensive way to make frozen margaritas for a large party. Keep some in the freezer for unexpected guests.*

Dudley Baker

Margarita

1 can (6 ounces) frozen	2 ounces triple sec
limeade concentrate	6 ounces lemon lime soda
6 ounces tequila	Lime slices

Blend all ingredients except lime slices. Fill blender with 5 cups crushed ice. Add mixture and blend until a slushy consistency. Pour into salt-rimmed margarita glasses and add lime slices. Serves 8.

Roger Borgelt

Margaritas on the Rocks

1 cup white tequila	1 cup fresh squeezed lime
1 cup triple sec	juice
	Crushed ice

Blend tequila, triple sec and lime juice in blender and pour over ice. Yields 3 cups.

Matt Martinez, Jr.

Sangria Blanc

2 bottles (4/5 quart each)	2 cups club soda
white wine	Lime slices
2 cans (6 ounces each)	
frozen lemonade	
concentrate, thawed	

Combine wine and lemonade. Add club soda just before serving. Garnish with lime slices. Yields 11 (8 ounce) servings.

Mrs. Tony Sessi (Alice)

Steve's Skinny Rita

1 cup tequila
1 cup freshly squeezed lime
juice
1 cup sparkling water

3 packages (.035 ounces
each) sugar substitute
Lime wedges for garnish

Combine all ingredients and stir well. Serves 4.

Steve McMillon

Tequila Sunrise

Ice
1½ ounces tequila

3 to 4 ounces orange juice
Splash of grenadine

Fill a 6 to 8 ounce bar glass with ice. Add tequila and orange juice and stir. Splash grenadine on top. Do not stir. It will begin to settle to the bottom, giving the streaks of a Mexican Sunrise. Serves 1.

Denman Smith

Mexican Martinis

¼ cup dry vermouth
1 fresh hot red or jalapeño
pepper, split lengthwise

1 quart vodka or gin

Combine vermouth and pepper in a quart canning jar. Add vodka to top of jar. Cover with air tight lid and refrigerate 6 hours. Taste mixture to gauge strength of pepper flavor. Remove pepper or continue steeping up to 6 more hours. Yields 1 quart.

Marcus Bone

Mexican Fizz

1½ ounces tequila
Dash grenadine
¼ cup orange juice

1½ ounces lemon juice
Ice

Mix all ingredients together and shake well with ice. Pour into 2 stemmed champagne glasses and enjoy. Serves 2.

Mrs. Denman Smith (Sandra)

Grenadine is made from pomegranate juice as well as from other fruit juices.

Mexican Soups

Crema Sopa de Salsa

3 to 4 tablespoons butter
2 cups chopped onion
3 garlic cloves, minced
1 teaspoon ground cumin

Pinch of white pepper
1½ cups chile salsa
4 cups half and half cream
Grated Cheddar cheese, garnish

Melt the butter in a skillet over medium heat. Add onion and garlic and sauté about 10 minutes, stirring occasionally, until soft. Stir in cumin and white pepper; set aside. Heat chile salsa in a 3 quart saucepan over medium heat. Do not boil. Add onion mixture and slowly stir in cream and heat through; do not boil. Ladle soup into heated bowls and sprinkle generously with Cheddar cheese. Serve immediately. Serves 6 to 8.

Mrs. Cecil Smith (Diana)

Green Chile Soup

1 large onion, thinly sliced
2 tablespoons butter
1 pound tenderized round steak, cut in thin strips
⅛ teaspoon garlic powder
2 cans (4 ounces each) whole green chilies
2 cans (14½ ounces each) stewed tomatoes

3 beef bouillon cubes
¼ cup hot water
½ teaspoon sweet basil
¼ teaspoon crushed celery seeds
30 ounces water
½ cup grated Longhorn cheese

In a 3 quart saucepan over low heat sauté onions in butter until limp. Add beef and garlic powder. Cook until steak has lost its pink color. Add green chilies, stewed tomatoes, beef bouillon, which has been dissolved in water, sweet basil and celery seeds. Boil gently, uncovered for 15 minutes, stirring occasionally. Add water and simmer 1 hour uncovered. When serving, sprinkle with 1 tablespoon grated cheese. Serves 4. *This soup will be mild to hot depending on the green chilies. Use 2 whole roasted and peeled chilies for each can of chilies if fresh chilies are desired.*

Mrs. Dan O'Donnell (Sharon)

Tostados are Mexican corn chips. They are corn tortillas which have been quartered and fried in hot oil. They are the favorite dippers for hot sauce, chile con queso or guacamole.

Clear Gazpacho

Soup:

2 pounds tomatoes, peeled and chopped

2 cans (2¼ ounces each) sliced ripe olives

¾ cup finely diced celery

¾ cup thinly sliced green onions

¾ cup chopped cucumbers

2 cloves garlic, minced

6 tablespoons red wine vinegar

2 teaspoons Worcestershire sauce

6 to 8 drops hot pepper sauce

1½ tablespoons olive oil

2 cans (14½ ounces each) chicken broth

¾ cup dry white wine

Salt and pepper to taste

Optional Garnishes:

Croutons

Fresh chives

Avocado slices

Lime slices

Cilantro

Combine soup ingredients and chill at least ½ hour or overnight. Serve in clear glass bowls with your choice of garnishes. Yields 8 cups.

Mrs. Larry Lerche (Gail)

Calabacita con Puerco

1 medium-sized pork loin roast, boned and cubed

3 tablespoons oil

3 ears of corn

1 large onion, chopped

4 cloves garlic, minced

1 teaspoon cumin

2 teaspoons chili powder

Dried red pepper to taste

Salt and pepper to taste

1 can (8 ounces) tomato sauce

Water

4 medium Mexican green squash or zucchini, chopped

Brown pork in oil, then drain. While pork is cooking, cut corn off cobs and scrape cobs. To the pork add corn, onion, garlic, spices, tomato sauce and enough water to cover. Bring to a boil, then simmer for 45 to 50 minutes. Add squash and additional water to cover, if necessary, and simmer another 30 minutes or until squash is tender. Serves 6 to 8. *Like any soup, calabacita is better warmed up — the only trouble is there's usually none left to reheat! This dish can also be made with chicken.*

Ken and Susan McGinnis

Mexican Pumpkin Soup

2 tablespoons butter
½ onion, chopped
1 clove garlic, minced
1 can (16 ounces) tomatoes
1 to 2 tablespoons picante
 sauce
¾ teaspoon salt

¼ teaspoon oregano
1 can (14½ ounces) chicken
 broth
4 cups cooked fresh
 pumpkin
Sour cream for garnish

Heat butter in a skillet and sauté onion and garlic until tender. Add tomatoes, picante sauce, salt and oregano and simmer for 3 to 4 minutes. Transfer onion mixture to a blender; add broth and pumpkin and blend on low until chopped. Return to pan and simmer for 15 to 20 minutes to blend flavors. Serve with a dollop of sour cream. Serves 6 to 8.

Mrs. Denman Smith (Sandra)

Sopa de Fideo

1 package (8 ounces) very
 thin vermicelli
Hot oil
1 can (8 ounces) tomato
 sauce

1 teaspoon chopped onion
¼ teaspoon minced garlic
4 cups chicken broth

Brown vermicelli in hot oil. Combine tomato sauce with onion and garlic. Add this to the browned pasta along with chicken broth. Boil about 10 minutes. Serves 6 to 8.

Mrs. Reece Goodman (Leslie)

Sopa de Arroz

1 cup brown rice
4 tablespoons bacon
 drippings
2 cloves garlic

1 medium tomato
½ onion
2 cups water
Salt and pepper to taste

Lightly brown rice in bacon drippings with garlic. Combine tomato, onion and water in blender and liquify. Pour over browned rice. Season with salt and pepper. Cover and simmer until rice is done. If liquid is consumed before rice is thoroughly cooked, sprinkle water on top. Remove garlic cloves before serving. Serves 2.

Mrs. Reece Goodman (Leslie)

Sopa de Pollo

2 to 3 pounds chicken breasts	½ teaspoon oregano
8 cups water	½ teaspoon thyme
2 cloves garlic, peeled	2 teaspoons chopped
1 carrot, peeled and sliced	cilantro
1 medium onion, chopped	¾ teaspoon ground cumin
1 bay leaf, crumbled	2 cups rice
2 ribs celery, sliced	2 to 3 ripe avocados, chopped
4 to 5 sprigs parsley	Juice of ½ lime
1 teaspoon salt	4 to 5 limes, quartered
½ teaspoon pepper	Hot pepper sauce to taste

In a large soup pot cook chicken in the water for 45 minutes or until done. Remove chicken from water, debone and cut into bite sized pieces. Return chicken to broth and add garlic, carrot, onion, bay leaf, celery, parsley, salt, pepper, oregano, thyme and cilantro. Simmer until vegetables are tender. Add cumin and rice, simmering until rice is done. Peel and pit avocados and cut into bite sized chunks and sprinkle with lime juice. To serve, top bowls of soup with avocados and a lime wedge. Serves 8.

Mrs. Erick Van Tongerloo (Anita)

Sopa de Tortilla

6 corn tortillas	2 quarts broth, chicken or
¼ cup oil	beef
1 onion, chopped	1 teaspoon fresh cilantro
½ cup tomato purée	Grated Monterey Jack cheese

Cut tortillas into strips about the size of macaroni; fry in oil until crisp, then remove from pan and drain on absorbent paper. Place in a large pot and add boiling broth which has been prepared in the following way: fry onion and tomato purée in the oil which was used to fry the tortillas; add the stock; mash the cilantro and add a little broth and strain into the stock. Serve with grated cheese on top. Serves 8.

Mrs. Ron Bruney (Carol)

Tortillas are the bread of Mexico. In various forms they are the base of tacos, burritos, enchiladas, tostados, flautas, and many other Mexican dishes. They may be made from corn or flour.

Mexican Salads

El Matt's Guacamole Salad

1   cup mashed avocado
¼   teaspoon salt
¼   teaspoon garlic powder
1   teaspoon cider vinegar
1   teaspoon vegetable oil
½   cup chopped tomatoes, optional

Blend all ingredients together well. Chill before serving. If using tomatoes, add ⅛ teaspoon more salt. Yields 1½ cups.

Matt Martinez, Jr.

Maude's Taco Salad

1   pound ground beef
1   package (1.5 ounces) taco seasoning
1   can (15 ounces) kidney beans, drained and rinsed
1   head of lettuce
2   avocados, chopped
2   tomatoes, chopped
4   green onions, chopped
1   bag (1¾ ounces) corn chips
1   can (2¼ ounces) ripe olives
1   bottle (8 ounces) sweet and spicy French dressing

Brown ground beef in skillet; drain and add taco seasoning and kidney beans. Wash lettuce and break into bite sized pieces and place in bowl. Add avocados, tomatoes, onions, corn chips and olives to lettuce, then add meat mixture. Toss with dressing. Serves 6.

Mrs. Randy Hagan (Robin Roberts)

Jicama Ensalada

1   cucumber, peeled
2   tomatoes, diced
1   medium jicama, peeled and grated
2   green onions, chopped
½   teaspoon chopped cilantro
½   pound salad shrimp, cooked, peeled and deveined, optional
1   avocado, diced
3   tablespoons olive oil
Juice of 2 limes
3   tablespoons picante sauce
Salt and pepper to taste

Halve the cucumber lengthwise, seed and slice thinly. Layer, beginning with cucumber, tomatoes, jicama; add green onions and cilantro. If desired, you may add shrimp, then top with the avocado. Mix the oil, lime juice and picante sauce together and pour over vegetables. Serves 4. *This is a very refreshing and colorful salad; it contains the colors of Mexico, red, white and green.*

Mrs. Denman Smith (Sandra)

Taos Salad Toss

1 large ripe avocado, chopped	2 cups shredded lettuce
½ cup sour cream	1 can (15 ounces) kidney beans, drained
2 tablespoons Italian salad dressing	2 tomatoes, chopped
¼ cup minced onion	½ cup sliced ripe olives
1 to 2 tablespoons chopped green chilies	½ cup shredded Cheddar cheese
¾ teaspoon chili powder	½ cup coarsely crushed corn chips
¼ teaspoon salt	Ripe olives for garnish
Dash of pepper	

Combine avocado, sour cream, Italian dressing, onion, green chilies, chili powder, salt and pepper; mix well and chill. Just before serving combine lettuce, beans, tomatoes and ripe olives. Mix avocado dressing into salad. Top with corn chips and cheese. Garnish with olive slices if desired. Serves 6 to 8.

Mrs. Marvin Sentell (Julie)

Tequila Sunrise Salad

2 watermelons	1 cup orange juice
4 large cantaloupes, peeled	1 cup powdered sugar
2 fresh pineapples, peeled	½ cup grenadine
2 cups tequila	

Cut the top off lengthwise from each watermelon, cutting about ¼ the distance from the top. Remove the meat from the rind, leaving about 1 inch inside the rind to form a shell. Remove seeds from the watermelon fruit and cut it into bite sized pieces; set aside. Cut a sawtoothed or scalloped pattern around the edge of the shells with a sharp knife; set aside. Cut cantaloupe and pineapple into bite sized pieces; combine with watermelon pieces and set aside. Combine the tequila, orange juice, powdered sugar and grenadine and mix well. Pour over the fruit and mix again. Spoon the fruit and liquid into melon shells; cover with plastic wrap and refrigerate overnight. Toss lightly before serving. Serves 20 to 24. *If fresh pineapple is not available, use 4 cans (15 ounces each) pineapple chunks, drained.*

Nancy Young Chandler

Jicama is a vegetable which looks like a cross between the potato and the turnip. After peeling, the inside meat resembles the potato and tastes like a water chestnut. Jicama may be used raw in salads or for dippers or may be cooked as a vegetable.

Mexican Vegetables

Arroz Con Tomaté

2 tablespoons olive oil
½ cup chopped green bell
pepper
¼ cup finely chopped onion
1 clove garlic, minced
½ teaspoon dried basil
½ teaspoon dried rosemary

1 cup long grain rice
1 cup peeled and chopped
tomato
1 teaspoon salt
⅛ teaspoon pepper
2 cups water
Jalapeño peppers, optional

In a skillet cook the bell pepper, onion, garlic, basil and rosemary in hot oil until tender. Stir in rice, chopped tomatoes, salt, pepper and water. Cover and cook over low heat for about 20 minutes or until rice is done. Serves 6.

Cyndee McBee

Black Beans

1 pound dried black beans
1 to 2 green onions, chopped
¼ pound bacon, slab or
sliced

1 tablespoon chopped
parsley or cilantro
1 teaspoon salt
½ teaspoon pepper
Sour cream, optional

Wash beans well and soak overnight. Drain off excess water, or add water, if necessary, to make 1½ quarts. Add onion, bacon, parsley, salt and pepper and bring to a boil. Reduce heat; cover and simmer until tender, approximately 3 hours. Remove cover and cook beans, stirring occasionally, an additional 30 to 45 minutes to reduce liquid. Beans should be slightly soupy. Correct seasonings to taste. If slab bacon was used, remove before serving. Serve with a dollop of sour cream if desired. Serves 10 to 12. *This dish is excellent with chicken enchiladas.*

Mrs. Marvin Sentell (Julie)

William B. Travis and James Bowie were the two leaders of the Texan forces at the Alamo.

Mexican Zucchini

Select several zucchini about the size and shape of a good cucumber; cut off ends and place in boiling salted water to cook until they are crisp tender. Slice them about ¼ to ½ inch thick and make sandwiches of them with small slices of Monterey Jack cheese in the middle. Press slices gently together, dip into a mixture of stiffly beaten egg whites to which a little flour and salt have been added along with the beaten egg yolks. It is very important to add the yolks to the whites rather than vice versa. Fry the zucchini sandwiches quickly until brown on both sides; they may be served dry or in a thin tomato sauce with slices of onion added. Serves 4 to 6.

Mrs. Reece Goodman (Leslie)

Cactus Mexicano

4 cups chopped cactus	1½ teaspoons salt
1 large fresh tomato, diced	½ teaspoon pepper
1 small onion, chopped	1 small garlic clove, minced
½ cup fresh chopped cilantro	

Remove thorns from cactus and peel. Boil in water over low flame about 30 to 45 minutes in a medium sized saucepan. When cooked, let stand until cool. Put cactus into a bowl and add fresh tomato, onion and cilantro. Add salt, pepper and garlic. Mix and serve. Serves 6 to 8.

Mrs. Bob Vasquez (Carmen)

Green Chili Rice Bake

1 cup uncooked long grain rice	1 cup half and half cream
2½ cups water	8 ounces Monterey Jack cheese, cubed
1 teaspoon salt	1 can (4 ounces) diced green chilies
2 tablespoons butter	2 cups sour cream
1 medium onion, chopped	
½ teaspoon salt	

Cook rice in salted water until tender. Sauté onion in melted butter until transparent. In a 1½ or 2 quart casserole, combine all ingredients and mix well. Bake at 325° for 30 minutes, or until bubbly. Serves 6 to 8.

Marsha Hynes

Mexican Rice

1½ cups long grain white rice
Hot water to cover
⅓ cup peanut oil
½ pound tomatoes, chopped
¾ cup chopped onion

½ tablespoon minced garlic
3½ cups chicken broth
½ teaspoon salt
⅛ teaspoon pepper

Wash rice in cold water 3 times. Pour hot water over rice in pot and let sit for 20 minutes. Drain rice and rinse well in cold water. Shake colander well and let drain for 10 minutes. Heat oil in skillet until it smokes. Give rice a final shake to remove moisture. Stir into hot oil until grains are well covered with oil; fry until light golden color, stirring and turning rice over to cook evenly and not stick to bottom of skillet, about 10 minutes. Be sure flame is high or rice will be mushy. Tip pan to one side and pour off any excess oil. Blend tomato, onion and garlic until smooth and add to fried rice. Cook over high heat, stirring and scraping pan until mixture is dry. Add broth, salt and pepper and stir well. Cook over medium heat uncovered, without stirring until liquid is absorbed and small air holes appear. Remove from heat; cover tightly with lid or aluminum foil for 30 minutes. Before serving, stir well from bottom of the pan. Serves 10.

S. D. Jackman

Potatoes and Corn Mexicano

2 pounds baking potatoes, peeled and sliced
Salt and pepper to taste
4 medium ears corn, grated
1 can (4 ounces) green chilies

5 tablespoons butter
2 cups buttermilk
2 tablespoons minced fresh chives
Monterey Jack cheese, grated

Arrange half of the potato slices in a single layer on bottom of a 9x13 inch buttered baking dish. Season with salt and pepper. Sprinkle with ½ cup corn and half the chilies; dot with butter. Repeat layering. Pour buttermilk over and bake at 375° for 1 hour. Remove from oven and sprinkle with chives and top with cheese; return to oven until cheese melts. Serves 6 to 8.

Mrs. Steve McMillon (Mary Beth)

Beef sold for 2½ cents per pound in 1836. The price of corn was 75 cents per bushel. Land in Texas sold for 50 cents an acre.

Spicy Pinto Beans

1 pound pinto beans
⅓ pound salt pork
3 pods garlic
1 large onion
1 tablespoon chili powder
3 to 4 jalapeños, seeds
removed

2 tablespoons seasoned salt
1 teaspoon brown sugar
1 bottle (10 ounces)
barbeque sauce
Dash of hot sauce

Wash beans and soak for at least 12 hours. Cut salt pork into ½ inch chunks. Slice garlic and onion. Bring 8 cups of water to a boil and add beans and remaining ingredients. Simmer, covered, for 5 to 6 hours. Spices may be varied to suit individual taste. Do not open pot except to check water. Serves 18.

Prosper A. Mika

Maquechou

8 ears fresh corn
2 tablespoons cooking oil
½ cup finely chopped onion
¼ cup finely chopped green
bell pepper

1 large tomato, peeled and
diced
1½ teaspoons sugar
¾ teaspoon salt
Dash of pepper

Score corn across top of each row of kernels. Cut off cob. Scrape cob to remove corn liquid. You should have about 4 cups. Heat oil in saucepan and add corn and remaining ingredients. Stir to combine. Reduce heat, cover and simmer 15 to 20 minutes, stirring occasionally. Serves 6.

Mrs. Marvin Sentell (Julie)

Calabaza Mexicana

2 tablespoons butter
3 medium zucchini, thinly
sliced
1 medium onion, finely
chopped
2 cloves garlic, minced

1 can (17 ounces) whole
kernel corn, drained
1 can (4 ounces) chopped
green chilies, drained
½ to ¾ cup grated sharp
Cheddar cheese

Melt butter in a large skillet and add zucchini, onion and garlic; sauté about 8 minutes or until squash is crisp tender. Stir in corn and chilies; spoon into a 1½ quart casserole. Top with cheese. Bake uncovered at 350° for 10 minutes or until cheese is melted. Serves 6.

Cyndee McBee

Lola's Mexican Beans

1	tablespoon butter	½	teaspoon salt
1	medium onion, chopped	⅛	teaspoon black pepper
1	green bell pepper, chopped	¼	teaspoon cumin
2	ribs celery, chopped	¼	teaspoon chili pepper
1	can (15 ounces) pinto ranch beans, undrained	1	package (12 count) tamales, shucks removed
2	cups canned whole kernel corn, drained	8	ounces Cheddar cheese, grated

Melt butter and sauté onion, bell pepper and celery until tender. Pour into a 2 quart casserole and add beans, corn and seasonings. Cut tamales into bite sized pieces, add to bean mixture, and stir gently. Bake at 375° for 30 to 40 minutes. Remove from oven, sprinkle cheese on top, and return to oven for 2 minutes to melt cheese. Serves 6 to 8.

Mrs. Andrew Tewell (Judy)

Zucchini Vera Cruz

1	small onion, chopped	½	teaspoon oregano
1	clove garlic, minced	½	teaspoon salt
2	tablespoons oil	¼	teaspoon pepper
1	pound zucchini, thinly sliced	1	can (12 ounces) corn, drained
1	can (16 ounces) tomatoes, drained		

Sauté the onion and garlic in oil until tender. Add zucchini to onion mixture. Break up tomatoes and add to zucchini mixture. Season with oregano, salt and pepper. Cover and simmer for 10 minutes, until zucchini is crisp-tender. Just before serving, add corn and stir until heated. Serves 8 to 10.

Mrs. Seale R. Doss (Vera)

 Chili powder is a seasoning which contains dried ground chilies and various other seasonings, such as comino, oregano, garlic cloves, salt, allspice and cilantro.

Mexican Main Dishes

Quickie Chili Relleños

2   cans (7 ounces each)
    whole green chilies
24 ounces Monterey Jack
    cheese, grated
8   ounces Cheddar cheese,
    grated

4   eggs
2   cups evaporated milk
½   cup flour
¾   teaspoon salt
1   clove garlic, minced
5   green onions, chopped

Lightly butter a 9x13 inch pan. Wash chilies, remove seeds and pat dry. Open chilies and cut into 2 inch squares. Layer bottom of casserole with chilies, then half the cheese. Repeat layers. Mix eggs, milk and seasonings with flour and pour over top. Bake at 325° for 45 minutes to 1 hour. Serves 8. *This is good even if you are not a chili lover.*

Mrs. Larry Morris (Diane)

Mexican Scrambled Eggs

6   flour tortillas
8   eggs
¼   cup water
2   tablespoons chopped
    green chilies
2   tablespoons picante sauce

¼   teaspoon salt
Dash pepper
Nonstick cooking spray
¾   cup picante sauce, divided
½   cup grated Cheddar
    cheese, divided

Wrap tortillas in foil; bake at 350° for 7 minutes. Set aside and keep warm. Combine eggs, water, green chilies, 2 tablespoons picante sauce, salt and pepper in a large bowl; mix well with a wire whisk. Pour egg mixture into a large skillet coated with nonstick cooking spray; cook over medium heat, stirring often, until eggs are firm but still moist. Spoon equal amount of egg mixture onto each tortilla. Top with 1 tablespoon picante sauce and 1 tablespoon cheese; fold opposite sides over. Garnish each tortilla with 1 tablespoon picante sauce and ½ tablespoon cheese. Serves 6.

Barbara Beall Stanley

Tamales

Husks:
½ pound tamale corn husks

To prepare husks, soak in warm water just until pliable. Remove any silks and wash husks thoroughly. Cover with warm water and soak at least 2 hours. Keep damp until used.

Filling:
1	small pork roast	1	teaspoon garlic powder
1	tablespoon salt	¾	teaspoon cumin

Cut pork roast into very small pieces. Place pork into a large pot with 2 cups water and add remaining filling ingredients. Cook for 1½ hours on medium heat; reduce to low and cook another 1½ hours. When meat is tender, drain juices into another pan and save them for the dough.

Dough:
2½ cups masa flour	½ teaspoon cumin
¾ cups lard	½ teaspoon garlic powder
Reserved meat juices	⅛ teaspoon red chili powder
¼ cup baking powder	

Place masa flour into a large bowl. Soften lard and work it, along with ¾ cup meat juice, into the masa. Add baking powder and spices. Combine until mixture is soft enough to spread. If dough is too stiff, add more of the meat juices.

Lay each husk flat on the working surface with the tip away from you and the smooth side up. Using 2½ tablespoons of dough for each husk, spread dough completely to the right edge and within 1 inch of the left side, 2 inches of the bottom, and 2 inches of the top. The rectangle should be about 4 or 5 inches in size. Spoon 2 tablespoons of meat mixture onto the dough in a line lengthwise. To enclose, turn the right side over to the center of the filling, then fold the left side over filling with the plain part of the husk wrapping around the tamale. Fold the bottom tip down and around tamale. Lay flat side down to hold husks.

Invert an aluminum pie plate in the bottom of a large pot and place some husks on top of the pie plate. Arrange tamales in the pot by placing them one by one, starting in the middle and working out, building a pyramid. Fill the pot about half full. Pour enough water seasoned with a little salt and chili powder into the pot to not quite touch the bottom of the tamales. Steam, covered about 3 hours on very low heat. Yields 4 dozen.

Mrs. Bob Vasquez (Carmen)

Migas con Chili

3 eggs
⅛ cup milk
⅛ teaspoon salt
⅛ teaspoon pepper
1½ cups coarsely crumbled
    tostado chips
1 tablespoon margarine

1 tomato, chopped
½ small onion, chopped
½ green bell pepper,
    chopped, optional
Your favorite chili, heated
2 cups grated Monterey
    Jack cheese

Mix eggs, milk, salt and pepper until smooth. Set aside; crumble tostados into a frying pan with melted margarine. Fry until beginning to brown. Add egg mixture and chopped vegetables. Scramble eggs until firm. Place on a plate and ladle on hot chili to cover; sprinkle generously with grated cheese and serve immediately while hot. Serves 2.

Dr. Gerald A. Beathard

Caldillo

2 pounds round steak, cubed
3 tablespoons oil
4 Anaheim peppers, sliced
    in thin strips
1 medium onion, coarsely
    chopped
½ teaspoon cumin
½ teaspoon chili powder

1 can (10 ounces) tomatoes
    and green chilies
1 can (4 ounces) diced green
    chilies
Dried red pepper to taste
½ cup tomato sauce
Salt and pepper to taste
Water
2 medium potatoes, diced

Brown meat in oil but do not drain. Add remaining ingredients except potatoes. Add enough water to cover and simmer for 45 minutes. Add potatoes and additional water, if necessary, to cover. Simmer another 30 to 40 minutes, or until liquid is cooked down to resemble a stew rather than a soup. Serves 6 to 8.

Ken and Susan McGinnis

A favorite Mexican breakfast, Huevos Rancheros, are usually fried eggs served on a corn tortilla topped with a chile sauce.

Chicken Tacos

4 chicken breast halves	½ teaspoon pepper
1 medium onion, chopped	¼ cup picante sauce
1 tablespoon margarine	¼ cup raisins, optional
1 cup fresh chopped	10 crisp taco shells
tomatoes	1 cup shredded lettuce
2 teaspoons cumin	1 cup grated Cheddar
½ teaspoon garlic salt	cheese
½ teaspoon salt	

Boil chicken in salted water. Drain, reserving ¼ cup broth; bone and cube chicken. In a large skillet sauté onion in margarine until soft. Add chicken, tomatoes, cumin, garlic salt, salt and pepper. Cover and simmer 5 minutes. Add broth, picante sauce and raisins if desired; simmer, uncovered 15 minutes. Spoon into heated taco shells and top with lettuce and cheese. Yields 10 tacos.

Mrs. Jerry Dow (Annette)

Layered Enchiladas

Filling:

2 pounds ground sirloin	¼ cup picante sauce
1 onion, chopped	1 teaspoon Worcestershire
½ green bell pepper,	sauce
chopped	1 tablespoon chili powder
¼ teaspoon coriander	½ cup chopped ripe olives
½ teaspoon chopped garlic	12 to 15 tortillas, quartered
1 can (10 ounces) chili	2 cups grated Cheddar
without beans	cheese
⅛ teaspoon hot pepper sauce	

Sauté ground sirloin, onion and bell pepper. Drain, then add remaining ingredients except tortillas and cheese.

Sauce:

½ cup butter, melted	1½ cups milk
2 tablespoons flour	2 cups sour cream

In a small saucepan combine butter and flour and mix well. Slowly add milk and cook until thickened and smooth. Cool, then add sour cream.

Spread a little of the sauce in the bottom of a 9x13 inch baking dish. Place one-half of the tortilla quarters over sauce and follow with one-half of meat mixture, one-half of white sauce, and one-half of cheese. Repeat layers, and bake at 375° for 20 minutes. Serves 6 to 8.

Mrs. John Biggar (Phyllis)

Green Chili Enchiladas

1 pound ground beef
1 onion, finely chopped
8 ounces American cheese, grated
8 ounces sharp Cheddar cheese, grated
1 can (4 ounces) chopped green chilies
1 jar (4 ounces) chopped pimiento
1 can (10 ounces) tomatoes with green chilies
1 teaspoon ground cumin
½ cup shortening
12 corn tortillas
1 can (10¾ ounces) cream of chicken soup
1 can (6 ounces) evaporated milk

Brown beef and onions; drain. Add both cheeses, green chilies, pimiento, tomatoes with chilies and cumin. Heat on low until cheeses melt, stirring to mix well. Heat shortening in another skillet and dip tortillas in hot shortening to soften. Place a portion of beef mixture in each tortilla and wrap securely. Arrange in a 9x13 inch baking dish. Combine soup and milk and pour over tortillas. Bake at 350° for 30 minutes. Serves 6. *Be sure to heat the tortillas until they are soft or they will split when you roll them. You can also top the enchiladas with additional grated cheese after baking and return to oven to melt cheese.*

Mrs. Marcus Bone (Beverly)

Sour Cream Chicken Enchiladas

3½ cups sour cream, divided
2 cups cooked chicken
1 can (4 ounces) green chilies, drained
⅓ cup diced onion
1 teaspoon chili powder
½ teaspoon salt
½ teaspoon garlic powder
¼ teaspoon pepper
Salad oil
12 corn tortillas
⅓ pound Cheddar cheese, grated

About 1 hour before serving, in a 13x9 inch pan, spread 1 cup sour cream; set aside. In a 2 quart saucepan, flake chicken; add ½ cup sour cream, green chilies, onion, chili powder, salt, garlic powder and pepper. Cook over low heat, stirring occasionally, just until heated. Preheat oven to 450°. In an 8 inch skillet with ½ inch salad oil, fry each tortilla a few seconds on each side or until soft. Spread ¼ cup chicken mixture along center of each tortilla. Fold sides over filling and place seam side down in sour cream. Spread enchiladas with remaining sour cream, then sprinkle with cheese. Bake 8 minutes or until cheese is melted. Serves 6.

Joyce Dailey

¡Enchiladas Gordas!

1 package (1.25 ounces) enchilada sauce mix	Hot oil
1 tablespoon bacon drippings	12 whole wheat flour tortillas
1 onion	1 cup grated Cheddar cheese
2 cloves garlic	1 carton (12 ounces) sour cream
1½ pounds lean ground beef	2 green onions, sliced
1 can (16 ounces) refried beans	¼ cup sliced ripe olives
Salt and pepper	¼ cup pecans
	Fresh green chilies, optional

Prepare enchilada sauce according to instructions. In bacon drippings, sauté onion and garlic. Add ground beef and cook until browned; drain. Add refried beans. Add, to taste, ¼ to ½ cup prepared enchilada sauce. Mix well. Salt and pepper to taste. Dip tortillas in hot oil to soften. On 1 tortilla at a time, spoon a tablespoon of sauce, followed by ¼ cup beef mixture. Roll up and place in a greased 9x13 inch casserole dish. When all 12 enchiladas are completed, pour remaining sauce over until nearly covered. Baste sauce over all enchiladas. Bake at 375° for 25 minutes. Lower oven to 350°; sprinkle on Cheddar cheese and bake 5 minutes more. Lower oven to 200° and bake 5 minutes. Sprinkle on garnishes of green onion, olives and pecans. Continue at 200° for a final 5 minutes. This slow reduction of temperature keeps the cheese from becoming oily and the sour cream from separating. Serve promptly. Serves 5 to 6. *If you have the "hots" for some really potent Mexican food, try chopping up some fresh green chilies, sprinkling some into each enchilada and some on top before serving. You'll think you've died and gone to heaven!*

Mrs. Dan Steakley (Susan)

Huevos Miguel

3 slices bacon	1 tablespoon picante sauce
2 eggs	⅓ cup grated Cheddar cheese
Dash of salt	
Dash of pepper	

Microwave bacon 2 to 3 minutes on HIGH or until done, but not quite crisp. Coat an individual casserole pan with nonstick vegetable cooking spray. Arrange bacon slices side by side in casserole pan. Carefully break eggs onto the bacon. Sprinkle with salt and pepper. Top eggs with picante sauce. Cover with waxed paper. Place in microwave on ROAST and cook until center of the eggs is set. Sprinkle with cheese and return to microwave until cheese is bubbly. Serves 1.

Mary Tawney

Monterey Chicken

4 chicken breasts, skinned,
  boned and halved
Salt and pepper
½ cup flour
½ cup butter, divided
½ cup chopped onion
1 clove garlic, minced
8 ounces mushrooms,
  chopped

2 tablespoons flour
1 teaspoon salt
½ teaspoon white pepper
½ cup chicken stock
½ cup white wine
1 avocado, mashed
1½ cups grated Monterey
  Jack cheese, divided
¼ cup chopped green chilies,
  optional

Place chicken between 2 sheets of waxed paper and pound until about ¼ to ½ inch thick. Sprinkle with salt, pepper and flour. Quickly sauté in ¼ cup butter until golden. Remove to plate and add remaining ¼ cup butter to pan and sauté onion, garlic and mushrooms slowly until cooked but not browned. Stir in flour, salt, pepper, chicken stock and wine. Cook until thickened, about 5 minutes. Stir in mashed avocados and ½ cup cheese. Arrange chicken breasts in glass baking dish. Top with sauce, remaining cheese and green chilies if desired. Bake at 350° for 10 minutes. Serves 8.

Mrs. Denman Smith (Sandra)

Spanish Style Chicken

5 pounds chicken pieces
Flour
Salt and pepper
4 tablespoons oil
½ cup minced onion
1 can (10¾ ounces) tomato
  soup

1 jar (6 ounces) stuffed
  olives, sliced
Dash of hot pepper sauce
1 can (10 ounces) green
  peas
1 jar (6 ounces) mushroom
  pieces

Salt and pepper chicken pieces and coat with flour. Heat oil in skillet and brown chicken. Remove chicken to warm platter. Remove all but 2 tablespoons of oil from skillet. Sauté onion, then add soup and olives and simmer for 10 minutes. Add chicken, hot pepper sauce, liquid from peas and mushrooms. Simmer until chicken is tender, about 30 minutes. Add peas and mushrooms. Thicken, if desired, with flour and cold water paste. Serve with rice. Serves 8 to 10.

S. D. Jackman

Pinto beans are the most common bean used for frijoles.

Mexican Fried Chicken

3 pounds chicken
2 teaspoons salt
½ cup flour
2 tablespoons chili powder, divided
½ cup shortening

½ cup uncooked rice
½ cup chopped onion
1 clove garlic, minced
1 cup chopped green bell pepper
1 cup chopped tomatoes

Cut chicken into pieces. Salt and roll each piece into mixture of flour and 1 tablespoon chili powder. Brown chicken in hot shortening. Reduce heat and add rice, onion, garlic, bell pepper, tomatoes and 1 tablespoon chili powder. Cover and simmer until well done, about 1 hour. Serves 6 to 8.

S. D. Jackman

Montezuma Pie

5 to 6 green tomatoes
2 green chilies
½ onion, chopped
12 flour tortillas
Oil
6 chicken breasts, cooked and chopped
1 can (8 ounces) green chili sauce

1 can (8 ounces) green chilies
1 cup sour cream
½ cup grated Monterey Jack cheese
½ cup grated Cheddar cheese

Boil green tomatoes and chilies together for 10 minutes. Drain and place in a blender and liquify with chopped onion. Quarter and fry tortillas in hot oil. Layer in a greased 9x13 inch casserole, chicken, tortillas, green chili sauce, green chilies, sour cream, and cheeses. Bake at 350° for 25 minutes. Serves 6.

Mrs. Reece Goodman (Leslie)

Texas is the only state in the United States to have had six flags and rulers.

Pollo de Rado

½ cup butter, softened
1 clove garlic, minced
1 fryer, cut into pieces
3 cups chicken broth, divided

Salt and pepper
Paprika
8 ounces fresh mushrooms
Chopped parsley for garnish

Combine butter and minced garlic and spread on chicken pieces. In a metal pan place chicken pieces skin side up. Add 1 cup chicken broth and broil until brown. Turn over and lightly broil the other side. Remove pan from the broiler and turn chicken skin side up. Add 2 cups of broth and season with salt, pepper and paprika. Lower oven temperature to 350° and bake chicken for 25 minutes. Add mushrooms, making certain mushrooms are covered with broth. Return pan to oven and bake until mushrooms are cooked to your taste. Serve chicken on a platter surrounded by mushrooms. Sprinkle a little chopped parsley on top. Serves 4 to 6.

Mrs. Jim Rado (Vicki)

Tamalitos

2¼ cups masa harina
1½ teaspoons salt, divided
1¼ cups chicken broth
½ cup oil
2 cups cooked chicken, cut in chunks

1 medium onion, chopped
1 can (4 ounces) chopped ripe olives
½ cup green chili salsa

Using a metal blade, process masa harina and ½ teaspoon salt for 2 seconds. With the motor running, pour chicken broth and oil through feed tube and process to make a thick paste; set aside. Still using metal blade, process chicken with on-off bursts until coarsely chopped; set aside. Process onion until coarsely chopped. Add remaining 1 teaspoon salt, olives, salsa and chopped chicken and mix with 2 on-off bursts. Cut 30 pieces of foil, each 6 inches square. Place about 1½ tablespoons masa paste on center of each foil square and spread it into a 3 inch square. Place about 1½ tablespoons chicken filling on each masa square, positioning it down the center. Fold foil edges together so that masa edges meet, then seal all sides. To cook tamalitos arrange in upper part of a steamer. Cover tightly and steam over boiling water for about 45 minutes. Unwrap and serve hot. Makes 30 small tamales. *This recipe will halve easily and is very tasty when covered with chili and grated cheese.*

Mrs. Tom Hollis (Doris)

Beef Empanadas

Filling:

1 pound lean ground beef	½ teaspoon salt
4 tablespoons chopped onion	¼ teaspoon pepper
	2 tablespoons cornstarch
4 tablespoons chopped green bell pepper	1 cup beef bouillon
	1 teaspoon cumin
5 tablespoons crushed plum tomatoes	5 tablespoons raisins
	5 tablespoons pecans

Brown beef in skillet with onion. Drain and add bell pepper, tomatoes, salt, pepper and cornstarch. Add bouillon, cumin, raisins and pecans. Simmer until thickened 3 to 5 minutes.

Dough:

1½ cups milk	1 teaspoon salt
1 cup butter	1 egg, separated
5 cups flour	1 teaspoon water
2 teaspoons baking powder	

Scald milk and add butter. After butter is melted, let cool. Combine flour, baking powder and salt. Mix well and add to cooled milk mixture. Add egg yolk. Knead, then let rest for 20 minutes. Divide dough into quarters and roll each piece into a 10x15 inch rectangle. Cut out squares or circles and spoon filling mixture evenly on 1 side of each pastry. Moisten edges of pastry with water, fold over and seal. Brush with egg white mixed with 1 teaspoon water. Bake at 400° for 15 to 20 minutes. Yields 7 dozen.

Mrs. Thomas Schwartz (Ellana)

Calabacita Con Carne

6 slices bacon	1 can (10 ounces) tomatoes with green chilies
1 pound ground beef	
1½ teaspoons salt	1 pound zucchini, sliced
1 large onion, chopped	

Fry bacon until crisp; remove and set aside. Salt beef and sauté with the onion in bacon drippings. Pour off drippings. Add tomatoes and zucchini. Cover and cook until squash is tender, about 5 to 10 minutes. Crumble bacon on top before serving. Serves 4. *This is very good served with tortillas and guacamole.*

Mrs. Larry Hanners (Sally)

Chili Powder

½ cup light chili powder
½ cup dark chili powder
½ cup ground cumin
2 tablespoons paprika

1 to 2 tablespoons cayenne
  pepper
¼ cup salt
1 to 2 tablespoons oregano

Mix all ingredients together and store in an airtight jar. If light and dark chili powders are not available, use 1 cup of what is available. Yields 2 cups. *This is a very good chili mix to use as a seasoning for taco meat, meat loaf or your favorite chili. Use 2 to 4 tablespoons for each pound of meat.*

Mrs. Denman Smith (Sandra)

Hot Red Chili

20 dried chili peppers
4 pounds chili meat
1 teaspoon oil
1 medium onion, chopped
4 to 5 cloves garlic, minced
1 teaspoon oregano

1 teaspoon comino
Salt and pepper to taste
1 can (10 ounces) tomato
  sauce
¾ cup water
2 to 3 tablespoons masa flour

Remove stems and seed from chili pods. Wash and put into a large pan and cover with water. Simmer until tender. Drain. Place peppers in food processor and purée. Put aside. Brown meat in small amount of oil. Add onion and garlic. Simmer for 10 minutes. Then add the oregano, comino, salt and pepper. Add peppers to the chili meat. Add tomato sauce and water, then bring to a boil. Reduce heat and simmer for 3 to 4 hours. More water may be added during cooking. When almost done, thicken with flour/water paste. Serves 8 to 10. *This recipe has a distinct Southwestern flavor.*

Mrs. A. S. Kallman (Janice)

Fajitas

½ cup oil
3 tablespoons lemon juice
1 tablespoon wine vinegar
½ teaspoon garlic salt
½ teaspoon whole thyme
½ teaspoon chili powder

1 teaspoon whole oregano
2 tablespoons minced dried
  onion
½ cup water
2 pounds skirt steak
Flour tortillas

Combine all ingredients in a bowl. Pour or spoon over 2 pounds of skirt steak in a shallow container. Place in refrigerator, covered, for about 6 to 8 hours, turning every few hours. Grill over hot coals about 10 minutes. Serve with flour tortillas and condiments. Serves 4 to 5.

Mrs. Jette Campbell (Sally)

East Texas Red Chili

2 tablespoons oil
2 pounds chili meat
2 large onions, finely chopped
1 teaspoon garlic powder
1 tablespoon leaf oregano
4 tablespoons paprika
½ teaspoon cumin
1 teaspoon salt

1 can (28 ounces) tomato sauce
1 can (28 ounces) whole tomatoes
3 cups water, divided
6 dried ancho chili peppers, stemmed and seeded
1 bar (4.5 ounces) milk chocolate candy

Place oil in a 5 to 6 quart pan with meat and onions. Sauté, stirring frequently. Add garlic powder, oregano, paprika, cumin, salt and tomato sauce. Chop the whole tomatoes into large pieces, then add to mixture. Heat 2 cups water to boiling and add ancho peppers. Stir occasionally, until peppers are soft. Drain and pureé in blender. Add peppers to the meat mixture. Rinse blender with the remaining cup of water and add to the meat mixture. Add the chocolate candy bar and allow to simmer for approximately 1 hour. Serves 8 to 10. *Ancho chilies are the large, black, dried peppers about 2 inches long and 1 inch wide. The number used may vary from 2 to 4 per pound of meat, depending on how spicy you like it. It is a good idea to add half the chilies, then taste and add more. If the dried chilies are not available, chili powder can be substituted: 1 tablespoon equals 1 chili pepper.*

Dr. Gerald A. Beathard

Jim's Texas Chili

3 pounds chili meat
2 cans (8 ounces each) tomato sauce
1 can (14½ ounces) whole tomatoes
1 tablespoon paprika
1 tablespoon salt

20 dashes hot pepper sauce
1 tablespoon cumin
1 tablespoon oregano
1 onion, diced
1½ tablespoons minced garlic
½ cup masa flour

In a large heavy pan sear the chili meat to a grayish color. Add tomato sauce and whole tomatoes to cover meat. Let mixture simmer. Add water if needed. Add all remaining ingredients except masa flour, mixing thoroughly. Simmer for 1½ hours, stirring every 15 minutes. Skim off any grease. Mix the flour with a little warm water and pour into chili while stirring vigorously. Cook another 15 minutes and taste. You are now ready for some good eating. Serves 6. *By the way, if you are a tenderfoot, I would suggest half the hot pepper sauce to start. You can always add more during the final 15 minutes.*

Jim Kimbell

Tacos de Fajitas al Carbon

4 ounces lime juice
2 ounces Mexican beer
1 ounce Worcestershire
   sauce
4 ounces olive oil
10 peppercorns
2 whole cloves
1 bay leaf
1 teaspoon marjoram
1 tablespoon celery powder
2 tablespoons paprika
2 tablespoons cumin
2 tablespoons brown sugar
1 large onion, peeled and
   sliced into thin rings

1 large garlic clove, minced
2 dry chili peppers,
   crumbled
1 cup chopped cilantro
2½ pounds skirt steak
Salt and pepper
1 tablespoon cumin
1 tablespoon paprika
1 teaspoon salt
1 teaspoon brown sugar
1 tablespoon pepper
Butter
Lime juice
Flour tortillas
Mexican condiments

To make marinade, combine lime juice, beer and Worcestershire
sauce in a glass bowl. With a whisk beat in oil a few drops at a time.
Add peppercorns, cloves, bay leaf, marjoram, celery powder,
paprika, cumin, brown sugar, onion, garlic, chili peppers and cilantro.
Stir vigorously. Trim fat from meat and sprinkle uniformly with salt
and pepper. Poke vigorously all over with a fork, piercing meat
completely. Turn over and repeat on the other side. Put meat into
marinade. Cover and refrigerate for 48 hours, stirring occasionally.
Combine cumin, paprika, salt, brown sugar, and pepper and set
aside. Prepare very hot fire on charcoal grill, adding chunks of moist
mesquite wood. You should not be able to hold your hand five inches
from grill. Remove meat from marinade and cook for 1½ minutes.
Turn over and brush with marinade; cook for 1½ minutes. Turn and
brush again. Cook for 4 minutes and sprinkle with cumin mixture.
Turn and sprinkle with seasoning. Top with several thin pats of butter
and a few drops of lime juice. Cook for 4 minutes more. Remove from
grill and let sit 5 minutes. Slice crosswise on bias. Serve on flour
tortillas topped with your choice of picante salsa, guacamole, grated
cheese, sour cream or sautéed onions. Serves 8.

Thomas Schwartz

*Fajitas make use of one of the least tender cuts of beef, the skirt
steak, which has long been a popular item in Mexican markets.
Because of the popularity of fajitas, the skirt steak, either tenderized or not, is now a staple in most Texas supermarkets.*

Fajitas Borrachos Olé

3   cans (12 ounces each) beer
1   jar (15.5 ounces) jalapeño
    slices, undrained
1   bottle (16 ounces) Italian
    salad dressing

10 pounds tenderized skirt
    steak
Flour tortillas

Mix first 3 ingredients together and pour over steak. Marinate for 24 to 48 hours. Cook over hot coals, turning often. Slice thinly across the grain and serve with flour tortillas. Top with your favorite condiments, such as guacamole, grated cheese, sautéed onions, sour cream, picante, pico de gallo, etc. Serves 20 to 24.

Rusty Batey

Pork with Frijoles

1   pound dried pinto beans
1   pork loin roast (3 pounds),
    trimmed
1   can (4 ounces) diced green
    chilies
1   jar (2 ounces) diced
    pimientos
½   cup chopped onion

2   cloves garlic, minced
7   cups water
1   tablespoon salt
2   tablespoons chili powder
1   tablespoon cumin
1   teaspoon oregano
Tortilla chips
Flour tortillas

In a large pot, soak beans overnight; drain. Add remaining ingredients and simmer 2 to 3 hours or until roast is very tender and "strings" easily. Remove roast from pot and shred meat. Return shredded meat to pot and simmer 30 to 45 minutes longer to thicken mixture and make beans tender. Serve over tortilla chips or in flour tortillas with condiments. Serves 8. *This is also very good on eggs for a Mexican breakfast.*

Mrs. N.W. Lipscomb (Charlotte)

There are twelve counties in Texas that are named after men who died at the Alamo: Bowie, Cochran, Cottle, Crockett, Dickens, Floyd, Kent, Kimble, King, Lynn, Taylor and Travis.

Chimichangas

2 pounds pork loin roast, cut into 1 inch pieces
Salt and pepper
4 tablespoons picante sauce
2 cloves garlic, minced
3 tablespoons red wine vinegar

½ teaspoon cumin
½ teaspoon oregano
Salt and pepper
Butter
10 flour tortillas
Sour cream
Guacamole

Cover pork with water and cook over medium heat for 2 hours. Season with salt and pepper. Drain and cool; shred meat with a fork. Add picante sauce, garlic, vinegar, cumin, oregano, salt and pepper. Cover and refrigerate overnight. Preheat oven to 450°. Generously butter 1 side of a tortilla. Place butter side down in a large skillet over medium heat and fry until soft, about 30 seconds. Remove from skillet. Spoon ½ cup pork mixture into center of uncooked side. Fold edges toward center and tuck ends under. Arrange seam side down in a baking dish. Repeat with remaining tortillas. Bake until golden brown, about 30 minutes. To serve, top each with a dollop of sour cream and guacamole. Serves 4 to 6.

Mrs. Marvin Sentell (Julie)

Ropa Vieja

2 pounds pork or beef stew meat
1⅓ cups water
⅛ teaspoon garlic salt
1 teaspoon salt
4 large tomatoes, peeled and chopped
1 medium onion, chopped
1 clove garlic, minced
3 tablespoons vinegar
¾ to 1 cup catsup

½ to 1 cup sliced jalapeño chilies
1 bay leaf
1 green bell pepper, sliced thin
½ cup beef broth
1 tablespoon jalapeño juice
½ teaspoon garlic salt
1 teaspoon salt
3 ancho chilies, dried

Cook the meat in a pressure cooker with 1⅓ cups water, ⅛ teaspoon garlic salt and 1 teaspoon salt for 35 minutes. Shred very finely. Make a sauce of the tomatoes, onion, garlic, vinegar, catsup, jalapeños, bay leaf and bell pepper. In a skillet cook until some of the juice has cooked down. Add the cooked meat and the remaining ingredients. Continue to cook until the flavor is well blended. If served as a hot hors d' oeuvre, Ropa Vieja should be dry enough so that it does not drip when eaten with tortilla chips. If used as a main dish over rice, retain more of the juice. Serves 15 as an hors d' oeuvre, 8 as a main course.

Mrs. Reece Goodman (Leslie)

Cabrito

1 goat shoulder and leg	Bar-b-que sauce
White vinegar	½ cup white vinegar
Salt and pepper	½ cup margarine, melted

Wash meat well. Rinse meat completely with vinegar. Salt and pepper. Smoke slowly for 5 to 6 hours over mesquite wood. Meat should not be over fire but smoked to one side of a covered bar-b-que pit. You will need to add wood throughout cooking time. After 3 hours, start basting with 1 cup of your favorite bar-b-que sauce, to which you have added ½ cup vinegar and ½ cup margarine. This meat should be cooked very slowly and completely. If you run out of time, or feel it may not be quite done, baste generously with sauce and place in a foil covered pan, and bake at 400° for 30 minutes. Serves 6.

Don Bradford

Mexican Breads

Mexican Cornbread

1 cup cornmeal	1 can (4 ounces) diced green
1 cup flour	chilies, drained
½ cup dry milk	1 cup water
2 tablespoons sugar	⅓ cup oil
4 teaspoons baking powder	2 eggs
½ teaspoon salt	1 tablespoon butter or
4 ounces grated Cheddar	bacon drippings
cheese	

Combine cornmeal, flour, dry milk, sugar, baking powder and salt in a bowl. Stir in cheese and chilies. Beat together water, oil and eggs. Stir into dry ingredients until just blended. Melt butter or bacon drippings in an 8 inch pan. Pour batter into pan and bake at 375° for 30 to 35 minutes. Yields 16 (2 inch) squares. *This cornbread freezes well.*

S. D. Jackman

Davy Crockett was the legendary hero who brought the Tennessee boys to help defend the Alamo.

Creamed Cornbread

1 can (17 ounces) cream
  style corn
1 cup cornmeal
1 cup butter, melted
¾ cup buttermilk
1 onion, finely chopped

2 eggs, beaten
½ teaspoon baking soda
2 cups grated sharp Cheddar
  cheese
2 jalapeño peppers, diced

In a large bowl combine creamed corn, cornmeal, melted butter, buttermilk, onion, eggs and baking soda. Mix well. Place half of batter into a 9 inch greased baking dish. Cover evenly with 1 cup of cheese, then all of the diced peppers. Cover with remaining batter and cheese. Bake at 350° for 1 hour. Let cool 15 minutes, then cut into squares. Serves 9.

Mrs. Marcus Bone (Beverly)

Homemade Flour Tortillas

4 cups flour
2 teaspoons salt
⅛ teaspoon baking powder

⅔ cup shortening
1 cup plus 3 tablespoons hot
  water

Combine flour, salt and baking powder, stirring well. Cut in shortening with a pastry blender until mixture resembles coarse meal. Gradually stir in water, mixing well. Shape dough into 1½ inch balls; roll each on a floured surface into a 6 inch circle. Cook tortillas in an ungreased skillet over medium heat about 2 minutes on each side or until lightly browned. Pat tortillas lightly with spatula while browning the second side if they puff during cooking. Serve hot. Yields 24.

Mrs. J. Edward Reed (Marian)

Robin's Whole Wheat Tortillas

2 cups whole wheat flour
1 teaspoon salt
1½ teaspoons baking powder

1 tablespoon shortening
⅔ cup cold water

Sift dry ingredients into a medium mixing bowl. Cut in shortening and add enough cold water to make a stiff dough. Knead on a lightly floured board. Make small balls; pat thin. Bake on a soapstone or lightly greased griddle. Yields 12. *It helps to have a tortilla press for gringos who have trouble patting them thinly enough! A standard tortilla is 6 inches in diameter.*

Mrs. Randy Hagan (Robin Roberts)

Mexican Desserts

Creamy Pralines

2½ cups sugar
1 cup buttermilk
1 teaspoon baking soda
¼ teaspoon salt

¼ cup butter
1 teaspoon vanilla extract
3 cups pecan halves

In a large, heavy saucepan combine sugar, buttermilk, soda and salt, stirring frequently, until sugar is dissolved. Continue, cooking over low heat to soft ball stage or 234°. Remove from heat and add butter and vanilla. Cool about 5 minutes. Beat until smooth and slightly thickened. Stir in pecans. Immediately drop from a tablespoon onto waxed paper. Yields 18 large pralines. *Do not attempt to make these pralines when it is humid.*

Mrs. Jim Stasswender (Linda)

Flan

1 cup sugar, divided
5 eggs
1 teaspoon vanilla extract

3¼ cups milk
¼ cup rum

Cook ½ cup sugar slowly in heavy skillet until melted, using a wooden spoon to stir. Beat eggs, sugar and vanilla. Add milk and rum. Pour into a buttered 5 cup ring mold on top of melted sugar. Place in a shallow pan filled with 1 inch of water. Bake at 325° for 1 to 1½ hours. Chill at least 1 hour before unmolding. Serves 4 to 6. *For a coffee flavored flan use 4 to 6 teaspoons instant coffee dissolved in ⅛ cup hot water.*

Mrs. Jim Rado (Vicki)

Mangos Flambé

1½ tablespoons butter
1½ tablespoons brown sugar
¼ cup orange marmalade
1 can (15 ounces) mangos, drained

2 ounces orange liqueur
4 to 6 vanilla or coconut ice cream balls

Melt butter in chafing dish. Add brown sugar and stir until dissolved. Stir in marmalade and mangos and heat about one minute. Add liqueur and stir just to warm. Ignite. Pour flaming over ice cream balls. Serves 4.

Mrs. Dave Buse (Marcy)

Sopaipillas

4 cups flour
1 tablespoon baking powder
1 teaspoon salt

3 tablespoons shortening
1¼ to 1½ cups cold water
Oil

Combine dry ingredients. Cut in shortening, and add water gradually to make a soft dough. Roll out as for pie crust and cut into 3 inch squares. Heat oil in a deep fryer, and fry sopaipillas until golden brown. Drain on paper towels and serve immediately with butter and honey. Yields 4 to 5 dozen.

Brandi and Cynthia Bradford

Flan Almendra

¾ cup sugar
1 cup almonds
2 cans (14 ounces each) sweetened condensed milk

1 cup milk
4 eggs
4 egg yolks
1 teaspoon vanilla extract

Melt sugar in a small saucepan until it forms a syrup. Pour this into a 10 inch pie pan. Allow to cool to form a hard layer. Chop almonds into coarse pieces. Toast under broiler until lightly browned. Mix remaining ingredients until completely blended. Add almonds to pie pan on top of sugar mixture. Let custard rest 10 minutes then pour on top of almonds; cover with foil and place pie pan in a larger pan containing ¼ to ½ inch of water. Bake at 350° for 1 hour. Chill for 20 to 30 minutes before serving. Loosen edge with knife and place a plate upside down on top of pie pan and invert quickly to remove flan from pan. Serves 8 to 10.

Dr. Gerald A. Beathard

Buñuelos

4 eggs
½ cup milk
¼ cup butter, melted
3 cups flour
1 tablespoon sugar

1 teaspoon salt
Oil
Sugar
Cinnamon

Beat eggs; add milk and melted butter. Stir in flour, sugar and salt to make a dough that is easily handled without sticking. Make into walnut sized balls. Roll each ball out on a floured surface until it is the shape of a tortilla. Fry in hot oil until golden brown. Combine sugar and cinnamon and sprinkle on each buñuelo. Serve warm. Yields approximately 5 to 6 dozen.

Traci Lerche

Cinnamon Flan

3 cups water
3 tablespoons sugar
1 can (14 ounces) sweetened
  condensed milk

14 ounces water
1½ teaspoons rum
4 eggs, slightly beaten
Ground cinnamon

Boil 3 cups water and pour into a 1½ quart glass bowl, to warm the bowl. Melt sugar in a small skillet over medium heat until caramelized, stirring occasionally. Mix milk, water and rum with eggs. Pour water out of the glass bowl into an iron skillet. Pour caramelized sugar into the glass bowl. Pour milk mixture over the top and sprinkle with cinnamon. Place bowl in the iron skillet; water should be about half as high as the mixture inside the bowl. Bake at 350° for 50 to 60 minutes. Run a knife blade around the sides to loosen flan. Invert a plate over the bowl; turn over quickly, and flan is ready to serve with its own sauce. Serves 8.

S. D. Jackman

Candied Mexican Orange Shells

4 large oranges
6 cups sugar
6 cups water

6 tablespoons glycerine
Granulated sugar

Wash oranges and cut a ½ inch thick lid off the top of each. With a curved grapefruit knife, cut fruit pulp away from rind, scraping any remaining membrane from rind with a heavy spoon. Scrape fruit pulp off lids. Reserve fruit pulp for other uses. Place shells and lids with cold water in a saucepan and cover. Bring to a boil and cook for 20 minutes. Drain well and set shells aside to cool. In a 4 quart pan, combine sugar and water. Add glycerine; heat until sugar dissolves. Add shells and lids; bring to a boil over high heat and boil, uncovered until syrup is medium thick, 220°. Remove from heat. Let shells and lids stand in syrup 24 hours, turning them several times. Bring syrup to a boil again and boil over high heat until syrup is thick, 232°, turning shells over several times to prevent scorching. Remove shells and lids from syrup carefully; turn each upside down over an inverted paper cup to drain and cool. When cool enough to handle, roll in granulated sugar, coating completely. Cool thoroughly; fill with sweet potatoes, ice cream or marmalade. Serves 4.

Mrs. Dudley Baker (Kathy)

Boscochitos

¾ cup sugar	1½ teaspoons baking powder
1 cup shortening	½ teaspoon salt
1 egg	¼ cup red wine or brandy
1 teaspoon anise seeds	¼ cup sugar
3 cups flour	½ teaspoon cinnamon

Cream sugar and shortening together. Add egg and anise seeds and cream again. Sift flour, baking powder and salt together and add to creamed mixture. Add wine or brandy and mix well. Roll out thinly on a floured board and cut into desired shapes. Mix sugar and cinnamon together and sprinkle on cookies. Bake at 350° for 10 to 15 minutes or until light brown. Yields 6 dozen cookies.

Mrs. Ron Bruney (Carol)

Pan Dulce

Bread:

1 package yeast	½ teaspoon salt
¾ cup warm water	½ teaspoon butter
3½ cups flour	2 eggs, slightly beaten
¾ cup sugar	

Dissolve yeast in the water. Sift flour, sugar and salt together in a bowl. Add the yeast mixture, butter and eggs; beat until smooth. Place dough in a greased bowl, cover and let rise in a warm place until doubled in bulk, about 1½ hours. Punch down and turn out onto a lightly floured board, and knead until smooth and elastic. Pinch off pieces of dough and shape into smooth rounded balls about 1¼ inches in diameter. Place balls of dough on a greased baking sheet, about 2 inches apart. With the palm of your hand, press each ball down, flattening it slightly.

Cinnamon-Flavored Topping:

1 cup sugar	1 egg, slightly beaten
1 cup flour	1 teaspoon cinnamon
½ cup butter, melted	Dash salt

Blend all ingredients together and mix well. Gently spread about 1 tablespoon topping on each bun, then let buns rise until double in bulk, about 30 minutes. Bake at 400° for 10 minutes, or until lightly browned. Serve warm. Yields 18.

Mrs. Dudley Baker (Kathy)

Pumpkin Empanadas

1 can (16 ounces) pumpkin	1 teaspoon salt
¾ cup sugar	1⅓ cups shortening
1 teaspoon ground allspice	1 cup milk
4 cups flour	Milk
½ cup sugar	1 egg white, beaten
1 tablespoon plus 1	¼ cup sugar
teaspoon baking powder	½ teaspoon cinnamon

Combine pumpkin, ¾ cup sugar and allspice; mix well and set aside. Combine flour, ½ cup sugar, baking powder and salt; cut in shortening with pastry blender until mixture resembles coarse meal. Sprinkle with 1 cup milk evenly over surface; stir with fork until all dry ingredients are moistened. Roll out to ⅛ inch thick and cut into 4 inch circles. Place 1 tablespoon pumpkin mixture in center of each circle. Moisten edges with additional milk. Fold in half and press edges together with a fork. Brush empanadas with egg white. Place on ungreased baking sheets. Bake at 450° for 8 to 10 minutes. Combine ¼ cup sugar and cinnamon and sprinkle over empanadas while still warm. Yields 18 empanadas.

Mrs. Marcus Bone (Beverly)

Churros

¾ cup water	1¼ cups flour
3 tablespoons butter, cut	3 eggs
into pieces	Oil
½ teaspoon salt	Powdered sugar
Pinch of grated nutmeg	Cinnamon, optional

Bring water to a boil in a saucepan; add butter, salt and nutmeg. When butter has melted, remove pan from heat and beat in flour until mixture pulls away from side of pan. Add eggs one at a time, beating well after each addition. Beat until thick and glossy. Set aside to cool. Spoon dough into a piping bag. Fill a large saucepan one-third full with oil and heat to 350°. Squeeze 8 inches of dough into hot oil. Deep fry for about 8 minutes. Using a slotted spoon, carefully remove churros from oil and drain. Sprinkle with powdered sugar and cinnamon, if desired. Serves 4. *These are traditionally served with cups of rich, steaming hot chocolate with a dash of cinnamon.*

Mrs. Marvin Sentell (Julie)

 Empanadas are small fried or baked turnovers. They may have a meat filling or a sweet dried fruit filling.

The Texas Gulf Coast is popular year round — it seems no one can resist the allure of the sea! Its wave-swept beaches stretch for hundreds of miles, providing a warm, sunny playground for dozens of water activities. But the Coast is much more than a winter haven from the Arctic cold; it supports a thriving fishing industry. Ports dot the coastline like precious gems on a necklace, with oysters, shrimp, crabs and a wide variety of other exotic fish brought in daily. This important resource is a true Texas treasure!

Main Dishes pictured: Shrimp Kabobs, Stuffed Texas Redfish, Shrimp Creole, Stuffed Avocado, Gulf Trout Almandine, Ceviche and Deviled Seafood.

Main Dishes

Crab Quiche

½ cup mayonnaise
2 tablespoons flour
2 eggs, beaten
½ cup milk
1 package (6 ounces) frozen crab meat

2 cups shredded Swiss cheese
⅓ cup chopped green onion
¼ teaspoon hot pepper sauce
1 baked 9 inch pastry shell

Combine mayonnaise, flour, eggs and milk. Add thawed and drained crab meat, cheese, green onion and hot pepper sauce. Pour into pie shell. Bake at 350° for 30 minutes, or until toothpick inserted in middle comes out clean. Serves 4 to 6. *This recipe is easily doubled and is wonderful for luncheons. I have also baked pastry shells the day before, mixed up the filling ingredients early in the morning and refrigerated them. About 45 minutes before serving, pour filling into pastry shell and bake.*

Mrs. Jim Schultz (Mary Kay)

Italian Broccoli Quiche

½ cup chopped onion
1 tablespoon oil
1 cup milk
½ teaspoon salt
¼ teaspoon Italian seasoning
4 eggs

1 package (10 ounces) frozen chopped broccoli, thawed and drained
½ cup grated Parmesan cheese, divided
4 slices bacon, cooked and crumbled

Sauté chopped onion in oil. Add milk, salt and Italian seasoning. Heat thoroughly. Beat eggs and gradually stir about ¼ of milk mixture into eggs; add to remaining milk mixture, stirring constantly. Add broccoli and ⅓ cup cheese; pour into a lightly greased 9 inch quiche dish. Sprinkle with bacon and remaining cheese. Bake at 350° for 25 minutes. Serves 6.

Barbara Beall Stanley

 There are four National Forests in Texas and thirty-five million acres of trees covering a land area the size of Maine, Vermont, New Hampshire and Massachusetts.

Mushroom Bacon Pie

1 pound fresh mushrooms, sliced	4 eggs, beaten
6 slices bacon, diced	1 cup grated Parmesan cheese
2 cloves garlic, minced	½ teaspoon salt
2 tablespoons chopped fresh parsley	⅛ teaspoon pepper
3 tablespoons olive oil	1 unbaked 9 inch pastry shell

Sauté mushrooms, bacon, garlic and parsley in olive oil until mushrooms are tender; drain. Cool 10 to 15 minutes. Combine eggs, cheese and seasonings. Mix well and add to mushroom mixture. Pour into pastry shell and bake at 350° for 30 minutes. Serves 6 to 8.

Mrs. Ed Fomby (Beaty)

Quiche Provencale

1 tablespoon oil	½ teaspoon crushed basil leaves
1 medium onion, sliced	
½ cup chopped green bell pepper	¼ teaspoon pepper
2 tomatoes, cut into wedges	6 eggs
1 cup sliced zucchini	1¼ cups half and half cream
1 tablespoon minced parsley	1 baked 9 inch deep dish pastry shell
1 teaspoon garlic salt	

Preheat oven to 375°. In a large skillet over medium heat, sauté the onion and bell pepper in oil until tender but not brown, about 5 minutes. Stir in tomatoes, zucchini and seasonings. Cook uncovered an additional 10 minutes, stirring frequently. Drain well and set aside. Beat together eggs and cream until well blended. Pour into baked pie shell. Spoon in reserved drained vegetable mixture. Bake at 375° for 30 to 35 minutes. Cook until knife inserted near center comes out clean. Let stand 5 minutes before serving. Serves 6.

Mrs. Ron Bruney (Carol)

Shirred Eggs

6 tablespoons half and half cream	6 teaspoons butter
12 eggs	6 ounces Swiss cheese, grated
Salt and pepper to taste	

Put 1 tablespoon cream in each of 6 custard cups. Break 2 eggs into each cup. Sprinkle with salt and pepper and dot each with 1 teaspoon butter. Top with grated cheese. Bake at 350° for 15 minutes. Serves 6.

Mrs. Terry Arndt (Barbara)

Swiss Zucchini Quiche

Quiche:

1½ cups sliced zucchini
¼ pound mushrooms, sliced
1 small onion, chopped
3 eggs, beaten
½ cup evaporated milk

¼ cup water
½ teaspoon salt
¼ teaspoon pepper
¾ cup shredded Swiss
    cheese, divided

Cook zucchini in a small amount of unsalted boiling water for 3 minutes. Drain and press gently to remove excess water. Spray a small skillet with cooking spray. Sauté mushrooms and onion in skillet over low heat until vegetables are tender but not brown; set aside. Combine eggs, milk, water, salt and pepper. Mix well. Add zucchini, mushroom mixture and ½ cup cheese. Stir well. Pour zucchini mixture into Rice-Cheese Shell; top with remaining ¼ cup cheese. Bake at 375° for 40 minutes.

Rice-Cheese Pastry Shell:

½ cup cooked rice
1 egg, beaten

¼ cup grated Swiss cheese

Spray a 10 inch pie plate with nonstick cooking spray. Combine rice, egg and Swiss cheese, stirring well. Press mixture into bottom and sides of a pie plate. Bake at 350° for 5 minutes. Serves 6 to 8.

Mrs. Kempe Hayes (Stephanie)

Scotch Eggs

1 pound bulk sausage
Fresh herbs or piquant sauce
4 hard cooked eggs
Flour, seasoned with salt and
    pepper

1 egg, beaten
Bread crumbs
Oil

Flavor sausage meat by adding a little chopped fresh herbs or piquant sauce. Divide meat into 4 equal portions. Shell the eggs and dip in seasoned flour. Coat each egg with sausage meat. Coat each sausage-covered egg with beaten egg and roll carefully in bread crumbs. Fry in smoking hot oil, until evenly browned and crisp; sufficient time must be allowed for sausage meat to cook through. Cut each egg in half. Serve hot with catsup or cold with a green salad. Serves 4. *This recipe has been handed down for many generations. It was given to me in 1967 as a "going to America" gift from my Aunt Annie. This recipe comes from South Wales, Great Britain.*

Mrs. Lawrence Christian (Joyce)

When buying mushrooms, look for tightly closed caps. It is better not to wash mushrooms before using as they absorb too much of the water; wipe them with a damp paper towel.

Tomato Quiche

1 baked 9 inch pastry shell
Salt and pepper
2 tomatoes, sliced
2 tablespoons flour
2 tablespoons oil
½ cup sliced olives
1 cup minced onion

3 slices Provolone cheese
6 ounces fresh mushrooms, sliced
2 eggs, beaten
1 cup half and half cream
1 cup grated Cheddar cheese

Salt and pepper the tomatoes and dust with flour. Sauté in oil. Arrange olives and onion in bottom of pie shell. Add the Provolone cheese, tomatoes and mushrooms. Beat eggs and cream together and add the Cheddar cheese. Spoon over layers. Bake at 350° for 40 minutes. Cool slightly before serving. Serves 6. *This freezes beautifully; just reheat before serving.*

Pam McKiernan

Crab Meat Scrambled Eggs

1 cup crab meat
4 eggs
½ teaspoon salt
¼ teaspoon pepper
1 tablespoon chopped scallions

3 tablespoons butter, divided
Paprika, optional
Toasted English muffins

Flake the crab meat, being sure to remove all cartilage. Beat eggs with the salt, pepper and scallions. In a skillet heat half the butter. Add the crab meat and cook gently until hot. Add the remaining butter and heat. Add the eggs and adjust the heat to high. With a fork, draw the solidified egg to the center of the skillet; tilt the skillet and let the uncooked egg run to the edge of the pan. Repeat until most of the egg has set. Serve immediately. Serves 4. *I prefer this over freshly buttered and toasted English muffins for breakfast.*

Mrs. Lawrence Christian (Joyce)

To make a more tender omelet, use water instead of milk for the liquid.

Eggs a la Sherry

¾ cup crushed crackers
3 tablespoons melted butter
12 hard cooked eggs, sliced
12 slices crisply cooked
bacon, crumbled
1 carton (16 ounces) sour
cream

2 tablespoons cream
1 teaspoon minced onion
1 teaspoon salt
¼ teaspoon seasoned salt
¼ teaspoon pepper
1 cup grated Cheddar
cheese

Mix crackers with butter and sprinkle on bottom of 9x13 inch baking dish. Arrange egg slices over crumbs. Combine bacon, sour cream, cream, onion and seasonings. Spoon over eggs and sprinkle with cheese. Bake at 350° for 20 minutes. Serves 4 to 6. *This may be assembled the day before, then cooked before the meal. If it is cooked the day before and reheated, it will be dry.*

Mrs. Ron Cass (Sherry)

Egg and Cheese Soufflé

6 eggs
1 cup milk
1½ cups grated sharp Cheddar
cheese
½ teaspoon salt

6 green onions, chopped
½ teaspoon dry mustard
⅛ teaspoon pepper
1 can (4.5 ounces)
mushrooms

Beat eggs well. Add remaining ingredients and blend thoroughly. Pour into a greased 1½ quart baking dish. Bake at 300° for 50 minutes. Serves 4.

Mrs. Cecil Smith (Diana)

Egg Sausage Casserole

1 pound bulk sausage,
crumbled and cooked
6 slices bread, cubed
1 pound Cheddar cheese,
grated
¼ pound fresh mushrooms,
sliced

2¼ cups milk
6 eggs
1 can (10¾ ounces) cream of
mushroom soup
1 teaspoon prepared
mustard

In a 9x12 inch casserole dish, layer the sausage, bread cubes, cheese and mushrooms. Mix the milk, eggs, soup and mustard in a bowl and beat together until well blended. Pour milk mixture over layers in casserole and refrigerate 24 hours. Bake at 350° for 1 hour. Let stand 15 minutes before serving. Serves 10 to 12.

Mrs. Howard Chance (Miriam)

Frittata

1 large onion, chopped	1 green bell pepper, chopped
1 can (4 ounces) chopped green chilies, drained	½ cup picante sauce
1 fresh jalapeño pepper, chopped	1 tablespoon chili powder
2 large garlic cloves, minced	2 tablespoons butter
16 little smoked sausages, cut into fourths	16 eggs, slightly beaten
1 cup peeled, steamed and diced potatoes	1½ cups grated Cheddar or Monterey Jack cheese

Sauté all ingredients except eggs and cheese in a large skillet with 2 tablespoons butter until the onion is translucent. Transfer to a lightly oiled 8x10 inch baking dish. Add eggs and 1 handful of cheese. Bake at 350° for 20 minutes. Remove and sprinkle remaining cheese on top. Lower temperature to 300°. Bake until brown and firm in center, 5 to 10 additional minutes. Serves 12.

Mrs. Larry Lerche (Gail)

Puffy Omelet

4 eggs, separated	⅛ teaspoon pepper
¼ cup water	1 tablespoon butter
½ teaspoon salt	

In a small mixing bowl beat egg whites with water and salt until stiff but not dry. In another bowl, beat egg yolks with pepper until thick and lemon colored. Fold into egg whites. Heat oven to 325°. Heat butter in a 10 inch skillet with oven-proof handle until just hot enough to sizzle a drop of water. Pour omelet mixture into skillet; level surface gently. Reduce heat. Cook slowly until puffy and lightly browned on bottom, about 5 minutes. Lift omelet at edge to judge color. Place in oven and bake 12 to 15 minutes or until knife inserted in center comes out clean. To serve, tip skillet, loosen omelet by slipping pancake turner or spatula under and fold omelet in half without breaking. Serves 2 to 3. *For a variation fold over with cheese and bacon, onion and sausage or sour cream and green chilies.*

Vanessa L. Hidell

Cover egg yolks with water to store in your refrigerator. They will keep for two or three days.

Artichoke Chicken Casserole

4 pounds chicken pieces
1 cup butter
½ cup flour
3½ cups milk
3 ounces Swiss cheese, cubed
2 ounces Cheddar cheese, cubed

2 cloves garlic, minced
½ tablespoon red pepper
1 can (6 ounces) mushrooms, drained
2 cans (14 ounces each) artichoke hearts, drained
1 package (12 ounces) noodles

Cook and debone chicken, saving broth. Cut chicken into bite sized pieces. In a saucepan make a cream sauce of the butter, flour and milk. Add cheeses, spices, mushrooms, artichokes and chicken. Cook noodles in chicken broth. Drain noodles and put into a 9x13 baking dish. Pour the chicken mixture over the noodles and bake at 350° for 30 minutes. Serves 8.

Mrs. Terry Jackson (Joyce)

Baked Chicken Breasts

4 whole chicken breasts, boned, skinned and halved
1 can (10¾ ounces) cream of mushroom soup

1 can (6 ounces) sliced mushrooms, drained
1 cup sour cream
⅓ cup dry sherry

Place chicken in baking dish. Combine remaining ingredients and pour over chicken. Cover with foil and bake at 325° for 1½ hours. Serves 4.

Mrs. Kempe Hayes (Stephanie)

Chicken Capers

2 tablespoons oil
1 onion, coarsely chopped
2 teaspoons Hungarian sweet paprika
1 pound boneless chicken breasts
1 tomato, cubed

½ teaspoon rosemary
½ cup vermouth
1 tablespoon capers
2 tablespoons tomato paste
Salt and pepper to taste
½ cup plain yogurt

Sauté onion and paprika in hot oil until onion is translucent. Add chicken breasts and cook quickly until they lose their pink color. Add tomato, rosemary, vermouth and capers. Cook over moderate heat for about 30 minutes. Stir in tomato paste. Season with salt and pepper. Stir in yogurt. Serves 2.

Mrs. Cecil Smith (Diana)

California Chicken with Spaghetti

California Chicken:

6	chicken breast halves, boned	¼	teaspoon pepper
½	onion, sliced	3	drops hot pepper sauce
⅔	cup red wine vinegar	1	cup pitted ripe olives, sliced
¼	cup olive oil, divided	1	tablespoon butter
1¾	teaspoons salt	1	can (14½ ounces) chopped tomatoes
1¼	teaspoons minced garlic	2	teaspoons cornstarch
1	teaspoon mixed Italian herbs	1	tablespoon cold water
1	teaspoon paprika		

Cut each half breast of chicken crosswise into 2 pieces and place in shallow dish to marinate. Add onion to chicken. In a small jar mix vinegar, 3 tablespoons oil, salt, garlic, herbs, paprika, pepper and pepper sauce; cover and shake. Pour over chicken to marinate. Refrigerate and let stand at least 2 hours, spooning marinade over chicken occasionally. Drain well, saving marinade. Drain ripe olives and cut into slices. Heat butter with remaining tablespoon of oil and brown chicken pieces slowly. Add ¼ cup of marinade to chicken. Cover and cook slowly for 10 minutes or longer until chicken is tender. Remove chicken from skillet. Mix olive slices and remaining marinade with liquid remaining in skillet. Add tomatoes and heat to boiling. Mix cornstarch with water and add to mixture. Cook, stirring, a minute or two. Add chicken and heat a few minutes longer.

Spaghetti with Cheese:

8	ounces uncooked spaghetti	¼	cup grated Parmesan cheese
6	cups boiling water	2	tablespoons olive oil
2	teaspoons salt	1	tablespoon chopped parsley

Cook spaghetti in salted boiling water about 3 minutes. Drain and rinse with hot water; toss with cheese, oil and parsley. Place on a platter topped with chicken and sauce. Serves 6.

Mrs. Maury Hafernick (Debbie)

 Texas may not be Vermont in the fall, but trees such as the Chinese tallow, the sweet gum and the sumac turn the country-side ablaze with their autumn colors.

Chicken and Chinese Noodle Casserole

1½ cups chopped celery
1 can (10¾ ounces) cream of mushroom soup
1 can (10¾ ounces) cream of chicken soup
1 can (6 ounces) evaporated milk
3 cups chow mein noodles
1½ cups cooked cubed chicken
1 can (4 ounces) mushroom pieces, undrained
½ cup toasted slivered almonds
1 cup chopped green bell pepper
¼ cup chopped pimiento
1 teaspoon crushed hot pepper
1½ tablespoons soy sauce

In a saucepan cook the celery in a small amount of salted water until tender. Drain. Combine soups and milk in a 2 quart casserole. Add celery and remaining ingredients. Stir to combine. Bake at 350° for 50 to 60 minutes. Serves 6 to 8.

Mrs. Cecil Smith (Diana)

Curried Chicken Divan

3 whole chicken breasts
2 packages (10 ounces each) broccoli spears
2 cans (10¾ ounces each) cream of chicken soup
1 cup sour cream
1 cup mayonnaise
1 cup grated sharp Cheddar cheese
1 tablespoon lemon juice
1 teaspoon curry powder
Parmesan cheese
Paprika
Butter

Cook and debone chicken. Cook broccoli just until tender. Mix soup, sour cream, mayonnaise, grated cheese, lemon juice and curry powder to make a sauce. Layer broccoli and deboned chicken in a 9x13 inch baking dish, sprinkling each layer with Parmesan cheese. Pour sauce over all and sprinkle with Parmesan cheese and paprika; dot with butter. Bake at 350° for 30 minutes. Serves 6.

Mrs. Tony Sessi (Alice)

Honey Curry Chicken

¼ cup butter
½ cup honey
¼ cup prepared mustard
1 teaspoon salt
1 teaspoon curry powder
1 chicken, cut into pieces

Preheat oven to 375°. Melt butter in a 9x13 inch baking dish. Stir in honey, mustard, salt and curry powder. Roll chicken in mixture and arrange in a single layer in dish. Bake uncovered for 1 hour or until tender, basting occasionally. Serves 4 to 6.

Mrs. Jim Rado (Vicki)

Chicken Kiev

8   chicken breasts
½   cup butter
1   clove garlic, crushed
2   tablespoons chopped
    chives
2   tablespoons chopped
    parsley
1½ teaspoons salt, divided

½   teaspoon pepper
½   teaspoon rosemary
2   tablespoons
    Worcestershire sauce
1   egg
½   cup cream
Flour
Cracker crumbs

Skin and bone chicken breasts and separate into 2 pieces each. Place filets between 2 sheets of waxed paper and flatten with cleaver. Cream butter with garlic, chives, parsley, ½ teaspoon salt, ½ teaspoon pepper, rosemary and Worcestershire sauce until smooth. Freeze until firm. Place 1 tablespoon cold butter mixture on each filet. Tuck in ends and roll tightly. Secure with toothpick. Beat egg and cream together. Roll filets in flour seasoned with remaining salt; dip in egg-cream and then in cracker crumbs. Fry in deep oil at 360° until golden. Serves 16. *You may use boneless chicken filets, but be sure there are no openings for the butter to seep through. Do not prick with fork while frying.*

Mrs. Art DeFelice (Connie)

Chicken Medallions with Peaches

2   whole chicken breasts,
    halved, skinned and boned
1   cup whole wheat flour
2   teaspoons dried rosemary,
    crushed
2   tablespoons butter,
    divided

2   peaches, peeled and
    halved
1¾ cups water
½   cup almonds

Remove any visible fat from chicken. Slice each piece of chicken into several medallions (small cutlets). Pat pieces dry with paper towels. Place medallions between sheets of waxed paper and flatten by pounding with a mallet until ¼ to ½ inch thick. Combine flour and rosemary on a plate and dredge the chicken to coat lightly. Shake off excess. Heat 1 tablespoon butter in a large frying pan. Add the peaches and sauté about 2 minutes on each side. Remove peaches from the pan and reserve. Add the remaining butter to pan. Add chicken and sauté over medium-high heat for 1 minute on each side. Remove from heat. Bring water to a boil in a saucepan. Add the almonds and blanch them for 2 minutes. Transfer the almonds and water to a blender. Starting on low speed and holding the lid firmly in place, process the almonds until finely chopped. Pour the mixture into the pan with the chicken. Add peaches and return to low heat for 10 minutes. Serves 4.

Mrs. Dan S. Steakley (Susan)

Italian Stuffed Game Hens

4 Rock Cornish Game Hens

Thaw hens; rinse; remove and boil giblets.

Stuffing:

1 recipe cornbread	½ teaspoon oregano
5 slices white bread	1 tablespoon sage
3 eggs, beaten	½ teaspoon Italian seasoning
1 cup margarine, divided	½ cup chicken broth
1 medium onion, chopped	Salt and pepper to taste
6 ribs celery, chopped	Minced garlic
2 cloves garlic, minced	

Bake cornbread. When cool, crumble cornbread and white bread into a large bowl. Add eggs and ½ cup melted margarine. Mix well. Sauté onions, celery and garlic in ¼ cup margarine until tender. Allow to cool slightly, then add to first mixture. Add oregano, sage and Italian seasoning, blending well. Chop half the giblets; add chopped giblets and ½ cup broth to bread mixture. Place hens in a large broiling pan. Stuff with dressing. Line pan with remaining dressing. Baste birds with remaining ¼ cup margarine and rub a little minced garlic on skin. Cover top of broiling pan with foil, seal and bake at 350° for 1½ to 2 hours. Remove foil and continue baking until hens are brown. Serves 4.

Mrs. James C. Doss (Charlene)

Chicken Asparagus Casserole

12 slices cooked, boned chicken	4 drops hot pepper sauce
1 pound cooked asparagus	4 tablespoons grated Parmesan cheese
2 cans (10½ ounces each) cream of mushroom soup	4 tablespoons chopped pimiento
1 cup whipping cream	Paprika
1 teaspoon curry powder	

Place chicken in a greased casserole. Arrange asparagus on top. Combine soup, cream, curry powder, hot pepper sauce and cheese. Heat, stirring constantly, until smooth. Add pimiento. Pour over chicken and asparagus. Sprinkle with paprika. Bake at 350° for 30 minutes. Serves 4 to 6.

Mrs. Gary McKenzie (Clare)

Chicken Marsala

1 teaspoon salt	4 tablespoons butter,
½ teaspoon pepper	divided
½ cup flour	1 cup sliced fresh
4 chicken breast halves,	mushrooms
skinned and boned	½ cup Marsala wine
2 tablespoons olive oil	½ cup chicken broth, divided

Combine salt, pepper and flour. Dredge chicken lightly on both sides. Shake off excess flour. Heat oil and 2 tablespoons butter in a skillet over medium heat. Brown chicken pieces for 3 minutes on each side; remove from skillet and keep warm. Sauté mushrooms in pan drippings. Add wine and ¼ cup broth. Boil for 2 minutes, stirring constantly. Return chicken to pan and simmer covered for 15 minutes. Remove chicken again to warm platter; add remaining broth and boil pan drippings until thickened. Remove from heat and stir in remaining 2 tablespoons butter. Pour over chicken and serve. Serves 4. *Serve with wild rice, fresh buttered carrots and a crisp green salad.*

David Bradberry

Chicken Americana

¼ cup melted butter	1 cup grated American
3 to 3½ pounds chicken	cheese
pieces	¾ teaspoon salt
¼ cup flour	¼ teaspoon crushed thyme
⅔ cup milk	⅛ teaspoon pepper
1 can (10¾ ounces) cream of	1 large onion, chopped
mushroom soup	¼ pound fresh mushrooms,
	sliced

Melt butter in a 12x7½x2 inch baking dish. Coat chicken pieces with flour. Arrange in single layer skin side down. Bake at 325° until brown, 15 to 20 minutes. Pour off excess fat. Combine milk, soup, cheese, salt, thyme and pepper. Add onions and mushrooms. Pour over chicken. Cover dish with foil and bake at 325° for 15 to 20 minutes. Serves 4 to 6.

Mrs. Tim Mizner (Carol)

Many settlers from the Old South established bases in East Texas, and towns such as Tyler, Jefferson and Nacogdoches with their pine trees, azaleas, magnolias and dogwoods remind the visitor of the historic South.

Hot Chicken Salad Casserole

4	cups diced cooked chicken	4	tablespoons freshly squeezed lemon juice
4	cups diced celery	2	cups mayonnaise
1	cup slivered almonds	2	cups grated sharp Cheddar cheese
1	teaspoon salt		
2	tablespoons grated onion	1½	cups broken potato chips

Mix chicken, celery, almonds, salt, onion, lemon juice and mayonnaise. Turn into a shallow buttered casserole. Combine cheese and potato chips and spread over top. Bake uncovered at 375° for 15 to 20 minutes. Serves 12 to 14. *This is good to serve at a bridal or baby shower.*

Mrs. Steve McMillon (Mary Beth)

Grandmother's Chicken Casserole

	Flour	2	bay leaves
	Salt and pepper to taste	6	small onions, peeled
	Ginger to taste	6	potatoes, peeled and quartered
	Breasts, thighs and drumsticks from 2 chickens	6	carrots, peeled and quartered
4	tablespoons butter	8	ounces mushrooms, sautéed in a small amount of butter
2	tablespoons flour		
1	cup water		
1	can (10¾ ounces) beef bouillon	1	can (8 ounces) English peas
1	tablespoon catsup		
1	tablespoon Worcestershire sauce		

Mix flour, salt, pepper and ginger and dredge chicken in the seasoned flour. Brown the floured chicken in a skillet with 4 tablespoons of melted butter. Remove pieces when brown and save the drippings. Put chicken pieces in a large casserole. Add flour to the drippings, making a paste. Stir in water, beef bouillon, catsup, Worcestershire sauce, bay leaves and whole onions. Pour over chicken and bake at 350° for 45 minutes. Add potatoes, carrots and mushrooms. Bake 35 minutes more. Add peas and bake 10 minutes longer. Serves 6. *This recipe is adapted from my great grandmother's handwritten recipe book, dated 1901, in Mt. Airy, Ohio.*

Mrs. Terry Arndt (Barbara)

Herb Buttered Chicken

2   chickens, cut into serving
    pieces
½   cup butter
½   teaspoon dried tarragon
1   teaspoon seasoned salt

Juice of 1 lemon
1   teaspoon dried marjoram
1   teaspoon instant minced
    garlic

Wash and pat chicken dry. Blend remaining ingredients to make a paste. Brush the chicken with herb butter paste and place on a broiler pan. Turn chicken at 10 minute intervals, brushing with herb butter with each turn. Continue to turn chicken pieces until they are tender and brown, about 1 hour. Serves 8 to 10.

Mrs. Bob Edgecomb (Mary)

King Ranch Chicken

1   chicken, 3 to 4 pounds
2   onions, chopped and
    divided
2   ribs celery, chopped
Salt and pepper
1   can (10¾ ounces) cream of
    mushroom soup
1   can (10¾ ounces) cream of
    chicken soup
8   ounces Cheddar cheese,
    grated

1   package (12 count) corn
    tortillas
1   large green bell pepper,
    chopped
Chili powder
Garlic salt
1   can (10 ounces) tomatoes
    with green chilies,
    undrained

Boil hen until tender in water seasoned with 1 onion, celery, salt and pepper. Remove chicken and cut into bite sized pieces. Reserve stock. Combine soups and grated cheese. Just before assembling casserole soak the tortillas in boiling chicken stock until softened. Start layering casserole in a 9x12 inch baking dish in this order: softened tortillas, chicken, onion, bell pepper; sprinkle to taste with chili powder and garlic salt; and soup mixture. Repeat the layers. Cover the casserole with the undrained tomatoes with chilies. Juices in the casserole should be about half the depth of the dish; if not, add a little more stock. Bake uncovered at 375° for 30 minutes. Serves 6 to 8. *This may be made and frozen several days ahead, but always make at least one day ahead and refrigerate so the flavors will blend.*

Mrs. Tony Hall (Jane)

Mushroom Stuffed Chicken

Stuffed Chicken:

4   chicken breast halves, boned
1   tablespoon butter
½   pound mushrooms, sliced
¼   cup shredded ham
½   tablespoon sherry
½   teaspoon lemon juice
¼   teaspoon tarragon
½   clove garlic, minced
1   cup grated Swiss cheese
Flour
Salt and pepper
¼   cup butter
4   tablespoons brandy

Wash chicken breasts and pat dry; set aside. In skillet melt butter and sauté mushrooms until tender; add ham, sherry, lemon juice, tarragon and garlic. Cook about 5 minutes; add Swiss cheese and simmer until cheese melts. Divide this mixture into 4 equal parts and use it to stuff each chicken breast. Fold the breast over and secure. Place in refrigerator or freezer for several hours to allow cheese to harden. Remove chicken from refrigerator and coat with flour which has been seasoned with salt and pepper. Quickly brown chicken on both sides in butter, then flame with brandy. Remove chicken from skillet and place in baking dish. Reserve pan drippings.

Sauce:

½   tablespoon tomato paste
½   teaspoon Dijon mustard
1½ tablespoons flour
¼   cup chicken broth
¾   cup whipping cream
1   tablespoon sherry
2   tablespoons dry white wine
½   teaspoon white pepper
½   cup grated Swiss cheese

Add tomato paste and mustard to drippings left in pan from flaming chicken. Mix the flour with a little of the chicken broth and add to pan. Add remaining chicken broth; gradually add cream. Stir in sherry, wine and white pepper. Simmer until somewhat thickened. Pour over chicken and bake at 350° for 45 to 50 minutes. Remove from oven; top with Swiss cheese, and return to oven for cheese to melt. Serve immediately. Serves 4.

Mrs. Marcus Bone (Beverly)

Instead of buying the more expensive ready made croutons in packages, make your own. Cube day old bread and saute in butter or toast in the oven.

Party Stuffed Chicken Breasts

4   whole chicken breasts,
    halved and boned
6   ounces Gruyere or Swiss
    cheese, grated
¼   pound salami, diced
½   cup chopped green onions
1   egg, beaten

1   package (3 ounces)
    chicken coating mix
¼   cup butter or margarine
¼   cup flour
2   cups milk
Parsley or watercress

Preheat oven to 400°. Put each piece of chicken between 2 sheets of waxed paper. Pound with mallet until ¼ inch thick; set aside. Toss 1 cup cheese, salami and green onion. Put ¼ cup cheese mixture in center of each breast. Roll up and fasten with toothpick. Dip chicken in beaten egg; then roll in coating mix. Place in 9x13 inch greased casserole. Bake for 40 minutes until brown. Meanwhile, make sauce. Melt butter in small saucepan. Stir in flour until bubbly and smooth. Gradually beat in milk. Cook and stir until thick. Add remaining cheese; remove from heat and stir until melted. Pour over baked chicken. Garnish with parsley or watercress. Serves 8. *Each serving contains about 360 calories.*

Mrs. Larry Lerche (Gail)

Chicken Stew

2   chickens
4   cups sliced okra
4   medium green bell
    peppers, chopped
2   jalapeño peppers, seeded
    and chopped
5   carrots, chopped

5   ribs celery, chopped
1   medium onion, minced
3   teaspoons salt
2   teaspoons pepper
2   teaspoons basil
1   teaspoon garlic powder
Cooked rice

Boil chicken and save broth. Remove from broth and debone, cutting chicken into bite sized pieces. Place okra, bell pepper, jalapeños, carrots, celery and onions in chicken broth. Cover and cook until tender. Add seasonings and chicken and cook until heated. Serves 8 to 10. *If desired, add one can of cream of mushroom, chicken, or celery soup. Serve over rice.*

Mrs. Charlie Tupa (Sidney)

Poulet Dijonnais

1 whole chicken, 3 to 4 pounds	Coarse salt
Fresh tarragon	Freshly ground pepper
2 tablespoons Dijon mustard	¼ cup brandy
2 tablespoons butter, softened	1 cup whipping cream
	1 teaspoon chopped fresh tarragon

Wash chicken and wipe with paper towels. Place small pieces of tarragon under the skin. Combine mustard and butter and spread over the chicken, putting a little of the mixture in the cavity. Season with salt and pepper and place in a roasting pan. Roast in a preheated 350° oven for 1 hour or until done. Remove to a plate and put the roasting pan on top of the range. Bring the cooking juices to a boil and add the brandy. Cook while stirring for a few minutes, then add the cream. Heat through and then add 1 teaspoon tarragon. Serve the sauce separately. Serves 4 to 6. *This dish goes well with rice and a green vegetable.*

Mrs. David King (Priscilla)

Island Chicken

1 can (8 ounces) pineapple chunks	1 tablespoon soy sauce
2 pounds chicken pieces	1 clove garlic, minced
2 tablespoons shortening	1 green bell pepper, seeds removed and cut in squares
1 can (10¾ ounces) chicken broth	4 tablespoons cornstarch
¼ cup white vinegar	¼ cup water
2 tablespoons brown sugar	

Drain pineapple chunks, saving syrup. Brown chicken slowly in shortening; pour off fat. Add reserved syrup, broth, vinegar, sugar, soy sauce and garlic. Cover; cook over low heat 40 minutes. Add bell pepper and pineapple chunks; cook 5 minutes more or until chicken is tender, stirring occasionally. Combine cornstarch and water; gradually stir into sauce. Cook, stirring, until thickened. Serve with cooked parsley rice. Serves 4.

Mrs. Ron Bruney (Carol)

To keep olive oil from becoming rancid, store in the refrigerator. It will harden, but will soon liquify if left at room temperature for a few minutes.

Szechuan Peanut Chicken

3   whole chicken breasts, halved, boned and skinned
1   tablespoon oil
1   slice fresh ginger, about ½ inch thick
1   clove garlic
2 to 3 dried red Szechuan peppers, cut into thirds

⅓   cup peanuts
½   pound snow peas
2   teaspoons soy sauce
1   teaspoon cornstarch
¾   cup chicken stock
2   scallions, cut in 1-inch pieces
Cooked brown rice

Cut each piece of chicken lengthwise into ½ inch wide strips. Heat the oil in a wok or heavy skillet; add ginger, garlic and peppers, and cook for 2 minutes over medium heat. Add the chicken and sauté for 2 minutes, stirring constantly. Add the peanuts, snow peas and soy sauce; stir and continue cooking another 1 to 2 minutes. Mix the cornstarch with the chicken stock until smooth; add to skillet and stir until sauce thickens. Add the scallions; reduce heat to low and cook for 30 seconds. Remove the garlic, peppers and ginger. Serves 4 to 6. *This is a wonderul recipe for both family and friends. It is low in calories and salt. I serve it with long grain brown rice to boost the fiber content.*

Mrs. Dan S. Steakley (Susan)

Yorkshire Chicken

Chicken:

¼   cup oil
⅓   cup flour
2   teaspoons salt

¼   teaspoon pepper
½   teaspoon sage
3   pounds chicken pieces

Pour oil into a 9x13 inch baking dish. Combine flour, salt, pepper and sage on waxed paper. Coat chicken with flour mixture. Rub chicken, skin-side down, in oil and turn. Do not add additional oil. Bake at 400° for 40 minutes. While chicken is cooking, prepare pudding.

Yorkshire Pudding:

1   cup flour
1   teaspoon baking powder
1   teaspoon salt

1½ cups milk
3   eggs
¼   cup fresh chopped parsley

Combine flour, baking powder and salt in medium mixing bowl. Gradually beat in milk, eggs and parsley. Pour pudding over chicken. Do not remove excess fat from baking dish. Place on cookie sheet to catch any overflow. Return to oven for 20 to 25 minutes or until puffed and brown. Serves 6.

Marsha Hynes

Turkey and Dressing

Turkey:

1   turkey, 18 to 20 pounds,
    preferably fresh
½   cup white wine

Salt and pepper
Sage to taste
½   cup butter, divided

Obtain a hypodermic needle from your doctor, pharmacy or feed store. The day before you plan to cook the turkey, inject it with white wine. I fill the needle twice for each side of the breast and once for each leg, a minimum of 6 times. Season inside of cavity with salt, pepper and sage. Rub inside with butter. Refrigerate overnight.

Dressing:

1   chicken, 3 to 4 pounds
2   onions
4   carrots
5 to 6 ribs celery, plus
    leaves
Salt to taste
6   whole peppercorns,
    optional
½   loaf French bread
½   loaf whole wheat bread

1   pan (8x8 inch) your
    favorite cornbread
10 to 12 mushrooms
2   tablespoons butter
1   cup chopped parsley
6   eggs, lightly beaten
2   teaspoons salt
1   teaspoon pepper
1   teaspoon sage

Boil chicken in water with ½ small onion, 1 carrot, 1 rib celery plus leaves from remaining ribs, salt and peppercorns or crushed pepper. When chicken comes away from the bone, remove from broth, debone and chop into pieces approximately ¼ to ½ inch square. Save chicken broth. Tear bread into ½ inch pieces. Crumble cornbread and mix with bread. This may be done the day before. Chop remaining onion, carrots, celery and mushrooms. Sauté on medium heat with 2 tablespoons butter or cook in microwave until tender. You should have approximately 2 cups sautéed vegetables. Combine bread crumbs, vegetables, parsley, chicken pieces and eggs. Season with salt, pepper and sage. Moisten with 1 to 2 cups broth from chicken or with enough broth to make the dressing stick together. Stuff turkey and place in roaster pan. Cover tightly with foil and bake at 250° for 10 hours. Remove foil for the last hour to brown. Serves 20. *Erma Bombeck says she has seen a 20 pound turkey cook in 30 minutes and an 8 pound turkey take 10 hours! I tend to agree! You just have to watch it.*

Mrs. Jim Rado (Vicki)

Rodeo in Texas is pronounced RO-de-o, not Ro-DAY-o. The popular sport was invented in the 1880's when cowboys from adjoining ranches got together to see who was better at such contests as bronco busting, calf roping and bulldogging.

Giblet Gravy

Giblets and neck from turkey
2 cups water, divided
2 cups pan drippings from
  baked turkey
¼ cup flour

Salt and pepper to taste
2 hard cooked eggs, thinly
  sliced
½ cup cooked chopped
  turkey

Cover giblets with water and simmer until tender, about 1 hour. Remove from heat and chop liver and gizzard. Remove meat from neck. Add to broth. Combine pan drippings with broth from giblets. Bring to a boil. Mix flour with 1 cup water. Spoon some of warm broth into water-flour mixture to warm and then add to broth. It might be necessary to add more flour and water mixture to make gravy the desired consistency. Add salt and pepper, eggs, chopped giblets and turkey just before serving. Yields 5 cups.

Mrs. Jim Rado (Vicki)

Turkey Patties

1 pound raw turkey, ground
2 tablespoons chopped fresh
  dill
½ cup finely chopped onion
½ cup plain yogurt

1 teaspoon salt
½ teaspoon pepper
1 egg, well beaten
½ cup bread crumbs
Oil

Mix turkey, dill, onion, yogurt, salt and pepper and shape into 4 patties. Dip each patty into the egg, then coat with bread crumbs. Fry in oil. Serves 4. *This is a low calorie dish, 350 calories per serving. You may also substitute 1 teaspoon oregano for the fresh dill, and add ½ cup grated Parmesan cheese.*

Mrs. Denman Smith (Sandra)

Scalloped Turkey Supreme

2 cups diced roast turkey
1 can (10¾ ounces) cream of
  celery soup
¼ teaspoon nutmeg
¼ teaspoon salt
¼ teaspoon pepper

1 green bell pepper,
  chopped
2 cups bread crumbs,
  divided
¼ cup grated Bleu cheese,
  divided
3 tablespoons butter, melted

Mix turkey, soup, nutmeg, salt and pepper. Add bell pepper, stirring well. Butter casserole dish and sprinkle 1 cup bread crumbs in bottom. Add turkey mixture and sprinkle with cheese. Add another layer of bread crumbs. Pour melted butter on top. Sprinkle grated cheese over all. Bake at 350° for 35 to 40 minutes. Serves 4.

Barbara Beall Stanley

Lemon-Herb Chicken Breasts

6 chicken breasts
3 large cloves garlic
Juice of 3 lemons
½ cup olive oil

1 teaspoon rosemary
1½ teaspoons pepper
1½ teaspoons salt

Rinse chicken breasts with skins on, pat dry and set aside. Combine remaining ingredients and mix well. Using a large freezer bag, combine chicken with liquid mixture and marinate for 12 hours. Turn bag occasionally. Remove chicken from bag and drain. Grill over mesquite chips, or bake uncovered at 350° for 1 hour. Serves 6. *This recipe takes only a few minutes in the morning to prepare, making the supper hour more relaxed and enjoyable.*

Mrs. Dan S. Steakley (Susan)

Turkey Tetrazzini

1 package (8 ounces) linguine noodles
7 tablespoons butter, divided
1 small onion, diced
¼ cup flour
3 cups milk
Fresh mushrooms, sliced

1 cup chicken or turkey broth
½ teaspoon salt
½ teaspoon pepper
¼ cup grated Parmesan cheese
4 slices bread
2 cups diced turkey or chicken

One hour before serving, cook linguine as label directs; drain; stir in 1 tablespoon butter and keep warm. Cook onion in 3 tablespoons butter; stir in flour. Gradually add milk, mushrooms, chicken broth, salt and pepper. Cook, stirring constantly, until thickened. Remove from heat and stir in cheese. Tear bread into small pieces to make 2 cups coarse bread crumbs. Melt 3 tablespoons butter in pan; sauté crumbs. Set aside. Add sauce and turkey to linguine. Spoon mixture into a 12x8 inch pan and top with bread crumbs. Bake at 350° for 20 minutes. Serves 6. *This dish can be made early in the day and stored in the refrigerator. When heating for dinner, extend baking time to 30 minutes.*

Mrs. Larry Keith (Virginia)

Turkey Loaf

1 pound raw turkey, ground	1 teaspoon salt
½ medium onion, grated	½ teaspoon white pepper
1 egg	½ teaspoon basil
1 teaspoon poultry seasoning	½ cup quick cooking oats

Mix all ingredients together and form into a loaf. Bake at 350° for 1 to 1½ hours. Serves 4. *This is a simple and low calorie dish. Each serving has less than 300 calories.*

Mrs. Denman Smith (Sandra)

Classic Beef Stroganoff

1 small onion, diced	¼ teaspoon garlic powder
4 ounces mushrooms, sliced	1 teaspoon minced parsley
4 tablespoons butter	1 teaspoon paprika
1 pound sirloin steak, cut into thin strips	1 cup sour cream
½ teaspoon salt	Cooked noodles
⅛ teaspoon coarsely ground pepper	

Sauté onion and mushrooms in butter. Add steak strips and simmer gently about 5 minutes. Do not brown the meat. Add seasonings and simmer, stirring, an additional 3 to 4 minutes. Stir in sour cream and continue cooking until sour cream is hot. Do not boil. Serve immediately over noodles. Serves 3 to 4. *This recipe is very quick, but the finished product gives the impression you worked long and hard!*

Mrs. J. P. Greve (Fran)

Beef with Peppers

1½ tablespoons oil	2 tablespoons cornstarch
1 clove garlic, crushed	1 tablespoon soy sauce
1 pound round steak, cut into small thin pieces	2 tablespoons water
1 teaspoon salt	1 cup green bell pepper, sliced lengthwise
¼ teaspoon pepper	½ teaspoon fresh ginger, finely chopped
1 cup beef stock	

Heat wok or skillet and add oil and garlic. Cook until garlic turns brown and remove. Add beef and fry a few minutes, seasoning with salt and pepper. Add beef stock and continue cooking a few seconds. This much may be done in advance. Mix cornstarch, soy sauce and water and add. Cook until sauce thickens, stirring slowly. Add bell peppers and ginger. Heat thoroughly and serve. Serves 4 to 6.

Mrs. Greg Gordon (Kathy)

Beef Tenderloin with Bearnaise Sauce

Beef Tenderloin:

2　beef tenderloins, 3½　　Garlic salt
　　pounds each　　　　　　Salt and pepper
Worcestershire sauce　　　12 bacon strips
Soy sauce

Tie two beef tenderloin strips together. Sprinkle generously with Worcestershire sauce, soy sauce, garlic salt, salt and pepper. Criss-cross bacon strips on top, securing with toothpicks. Let stand at room temperature 3 hours. Bake at 475° for 45 minutes or at 500° for 30 minutes.

Bearnaise Sauce:

½　cup sour cream　　　　1　teaspoon tarragon leaves
½　cup mayonnaise　　　　½　teaspoon dried shredded
½　teaspoon salt　　　　　　　green onions
2　tablespoons white
　　vinegar

Combine sour cream, mayonnaise, salt, vinegar, tarragon leaves and onions. Cover and refrigerate. Warm gently before serving. Serves 12 to 14. *This dish can be served warm or cold with the sauce. If served cold, do not heat sauce, serve cold.*

Mrs. David Sandberg (Bonnie)

Party Beef Tenderloin

1　whole beef tenderloin　　Teriyaki sauce
Salt　　　　　　　　　　　　Worcestershire sauce
Black peppercorns, ground　Garlic powder
Soy sauce

Allow ½ pound serving per person. Sprinkle meat generously with all the seasonings and bake at 425° for 15 to 20 minutes per pound. The ends will be well done and the center will be medium rare. Let stand 15 minutes before carving. *You can season ahead of time and pop in the oven after guests arrive and are having cocktails.* Yields ½ pound per person.

Mrs. Steve McMillon (Mary Beth)

When grilling meat outside, it is better to bring the meat to room temperature. It will cook faster and more evenly.

Standing Rib Roast

1 rib roast, 6 to 7 pounds	1 onion
Coarse salt	1 carrot
Freshly ground pepper	3 sprigs parsley
Garlic cloves	

You need at least 3 ribs on a roast for it to stand properly and to feed 5 to 6 people. Rub the roast with lots of salt and freshly ground pepper. Peel 1 clove of garlic and push it between 2 ribs. Add a whole, peeled onion and a carrot to the pan. Roast, standing on ribs, uncovered at 350°. For rare, roast 15 to 18 minutes per pound; medium 20 to 25 minutes; and well done, 30 minutes per pound. Serves 6.

Mrs. Marcus Bone (Beverly)

Lobster Stuffed Tenderloin

2 lobster tails, 4 ounces each	½ cup chopped green onion
3 to 4 pounds whole beef tenderloin	½ cup butter
1 tablespoon butter, melted	½ pound fresh mushrooms
1½ teaspoons lemon juice	½ cup dry white wine
6 slices bacon, partially cooked	⅛ teaspoon garlic salt

Place lobster tails in boiling salted water to cover. Return to boiling, reduce heat, and simmer for 5 to 7 minutes. Cut beef tenderloin lengthwise to within ½ inch of bottom to butterfly. Carefully remove lobster from shells. Cut in half lengthwise. Place lobster end to end, inside beef. Combine 1 tablespoon melted butter with lemon juice and drizzle on lobster. Close meat around lobster and tie roast with string at 1 inch intervals. Place on a rack in a shallow roasting pan. Roast at 425° for 25 minutes for rare. Lay partially cooked bacon slices on top and roast 5 minutes more. Meanwhile, in a saucepan cook green onions in remaining butter; add mushrooms and sauté until tender. Add wine and garlic salt and heat through, stirring frequently. To serve, slice roast and spoon on wine sauce. Serves 8.

Mrs. John Wilbur (Nancy)

Nearly every country of the world has its own popular sausage or sausages.

Rouladen

2 pounds thin round steak
Salt
Pepper
Onion, cut in small wedges

Bacon, cut in small pieces
Flour
Oil

Cut steak in pieces about 2x4 inches each. Sprinkle with salt and pepper; place small piece of onion and bacon on top of each piece of meat. Roll each piece and fasten with toothpicks. Roll in flour and brown in hot oil. Add small amount of water. Cover and simmer about 2½ to 3 hours, or until tender. Add water if needed. Serves 6 to 8. *A small raw baby carrot can be used in place of bacon.*

Mrs. Ron Dorst (Clarice)

Empress Beef

3 tablespoons vegetable oil
¼ teaspoon salt
½ pound boneless sirloin steak cut into shoestring strips
1 large onion, thinly sliced
3 ribs celery, coarsely chopped
¼ pound fresh or frozen snow peas, each cut in half

4 ounces fresh whole mushrooms, thinly sliced
½ cup coarsely chopped water chestnuts
1 tablespoon cornstarch
½ tablespoon sugar
5 tablespoons soy sauce
½ cup water
Cooked rice

Heat oil in large skillet; add salt, then beef. Cook over high heat about 5 minutes, stirring often to brown meat. Add onion, celery, snow peas, mushrooms and water chestnuts. Continue cooking over high heat, stirring constantly, 2 to 3 minutes. Combine cornstarch, sugar, soy sauce and water in a small dish; mix well. Add to skillet; cook, stirring constantly, until mixture thickens and bubbles, about 1 minute. Serve immediately over fluffy steamed rice. Serves 2 to 3.

Mrs. Larry Lerche (Gail)

Best Ever Brisket

Preheat gas grill to low. Wash a 6 to 8 pound brisket. Trim loose fat and dry. Rub both sides liberally with coarse salt. Place on grill for 30 minutes, turning every 15 minutes. Turn grill to low and place meat off fire. Cook for 1 hour turning every 30 minutes. Heat oven to 250°. Place 1 tablespoon flour in cooking bag and shake to coat. Put brisket in bag, make 2 or 3 small slits and bake for 2½ hours. Slice and serve. Serves 12 to 16. *This method assures the meat will be tender and good without a sauce.*

Mrs. Bob Bluntzer (Jo)

Cantonese Pepper Steak

2 pounds round steak, cut
  into thin strips
Pepper to taste
Garlic powder to taste
¼ cup oil
4 cups water
¼ cup soy sauce
2 beef bouillon cubes
2 green bell peppers, diced
4 ribs celery, diced
1 onion, cut in wedges
1 can (8 ounces) sliced
  water chestnuts
8 ounces bamboo shoots
5 to 6 tablespoons cornstarch
Water
2½ cups cooked rice

Season steak with pepper and garlic powder and brown in hot oil in a large skillet. Add water, soy sauce and bouillon cubes and simmer until steak is tender, about 30 minutes. Add bell pepper, celery, onion, water chestnuts and bamboo shoots to meat mixture. Cook 5 more minutes. In a large measuring cup, add enough water to the cornstarch to get a heavy cream consistency. Slowly add to meat and vegetable mixture until desired thickness. Stir constantly. Serves 6.

Joan Winkelman

Portuguese Roast Beef

5 pound roast
4 tablespoons Mexican hot
  salsa
2 teaspoons garlic powder
2 teaspoons salt
1½ teaspoons paprika
2 bay leaves, crushed
1 large onion, diced
1 can (15 ounces) tomato
  sauce
15 ounces water
5 or 6 medium potatoes, cut
  into large chunks
1 link hot sausage, cut into
  thick slices

Preheat oven to 300°. Mix hot salsa, garlic powder, salt, paprika and bay leaves and spread over roast at least 2 hours before baking. Place roast, marinade, onion, tomato sauce and water in heavy Dutch oven or roasting pan. Cook about 1½ to 2 hours, basting each half hour. Add potatoes and sausage and cook another ¾ to 1 hour. Baste potatoes once or twice while cooking. To serve, remove roast and slice. Put potatoes and sausage in separate bowl. Pour marinade and cooking sauce into a separate bowl to serve as gravy for the roast. Serves 8 to 10.

Joan Winkelman

Estopado

1	pound lean beef, cut into 1 inch cubes
1	tablespoon oil
1	cup dry red wine
1	can (8 ounces) tomatoes
1	large onion, sliced
1	green bell pepper, cut in strips
¼	cup raisins
¼	cup dried apricots, halved
1	clove garlic, minced
1½	teaspoons salt
⅛	teaspoon pepper
1	teaspoon dried basil
1	teaspoon dried thyme
1	teaspoon dried tarragon
1	bay leaf
½	cup sliced fresh mushrooms
¼	cup sliced ripe olives
1	tablespoon flour
¾ to 1	cup cold water

In a large skillet, brown meat in hot oil. Add red wine, tomatoes, onion, bell pepper, raisins, apricots, garlic, salt and pepper. In a cheese cloth tie the basil, thyme, tarragon and bay leaf together and add to skillet. Simmer, covered 1 hour. Add mushrooms and olives; simmer 30 minutes more. Discard cheese cloth with spices. Combine flour and cold water; stir into stew. Cook, stirring constantly, until mixture thickens and bubbles. Serve over hot cooked rice or risotto. Serves 6 to 8.

Betty M. Williams

Steak Diane

4	beef tenderloin steaks, 4 to 6 ounces each
2	tablespoons flour
½	teaspoon salt
⅛	teaspoon pepper
4	tablespoons butter, divided
1½	tablespoons Dijon mustard
2	teaspoons Worcestershire sauce
2	cups thinly sliced mushrooms
2	tablespoons minced onions
¼	cup brandy
½	cup beef bouillon

Coat steaks with flour which has been seasoned with salt and pepper. Melt 2 tablespoons butter in a skillet and brown steak. When brown, remove meat from skillet and add mustard and Worcestershire to the pan drippings to make a roux. Add the remaining 2 tablespoons butter and sauté mushrooms and onions. When onions are soft, add brandy and bouillon and return steaks to the skillet. Simmer until done, about 15 to 20 minutes. Serves 4.

Mrs. Andrew Tewell (Judy)

Peppered Beef Flambé

Beef:

3 to 3½ pound rolled rump
    beef roast
1 tablespoon black
    peppercorns
Watercress or parsley

Tomato wedges, optional
¼ cup cognac
Sesame Butter, Lemon or
    Horseradish Butter

Heat oven to 325°. Place peppercorns in a plastic bag; hit them with a mallet until coarsely cracked. Roll beef roast in cracked pepper and press pepper into beef with heels of hand. Place beef on rack in a shallow roasting pan. Roast uncovered to desired doneness, 25 to 30 minutes per pound. Remove beef from oven and garnish with watercress or parsley and tomato wedges. Heat cognac in small saucepan just until warm. Ignite and pour the flaming cognac over the beef. Slice and serve with any of the following sauces. Serves 12 to 16.

Sesame Butter Sauce:

½ cup butter, softened
3 tablespoons toasted
    sesame seeds

Dash hot pepper sauce

Beat softened butter with sesame seeds and hot pepper sauce.

Lemon Butter Sauce:

½ cup butter
¼ cup parsley

½ teaspoon finely grated
    lemon peel
1 teaspoon lemon juice

Combine butter with parsley, lemon peel and lemon juice.

Horseradish Butter Sauce:

½ cup butter, softened

2½ tablespoons prepared
    horseradish

Beat softened butter with prepared horseradish.

Mrs. J. Edward Reed (Marian)

The Texas State Legislature in 1977 adopted a state dish, chili, a fiery stew brewed with Texas pride, and occasionally with a touch of Texas beer.

Just for Two

½ pound sirloin tip, thinly sliced	1 potato, peeled and diced
1 teaspoon oil	1 carrot, peeled and sliced
¼ teaspoon salt	¼ green bell pepper, chopped
½ teaspoon pepper	⅛ red bell pepper, chopped
¼ teaspoon crushed red pepper	1 zucchini, sliced
1 can (10¾ ounces) beef broth	¼ jalapeño, seeded and chopped
¾ soup can of water	1½ teaspoons flour
	¼ cup water

Pour yourself a glass of wine. Using an 11 inch cast iron skillet, brown the meat in oil and add salt, pepper and red pepper. After the meat is browned, add beef broth, water, potato, carrot, green and red peppers, zucchini and jalapeño. Mix flour and water together and add to meat mixture to thicken. Bring to a boil, reduce heat to low, and cook until the vegetables are tender, approximately 30 to 45 minutes. Serves 2.

Larry Lerche

Cornish Pastries

4 sticks or 2 packets of pie crust mix	1 cup diced onion
1 pound beef chuck or round steak, cut into 1/4 inch strips	1 cup diced turnips
	Pepper
2 cups pared, diced potatoes	4 tablespoons butter
2 teaspoons salt, divided	4 tablespoons water
2 cups diced carrots	Milk
	Chili sauce or pickles

Preheat oven to 350°. Prepare pastry for 2 pies as directed on package, except divide dough into 4 rounds. Roll 1 round into a 12 inch circle and place on 1 end of an ungreased baking sheet. On half the circle, spoon ¼ each of the meat and potatoes. Sprinkle each with ¼ teaspoon salt. On potatoes, layer ¼ each of the carrots, onions and turnips. Sprinkle with pepper and ¼ teaspoon salt; dot with 1 table-spoon butter and sprinkle with 1 tablespoon water. Brush edge of pastry with water; fold pastry half over filling. Fill and roll lower edge of pastry over top edge; seal and flute. Cut slits on top; brush with milk. Repeat with remaining pastry rounds and filling, placing second pastry circle on other end of baking sheet. Use another baking sheet for remaining 2 circles. Bake at 350° for 1 hour. Serve hot or cold with relishes. Serves 4.

Mrs. J. Edward Reed (Marian)

Green Pepper Swiss Steak

2 pounds tenderized round
  steak
Flour
2 tablespoons oil
1 cup chopped onion
1 cup chopped green bell
  pepper
1 cup chopped celery

1½ cups vegetable cocktail
  juice
1 beef bouillon cube
½ teaspoon salt
¼ teaspoon pepper
2 tablespoons cornstarch
¼ cup water

Cut meat into serving size pieces. Dip in flour and brown well in a large skillet in 2 tablespoons oil. Add remaining ingredients, except cornstarch and water. Cover and simmer until meat is tender, about 1 to 1½ hours. Thicken gravy with cornstarch water mixture. Serves 6 to 8.

Mrs. Sid Mann (Kathi)

Mustard Topped Steak

2 pounds top round steak,
  about 1¼ inches thick
¾ cup mayonnaise

¼ cup bread crumbs
2 tablespoons prepared
  mustard

Broil steak 3 to 5 inches from heat source for 10 minutes on each side. While broiling, mix mayonnaise, bread crumbs and mustard. When steak is done, spread mixture on top and broil 2 minutes longer, or until the topping is hot and bubbly. To serve, place steak on cutting board and slice diagonally. Serves 6 to 8. *This is an easy company meal with spinach salad and twice baked potatoes.*

Mrs. Daniel O'Donnell (Sharon)

Rolled Stuffed Steak

1 round steak, 14 to 16
  inches in diameter
4 cloves garlic, minced
3 medium onions, chopped
1 medium green bell pepper,
  chopped

1 cup chopped celery
⅓ cup dry bread crumbs
1 pound bulk pork sausage

Season steak to taste. Mix remaining ingredients together and spread on top of steak. Roll meat up in jelly roll fashion and fasten the edges with toothpicks. Place in a flat baking pan and bake at 325° for 2 hours, or until tender. Baste meat occasionally with juices from pan. Serves 6.

Mrs. Ken Moyer (Bonnie)

Stuffed Bell Peppers

6   green bell peppers
1   pound ground beef
⅓   cup chopped onion
1   can (16 ounces) stewed
    tomatoes
¾   cup rice

2   tablespoons
    Worcestershire sauce
Salt and pepper to taste
1½ cups grated Cheddar
    cheese, divided

Cut off tops of bell peppers, remove seeds and membranes and cook in boiling, salted water until tender-crisp; set aside. Brown ground beef with onion; drain, then add tomatoes, rice, Worcestershire sauce, salt and pepper and simmer about 5 minutes. Remove from heat and add 1 cup cheese. Stuff the peppers with the mixture and set upright in a baking dish; pour the rest of filling around peppers. Bake uncovered at 350° for 25 minutes. Sprinkle remaining cheese on top and return to oven for 5 minutes. Serves 6.

Mrs. Sid Mann (Kathi)

Royal Beef

2   pounds round steak
2   tablespoons butter
3   tablespoons flour
½   cup dry sherry
5   slices bacon
24 small onions, peeled
1   pound small fresh
    mushrooms
¾   cup beef consommé

¼   cup water
1   cup Burgundy wine
2   tablespoons tomato paste
2   bay leaves
⅛   teaspoon chives
⅛   teaspoon crushed thyme
⅛   teaspoon tarragon
⅛   teaspoon dried parsley
    flakes

Brown steak in butter in a heavy Dutch oven. Combine flour and sherry; stir into steak. Cook bacon until crisp; drain and crumble; add to steak. Sauté onions in bacon drippings until tender; remove with slotted spoon and add to steak. Sauté mushrooms in bacon drippings; drain well and set aside. Add remaining ingredients, except mushrooms, to steak and simmer covered for 1½ hours. Add mushrooms and simmer 30 minutes more. Remove bay leaves before serving. Serves 8 to 10.

Betty M. Williams

Ground round is the most expensive type of hamburger meat because it is the leanest.

Steak San Marco

2 pounds round steak, cut
   into serving pieces
1 envelope (1.25 ounces)
   onion soup mix
1 can (16 ounces) peeled
   tomatoes

1 teaspoon oregano
Pepper
Garlic powder to taste
2 tablespoons oil
2 tablespoons wine vinegar

Arrange meat in a large skillet or electric frying pan. Sprinkle soup mix evenly over meat. Add tomatoes and sprinkle with oregano, pepper and garlic powder. Then sprinkle oil and vinegar over top. Simmer, covered, for about 1½ hours or until meat is fork tender. Serves 4 to 6. *Serve over rice with a green salad for an easy, tasty meal.*

Mrs. Greg Gordon (Kathy)

Swiss Steak Au Gratin

1 cup thinly sliced onion
Water
2 pounds round steak
Flour
2 teaspoons salt

¼ teaspoon pepper
¼ cup bacon drippings
2 cups canned tomatoes
1 cup grated sharp Cheddar
   or Swiss cheese

Place onions in a skillet with sufficient water to cover. Cook uncovered until all the water is consumed. Cut meat into serving size pieces. Pound flour, salt and pepper lightly into both sides of meat. Heat bacon drippings in skillet and sauté meat until brown. In a large casserole place layers of meat and onions. Add tomatoes. Cover casserole tightly and bake at 275° for 2 hours. A few minutes before serving, place meat in a shallow baking dish so that each serving may be sprinkled with grated cheese. Put uncovered baking dish in a hot oven until cheese melts and seeps through into the sauce. Serves 6 to 8. *This method of preparing the onions has a unique flavor for casserole dishes.*

Veronica Toce Robert

Texas Goulash

2 teaspoons butter
1 cup chopped onion
1 cup chopped green bell
   pepper
1 pound ground beef

1 cup raw rice
1 can (16 ounces) whole
   tomatoes
1 tablespoon chili powder
Salt and pepper to taste

Sauté onion and bell pepper in butter until soft. Add ground beef and stir until brown. Add rice, tomatoes, chili powder, salt and pepper. Bake at 350° for 1 hour. Serves 4 to 6. *This freezes well.*

Mrs. James Albrecht (Donne)

White House Swiss Steak

1 onion, sliced	1 cup vegetable cocktail
2 tablespoons oil, divided	juice
¼ teaspoon thyme	1 cup beef bouillon
Seasoned salt	1 cup julienne sliced carrots
6 top round steaks, 8 ounces	1 cup julienne sliced celery
each	1 teaspoon chopped parsley
Flour	Cooked rice

Simmer onion in 1 tablespoon oil until golden. Remove pan from heat and add thyme. Season and sprinkle steaks on both sides with flour. Brown steaks in 1 tablespoon oil on both sides in an iron skillet. Transfer steaks to pan with the onions. Pour vegetable juice and bouillon over steaks. Cover pan and simmer very slowly for 1 hour in the oven or on top of the stove. After 1 hour of cooking time, turn steaks over and cover the steaks with the vegetables and continue cooking for 30 minutes. Sprinkle with parsley and serve over rice. Serves 6. *This recipe came as a framed print from my husband's grandmother. It was served during President Johnson's administration.*
Mrs. William Steigelman (Kathleen)

Steak Au Poivre

4 boneless steaks (sirloin,	½ cup white wine
ribeye, filet, strip)	¼ cup brandy
⅓ cup peppercorns	¼ cup whipping cream
3 tablespoons butter	Coarse salt
1 tablespoon oil	

Trim steaks; crush peppercorns. With the heel of your hand, press the peppercorns firmly into the meat on both sides. Heat butter and oil in a heavy skillet and cook the steaks over high heat. Remove to a warm plate. Add the wine; bring to a boil. Add the brandy; cook for a minute, enough to boil off alcohol, scraping the cooking juices. Add cream and heat through. Season with coarse salt and pour over steaks. Serves 4. *To crush peppercorns, use a pestle and mortar or put in cloth and smash with a hammer. A peppermill crushes too finely.*
Mrs. David King (Priscila)

Catsup stays fresh longer when stored in the refrigerator.

Veal Cordon Bleu

4	boneless veal cutlets	¼	teaspoon pepper
4	thin slices boiled or cooked ham	¼	teaspoon allspice
		1	egg, slightly beaten
4	thin slices Swiss cheese	½	cup dry bread crumbs
2	tablespoons flour	3	tablespoons butter
½	teaspoon salt	2	tablespoons water

Pound cutlets until ¼ inch thick. Place a slice of ham and cheese on each cutlet. Roll up carefully and secure with wooden skewers or picks. Mix flour, salt, pepper and allspice. Coat the veal rolls with flour mixture. Dip into egg, then roll in bread crumbs. In a large skillet brown the veal rolls in the butter for about 5 minutes. When brown, remove from skillet and place in a baking dish. Add water and bake at 350° for 45 minutes. Serves 4.

Mrs. J. Edward Reed (Marian)

Veal Parmigiana

½	cup chopped onion	1	pound veal, thinly sliced
2	tablespoons olive oil	2	eggs, beaten
Dash of garlic salt		1	cup seasoned bread crumbs
1	can (14½ ounces) tomato wedges		
		½	cup olive oil, divided
2	teaspoons sugar	6	ounces Mozzarella cheese, sliced
¾	teaspoon salt		
½	teaspoon oregano	¼	cup grated Parmesan cheese
¼	teaspoon basil		
¼	teaspoon pepper		

Sauté onion in oil with garlic salt for 5 minutes. Add tomatoes, sugar, salt, oregano, basil and pepper. Mix well, mashing tomatoes with fork, and bring to a boil. Reduce heat and simmer covered for 10 minutes. Wipe veal with damp paper towels. Dip veal in eggs, then in bread crumbs. Brown veal in ¼ cup oil about 3 minutes on each side, adding oil as needed. Place veal in a baking dish. Cover with the tomato sauce; sprinkle with Parmesan cheese and top each cutlet with a slice of Mozzarella cheese. *Do not layer.* Cover and bake at 350° for 30 minutes. Serves 4 to 6.

Mrs. Ron Bruney (Carol)

Oregano has a natural affinity for tomato sauces.

Beef Curry

Curry Powder:

¼ cup ground cinnamon
2½ tablespoons ground coriander
2½ tablespoons ground turmeric
3 tablespoons ground cumin
1 tablespoon ground fenugreek
2 tablespoons dry mustard

2 tablespoons ground cardamon
2 tablespoons garlic salt
2 tablespoons ground poppy seeds
2½ tablespoons ground dried chilies
2½ tablespoons ground black pepper
1 tablespoon ginger

Blend spices well. If dust from the spices is a bother, sprinkle with a few drops of vinegar. Seal tightly and store.

Beef Mixture:

⅔ cup oil
¼ cup curry powder
2 teaspoons paprika
3 onions, chopped
2½ cups beef stock
1¼ cups tomato juice
2 ribs celery, chopped

1 tablespoon dried apricots, chopped
2 pounds lean stewing beef, cubed
1 bay leaf
Salt to taste

Heat the oil and gently fry the curry powder and paprika for 3 minutes. Add onions and fry until transparent. Add stock, tomato juice, celery, apricots to the onions and cook gently for 15 minutes. Add meat and bay leaf, salting to taste. Cook on low heat for 2 to 2½ hours. This stew is best cooked the day before, cooled and then reheated. Serves 6. *Serve over steamed rice with fruit and/or vegetable side dishes. This recipe comes from my aunt who spent several years in Tripoli, Libya. The 'homemade' curry powder requires a little extra shopping, but can't be beat. If you can't find all the spices at your supermarket, go to a health food store.*

Mrs. Ron Bruney (Carol)

Some curry powder is hotter than other. Indian style curry powder will have more fire.

Everyday Meatloaf

Meatloaf:

¾ cup oatmeal
1 egg, beaten
1 can (8 ounces) tomato
  sauce
1 pound ground beef

¼ cup grated onion
1 teaspoon salt
½ teaspoon pepper
½ teaspoon Italian seasoning

Combine all ingredients and mix well. Form into a loaf pan and cover with sauce.

Sauce:

3 tablespoons brown
  sugar
¼ cup catsup

¼ teaspoon nutmeg
1 teaspoon dry mustard

Mix sauce ingredients together and pour over meatloaf. Bake at 350° for 45 minutes to 1 hour. Serves 4.

Mrs. William A. Bone (Chris)

Italian Meatloaf

2 medium onions, chopped
2 tablespoons olive oil
½ cup water
1 pound ground beef
½ pound ground pork

½ pound mild bulk Italian
  sausage
1 cup Italian bread crumbs
2 eggs, lightly beaten
Parsley to taste
Salt and pepper to taste

Cook onions in a covered saucepan with olive oil and water until onions are clear, not browned. Mix beef, pork and sausage together in large mixing bowl. Add onions with the pan juices and mix well. Stir in bread crumbs. Add beaten eggs, parsley, salt and pepper. Mix thoroughly. Adjust to the amount of moistness you prefer by adding water or bread crumbs. Form into a loaf and bake at 350° for 30 minutes. Serves 4 to 6. *You can make meat balls from this mixture if you want and add to your favorite tomato sauce. This makes a good meal served with green beans Italiano and a tossed green salad. Potatoes are a nice addition also.*

Mrs. Jim Rado (Vicki)

Lasagne

2 pounds ground beef
2 cloves garlic, minced
2 cans (28 ounces each) whole tomatoes
1¾ teaspoons salt
¾ teaspoon pepper
2 teaspoons oregano
1 can (6 ounces) tomato paste
1 box (8 ounces) lasagne noodles
12 ounces Mozzarella cheese
1 carton (16 ounces) cottage cheese or Ricotta cheese

Brown ground beef and garlic. Add tomatoes and the juice from one can, salt, pepper, oregano and tomato paste. Simmer for 20 minutes. Boil noodles according to package directions and drain. In a 9x13 inch pan, layer noodles, strips of Mozzarella cheese, cottage cheese and meat sauce. Repeat layers. Bake at 400° for 40 minutes. Serves 8 to 10.

Mrs. Fred Markham (Marilyn)

Italian Casserole

2 pounds ground beef
½ cup chopped onion
1 red or green bell pepper, diced, optional
1 tablespoon chopped garlic
1 bottle (32 ounces) spaghetti sauce
2 cans (8 ounces each) mushroom stems and pieces
½ teaspoon oregano
½ teaspoon salt
¼ teapoon pepper
1 package (10 ounces) medium egg noodles
8 ounces cream cheese
1 carton (16 ounces) sour cream
1 cup grated Parmesan cheese
1 pound Mozzarella cheese, grated

Brown ground beef, onion, bell pepper and garlic. Drain; add spaghetti sauce, mushrooms and seasonings, and simmer 10 to 15 minutes. Cook egg noodles according to package directions; drain and mix with cream cheese, sour cream and other cheeses. Layer noodles, meat mixture and cheese in 2 layers in a deep 9x13 pan. Bake at 350° for 30 minutes. Serves 8 to 12.

Mrs. Denman Smith (Sandra)

A red bell pepper is simply a more mature green bell pepper.

Tavern Sloppy Joes

1½ pounds ground beef
½ cup catsup
2 teaspoons prepared
mustard
1 teaspoon white vinegar
2 tablespoons bar-b-que
sauce
½ cup chopped onion
1 tablespoon Worcestershire
sauce

Mix all ingredients together and cook in a crock pot for 3 to 4 hours on high. For the last ½ hour remove cover. Serve on hamburger buns. Serves 6.

Mrs. Doug Lapham (Debbie)

Pecan Glazed Ham

1 whole boneless, fully
cooked ham
Whole cloves
Honey
1 cup firmly packed brown
sugar
½ cup fine soft white bread
crumbs
1½ teaspoons dry mustard
½ cup coarsely chopped
pecans

Place ham in roasting pan. Add water to a depth of approximately 2 inches; bring to a boil. Reduce heat and simmer, covered for 2 hours. Remove ham from pan; score with diagonal cuts and stud each corner of diamonds with whole cloves. Coat with honey. Mix brown sugar, bread crumbs, mustard and pecans and pat onto ham. Bake at 325° for 30 minutes. Serves 12. *This ham is a favorite of my mother's for Christmas gift giving.*

Mrs. Marvin Sentell (Julie)

Baked Ham

10 to 12 pound fully cooked
ham
Juice of 2 oranges
½ cup pineapple juice
½ cup light corn syrup
½ cup brown sugar
1 cup apricot preserves

Make diagonal slits, ¼ inch deep, across ham to get a crisscross pattern. Bake at 300° for 1½ hours, basting often with a combination of orange juice, pineapple juice, corn syrup and brown sugar. Spoon preserves over ham and bake 30 minutes longer. Cool slightly before slicing. Serves 12 to 16. *I serve this every Easter along with mustard sauce.*

Mrs. Jim Rado (Vicki)

Creamy Ham Casserole

1 medium head cauliflower, broken into flowerets	½ cup sour cream
4 tablespoons butter	4 cups cubed cooked ham
⅓ cup flour	1 can (3 ounces) sliced mushrooms, drained
1 cup milk, heated	1 cup soft bread crumbs
1½ cups cubed processed cheese	1 tablespoon butter, melted

Cook cauliflower in boiling water for 10 minutes. Drain well. In a large saucepan melt 4 tablespoons butter; stir in flour and cook for a moment. Add milk all at once; cook until thickened. Add cheese and sour cream. Cook until cheese melts. Combine with cauliflower, ham and mushrooms. Turn into a 3 quart casserole. Combine bread crumbs and melted butter. Sprinkle over top of casserole. Bake at 350° for 40 minutes until hot and bubbly. Serves 8.

Mrs. Sid Mann (Kathi)

To keep extracts and spices fresher longer, store in the refrigerator.

Chop Suey

2½ pounds lean pork, cubed	3 tablespoons cornstarch
1 tablespoon soy sauce	⅛ teaspoon pepper
2 cups water	1 teaspoon salt
2 cups coarsely chopped celery	1 can (8 ounces) sliced water chestnuts, drained
1 medium onion, sliced	1 can (14 ounces) bean sprouts, well drained
2 cans (4 ounces each) mushrooms, and liquid	Rice or chow mein noodles
¼ cup soy sauce	

Brown pork in electric skillet over medium-high heat until well done. Add 1 tablespoon soy sauce and water and simmer 5 minutes. Add celery and onion and cook on low 5 minutes. Add mushrooms. Mix soy sauce and cornstarch until smooth. Slowly stir cornstarch mixture into hot liquid. Cook, stirring constantly until thick. Reduce heat to warm and add water chestnuts and bean sprouts. Serve over rice or chow mein noodles. Serves 6.

Mrs. Ron Bruney (Carol)

Frankie's Pork Chops

½ cup catsup
⅓ cup chili sauce
½ cup brown sugar
1 cup water

1 onion, chopped
1 tablespoon hot pepper
sauce
6 to 8 loin pork chops

Bring all ingredients except pork chops to a boil and cook 2 minutes. Trim all fat from pork chops; put into baking dish. Pour sauce over the chops and bake at 325° for 1 hour. Serves 4 to 6. *This is a fast, tasty recipe, especially since the pork chops don't have to be browned first.*

Mrs. Willie Miles (Frankie)

Hungarian Pork Chops

4 thick pork chops
2 tablespoons butter
Dash of olive oil
1 clove garlic, chopped
1 teaspoon marjoram

1 tablespoon Hungarian
paprika
1 cup dry white wine
Coarse salt and freshly
ground pepper

Trim the pork chops and wipe them dry with paper towels. In a casserole that will go both on top of the stove and inside oven, brown the chops in butter and oil. *Oil is added to prevent the butter from burning.* Remove the chops and sauté the garlic for a few minutes. Return the chops with the remaining ingredients and cook in a preheated 350° oven for 45 minutes to 1 hour. Serves 4. *Pasta and a salad go with this simple dish.*

Mrs. David King (Priscilla)

Hearty Sausage Bake

2½ cups herb stuffing
2 cups grated sharp Cheddar
cheese
2 pounds bulk sausage
4 eggs
2½ cups milk

1 can (10¾ ounces)
mushroom soup
¾ teaspoon dry mustard
1 can (8 ounces)
mushrooms, drained

Layer stuffing then cheese in a 9x13 inch casserole dish. Fry sausage and drain very well. Add a layer of sausage. Beat eggs and add milk, soup and mustard, mixing until smooth. Add mushrooms. Pour over first layers. Bake at 350° for 1½ hours. Cut into squares and serve. Serves 12 to 16.

Mrs. Bob Reynolds (Carol)

Peachy Pork Chops

10 to 12 fresh Texas peaches,
    unpeeled
4   tablespoons lemon juice,
    divided
⅓   cup soy sauce
⅓   cup honey

1   clove garlic, minced
¼   teaspoon ginger
⅛   teaspoon pepper
12 pork chops
1   tablespoon lemon rind

Cut peaches in half and remove pits. Crush or purée 10 of the peach halves in a blender to make 2 cups pulp. Blend 1 cup of pulp with 1 tablespoon lemon juice. Cover and refrigerate for the sauce that will be served with the meat. Mix second cup of pulp with the remaining lemon juice, soy sauce, honey, garlic, ginger and pepper. Pour over pork chops. Let stand several hours, turning several times. Drain and save marinade. Place chops on grill. Cook for 15 to 20 minutes, turning for more even cooking. During the last 10 minutes baste often with marinade. At the same time the meat is placed on the grill, arrange the remaining peach halves at the edge of the grill. Sprinkle with lemon rind and brush with marinade. Cook about 15 to 20 minutes or until chops are done. Serve as garnish with chops. Add the reserved cup of peach pulp and lemon juice mixture to the remaining marinade. Heat and serve with the pork. Serves 12.

Mrs. Lee Provinse (Dottie)

Jim Hogg was the first Texas-born Governor of the State.

Pork Chop Casserole

2   tablespoons oil
6   pork chops, ½ inch thick
1   can (10¾ ounces) cream of
    mushroom soup
¾   cup sour cream

1   tablespoon parsley
½   cup milk or cream
4 to 5 medium potatoes,
    peeled and sliced very
    thin

Brown pork chops in oil and drain on paper towels. Mix soup, sour cream, parsley and milk. In a greased 2 quart casserole, layer potatoes, then soup mixture, then pork chops, ending with soup. Sprinkle with paprika if desired. Bake at 325° for 1 hour and 20 minutes. Serves 6.

Mrs. Wayne Bowles (Carolyn)

Spare Ribs José

1 cup water
½ cup sherry
2 tablespoons soy sauce

1 tablespoon sugar
2 pounds spareribs, cut apart

In a large saucepan, combine water, sherry, soy sauce and sugar. Bring to a boil. Reduce heat; add ribs and simmer 1 to 2 hours. Serves 4.

Mrs. Bob Edgecomb (Mary)

Sausage Stuffed Turban Squash

1 turban squash, approximately 3 pounds
Salt
1 pound bulk pork sausage
1 cup chopped celery
½ cup fresh sliced mushrooms

¼ cup chopped onions
1 egg, slightly beaten
½ cup sour cream
¼ cup grated Parmesan cheese
¼ teaspoon salt

Cut a slice from the stem end of squash so it will stand upright. Cut out turban end; scoop out seeds. Lightly salt inside. Place squash, scooped end down, in shallow baking dish. Bake at 375° until tender, about 1 hour. Meanwhile, in a skillet combine pork sausage, celery, mushrooms and onions. Cook until vegetables are tender and meat is brown. Drain well. Combine egg, sour cream, Parmesan cheese and salt. Stir into sausage mixture. Turn squash over and fill with sausage mixture. Bake at 375° for 20 to 25 minutes. Serves 6.

Mrs. J. Edward Reed (Marian)

Sausage Bread

1 pound hot bulk sausage
1 cup chopped onion
¼ cup grated Parmesan cheese
1 cup grated Swiss cheese
1 egg, beaten
¼ teaspoon hot pepper sauce

1½ teaspoons salt
2 tablespoons chopped parsley
3 cups biscuit mix
1 cup milk
½ cup mayonnaise
1 egg yolk, beaten

Cook crumbled sausage and onion until brown; drain. Add cheeses, beaten egg and seasonings. Set aside. Make a dough of biscuit mix, milk and mayonnaise. Grease a 9 inch pan and spread half the dough in pan. Top with sausage mixture, then remaining dough. Brush with egg yolk and bake at 400° for 25 to 30 minutes. Serves 6.

Mrs. Bill Zapalac (Michelle)

Portuguese Marinated Ribs

1 cup water
¾ cup white vinegar
3 tablespoons lemon juice
½ teaspoon grated lemon
  peel
1 clove garlic, crushed
1 dried red chili pepper,
  seeded and crushed

1 teaspoon salt
¼ teaspoon pepper
2 teaspoons cumin seed,
  crushed
4 pounds pork spareribs, cut
  into serving pieces

Place large plastic bag in a large bowl and combine all ingredients except ribs. Mix well. Add ribs and close bag tightly. Refrigerate at least 6 hours or overnight, turning bag several times to distribute marinade. Drain ribs; discard marinade. Place meat in a 16x10x4 inch roasting pan. Roast uncovered at 450° for 25 minutes. Drain off fat and reduce heat to 350°. Roast, covered, 30 minutes. Uncover and roast 30 minutes longer. Serves 4 to 6.

Mrs. Joe Bowles (Mary)

Quail in Orange Sauce

1 teaspoon seasoned salt
½ cup flour
¼ teaspoon pepper
8 quail
½ cup oil
½ cup chopped onion
½ green bell pepper,
  chopped
2 cloves garlic, minced

1 carrot, peeled and thinly
  sliced
1 cup chicken broth
1 cup dry white wine
1 tablespoon grated orange
  peel
1 teaspoon Worcestershire
  sauce
Sour cream for garnish

Combine salt, flour and pepper in a paper bag. Shake quail, 1 at a time in the bag, until lightly coated. Brown quail in hot oil. Remove to an oven proof casserole dish. Sauté the onion, bell pepper and garlic in the remaining oil. Add the carrot, broth and wine. Cover and simmer 15 minutes. Strain sauce over birds and sprinkle with orange rind and Worcestershire sauce. Cover and bake 45 minutes. Turn off heat and leave in oven 30 minutes. Serve with a dollop of sour cream. Serves 8.

Mrs. Jim Rado (Vicki)

America was found because of Christopher Columbus' quest for a route to the Spice Islands.

Platte River Duck

1 duck	Salt and pepper to taste
1 small onion, chopped	6 tablespoons barbecue
1 small orange, peeled and	sauce
sliced	6 tablespoons dry sherry

Stuff duck with onion and orange. Rub well with salt and pepper. Place breast down in heavy foil, large enough to completely seal duck. Pour barbecue sauce and sherry over duck and seal. Bake at 275° for 3 hours. Serves 2.

Mrs. Kempe Hayes (Stephanie)

Brazos Valley Doves

6 doves, cleaned	1 cup chopped mushrooms
¾ cup butter, melted	½ teaspoon nutmeg
1 tablespoon Worcestershire	Salt and pepper to taste
sauce	⅓ cup flour
1 teaspoon garlic salt	Toast
⅓ cup cooking sherry	

Brown doves on all sides in melted butter in a large skillet. After doves are browned, add Worcestershire, garlic salt, sherry, mushrooms, nutmeg, salt and pepper to make sauce. Cover skillet and allow to simmer for 20 minutes. Remove the doves from skillet and add flour to the sauce to make a roux. Place doves on toast and top with sauce. Serves 3.

Joe Bowles

Doves in Madeira

1 cup uncooked rice	½ teaspoon rosemary,
3 tablespoons butter	crumbled
4 doves	8 small white onions
Lemon juice	½ pound mushrooms
Salt and pepper	1 cup chicken broth
	1 cup Madeira

Sauté rice in butter, allowing the rice to brown but not burn. Place in the bottom of a casserole. Rub the doves inside and out with lemon juice, then with salt, pepper and rosemary. Place doves on the rice and surround with onions and mushrooms. Combine chicken broth and Madeira, and pour over doves; cover and bake at 350° for 30 to 40 minutes. Serves 2.

Denman Smith

Creole Duck Stew

3 ducks, mallards or teal are best
4 tablespoons flour
Salt and pepper to taste
4 tablespoons peanut oil
½ cup chopped onion
¾ cup chopped green bell pepper
¼ cup flour
3 chicken bouillon cubes
3 cups hot water

Cut ducks into serving size pieces. Dredge in 4 tablespoons flour, salt and pepper. Brown in peanut oil in a heavy skillet. Remove ducks. Add onion, bell pepper and flour, cooking until flour is browned. Add bouillon cubes to hot water and stir until dissolved. Add to browned flour mixture in skillet, along with ducks and vegetables. Cook over low heat for 1½ to 2 hours. Serve with hot, fluffy rice tossed with chopped parsley or chopped bell pepper. Serves 3 to 6.

Marcus R. Bone

Pheasant in Red Wine Sauce

10½ tablespoons butter, divided
12 small mushrooms, caps and stems separated
Salt and pepper to taste
12 small white onions
1 to 2 tablespoons sugar
2 pheasants, with livers
4 shallots, finely chopped
2 tablespoons olive oil
2½ cups dry red wine
2 tablespoons flour

Sauté mushroom caps in 2 tablespoons melted butter. Season with salt and pepper and set aside. Cook onions in gently boiling salted water until tender and drain. Add 2 tablespoons butter to onions. When butter has melted, add sugar and stir until well blended. Return onions to pan and cook until glazed. Keep warm. Chop liver finely and sauté in ½ tablespoon butter. Mix with shallots and place in cavities of cleaned birds. Slice pheasants' breasts into thin slices and sauté in 4 tablespoons butter with a dash of oil until golden on all sides. Transfer to covered casserole and keep warm. Pour wine into same pan and add mushroom stems and continue cooking until liquid is reduced by half. Thicken sauce by mixing last 2 tablespoons butter with flour and dropping into liquid, stirring constantly. Simmer for several minutes. Strain into bowl, cool and skim off grease. Pour over pheasant. Add onions and mushroom caps. Cover and bake at 325° for 1½ to 2 hours, or until tender. Serves 4.

Mrs. Jim Rado (Vicki)

Bar-B-Q Venison Roast

1   hindquarter venison roast
2   cups white vinegar
1   cup oil
½   cup dry onion soup mix
1   can (12 ounces) beer
1   tablespoon salt
1   tablespoon pepper
1   teaspoon garlic powder
4   cloves garlic, quartered
6   slices bacon
Barbecue sauce

Combine vinegar, oil, soup mix, beer, salt, pepper and garlic powder for marinade. Marinate roast for 24 hours, turning frequently. Pierce the surface of the roast with a sharp knife every 2 inches; insert ¼ clove garlic in each hole. Cover thickest side of roast with 6 slices of bacon, securing with toothpicks. Smoke the roast for 8 to 10 hours. Baste with your favorite barbecue sauce the last 2 to 3 hours of smoking. Serves 6 to 8.

Don Bradford

Butler's Venison Stew

4   tablespoons butter or oil
1   clove garlic, minced
½   onion, minced
¼   cup flour
½   teaspoon salt
⅛   teaspoon black pepper
2   pounds venison, cubed
2   cups vegetable cocktail juice
1   cup red wine
½   pound fresh mushrooms, sliced
1   onion, cut into eighths
2   bay leaves
½   teaspoon thyme
Dash of oregano
3   dashes of hot pepper sauce
Water to cover
4   teaspoons aromatic bitters
3   potatoes, cut into ½ inch thick slices
4   carrots, cut into ½ inch thick rounds
Beef broth or water to cover

Brown garlic and onion in butter in a large pot or Dutch oven. In a paper bag combine flour, salt, pepper and meat and shake until well coated. Add meat and remainder of flour mixture to pot and brown over medium heat, stirring constantly to prevent sticking. Turn down heat to very low when the meat has browned. Add vegetable cocktail juice, wine, mushrooms, onion, bay leaves, thyme, oregano and hot pepper sauce. Cover with water and bring to a boil. Reduce heat and simmer covered for 2 hours, stirring occasionally. Add bitters, potatoes, carrots and beef broth to cover and simmer for another ½ hour, or until potatoes and carrots are tender, but not mushy. Serves 8 to 12. *What makes this stew so good and the venison not taste like vension is the vegetable cocktail juice and aromatic bitters.*

Robert Bluntzer

Cecil's Chili Verde

2 large onions, finely
   chopped
5 cloves garlic, minced
2 jalapeño peppers,
   stemmed, seeded and
   finely chopped
5 serrano peppers,
   stemmed, seeded and
   finely chopped
1 large red pepper, chopped
3 tablespoons bacon
   drippings, divided
¼ cup jalapeño juice
1 can (14 ounces) beef broth
1 can (12 ounces) Mexican
   beer

2 pounds venison, cubed
1½ pounds chili meat
½ pound hot pork sausage
6 tablespoons ground red
   chili pepper, divided
4 teaspoons cumin, divided
¼ teaspoon oregano
1½ teaspoons cayenne pepper
½ teaspoon white pepper
¼ teaspoon cascabel pepper
4 teaspoons paprika
1 cup tomato sauce
4 tablespoons masa flour
Grated cheese and onion for
   garnish

Sauté onion, garlic, jalapeños, serranos and red pepper in 1 table-spoon bacon drippings. Add jalapeño juice, broth and beer and bring to a simmer. Meanwhile, divide meat in half and brown half at a time in 1 tablespoon bacon drippings. Sprinkle 1 tablespoon chili pepper over each half. When brown, place meat into pot with liquid. Add 1 tablespoon chili pepper and 1 teaspoon cumin. Bring meat to a boil, cover and simmer 1½ hours. Mix remaining spices together and add with tomato sauce. Simmer 1 hour covered. Serves 6 to 8. *Top with grated cheese and grated onion. Serve accompanied by a cold beer.*

Cecil E. Smith

Venison

3 pounds venison
Salt and pepper
2 tablespoons butter
1 onion, chopped
1 slice ham, minced
1 clove garlic, minced
2 bay leaves

2 sprigs thyme, crushed
1 tablespoon flour
2 cups warm water
4 cups consommé
½ pound fresh mushrooms,
   sliced
Grated rind of 1 lemon

Cut venison into 2 inch square pieces. Salt and pepper generously. Heat butter in skillet and brown venison slowly. When almost brown, add onion; brown slightly. Stir in ham, garlic, bay leaves and thyme. Simmer, stirring for 2 minutes. Add the flour and cook a few minutes longer. Add warm water and simmer. Add consommé and cook slowly for 1 hour. Season again according to taste; then add mush-rooms and grated lemon rind. Let cook for 30 minutes longer. Serve on a very hot plate. Serves 6 to 8.

Marcus R. Bone

Lamb with Peaches

1 cup white wine	1 tablespoon garlic, minced
1 cup olive oil	½ cup brown sugar
½ cup white vinegar	8 peach halves
¼ cup minced onion	1 leg of lamb, 5 to 6 pounds
1 cup peach marmalade	1 cup peach chutney
1 teaspooon rosemary	1 cup herb stuffing mix
1 tablespoon thyme	Peach halves for garnish

In a saucepan combine all ingredients except lamb, peach chutney and stuffing mix. Bring to a boil; pour over lamb and marinate overnight. Remove from marinade and mix chutney and stuffing mix together and place in lamb. Roll and tie. Bake at 350° for 2 to 3 hours. Garnish with peach halves. Serves 6 to 8.

Mrs. Denman Smith (Sandra)

Grecian Stuffed Lamb

1 leg of lamb, 6 to 8 pounds, boned	1 tablespoon grated orange peel
Salt	¼ cup soft bread crumbs
¼ pound ground pork	½ teaspoon pepper
¼ pound ground cooked ham	½ teaspoon thyme
1 bunch green onions, chopped	1 egg, beaten
½ cup parsley, chopped	¼ cup milk
1 clove garlic, minced	½ cup pine nuts

Rub lamb inside and out with salt. Combine the rest of ingredients and mix well. Fill cavity. Tie lamb and place on rack in shallow roasting pan. Bake in 325° oven for 2¼ to 2½ hours, or to desired doneness. Roast to 175° on a meat thermometer for medium done meat. Serves 8 to 12.

Mrs. Dudley Baker (Kathy)

Grilled Lamb Chops with Minted Grapefruit

6 to 8 lamb chops	3 Texas Ruby Red grapefruit, sectioned
1 clove garlic	
1 cup mint jelly	

Rub chops with garlic. Pan broil or grill lamb chops until tender. In a skillet melt mint jelly and add grapefruit sections. Serve on top of lamb. Serves 6 to 8.

Mrs. Dudley Baker (Kathy)

Marinated Grilled Lamb

6   pound leg of lamb,
    deboned and butterflied
    by butcher
¼   cup olive oil
¾   cup soy sauce
¼   cup Worcestershire sauce
2   tablespoons dry mustard

2¼ teaspoons salt
1   tablespoon ground pepper
¼   cup red wine vinegar
½   teaspoon dried parsley
    flakes
⅓   cup fresh lemon juice
2   garlic cloves, crushed

Mix all ingredients together and marinate the leg of lamb overnight. Remove from marinade and reserve for basting. Cook on grill for 45 minutes to 1 hour, basting occasionally. Serves 10 to 12.

Mrs. Bill Wittenbrook (Linda)

To get the most juice from a lemon, have it at room temperature. Then roll it along your kitchen counter before cutting it.

Lemon Honey Lamb Chops

3   tablespoons lemon juice
2   tablespoons honey
2   tablespoons red wine
    vinegar
2   teaspoons dried oregano
1   teaspoon rosemary,
    crumbled

1   teaspoon minced garlic
1   teaspoon salt
2   tablespoons olive oil
⅔   cup oil
8   lamb chops, 1½ inch thick

For marinade, combine all ingredients except oils and lamb chops in food processor. Let stand 2 minutes. With processor running add oils through feeder tube. Let stand overnight. Score fat on lamb at 2 inch intervals. Place lamb in shallow dish. Whisk marinade and pour over lamb chops. Turn to cover both sides. Let stand at room temperature for 2 hours or refrigerate overnight, turning occasionally. Preheat broiler. Broil 4 minutes per side for medium rare or until desired doneness. Transfer to serving platter. Serves 8. *This is good served with jalapeño jelly as an accompaniment.*

Mrs. Jim Rado (Vicki)

Crab Casserole

1 pound cod fillets	1 egg, beaten
⅔ cup butter, melted	2 tablespoons chopped
1½ cups crushed herb	parsley
seasoned stuffing mix,	¼ teaspoon salt
divided	2 tablespoons lemon juice
6 ounces crab meat, drained	¼ teaspoon hot pepper sauce
4 ounces mushrooms, sliced	2 tablespoons butter, melted

Place cod fillets in an ungreased 8x8 inch baking dish. Combine ⅔ cup melted butter, 1 cup stuffing mix, crabmeat, mushrooms, egg, parsley, salt, lemon juice and hot pepper sauce. Mix well and spread over cod fillets. Combine ½ cup stuffing mix with 2 tablespoons melted butter and sprinkle over casserole. Bake at 350° for 30 to 35 minutes. Serves 4 to 6.

Mrs. Bill Zapalac (Michelle)

Fried Crab Cakes

1 pound crab meat	1 tablespoon prepared
¾ cup cracker crumbs	mustard
1 egg, slightly beaten	¾ teaspoon hot pepper sauce
2 tablespoons minced onion	1 teaspoon salt
2 tablespoons mayonnaise	½ teaspoon pepper
1 tablespoon Worcestershire	Saltine cracker crumbs
sauce	Oil

Flake crab meat with fork and mix with cracker crumbs, egg, onion, mayonnaise, Worcestershire, mustard, hot pepper sauce, salt and pepper. Form into six 3-inch patties and roll in cracker crumbs. Heat oil in an electric skillet to 375° and fry cakes until golden brown, about 3 minutes per side. Serve immediately. Serves 6.

Mrs. Marcus Bone (Beverly)

Tom's Mustard Fried Fish

Cut fish into desired size. Dilute prepared mustard with Worcestershire sauce to a thin paste consistency; the mustard taste should not be prominent. Dip fish into mustard mixture. Shake fish in a paper sack of cornmeal seasoned with salt and pepper. Fry in cooking oil or lard that is hot enough to light a wooden match; use enough so fish will float when done. *Do not overcook.* For best reults, if pieces are thick or large, fry only one layer of fish at a time. About every third batch, cook French fries or skim to remove excess cornmeal. Yields ½ pound fish per person.

The Honorable W. T. McDonald, Jr.

Shrimp Creole

¼ cup margarine
1 large onion, chopped
1 large clove garlic, minced
½ cup chopped green bell pepper
½ cup chopped celery
2 tablespoons flour
1 to 2 tablespoons salt
½ teaspoon pepper
¼ teaspoon red pepper

1 can (16 ounces) tomatoes
1 can (8 ounces) tomato sauce
3 sprigs parsley, chopped
4 small green onions, chopped
½ cup water
1 pound shrimp, peeled and deveined
Cooked rice

Melt margarine in skillet; sauté onion, garlic, bell pepper and celery until onion is lightly browned. Blend in flour. Add all remaining ingredients except shrimp. Mix well. Bring to a boil, cover and simmer 30 minutes. Stir in shrimp. Cover and cook 10 minutes longer. Serve over rice. Serves 4 to 6.

Mrs. Larry Hanners (Sally)

Shrimp au Vin

4 tablespoons butter
1 onion, minced
2 tablespoons tomato paste
½ cup white wine
3 to 4 tablespoons chopped fresh parsley
1 clove garlic, minced

¾ teaspoon salt
⅛ teaspoon pepper
½ teaspoon thyme
2 pounds shrimp, shelled and deveined
Cooked rice for 4

Melt butter in pan and sauté onion to light brown. Add tomato paste, wine, parsley and seasonings. Blend well. Mix in shrimp and simmer about 15 minutes. Serve with rice. Serves 4.

Mrs. Bill Wittenbrook (Linda)

The Gulf Coast of Texas beckons the vacationer and the fisherman with its 624 mile stretch of sandy beach. Sailing, swimming and sunbathing bring thousands of people to the Coast from March until well after the first norther. For the serious fisherman there is the lure of snapper, marlin or redfish, to name a few of the many varieties of fish who make their home in the Gulf of Mexico. And always there is the promise of finding that perfect sanddollar along some secluded beach.

Baked Scallops

½ cup butter
¾ cup round rich cracker
   crumbs
¾ cup seasoned bread
   crumbs
1 teaspoon seasoned salt

½ teaspoon pepper
½ teaspoon garlic powder
1½ pounds scallops, quartered
   or whole bay scallops
1 cup whipping cream

Melt butter in a large pan. Combine crumbs and seasonings and mix. Fold in scallops. Place in an ungreased 4 quart casserole. Pour cream evenly over the top. Bake at 350° for 45 minutes or until golden brown. Serves 8.

Mrs. Ron Cass (Sherry)

Shrimp and Green Noodle Casserole

4 tablespoons melted butter,
   divided
4 green onions, chopped
3 pounds raw shrimp
1 package (6 ounces) green
   noodles
1 cup mayonnaise
1 cup sour cream

1 can (10¾ ounces) cream of
   mushroom soup
1½ teaspoons prepared
   mustard
3 tablespoons dry vermouth
6 ounces grated Cheddar
   cheese

Sauté onions in 2 tablespoons butter. Cook and peel shrimp. Cook and drain noodles and toss with remaining melted butter. Place noodles in a buttered casserole. Cover with shrimp and green onions. Mix remaining ingredients and pour over onions and shrimp. Adjust seasoning and bake at 350° for 30 to 40 minutes. Serves 6 to 8.

Mrs. Bill Hayes (Ginger)

Shrimp Curry

2 tablespoons butter
1 green bell pepper,
   chopped
1 onion, chopped
1 pound shrimp, cooked,
   peeled and deveined

1 to 2 teaspoons curry powder
1 jar (4.5 ounces) whole
   mushrooms
⅓ cup white wine or sherry
Cooked rice for 4

Sauté bell pepper and onion in butter. Add remaining ingredients and simmer 5 minutes. Serve over rice. Serves 4.

Mrs. Linden Welsch (Phyllis)

Deviled Seafood

¼ cup finely chopped onion
1 cup finely chopped celery
1 teaspoon Worcestershire sauce
½ teaspoon salt
8 ounces shrimp, cooked, shelled and deveined
8 ounces crab meat, flaked
1 to 2 cups herb stuffing mix, crushed
1 cup mayonnaise
Lemon wedges, optional
Tartar sauce, optional

Stir together all ingredients except lemon wedges and tartar sauce, until blended. Spoon into a shallow 1 quart casserole or into 8 oven proof shells. Bake at 350° for 30 minutes or until browned. Serve with lemon wedges or tartar sauce if desired. Serves 6 to 8.

Mrs. Larry Nau (Rose)

Shrimp Jambalaya

3 tablespoons butter
½ cup chopped onion
½ cup chopped green bell pepper
½ cup chopped green onion
½ cup chopped celery
¼ pound diced cooked ham
2 cloves garlic, crushed
1 can (10¾ ounces) chicken broth
3 to 4 medium tomatoes, chopped
¼ cup chopped parsley
½ teaspoon salt
⅛ teaspoon pepper
⅛ teaspoon cayenne pepper
1 bay leaf
1 cup uncooked white rice
1½ pounds shrimp, cooked, peeled and deveined
¼ cup green bell pepper for garnish

Sauté onion, bell pepper, green onion, celery, ham and garlic in butter. Stir in the chicken broth, tomatoes, parsley, salt, peppers, bay leaf and rice and bring to a boil. Simmer 20 minutes until rice is tender. Mix in shrimp and bell pepper and serve when shrimp is hot. Serves 6.

Mrs. Gary McKenzie (Clare)

Tarragon added to melted butter makes a nice sauce for fresh seafood or vegetables.

Shrimp and Linguini

2 tablespoons minced garlic
8 tablespoons olive oil, divided
4 cups tomatoes, peeled, seeded and chopped
3 tablespoons minced parsley
2 teaspoons dried basil
1 teaspoon salt
½ teaspoon pepper
1½ cups half and half cream
2 pounds medium shrimp, shelled and deveined
16 ounces spinach linguini, cooked
Parchment paper or foil
⅛ cup grated Romano cheese

In a skillet, sauté the garlic in 6 tablespoons olive oil for 1 minute. Add tomatoes, parsley, basil, salt and pepper. Simmer for 15 minutes. Add cream and shrimp and continue to simmer for 2 minutes. Drain cooked pasta and toss with 2 tablespoons olive oil, salt and pepper to taste. Cut 10 to 12 pieces of foil 12 inches square. Divide pasta and place a portion in each piece of foil. Divide shrimp mixture and place on top of pasta. Close foil and crimp edges to seal. Place foil packets on a cookie sheet and bake at 400° for 10 to 15 minutes. Serves 12.

S. D. Jackman

Frog Legs in Cream Sauce

8 pairs frog legs
4 tablespoons butter, divided
3 tablespoons finely chopped shallots
3 cups quartered mushrooms
Salt and pepper to taste
½ cup dry white wine
1 cup whipping cream
2 teaspoons flour
1 egg yolk, lightly beaten
Juice of ½ lemon
¼ teaspoon cayenne pepper
3 tablespoons finely chopped chives

Pat the frog legs dry. Cut off and discard the bottom end of each leg. In a large skillet heat 2 tablespoons butter. Add the shallots and cook briefly. Add the frog legs, mushrooms, salt and pepper. Cook 1 minute, stirring constantly. Add wine and cook for 5 minutes. Transfer frog legs to a warm serving platter. Bring the cooking liquid to boil over high heat and cook down to ⅓ cup. Add the cream and cook 1 minute. Blend flour with remaining two tablespoons butter and mix thoroughly. Gradually add to sauce and simmer. Add lemon juice and cayenne pepper. Pour sauce over frog legs and sprinkle with chopped chives. Serves 4.

Mrs. Cecil Smith (Diana)

Shrimp Kabobs

1   bottle (8 ounces) Italian
    dressing
1 to 2 tablespoons picante
    sauce
1 to 2 tablespoons soy sauce
3 to 4 pounds shrimp, peeled
1   can (8 ounces) artichoke
    hearts

1   package cherry tomatoes
1   package (16 ounces) fresh
    mushrooms
4   green bell peppers,
    quartered
4   onions, peeled and
    quartered

Mix Italian dressing, picante sauce and soy sauce in a large bowl. Add shrimp and marinate overnight. Remove shrimp from marinade and skewer with artichoke hearts, tomatoes, mushrooms, bell peppers and onions. Grill for 5 to 10 minutes, or until shrimp is done. Serves 6 to 8.

Mrs. Denman Smith (Sandra)

Fish with Vegetables

1   tablespoon butter
1½ pounds mild fish fillets
1   tomato, peeled and
    chopped
1   onion, chopped

¼   cup chopped green bell
    pepper
8   mushrooms, sliced
1   tablespoon lemon juice
Salt and pepper to taste

Grease a 9x14 inch casserole with butter. Place fish flat in casserole. Top with a mixture of tomato, onion, bell pepper and mushrooms. Sprinkle with lemon juice and seasonings. Cover with foil and bake at 350° for 30 to 45 minutes. Serves 4 to 6.

Mrs. Terry Arndt (Barbara)

Stuffed Crab a la Irma

1   bunch green onions,
    minced
1   green bell pepper, minced
3   ribs celery, chopped
6   cloves garlic, minced
2   tablespoons butter

Salt and pepper
3   eggs
1   cup bread crumbs
3   pounds fresh crab meat
2   tablespoons minced
    parsley

Sauté vegetables and garlic in butter. Season with salt and pepper to taste. Add eggs and mix together. Sprinkle in bread crumbs which have been moistened with a little water and add crab meat last. Place in 9x13 inch baking dish and dot with butter and bake at 375° for 20 to 25 minutes. Serves 8 to 10. *My mother-in-law serves this delicious dish to entice her children and grandchildren to return to Galveston Island during the summer months for vacation.*

Mrs. Adrian Piperi (Carole)

Danish Fish Fillets

6 fish fillets
Milk
1 can (10¾ ounces) chicken
   broth
Juice of ½ lemon

3 tablespoons butter
2 tablespoons flour
Dash of white pepper
⅓ cup sour cream
1½ teaspoons dill weed

Soak fish in milk for 2 hours. Remove fish and place in a large glass baking dish; discard milk. Cover with broth and lemon juice. Bake covered at 350° for 15 minutes. Transfer fish to platter. Measure out 1 cup of liquid fish was cooked in. Melt butter in a saucepan and add flour and pepper and cook several minutes. Do not brown. Remove from heat and add sour cream and dill. Return fish to baking dish and spoon sauce over fish. Bake uncovered 10 to 12 minutes until sauce is bubbly around edges. Serves 6.

Mrs. Sid Mann (Kathi)

Have all ingredients at room temperature unless otherwise stated in recipe.

Savory Baked Flounder Fillets

2 pounds flounder fillets
2 teaspoons lemon juice
Dash pepper
6 slices bacon

1 medium onion, thinly
   sliced
½ cup soft bread crumbs
2 tablespoons chopped
   parsley

Preheat oven to 350°. Place fillets in a single layer in a greased baking dish. Sprinkle with lemon juice and pepper. Fry bacon until crisp, remove from drippings and crumble. Cook onion rings in bacon drippings until tender and arrange evenly over fillets. Combine bacon, bread crumbs and parsley. Sprinkle mixture over fillets and onion. Bake at 350° for 25 to 30 minutes. Serves 4 to 6.

Mrs. Chris John (Anne)

Poached Flounder Rolls in Mushroom Sauce

1 can (4.5 ounces) sliced mushrooms	2 teaspoons lemon juice
Water	1 teaspoon browning sauce
¼ cup dry white wine	Salt and pepper to taste
¼ teaspoon fennel	½ pound cooked shrimp
1 pound flounder fillets	1 tablespoon cornstarch
2 tablespoons butter	½ cup whipping cream
	¼ teaspoon salt

Drain liquid from mushrooms; add water to make 1 cup and pour into large saucepan. Add wine and fennel. Cover, bring to a boil and simmer. Slice fillets in half lengthwise. Pat dry. Combine butter, lemon juice and browning sauce. Brush 1 side of fish with the mixture. Sprinkle with salt and pepper. Roll each piece of fish, butter side in, around shrimp. Secure with wooden picks. Place fish rolls in the wine mixture in the saucepan. Cover and cook over low heat 4 minutes. Remove fish from pan to a warm plate. Combine cornstarch, cream and salt. Add to the wine mixture and cook until sauce is thickened. Heat the mushrooms and remaining shrimp in the sauce and pour over fish rolls. Serves 4. *This is easy, elegant and absolutely delicious.*

Mrs. Lee Richard Dickerson (Carol)

Fillet of Turbot in Tarragon Butter

6 tablespoons butter, divided	1 to 1½ pounds turbot fillets
¼ pound fresh mushrooms, sliced	¼ cup dry vermouth
1 small onion, minced	2 tablespoons tarragon
	Salt and pepper

Preheat oven to 350°. Line a 9x13 inch baking dish with foil. Melt 2 tablespoons butter in medium skillet over medium high heat. Add mushrooms and onion and sauté until softened, about 5 minutes. Arrange fillets in dish. Pour vermouth over fish. Dot each piece generously with butter and sprinkle with tarragon, salt and pepper. Spoon mushroom mixture evenly over top. Cover with foil and bake until fish flakes easily, about 40 minutes. Serves 3 to 4.

Mrs. Sid Mann (Kathi)

Trout Amandine

2 pounds Gulf trout fillets	½ cup sliced almonds
¼ cup flour	2 tablespoons lemon juice
1 teaspoon seasoned salt	4 to 5 drops hot pepper sauce
1 teaspoon paprika	1 tablespoon chopped
¼ cup melted butter, divided	parsley

Cut fillets into 6 portions. Combine flour, seasoned salt and paprika and sprinkle over fillets. Roll fillets and place in a single layer, skin down, in a well-greased baking dish. Drizzle 2 tablespoons melted butter over portions. Broil about 4 inches from source of heat for 10 to 15 minutes, or until fish flakes easily when tested with a fork. While fish is broiling, sauté almonds in remaining butter until golden brown, stirring constantly. Remove from heat and mix in lemon juice, hot pepper sauce and parsley. Pour over fillets and serve at once. Serves 4 to 6.

Mrs. O. B. Carlson (Marie)

Salmon Croquettes

Croquettes:

1 can (15½ ounces) salmon, drained, boned and flaked	Dash pepper
1 to 1½ cups mashed potatoes	1 teaspoon dried parsley flakes
1 egg	¼ cup seasoned bread crumbs
1 tablespoon grated onion	1 to 2 tablespoons flour, optional
Juice of ½ lemon	

Mix all ingredients well. If mixture is too mushy, add additional flour, 1 tablespoon at a time. Shape into 6 croquettes. If mixture seems hard to handle, refrigrate for 1 hour to firm up.

Coating:

1 cup flour	1 tablespoon water
Dash of garlic powder	1 cup seasoned bread crumbs
Dash of pepper	
1 egg	Oil

Roll croquettes in flour which has been seasoned with garlic powder and pepper, then in egg and water mixture. Coat with breadcrumbs. Refrigerate croquettes for about 30 minutes; this keeps the coating on. Fry croquettes in ¼ inch oil over medium-high heat. Brown well on both sides. Drain. Serves 6.

Mrs. Bob McGoldrick (Fran)

Shrimp Zucchini Casserole

2   medium tomatoes, sliced
    ⅛ inch thick
3   small zucchini, sliced
1   green onion, chopped,
    tops included
1   pound shrimp, cooked,
    peeled and deveined
4   ounces Mozzarella cheese,
    grated

½   teaspoon salt
¼   teaspoon pepper
½   teaspoon thyme
¼   cup seasoned bread
    crumbs
⅛   cup white wine

Grease a 2 quart casserole and layer with half the tomatoes, zucchini, onions, shrimp and cheese. Repeat layers, except for cheese, and sprinkle with salt, pepper and thyme. Top with remaining cheese, bread crumbs and wine. Cover with foil and bake at 375° for 40 minutes. Uncover and broil briefly to brown. Serves 4.

Mrs. John Wilbur (Nancy)

Tuna Noodle Crisp

4   ounces uncooked noodles
¼   cup butter
⅓   cup chopped onion
2   tablespoons chopped
    green bell pepper
1   can (10½ ounces) Cheddar
    cheese soup
½   cup milk

1   tablespoon chopped
    pimiento
1   teaspoon salt
⅛   teaspoon pepper
1   can (6½ ounces) tuna,
    drained
½   cup bread crumbs

Cook noodles according to package directions. Melt butter in large skillet; add onion and green pepper and cook until tender. Stir in soup, milk, pimiento, salt and pepper and bring to a boil. Add cooked noodles and tuna. Pour mixture into a 2 quart casserole dish. Sprinkle top with bread crumbs and bake at 350° for 30 minutes or until bubbly. Serves 4 to 6.

Mrs. Tommy Gardner (Peggy)

Although dry pasta is more common and stores longer, fresh pasta is becoming more available and is tastier.

Seafood Lasagna

1   package (8 ounces)
    lasagna noodles
1   cup chopped green onions
2   tablespoons butter
8   ounces cream cheese
1½ cups cottage cheese
1   egg, beaten
2   tablespoons basil
Salt and pepper to taste
2   cans (10¾ ounces each)
    cream of mushroom soup

⅓   cup milk
⅓   cup dry white wine
1   pound shrimp, cooked,
    peeled and deveined
1   pound crab meat
¼   cup grated Parmesan
    cheese
½   cup grated Cheddar
    cheese
½   cup grated Mozzarella
    cheese

Cook noodles according to package directions; drain. Sauté onions in butter. Combine cream cheese, cottage cheese, egg and basil. Add onions; salt and pepper to taste. Line lasagna pan with a layer of noodles. Layer with one-half of the cottage cheese mixture. Over cottage cheese layer, spread 1 can of cream of mushroom soup. Combine milk, wine, shrimp and crab meat. Spread one-half of seafood mixture over soup layer. Repeat layers. Sprinkle top with Parmesan cheese and bake at 350° for 45 minutes. Sprinkle top with remaining cheeses and bake an additional 2 to 3 minutes or until cheese is melted and browned slightly. Let stand 15 minutes before serving. Serves 8 to 10.

Mrs. Chris Wegmann (Eva)

Stuffed Texas Redfish

1   medium onion, chopped
2   cups chopped celery
1   cup butter, divided
2   teaspoons parsley
1   teaspoon dill weed
1 to 2 teaspoons basil
½   cup white wine
½   cup chicken broth

3   cups herb stuffing mix
1   cup cooked rice
1   can (12 ounces) crab meat
1   redfish, 3 to 5 pounds
1 to 2 limes
Salt and pepper
Paprika

Sauté onion and celery in ½ cup butter until crisp tender. Add remaining butter, parsley, dill weed, basil, wine and chicken broth, simmering for 5 minutes. In a large bowl toss stuffing mix, rice and crab; add to broth mixture. This stuffing mix may be made a day ahead to allow the flavors to blend. Using a pan large enough to hold the fish, spoon half the dressing mixture into pan and top with fish. Fill cavity of the fish with remaining stuffing. Generously squeeze lime juice over fish and sprinkle with salt, pepper and paprika. Bake at 350° for approximately 1 hour. Serves 8 to 10.

Mrs. Denman Smith (Sandra)

Calabrian Style Pasta with Broccoli

1   bunch broccoli, broken
    into pieces
2   teaspoons olive oil
2   cloves garlic, minced
2   pounds ripe tomatoes,
    coarsely chopped
3   tablespoons raisins

2 to 3 tablespoons sunflower
    seeds
Salt and pepper
¼   teaspoon oregano
¼   teaspoon sweet basil
1   pound tortellini pasta
3   tablespoons minced
    parsley for garnish

Steam broccoli until it is a tender, bright green, about 7 minutes.
Rinse under cold water and set aside. Heat oil in a heavy saucepan
and sauté the garlic until it is golden brown. Add tomatoes and
simmer 15 minutes, uncovered. Add raisins and sunflower seeds and
simmer 5 minutes. Season with salt, pepper, oregano and sweet basil.
While sauce is simmering, heat the water for pasta and cook about 6
to 8 minutes at full boil. Spoon cooked pasta into a large, warmed
serving dish. Spoon on the sauce, add broccoli and toss. Garnish with
parsley. Serves 6 to 8.

Mrs. Don Bradford (Melinda)

Fettucine Alla Carbonara

¼   pound thick sliced bacon
¾   pound fettucine
1   tablespoon olive oil
6   cloves garlic, minced
¼   cup dry white wine
2   eggs, room temperature

½   cup heavy cream, room
    temperature
½   cup grated Parmesan
    cheese
½   teaspoon black pepper
½   teaspoon red pepper
¼   cup chopped parsley

Slice bacon into ¼ to ½ inch pieces and blanch in boiling water for 2
minutes. Drain well. Cook fettucine according to package directions.
Heat olive oil and and sauté bacon until it starts to brown. Add the
garlic and sauté for 1 to 2 minutes. Add the wine and simmer until
wine evaporates. Mix eggs, cream and cheese in a small bowl. Drain
cooked pasta well and add to skillet with bacon mixture. Toss and
add the egg mixture; toss again, adding the peppers and parsley.
Serve immediately. Serves 4. *You can easily change this recipe by
sautéing any fresh vegetables you have on hand, such as carrots, peas,
or cauliflower. This makes a good light supper with a tossed salad.*

Mrs. Jim Rado (Vicki)

Pasta Ricotta

⅔ cup ricotta or cottage cheese
½ cup grated Parmesan cheese

Dash of nutmeg
1 package (8 ounces) pasta
2 tablespoons butter
Salt and pepper to taste

Mash cheeses together and add seasoning. Cook pasta in salted, boiling water and place into a hot buttered casserole. Stir in cheese mixture add butter and bake at 350° for 5 to 7 minutes. Serves 4. *This pasta goes great with anything or eat it alone with a glass of good red wine.*

Mrs. Joe Bowles (Mary)

Fettuccine Supreme

1 package (8 ounces) fettuccine
¼ cup whipping cream
½ cup butter, melted
½ teaspoon dried basil

¼ cup minced fresh parsley
Dash of pepper
1 cup freshly grated Parmesan cheese

Cook fettuccine according to package directions; drain well. Add whipping cream, butter, basil, parsley and pepper. Toss until noodles are well-coated. Add Parmesan cheese and toss gently. Serve immediately. Serves 6.

Mrs. Marcus Bone (Beverly)

Pasta with Texas Pecan Sauce

1 pound fettucine or linguine
1 clove garlic, minced
2 tablespoons olive oil
½ cup butter, melted

1½ to 2 cups Texas pecans
¼ cup chopped parsley or spinach
Salt and white pepper to taste

Cook pasta al dente. While pasta is cooking, sauté garlic in olive oil and mix with melted butter. Finely chop pecans and parsley or spinach in food processor. Drain cooked pasta and immediately toss with butter and garlic mixture. Add pecans and parsley or spinach and season to taste with salt and white pepper. Serves 4 to 6.

Mrs. Denman Smith (Sandra)

The Daniel H. Caswell House in Austin is a tribute both to the gracious lifestyle of yesteryear and to those who seek to preserve the rich heritage of the past. Perhaps it was wanderlust which encouraged Mr. Caswell to leave a thriving business behind in Tennessee and transplant his family to the wide open spaces of Texas. In 1899 he commissioned the construction of his stately family home on the crest of a hill overlooking the new Capitol building to the east and the distant hills to the west. Since then, the colorful history of the residence has included division into apartments during the '30's and at least one near-brush with demolition crews. In 1979 the women of Austin Junior Forum committed themselves to the permanent preservation of the Caswell House. In fact, with its purchase, the idea for LONE STAR LEGACY was born. In order to support the renovation and restoration of this historical home, a continuous source of revenue was necessary. The cookbook was created for this purpose. In 1983 the Caswell House doors were opened once again. From the attic, which houses our cookbook offices, to the basement, where a Senior Nutrition program is in operation, the Caswell House is vibrantly, majestically alive, establishing a new tradition as a center for community service.

Breads pictured: Twisted French Rolls, Coffee Cake with Almonds, Sweet Rolls and Breads and Popovers.

Breads and Sweet Breads

Sour Dough Bread Starter

¼ cup milk
½ cup water
2 teaspoons vegetable oil
1 package yeast

¼ cup warm water
2 teaspoons sugar
1½ teaspoons salt
1½ cups flour

Combine milk, water and oil; bring to a boil. Cool to lukewarm. Dissolve yeast in water. Add with sugar and salt to cooled milk mixture. Cover. Let stand 12 to 18 hours to sour. Add flour and stir well. Yields 2½ cups.

Mrs. Ernest Butler (Sarah)

Sour Dough French Bread

½ cup milk
1 cup water
1½ tablespoons oil
1 package yeast
¼ cup warm water

1½ tablespoons sugar
2½ teaspoons salt
4¾ cups flour
2 tablespoons starter dough

Combine milk, water and oil and bring to a boil. Cool to lukewarm. Dissolve yeast in water and add with sugar and salt to cooled milk mixture. Place flour in a large bowl; pour milk into well made in center of flour; add starter and blend well. *Do not knead.* Place in a greased bowl; cover and let rise until double. Turn onto lightly floured board. Divide into half. Roll each into a 15x10 inch rectangle. Roll the oblong up tightly towards you. Taper ends by rolling. With scissors make cuts ¼ inch deep diagonally along loaf 2 inches apart. Let rise uncovered until double. Bake at 425° for 15 minutes. Reduce heat to 350° and bake 15 to 20 minutes. Brush top with ¼ teaspoon salt dissolved in ½ cup water and bake another 5 minutes. Cool in a drafty place for crisp crust. Yields 1 loaf.

Mrs. Ernest Butler (Sarah)

Always dissolve yeast by sprinkling on top of warm water. Ideal temperature of liquid for dissolving yeast is 105° to 115°. If water is too cool, action of yeast will be slowed, but will work eventually. If water is too hot, action of yeast will be killed completely.

Very Easy White Bread

2   packages yeast
¼   cup warm water
2   cups warm milk
4   tablespoons sugar

2   teaspoons salt
1   tablespoon shortening
6   cups flour

Soften yeast in warm water. Combine warm milk, sugar, salt and shortening. Add yeast and mix well. Add 2 cups of flour at a time. Knead about 5 minutes, adding more flour until the dough does not stick to your fingers. Put dough into 2 greased loaf pans. Let rise until double in size, about 1 hour. Bake at 350° for 40 to 45 minutes. Yields 2 loaves.

Mrs. Hal Williamson (Gayle)

Golden Brown Yeast Bread – "Challah"

2   packages dry yeast
2   cups warm water
½   cup sugar
4   teaspoons salt
1¼ cups oil

3   eggs, beaten
8 to 9 cups sifted flour,
     divided
1   egg yolk
1   teaspoon water

In a large bowl combine yeast, water and sugar and stir well. Set aside for a few minutes. Add salt, oil, eggs and half the flour; stir well. Add the remaining flour 1 cup at a time, stirring well between each addition, until dough is stiff. Turn out onto a lightly floured board and knead until satiny-smooth. Place dough into a greased bowl, cover with a clean cloth, and let rise in a warm place until doubled in bulk over an hour. When dough has doubled in bulk, punch down and turn out onto lightly floured board. Cut into 4 equal portions. Shape each portion into a 4x10 inch oblong length, then cut the oblong into thirds lengthwise up to 1 inch from the top end. Braid strips and tuck ends underneath loaf. Place loaves on a lightly greased cookie sheet, cover with a clean cloth, and let rise for an hour. Combine egg yolk and 1 teaspoon water, and brush loaves with "egg wash". Bake at 350° for approximately 30 minutes. Yields 4 loaves. *This recipe was handed down to me by my mother. It can be sprinkled with poppy seeds if desired.*

Mrs. Louis Henna, Jr. (Marci)

Best Rye Bread

2 packages yeast
1½ cups warm water
¼ cup molasses
⅓ cup sugar
1 tablespoon salt
2 tablespoons shortening

3 to 4 tablespoons grated
   orange peel
2½ cups rye flour
2¼ to 2¾ cups flour
Cornmeal

In a mixing bowl dissolve yeast in warm water; stir in molasses, sugar, salt, shortening and orange peel. Mix in rye flour with a spoon until smooth. Stir in flour, mixing with hands until thoroughly blended. Turn out onto a lightly floured board. Cover and let rest 10 to 15 minutes. Knead until smooth. Place in a greased bowl; turn greased side up. Cover and let rise in a warm place until double, about 1 hour. Punch dough down, round up, cover and let rise again until double, about 40 minutes. Punch down; divide dough in half; shape into two round loaves. Grease a baking sheet and sprinkle with cornmeal. Place loaves on opposite corners of baking sheet. Cover and let rise 1 hour. Bake at 375° for 30 to 35 minutes. Yields 2 loaves.

Mrs. Marcus Bone (Beverly)

Peppery Cheese Bread

1 package yeast
¼ cup hottest tap water
2⅓ cups flour, divided
2 tablespoons sugar
1 teaspoon salt
¼ teaspoon baking soda
1 cup sour cream

1 egg
1 cup grated Cheddar
   cheese
⅛ teaspoon pepper
2 jalapeños, minced,
   optional

Grease two 1 pound coffee cans. In a large mixing bowl dissolve yeast in hot water. Add 1⅓ cups of flour, sugar, salt, soda, sour cream and egg. Blend ½ minute on low speed, scraping bowl constantly. Beat 2 minutes on high speed scraping bowl occasionally. Stir in remaining flour, the cheese, pepper and jalapeños. Divide batter between cans. Let rise in a warm place 50 minutes. Batter will rise slightly but will not double. Bake at 350° for 40 minutes or until golden brown. Immediately remove from cans. Cool slightly before slicing. Yields 2 loaves.

Mrs. J. Edward Reed (Marian)

Peach Flip

2 packages dry yeast
½ cup warm water
½ cup sugar
½ cup margarine

½ cup hot, scalded milk
2 teaspoons salt
3 unbeaten eggs
5 to 5½ cups flour

Soften yeast in warm water. Combine in mixing bowl sugar, margarine, scalded milk and salt. Stir to melt butter. Cool to lukewarm. Blend in eggs and softened yeast. Gradually add flour to form stiff dough. Knead on floured board until smooth and satiny, 3 to 5 minutes. Place in greased bowl; cover. Let rise in warm place until light and doubled in size, 1 to 1½ hours.

Filling:
⅔ cup sugar
2 teaspoons cinnamon
1 cup chopped walnuts

2 tablespoons soft butter
¼ cup peach or apricot preserves

Combine sugar, cinnamon, and walnuts. Set aside. Roll out ½ of dough on floured board to a 20x10 inch rectangle. Spread with butter and preserves. Sprinkle with ½ the cinnamon, sugar mixture. Roll up starting with the 20 inch side. Seal edge and ends. Place seam side down on greased cookie sheet, curving ends to make "U" shape. With scissors, make a cut down the center, ⅓ of the way through roll, to within 2 inches of ends. Repeat with remaining dough. Let rise in warm place about 30 minutes until light. Spoon ¼ cup preserves down center of each. Bake at 350° for 20 to 25 minutes until golden brown. Yields 2 loaves.

Frosting:
1 cup powdered sugar
1 teaspoon vanilla

2 to 3 teaspoons milk

Frost with powdered sugar, vanilla and milk mixture.

Donna Haverkamp

Easter Bread

2 loaves frozen yeast bread
6 raw eggs, dyed

Defrost bread but do not allow to rise. On a floured work surface roll and stretch each loaf into a 36 inch rope *or as close as you can get to 36 inches.* Now twist the two ropes together into one long rope. Form into a ring on a greased cookie sheet and seal ends together. Evenly space eggs into dough; cover and let rise for 30 to 45 minutes in a warm place. Bake at 375° for 20 to 25 minutes or until browned. Yields 1 loaf. *This is a very pretty treat for Easter morning and the eggs do cook in the oven!*
Mrs. Denman Smith (Sandra)

Cinnamon Raisin Bread

5½ to 6 cups flour, divided
2   packages dry yeast
1   cup milk
¾   cup water
¼   cup sugar
¼   cup oil

2   teaspoons salt
1   egg
1   cup raisins
1   cup sugar
1   tablespoon cinnamon
2   tablespoons butter, melted

Combine 2 cups of flour with yeast. Heat milk, water, ¼ cup sugar, oil and salt over low heat until warm (120° to 130°). Add warm liquids to flour-yeast mixture and beat until smooth with an electric mixer. Blend in egg. Stir in raisins. Add more flour to make a moderately soft dough. Turn out on a lightly floured surface and knead until smooth and shiny, about 5 to 10 minutes. Cover dough with bowl and let rest 20 minutes. Combine 1 cup sugar with cinnamon. Divide dough in half. Roll each portion into a 7x14 inch rectangle. Brush with melted butter and sprinkle with the sugar-cinnamon mixture. Beginning at narrow side, roll dough tightly into loaves. Fold ends under and seal. Place in two greased 9x5 inch loaf pans and brush tops with melted butter. Let rise in a warm place until doubled, about 45 minutes. Bake in a 375° oven for 35 to 40 minutes. Remove from pans immediately and cool on rack. Yields 2 loaves.

Mrs. Jim Schultz (Mary Kay)

Oatmeal Cheese Bread

2   packages dry yeast
1   cup warm water
2   cups quick oats
1   cup scalded milk
1   cup hot water
4   cups grated Cheddar
    cheese

3   tablespoons sugar
1   tablespoon salt
2   teaspoons dill weed,
    optional
6 to 6½ cups flour

Soften yeast in warm water. In a large bowl combine oatmeal, milk and hot water and set aside to cool. Add yeast, cheese, sugar, salt and dill, if desired. Slowly stir in flour one cup at a time until almost all flour is used and the dough is easy to handle. On a floured surface turn dough out and knead for 3 to 5 minutes. Place in a greased bowl; cover and let rise in a warm place one hour or until doubled. Punch down, and divide into 2 portions. Place in 2 greased 9x5 inch loaf pans. Cover and allow to rise in a warm place for 30 minutes. Bake at 350° for 45 to 50 minutes or until brown. Remove from pans and cool on a wire rack. Yields 2 loaves.

Mrs. Marcus Bone (Beverly)

Polenta

1 cup yellow cornmeal,
  divided
2 tablespoons sugar
2 teaspoons salt
8 slices bacon, cooked,
  crumbled and drippings
  reserved
1 cup boiling water

2 packages dry yeast
1¼ cups warm water
2 tablespoons chopped
  parsley
2 tablespoons chopped
  chives
4 cups flour

Combine ¾ cup cornmeal, sugar, salt and 2 tablespoons bacon drippings. Pour boiling water over cornmeal mixture. In another large bowl sprinkle yeast over warm water and stir to dissolve. Let rest a few minutes, then add to cornmeal mixture. Stir in crumbled bacon, parsley and chives. Slowly add flour one cup at a time until well blended and smooth. Place bowl in a warm place, cover and allow to rise one hour or until doubled. Punch dough down and beat with a wooden spoon. Divide dough between two quart casseroles which have been greased and sprinkled with some of the reserved cornmeal. Let rise an additional 30 minutes. Sprinkle top with more of the cornmeal. Bake at 350° for 55 to 60 minutes or until golden brown. Remove from casseroles and cool on a wire rack. Yields 2 rounds.

Mrs. Denman Smith (Sandra)

Butter Crescent Rolls

1 package yeast
1 cup warm water
1 cup melted butter, divided
½ cup sugar

3 eggs, beaten
¾ teaspoon salt
4½ cups flour

Dissolve yeast in warm water in a large mixing bowl. Add ½ cup melted butter, sugar, eggs and salt; stir well. Gradually add flour, mixing well. Cover and let rise 4 hours in a warm, 85°, draft-free place. Divide dough into 2 equal parts. Knead each part 4 or 5 times on lightly floured board. Roll into 12 inch circles and brush with remaining melted butter. Cut each circle into 12 wedges. Roll up each wedge, beginning at wide end. Place on lightly greased cookie sheets and let rise 1 hour in a warm, draft-free place. Bake at 400° for 10 minutes or until light brown. Yields 24 rolls. *These freeze beautifully. After thawing, place in preheated 350° oven 2 to 3 minutes. This will crisp the rolls as though they were freshly baked.*

Mrs. Ron Bruney (Carol)

Buttermilk Rolls

1½ packages yeast	½ teaspoon baking powder
¼ cup warm water	½ teaspoon baking soda
1 cup buttermilk	3 cups flour
3 tablespoons sugar	1 teaspoon salt, optional
3 tablespoons oil	Melted butter

Dissolve yeast in warm water. In large mixing bowl mix buttermilk, sugar, oil, baking powder and baking soda. Add yeast after it is dissolved. Add enough flour to make a stiff dough. Let rise until double in size. Punch down and then shape as desired. Place in greased muffin tins and let rise until doubled. Bake at 400° for 8 to 10 minutes. Yields 18 rolls. *After baking, brush the tops with melted butter.*

Linda Kelley

Old South Refrigerator Rolls

1 cup mashed potatoes	1 yeast cake
1 cup potato water	1 cup lukewarm water
1 cup sugar	1 tablespoon salt
1 cup shortening	4 cups flour, sifted
2 eggs	

Combine mashed potatoes, potato water, sugar and shortening. Beat in eggs 1 at a time and cream well. Dissolve yeast cake in 1 cup lukewarm water and add to potato mixture. Add salt to the first sifter of flour. Add enough flour to the potato mixture to make a stiff handling dough. Put into a large bowl, cover tightly, and place in refrigerator. Pinch off dough as needed. Roll, cut and let rise. Bake at 450° for 10 to 12 minutes. Yields 16 rolls.

Barbara Beall Stanley

Heavenly Biscuits

5 cups flour	1 cup shortening
¼ cup sugar	2 cups buttermilk
1 teaspoon baking soda	1 package yeast
3 teaspoons baking powder	¼ cup very warm water
¾ teaspoon salt	

Sift together flour, sugar, soda, baking powder and salt. Cut in shortening and add buttermilk. Mix yeast with water and add to mixture. Roll out dough and cut with biscuit cutter; place in greased pan. Let rise 30 minutes. Bake at 400° for 15 minutes. Yields 48.

Mrs. Rick Denbow (Susan)

Quick Pancakes

⅔ cup warm water
2   packages yeast
2   cups biscuit mix

1   egg
1   cup milk

Make the batter by mixing all ingredients together and chill in the refrigerator. When ready to serve, pour out onto a greased griddle or skillet. Brown lightly on one side until the batter is bubbly. Turn to brown on the other side. Serves 4. *This batter can be frozen. This is a great recipe to use when feeding a crowd because the portions can easily be doubled or tripled.*

Mrs. James Albrecht (Donne)

Wondrous Waffles

2   eggs, separated
4 to 6 tablespoons oil
2   tablespoons honey
2   cups milk

1   cup white flour
1   cup whole wheat flour
2   teaspoons baking powder
¼   teaspoon salt

Beat egg whites until stiff and set aside. In a large mixing bowl, beat egg yolks, then mix in oil, honey and milk. Add dry ingredients and mix until just moistened. Fold in beaten egg whites. Preheat waffle iron to medium-high setting. Pour approximately one cup batter onto waffle iron. Cook for 6 to 7 minutes. Yields 6 to 7 batches of waffles. *Buttermilk or plain yogurt may be substituted for one of the cups of milk for a tasty variation.*

Mrs. Dan S. Steakley (Susan)

Waffles

1¾ cups flour
1   tablespoon baking powder
½   teaspoon salt
2   egg yolks, beaten

1¼ cups milk
½   cup oil
2   egg whites, stiffly beaten

Sift flour, baking powder and salt together. Mix egg yolks, milk and oil; add to dry ingredients. Fold in egg whites gently. Heat waffle iron and pour in 1½ cups of batter per waffle. Yields 8 waffles.

Mrs. John Perkins (Sandy)

Sugar, honey or cornmeal increases action of yeast. Salt retards action, so mix it in after some flour has been added to yeast mixture.

French Toast

14 slices buttered bread	3 tablespoons cinnamon
7 eggs	sugar or honey
½ cup milk	½ teaspoon nutmeg
	½ teaspoon vanilla extract

Arrange buttered bread slices in a rimmed baking pan. In a medium bowl, beat together eggs, milk, cinnamon sugar, nutmeg and vanilla. Pour half of the egg mixture over bread, spreading evenly. Bake at 400 to 425° for 10 minutes. Turn and bake about 10 minutes more or until lightly browned. Let cool. Yields 14. *Slices can be frozen on the pan before they are baked. When firm, seal slices in airtight wrap and return to freezer. To serve place frozen slices on lightly greased baking sheet and bake at 500° for 7 minutes. Turn and bake 8 minutes more until browned.*

Mrs. Larry Lerche (Gail)

Baby German Pancake

3 eggs, beaten	½ cup milk
½ cup flour	2 tablespoons butter, melted
¼ teaspoon salt	

Slowly add flour to beaten eggs, beating constantly. Stir in remaining ingredients. Grease a 10 inch ovenproof skillet. Pour batter into cold pan. Bake at 450° for 18 minutes, then lower temperature to 350° and bake 10 minutes longer. Serves 6 to 8. *This makes an unusual breakfast treat served with melted butter, powdered sugar and lemon wedges.*

Mrs. Drue Denton (Jan)

Swedish Aggkaka

2 tablespoons margarine	1 cup flour
3 eggs	2 tablespoons sugar
2 cups milk	1 teaspoon salt

Put margarine into a 9x9 inch baking pan and melt in a 425° oven. Beat eggs and add remaining ingredients. Pour batter into the pan when the margarine is hot. Bake for 20 to 25 minutes, or until the aggkaka has risen and is lightly browned. Serves 8 to 10. *Aggkaka 'falls' when it is removed from the oven and cools, so pull everyone into the kitchen to see it in all its glory - risen and waiting. Serve with syrup, jam or berries. Aggkaka is Swedish for 'egg cake'.*

David Farris

Applesauce Doughnuts

3⅓ cups flour, divided
1 cup applesauce
¾ cup sugar
2 tablespoons shortening
2 eggs

3 teaspoons baking powder
¾ teaspoon ground nutmeg
½ teaspoon salt
¼ teaspoon ground cloves
Oil

Beat 1⅓ cups of the flour and the remaining ingredients except oil in a large mixing bowl on low speed. Scrape bowl constantly until mixture is blended. Beat on medium speed for 2 minutes. Stir in the remaining flour. Cover and refrigerate for at least 1 hour. Heat 2 to 3 inches of oil to 375° in deep fat fryer or a 3 quart saucepan. Turn half of the dough onto well floured cloth covered board. Roll dough gently to ⅜ inch thick. Cut the dough with a floured doughnut cutter and then repeat with the remaining dough. Slide doughnuts into hot oil with a wide spatula. Turn the doughnuts as they rise to the surface. Fry until golden brown, 1 to 1½ minutes per side. Remove carefully without pricking the surfaces. Drain. Serve plain or sugared. Yields 18.

Mrs. J. Edward Reed (Marian)

Donut Balls

3 cups pancake mix
1½ teaspoons cinnamon
⅓ cup sugar
½ teaspoon nutmeg

2 eggs, beaten
2 tablespoons oil
¾ cup milk
Powdered sugar

Combine pancake mix, cinnamon, sugar and nutmeg. Add eggs, oil and milk, stirring only until blended. If dough is too stiff, add 1 more teaspoon of milk. Drop batter into deep 325° oil and fry for 2 to 2½ minutes or until brown. Drain on paper towels and dust with powdered sugar. Yields 24.

Mrs. Leo Mueller (Nancy)

Popovers

3 eggs
1 cup milk

1 cup flour
½ teaspoon salt

Grease and lightly flour muffin tins. Place in the coldest part of refrigerator while preparing batter. Beat eggs in a bowl and add milk, flour and salt. Mix well with a wire whip or spoon, disregarding lumps. Fill cold muffin tins ⅔ full. Put in cold oven and turn on heat to 450° and bake for 35 minutes without opening oven. Yields 6.

Mrs. Bob Edgecomb (Mary)

Sour Cream Corn Muffins

1 cup yellow cornmeal	½ teaspoon baking soda
1 cup flour	1 cup sour cream
¼ cup sugar	2 eggs, slightly beaten
2 teaspoons baking powder	¼ cup butter, melted
1½ teaspoons salt	

Generously butter 12 muffin tins. Mix dry ingredients in a medium bowl. Stir sour cream, eggs and melted butter together in a small bowl to blend. Add to dry ingredients and stir just until evenly moistened; do not overmix. Turn batter into prepared muffin tins. Bake at 425° for 25 to 30 minutes. Cool in pans for 5 minutes before removing. Yields 12.

Mrs. Don Bradford (Melinda)

Good Texas Cornbread

1 cup yellow cornmeal	1 cup buttermilk
½ cup flour	½ cup milk
1 teaspoon salt	1 egg
1 tablespoon baking powder	¼ cup margarine, melted
½ teaspoon baking soda	

Mix together cornmeal, flour, salt, baking powder and baking soda. Stir in remaining ingredients. Pour into greased muffin tins and bake at 425° for 20 to 25 minutes. Yields 12 muffins.

Mrs. Bob Edgecomb (Mary)

Jambalaya Cornbread Muffins

3 tablespoons butter	1 teaspoon salt
½ cup finely chopped green bell pepper	2 eggs
	2 cups buttermilk
½ cup finely chopped green onions	1 cup finely chopped, cooked ham
1 cup yellow cornmeal	1 cup finely crumbled, cooked bulk sausage
1¼ cups flour	
2 teaspoons baking soda	

Melt butter in a skillet and sauté bell pepper and onion until soft and clear but not brown. Remove from heat. In a large bowl sift together dry ingredients. In a smaller bowl beat eggs and stir in buttermilk. Add the egg mixture to the flour mixture all at once, stirring only until mixed. Carefully fold in ham, sausage, bell pepper and onion. Spoon into well greased muffin tins, filling ⅔ full. Bake at 400° for 30 minutes or until nicely browned. Serve with hot butter. Yields 12.

Mrs. Charles Smith (Jeannie)

Beer Puppies

4   cups stone ground
    cornmeal
2   cups flour
1   tablespoon baking powder
1¼ teaspoons salt
2 to 2½ cups beer

1   medium onion, minced
1   egg
¼   cup chopped parsley
1½ teaspoons pepper
3   quarts peanut oil

Sift cornmeal, flour, baking powder and salt into bowl. Add beer, onion, egg, parsley and pepper. Stir quickly until moist; do not over stir. If batter seems too thick, add ½ cup beer. Preheat oven to 250°. Heat oil in an electric skillet to 365°. Drop batter by rounded teaspoons into hot oil and cook until brown, about 2 minutes. Drain and keep warm in oven. Serve hot. Yields 6 dozen.

Mrs. Marcus Bone (Beverly)

Walnut Wheat Muffins

1½ cups whole wheat flour
2¼ teaspoons baking powder
1   teaspoon salt
3   tablespoons wheat germ
1   egg, lightly beaten

1   cup milk
1   tablespoon honey
1   cup chopped walnuts,
    lightly toasted

Sift together flour, baking powder and salt. Stir in wheat germ. In a small bowl beat together the egg, milk and honey. Add liquid to the flour mixture along with walnuts. Stir the mixture until it is just moist. Let the batter stand for 5 minutes and then spoon into 12 greased muffin tins, filling them ¾ full. Bake at 400° for 30 minutes. Yields 12 muffins.

Mrs. Ernest Butler (Sarah)

Spoon Bread

1   cup cooked grits
½   cup cornmeal
3   teaspoons baking powder
1   teaspoon sugar

1   teaspoon salt
1   cup milk
2   eggs, beaten
5   tablespoons butter, melted

If grits are cold, mash with fork until smooth. Add cornmeal, baking powder, sugar and salt. Mix well. Add milk, eggs and melted butter. Pour into a greased dish and bake at 350° for 45 minutes to an hour. Serves 8.

Mrs. Bob Edgecomb (Mary)

Cheese Spoon Bread

2½ cups milk
1 cup yellow cornmeal
2 tablespoons butter, melted
1 teaspoon baking powder
1 teaspoon salt

4 ounces Cheddar cheese, grated
4 eggs, separated
¼ teaspoon cream of tartar

Grease a 2 quart soufflé dish. Warm milk in a large saucepan over medium heat until hot. Gradually add cornmeal, stirring constantly. Blend in melted butter, baking powder and salt and cook until mixture is smooth and very thick. Stir in cheese. Beat yolks in medium bowl until light. Gradually stir into cornmeal mixture. Beat whites with cream of tartar in a large bowl until stiff, but not dry. Fold into cornmeal. Turn mixture into prepared dish. Bake at 375° for 40 minutes, until puffed. Serves 6 to 8.

Nikki Kincaid Keller

Carrot Cake Muffins

1 cup grated carrots
1¼ cups whole wheat flour
1 egg
½ cup honey
½ cup butter, melted

½ teaspoon cinnamon
1 teaspoon baking soda
2 teaspoons baking powder
¼ cup lemon juice

In a large bowl combine all ingredients and mix well. Pour into buttered muffin tins. Bake at 350° for 20 minutes. Yields 12 muffins.

Betsey Bishop

Broiled Parmesan Toast

French bread, thinly sliced
Butter or margarine
½ cup mayonnaise
¼ cup grated Parmesan cheese

½ cup finely chopped onion
1 teaspoon Worcestershire sauce
Paprika

Spread French bread slices completely with butter and place on cookie sheet. Mix together mayonnaise, cheese, onion and Worcestershire sauce. Spread mixture on buttered bread, then sprinkle with paprika. Broil in oven until golden brown. Serve immediately. Serves 8 to 10. *This could also be placed on smaller slices and be served as an appetizer.*

Mrs. Tom Russell (Ann)

Dark Brown Bread

2	cups buttermilk	2	tablespoons shortening
⅔	cup molasses	2	cups flour
1	teaspoon sugar	2	cups graham flour
2	teaspoons baking soda	1	cup raisins

Combine all ingredients and bake at 325° for 1 hour. Makes 2 large loaves or one 9x13 inch loaf. *I remember watching my grandmother make this bread when I was a child. My mother passed it on to me when I got married.*

Mrs. Bob Vossman (Nancy)

My Favorite Cheese Bread

1	cup margarine	¼	teaspoon garlic powder
12	ounces Cheddar cheese, grated	¼	teaspoon paprika
½	cup grated Parmesan cheese	½	teaspoon seasoned salt
1	teaspoon Worcestershire sauce	1	loaf French bread, sliced in half lengthwise

Have all ingredients at room temperature. Mix together all ingredients except bread. Broil bread slices on 1 side until brown; remove from broiler. Spread cheese mixture on the other side of the bread; broil until bubbly. Watch carefully. Yields 12 slices of bread. *Mozzarella cheese may be used instead of Cheddar cheese. The cheese mixture freezes well. This is wonderful at barbecues.*

Mrs. David King (Priscilla)

Cheddar Nut Bread

3¾	cups biscuit mix	1	egg, slightly beaten
1½	cups grated sharp Cheddar cheese	1	cup evaporated milk
¼	teaspoon salt	½	cup water
		½	cup chopped pecans

Combine biscuit mix, cheese and salt in a large bowl; set aside. Combine egg, milk and water; add to dry ingredients, and stir until moistened. Stir in pecans. Spoon batter into a lightly greased 9x5x3 inch loaf pan. Bake at 350° for 55 to 60 minutes. Let cool in pan 10 minutes. Yields 1 loaf.

Barbara Beall Stanley

Grandmother's Buttermilk Biscuits

2 cups flour	½ teaspoon baking soda
1 teaspoon salt	6 to 7 tablespoons shortening
4 teaspoons baking powder	1 cup buttermilk

In a mixing bowl sift dry ingredients together. Cut shortening into flour mixture; gradually add buttermilk. Turn out onto a floured board and knead a few times. Roll dough out to ½ to ¾ inch thickness and cut with a biscuit cutter. Place biscuits with sides touching on a cookie sheet and bake at 450° for 12 to 15 minutes. Yields 12 biscuits. *My grandson loves these biscuits and makes them all the time.*

Mrs. Jack Allen Bone (Joyce)

Irish Soda Bread

3¼ cups sifted flour	1½ teaspoons caraway seeds
1 tablespoon baking powder	1 cup seedless raisins
1 teaspoon baking soda	2 eggs, slightly beaten
1 teaspoon salt	1 cup buttermilk
¼ cup light brown sugar	1 tablespoon melted butter
3 tablespoons corn oil	1 tablespoon sugar

Resift flour with baking powder, soda and salt. Add brown sugar and corn oil. Mix with fork until mixture resembles fine crumbs. Stir in caraway seeds and raisins. Combine eggs with buttermilk. Add gradually to flour mixture and stir until soft dough forms. Turn onto floured board and knead 10 times, adding more flour as needed. Grease an 8 or 9 inch cake pan; shape dough into a round and place into pan. Flatten slightly. Cross with knife into quarters about ⅔ way through dough. Brush top with melted butter and sprinkle with 1 tablespoon sugar. Bake at 350° for 30 to 40 minutes. Yields 1 loaf.

Mrs. W. H. Heggen III (Maryellen)

Jan's Shortbread

4 cups flour	1¼ cups powdered sugar
2 cups butter, softened	1 teaspoon baking powder

Mix all ingredients together with hands until sticky. Pat into two 9 inch cake pans. Bake at 350° for 30 to 45 minutes, until lightly brown at edges. Cool 5 minutes and cut into 12 pie-shaped pieces while still warm. Yields 12 pieces. *This is a very rich bread.*

Mrs. W. H. Heggen III (Maryellen)

Blueberry Coffee Cake

Cake:

½ cup butter	1½ teaspoons baking powder
¾ cup sugar	½ teaspoon salt
1 egg	½ cup milk
1½ cups flour	1 cup blueberry pie filling

Cream butter and sugar together; stir in egg. Mix flour, baking powder and salt together. Add to butter mixture, alternating with milk. Pour half the mixture into an 8x8 inch greased pan. Cover with blueberry pie filling. Pour remaining batter over pie filling.

Topping:

½ cup brown sugar	1½ teaspoons cinnamon
2 tablespoons butter, melted	½ cup chopped pecans
	1½ tablespoons flour

Mix all ingredients together and sprinkle on top of batter. Bake at 350° for 50 minutes. Serves 8.

Mrs. Thomas Schwartz (Ellana)

Armenian Coffee Cake

2 cups brown sugar	2 teaspoons grated orange peel
2 cups flour	
½ cup butter	1 cup sour cream
½ teaspoon salt	1 egg
½ teaspoon allspice	½ cup chopped pecans
1 teaspoon baking soda	

Blend brown sugar, flour, butter, salt and allspice until crumbly. Pour half this mixture into a 9 inch buttered cake pan. Stir soda and orange peel into sour cream and mix with remaining crumb mixture. Blend in egg. Pour batter over crumbs and sprinkle with pecans. Bake at 350° for 40 to 45 minutes. Serves 6 to 8.

Mrs. W. H. Heggen III (Maryellen)

To help the bread rise faster, preheat the oven to 140° as you begin kneading the dough. After you have put the dough into the bread pans, turn off the oven and put the bread inside. It should be ready to bake in 20 minutes. Be sure not to get the oven too hot, and don't leave it on during the rising process or a crust will form as the bread rises, causing the bread to crack during baking.

Spicy Buttermilk Coffee Cake

2½ cups flour
½ teaspoon salt
2 teaspoons cinnamon,
   divided
¼ teaspoon ginger
1 cup brown sugar
¾ cup sugar

¾ cup oil
1 cup chopped walnuts or
   pecans
1 teaspoon baking soda
1 teaspoon baking powder
1 egg, beaten
1 cup buttermilk

Mix flour, salt, 1 teaspoon cinnamon, ginger, sugars and oil together in a bowl. Remove ¾ cup of this mixture and add it to the walnuts with 1 teaspoon cinnamon. Mix well and set aside. To the remaining batter, add baking soda, baking powder, egg and buttermilk and mix. Pour batter into a well greased 9x13 inch pan and sprinkle the topping mixture evenly over the surface. Bake at 350° for 35 to 40 minutes. Serves 12.

Mrs. Larry Crain (Pat)

Cocoa Coffee Ring

1½ cups sugar, divided
1 cup chopped pecans
2 tablespoons cocoa
1 teaspoon cinnamon
3 cups flour

1 tablespoon baking powder
1 teaspoon baking soda
½ cup butter
3 eggs
1½ cups sour cream

Combine ½ cup sugar with pecans, cocoa and cinnamon; set aside. Mix flour, baking powder and baking soda. Cream butter and 1 cup sugar. Add eggs 1 at a time and beat well. Add butter mixture to dry ingredients alternately with sour cream. Pour half the batter into a greased tube pan, then sprinkle with all pecan mixture. Top with remaining batter and bake at 375° for 1 hour. Serves 8.

Mrs. Denman Smith (Sandra)

Carrot Bread

½ to ¾ cup oil
1 cup sugar
1½ cups flour
1 teaspoon baking soda
1 teaspoon cinnamon

¼ teaspoon salt
1 cup grated carrots
2 eggs, beaten slightly
1 teaspoon vanilla extract
½ cup chopped pecans

Combine all ingredients in the order given and spoon into a greased 9x5 inch loaf pan. Bake at 325° for 45 to 55 minutes. Remove from pan and cool on a rack. Yields 1 loaf. *Start with ½ cup of oil and add more as needed to mix easily.*

Mrs. Ken McConchie (Paulette)

Sour Cream Coffee Cake

2 eggs	¼ teaspoon salt
1 cup butter	1 teaspoon baking powder
2 cups sugar	1 cup chopped pecans
1 cup sour cream	2 teaspoons cinnamon
1 teaspoon vanilla extract	½ cup brown sugar
2 cups flour	

Cream together eggs, butter and sugar. Add the sour cream and vanilla and mix. Slowly stir in flour, salt and baking powder. For the nut mixture, combine pecans, cinnamon and brown sugar in a separate bowl. Place half the nut mixture in the bottom of a well greased bundt pan; add half the cake batter; then the remaining nut mixture; end with cake batter. Place in a preheated 350° oven and bake for 55 minutes. Serves 12 to 16. *The cake should be very moist, but done. This is a favorite family recipe.*

Mrs. Bill Pohl (Kelly)

Autumn Apple Bread

¼ cup shortening	1 teaspoon salt
⅔ cup sugar	2 cups peeled, coarsely
2 eggs, beaten	grated tart apples
2 cups sifted flour	1 teaspoon grated lemon
1 teaspoon baking powder	rind
1 teaspoon baking soda	⅔ cup chopped walnuts

Cream shortening and sugar until light and fluffy. Beat in eggs. Sift dry ingredients together. Add alternately with the apple to the egg mixture. Stir in lemon rind and nuts. Bake in greased and floured 9x5 inch loaf pan at 350° for 50 to 60 minutes. Cool completely before slicing. Yields 1 loaf.

Mrs. Marcus Bone (Beverly)

Super Quick Banana Bread

1 package (18.5 ounces) nut bread mix	½ teaspoon vanilla extract
1 cup mashed ripe bananas	1 egg
2 tablespoons water	⅓ cup chopped walnuts, optional

Grease and flour the bottom of a loaf pan. Mix all ingredients with a spoon for 40 to 50 strokes until well blended. Pour into pan. Bake at 350° for 50 to 55 minutes until a toothpick comes out clean. Cool in pan for 15 minutes. Remove from pan and cool completely before wrapping. Yields 1 loaf. *This freezes well.*

Mrs. Sid Mann (Kathi)

Banana Butterscotch Bread

1¾ cups flour	2 eggs
2 teaspoons baking powder	¼ cup margarine, melted
½ teaspoon baking soda	¼ cup milk
½ teaspoon salt	1 package (6 ounces)
½ teaspoon cinnamon	butterscotch morsels
½ teaspoon nutmeg	1 cup chopped pecans,
1 cup mashed bananas	divided
¾ cup sugar	

Combine flour, baking powder, baking soda, salt, cinnamon and nutmeg. Set aside. In a small bowl mix bananas, sugar, eggs and margarine. Add banana mixture to flour mixture alternately with milk, beating well with an electric mixer. Stir in butterscotch morsels and ⅔ cup pecans. Line bottom of a 9x5x3 inch loaf pan with waxed paper. Grease waxed paper and side of pan. Spoon batter into pan and sprinkle with remaining pecans. Bake at 350° for 80 minutes. Cool 30 minutes before removing from pan. Yields 1 loaf.

Mrs. Don Kothmann (Sheila)

Cherry Pecan Bread

½ cup butter	½ teaspoon salt
¾ cup sugar	1 scant cup buttermilk
2 eggs	1 cup chopped pecans
1 teaspoon vanilla extract	1 jar (10 ounces) maraschino
2 cups flour	cherries, drained and
1 teaspoon baking soda	chopped

Beat butter and sugar until fluffy. Beat in eggs and vanilla. Stir together flour, baking soda and salt; add alternately with buttermilk to creamed mixture, blending well. Fold in pecans and cherries. Turn into a greased 9x5 inch loaf pan or 2 small loaf pans. Bake at 350° for 55 to 60 minutes or until toothpick comes out clean. Cool in pan at least 10 minutes, then remove and cool completely before wrapping. Yields 1 large or 2 small loaves. *This is a soft loaf, so handle it carefully while warm. It freezes well.*

Mrs. Sid Mann (Kathi)

Always dissolve yeast by sprinkling on top of warm water. Ideal temperature of liquid for dissolving yeast is 105° to 115°. If water is too cool, action of yeast will be slowed, but will work eventually. If water is too hot, action of yeast will be killed completely.

Zucchini Fritters

2 medium zucchini, grated
1 teaspoon salt
1 carrot, grated
½ onion, minced
2 tablespoons minced
   parsley

1 egg, beaten
½ cup flour
Dash pepper
Vegetable oil

Combine zucchini and salt in colander. Drain 15 to 30 minutes. Squeeze zucchini as dry as possible. Combine zucchini with remaining ingredients except oil. Drop by tablespoons into hot oil. Brown on both sides. Yields approximately 12 fritters.

Mrs. Charles Denton (Carole)

Strawberry Bread

2 cups margarine
3 cups sugar
2 teaspoons vanilla extract
½ teaspoon lemon extract
8 eggs
6 cups flour

2 teaspoons salt
2 teaspoons cream of tartar
1 teaspoon baking soda
2 cups strawberry preserves
1 cup sour cream
2 cups chopped pecans

Cream margarine, sugar and extracts; add eggs, one at a time and beat well after each addition. Sift dry ingredients together. Combine preserves and sour cream and add to creamed mixture, alternating with flour mixture. Stir in pecans and place in 4 well greased and floured 9x5 inch loaf pans. Bake at 350° for 50 to 55 minutes. Yields 4 loaves.

Mrs. Thomas Price (Marie)

Processor Zucchini Bread

1 cup whole wheat flour
½ cup flour
½ teaspoon salt
½ teaspoon baking soda
½ teaspoon baking powder
¼ teaspoon ginger

1 medium zucchini
½ cup chopped pecans
2 eggs
1 cup sugar
½ cup oil
1 teaspoon fresh lemon rind

Sift dry ingredients together into a bowl and set aside. Grate zucchini in processor and set aside. Chop nuts in processor and set aside. Place eggs, sugar and oil in processor bowl and mix well. Continue to process, adding dry ingredients through the chute. Process a few seconds, then scrape mixture down from sides of bowl. Add zucchini, nuts and lemon rind. Process just to mix. Pour into a well greased 8x4 inch loaf pan. Bake at 350° for 1 hour. Yields 1 loaf.

Mrs. Clark E. Rector (Sue)

Blueberry Muffins

2 cups flour
½ cup sugar
3 teaspoons baking powder
½ teaspoon salt
1 cup fresh blueberries

1 cup milk
⅓ cup oil
1 egg, slightly beaten
Sugar for garnish

In a large bowl combine flour, sugar, baking powder and salt. Stir in blueberries. Preheat oven to 400°. Combine milk, oil and egg and beat with fork to mix. Make a well in center of flour-blueberry mixture. Pour in milk mixture all at once. Stir quickly with fork, just until dry ingredients are moistened. Do not over mix; batter will be lumpy. Spoon batter into greased muffin pan. Sprinkle tops lightly with sugar. Bake at 400° for 20 to 25 minutes. Yields 12 muffins.

Mrs. Bill Hayes (Ginger)

Applesauce Muffins

2 teaspoons baking soda
1½ cups applesauce, heated
⅔ cup margarine, melted
1 cup sugar

2 cups flour
1 teaspoon cinnamon
½ teaspoon ground cloves
½ teaspoon allspice

Add soda to hot applesauce. Mix in melted margarine. Mix all dry ingredients together and add to applesauce mixture. Pour into greased muffin tins and bake at 350° for 10 to 12 minutes. For a variation you may add 1 cup raisins that have been plumped in simmering water and/or 2 cups finely chopped pecans. Yields 12.

Mrs. Mark White (Linda Gayle)

Apple-Oatmeal Muffins

1 cup oatmeal
½ cup whole wheat flour
½ cup flour
2 teaspoons baking powder
½ teaspoon salt
½ teaspoon cinnamon

2 eggs
⅔ cup honey
2 apples, finely chopped
2 tablespoons butter, melted
Cinnamon sugar, optional

Mix oatmeal, flours, baking powder, salt and cinnamon together. Stir in eggs, honey, apples and butter just until mixed. Pour into greased muffin tins and sprinkle with cinnamon sugar if desired. Bake at 400° for 20 to 25 minutes. Yields 12 large or 24 small muffins.

Mrs. Denman Smith (Sandra)

Easy Apricot Bread

Bread:

2   cups self-rising flour
1   teaspoon cinnamon
2   cups sugar
4   eggs
1   cup oil

2   jars (4¼ ounces each)
    baby food apricots with
    tapioca
1   cup chopped pecans
Dash of allspice

Combine all ingredients and mix well. Pour batter into a greased 9x5 inch loaf pan and bake at 325° for 60 minutes, or until toothpick inserted comes out clean.

Glaze:

½   cup powdered sugar
Juice of 1 lemon

¼   cup chopped pecans,
    optional

Combine powdered sugar and lemon juice for glaze. Immediately after removing from oven, top with glaze. Remove from pan; sprinkle with pecans and cool. Yields 1 loaf.

Mrs. Ron Bruney (Carol)

Orange Muffins

Muffins:

½   cup shortening
1   cup brown sugar
4   eggs
2   cups flour
½   teaspoon salt

1   teaspoon baking soda
1   cup buttermilk
¾   cup chopped pecans
1   tablespoon grated orange
    rind

Cream shortening and brown sugar together. Add eggs one at a time. Sift flour and salt together. Add soda to buttermilk. Add flour and buttermilk alternately to the creamed mixture. Then add pecans and orange rind. Fill small greased muffin tins ⅔ full. Bake at 350° for 15 minutes. While still hot remove from tins and dip into the glaze. Drain and place on waxed paper.

Glaze:

1½   cups sugar
¾   cup orange juice

1   tablespoon grated orange
    rind

Heat sugar, juice and rind in a saucepan. Do not boil. Yields 6 dozen bite sized muffins.

Mrs. John Bosch (Nancy)

Texans look with pride at the rich heritage and warm hospitality associated with the Governor's Mansion. It has stood like a gracious hostess — stately and regal — in the shade of the Capitol grounds since its completion in 1856. The hand-crafted pine floors in the original house were cut from trees in the "lost pines" of nearby Bastrop, and the charming carriage house served as stables for the Mansion's first occupants. In 1900 the stucco-colored exterior was painted white and four years later, the addition of a conservatory and several upstairs rooms enlarged the home from eleven to twenty-one rooms. In 1979 the Mansion received extensive restoration and redecoration. Of the three million dollars required to accomplish the task, only one-third came from State appropriations.

Desserts pictured: Raspberry Sherbert, Grapefruit Sorbet, Apricot Cake, Cheese Cake, Trifle, Cherry Topped Pie, Baklava and Harriette's Winter Strawberries.

Desserts

Apricot Brandy Cake

Cake:

1 cup butter	1 teaspoon baking soda
1 cup sugar	1¼ cups sour cream
3 eggs, separated	1 cup chopped pecans,
2 cups flour	optional
1 teaspoon baking powder	

Cream butter with sugar until fluffy. Add egg yolks one at a time. Mix flour, baking powder and soda, and add alternately with sour cream. Mix until smooth. Add pecans and fold in stiffly beaten egg whites. Pour into a greased and floured tube pan. Bake at 350° for 50 to 55 minutes.

Topping:

½ cup apricot brandy	1 carton (8 ounces) whipped
½ cup sugar	topping
¾ cup apricot nectar	1 can (16 ounces) apricot
	halves, drained

Combine brandy, sugar and nectar. Pour on warm cake. Let sit until cool. Carefully remove from pan. Frost with whipped topping and garnish with apricots. Serves 12 to 14.

Florence Batey

Pound Cake

1 cup butter	2 cups sifted flour
2 cups sugar	1½ teaspoons lemon extract
5 eggs	

Cream butter and sugar. Add eggs one at a time, mixing well before adding next egg. Add flour and mix well. Add lemon extract. Pour into a greased and floured tube pan. Bake at 275° for 1¼ hours to 1½ hours. The cake should be brown and crusty on top and moist on the inside. Go around sides of tube with knife, then let cool in pan about 15 minutes. Serves 16. *This cake stays very moist. It is my family's favorite, a recipe we have been using for 30 years.*

Mrs. John Reesing (Hallie Jo)

Blueberry Pound Cake

Cake:

2 cups sugar	3 tablespoons lemon extract
1 cup shortening	½ cup buttermilk
4 eggs	3 cups flour
¼ teaspoon yellow food coloring	½ teaspoon salt
½ teaspoon almond extract	1 teaspoon baking powder
1½ teaspoons vanilla extract	1 teaspoon baking soda
2 tablespoons butter flavoring	2½ cups whole blueberries, rinsed and drained

Preheat oven to 325°. Cream sugar and shortening. Beat in eggs one at a time. Add food coloring, almond extract, vanilla, butter flavoring and lemon extract to buttermilk; blend well and set aside. Sift flour with salt, baking powder and baking soda. Add to batter, alternating with buttermilk, until evenly distributed. Fold in blueberries, reserving a few for garnish. Pour into a greased bundt pan and bake at 325° for 1 hour and 10 minutes. Allow cake to cool 15 minutes. While cake is still warm, brush on glaze, covering top and sides.

Glaze:

½ cup sugar	½ teaspoon butter flavoring
¼ cup water	2 teaspoons lemon extract, divided
¼ teaspoon almond extract	3 tablespoons milk
½ teaspoon vanilla extract	2 cups powdered sugar

Combine sugar, water and flavorings except one teaspoon lemon extract in a small saucepan. Bring slowly to a boil, stirring frequently. Simmer 3 to 4 minutes. Apply to cake while still warm. Combine 1 teaspoon lemon extract with milk and add to powdered sugar, blending well. Drizzle on cake and garnish with a few reserved blueberries. Serves 16 to 18.

Mrs. Ron Bruney (Carol)

Poppy Seed Cake

1½ cups sugar	1 teaspoon baking soda
1 cup margarine	1 cup sour cream
4 eggs, separated	2 cups sifted flour
⅓ cup poppy seeds	

Cream sugar and margarine. Beat egg yolks and add to creamed mixture. Add poppy seeds. Dissolve soda in sour cream and add the sour cream alternately with flour to the mixture. Beat egg whites until stiff and fold in. Pour into a lightly greased tube pan and bake at 350° for 1 hour. Serves 16. *This makes a good morning cake for coffee.*

Mrs. Greg Gordon (Kathy)

Joyce's Banana Pound Cake

1	package (9.9 ounces) butter pecan frosting mix	1	package (3½ ounces) instant banana pudding
5	tablespoons butter, softened	1	cup sour cream
1	package (18.5 ounces) yellow cake mix	4	eggs
		1½	cups thinly sliced bananas

Stir butter pecan frosting mix and butter together to form a crumb mixture; set aside. Combine yellow cake mix, pudding mix, sour cream and eggs. Fold in bananas. In a greased and floured tube pan, pour half the batter, then half the crumb mixture; repeat, ending with crumb mixture. Bake at 350° for 50 to 60 minutes. Cool 20 to 30 minutes. Serves 18.

Mrs. Tom Aiken (Joyce)

Chocolate Pound Cake

1	cup butter	4 to 5	tablespoons cocoa
1	cup shortening	¾	teaspoon salt
3	cups sugar	1	cup milk
5	eggs	1	teaspoon vanilla extract
3	cups flour		Powdered sugar, optional
¾	teaspoon baking powder		

Cream butter, shortening and sugar. Add eggs, one at a time, beating well after each. Sift together dry ingredients and add to creamed mixture alternately with milk. Add vanilla and mix. Pour into a greased 10 inch tube pan and bake at 350° for 1¼ to 1½ hours. Cool in pan. Serves 15 to 20. *This cake is even better if dusted with powdered sugar or topped with an orange or mint glaze.*

Mrs. Edward Sternen (Suzanne)

Vanilla Wafer Cake

1	cup butter	1	cup broken pecans
2	cups sugar	2	cups flaked coconut
6	eggs		Powdered sugar for garnish
½	cup milk		
1	box (12 ounces) vanilla wafers, crushed		

Cream butter and sugar with an electric mixer. Add one egg at a time, beating continuously. Add milk alternately with remaining dry ingredients until all are used, beating continuously. Bake in a well greased and floured tube or bundt pan at 325° for 1½ hours. Sprinkle top with powdered sugar. Serves 14 to 16.

The Cookbook Committee

Chocolate Chip Pound Cake

2   cups sugar
1   cup shortening
4   eggs
3   cups flour
½   teaspoon salt
1½ tablespoons cocoa

1   teaspoon baking soda
1   cup buttermilk
1   teaspoon vanilla extract
1   package (6 ounces)
    semisweet chocolate chips
1   cup chopped pecans

Cream sugar and shortening; add eggs one at a time, beating well after each addition. Stir together flour, salt and cocoa. Add soda to buttermilk. Add flour to creamed mixture alternately with buttermilk mixture. Add vanilla, chocolate chips and pecans. Pour into a greased and floured 10 inch tube pan and bake at 325° for 1¼ to 1½ hours. Serves 15 to 20.

Mrs. W. H. Heggen III (Maryellen)

Bavarian Chocolate Pound Cake

1   bar (4 ounces) sweet
    baking chocolate
1   cup shortening
2   cups sugar
4   eggs
2   teaspoons vanilla extract

2   teaspoons butter flavoring
1   cup buttermilk
3   cups flour
1   teaspoon baking soda
1   teaspoon salt

Partially melt chocolate in top of double boiler. Remove and stir rapidly until melted; cool. Cream shortening and sugar, adding sugar gradually. Add eggs, flavorings and buttermilk. Sift together dry ingredients and add to batter a little at a time. Mix well. Blend in chocolate. Pour into a well greased and floured tube pan and bake at 300° for about 1½ hours. Remove from pan while hot and cover until thoroughly cooled. Serves 16 to 18. *This is great topped with vanilla ice cream.*

Mrs. Ron Bruney (Carol)

When baking cakes or cookies, add the flavoring extracts with the liquids, and they will be more easily distributed.

Brownstone Front Cake

Cake:

1   cup margarine, softened
2   cups sugar
3   eggs
1   cup buttermilk
1   teaspoon baking soda

1   square unsweetened
     baking chocolate, melted
3   cups flour
½   cup warm water
1   teaspoon vanilla extract
¼   teaspoon salt

Combine all cake ingredients and mix well. Bake in 2 greased and floured 9 inch cake pans at 350° for 35 to 40 minutes. Cool.

Frosting:

2   cups sugar
1   cup margarine

1   cup milk

Put all ingredients in a heavy saucepan and cook over low heat for 1 hour, boiling gently. Frosting will turn a caramel color. It does not have to be stirred continuously, but must be watched or it will boil over. Remove from heat and beat until thick and spreadable. Frost cooled cake. Serves 12 to 16.

Mrs. Robert Schnautz (Alma)

Oatmeal Chocolate Chip Walnut Cake

1¾ cups boiling water
1   cup quick oatmeal,
     uncooked
1   cup lightly packed brown
     sugar
1   cup sugar
½   cup margarine
2   eggs

1¾ cups unsifted flour
1   teaspoon baking soda
½   teaspoon salt
1   tablespoon cocoa
1   package (12 ounces)
     semisweet chocolate
     chips, divided
¾   cup chopped walnuts

Pour boiling water over oatmeal. Let stand 10 minutes. Add sugars and margarine. Stir until margarine melts. Add eggs and blend. Sift together flour, soda, salt and cocoa. Add flour to sugar mixture; blend well. Add about half the package of chocolate chips. Pour batter into a greased and floured 9x13 inch pan. Sprinkle the walnuts and remaining chocolate chips on top. Bake at 350° for 40 minutes or until done. Serves 16.

Mrs. Steve Prough (Susan)

Sweet Chocolate Cake

Cake:

1   bar (4 ounces) sweet
    baking chocolate
½   cup boiling water
1   cup butter
2   cups sugar
4   eggs, separated

1   teaspoon vanilla extract
½   teaspoon salt
1   teaspoon baking soda
2½ cups cake flour
1   cup buttermilk

Melt chocolate in boiling water. Cool. Cream butter and sugar until fluffy. Add egg yolks one at a time, beating well. Add melted chocolate and vanilla; mix well. Sift dry ingredients together and add alternately with buttermilk to chocolate mixture. Beat until smooth. Beat egg whites until stiff and fold into mixture. Pour into 3 cake pans, 8 inches each, lined with waxed paper. Bake at 350° for 30 to 40 minutes. Cool. Fill layers and frost.

Frosting:

1   cup evaporated milk
1   cup sugar
3   egg yolks
½   cup margarine

1   teaspoon vanilla extract
1   cup chopped pecans
1⅓ cups coconut

Combine milk, sugar, egg yolks, margarine, and vanilla. Cook over low heat, stirring constantly until thickened, about 12 minutes. Add pecans and coconut and beat until thick enough to spread. Frost cake. Serves 12 to 16.

Mrs. Jack A. Bone (Joyce)

Seduction Cake

1   package (6 ounces)
    semisweet chocolate chips
¾   cup chopped pecans
1   box (18.5 ounces)
    chocolate butter cake mix
4   eggs
½   cup oil

¼   cup water
1   teaspoon vanilla extract
1   box (3½ ounces) instant
    chocolate pudding
1   carton (8 ounces) sour
    cream

Coat chocolate chips and pecans in a spoon or two of dry cake mix. Mix remaining ingredients together and fold in chocolate chips and pecans. Pour into a greased and floured bundt or tube pan. Bake at 350° for 50 minutes. Serves 16.

Mrs. Ted M. Linder (Michelle Just)

My Favorite Chocolate Cake

1   box (18.5 ounces) devil's
    food cake mix
1   box (3½ ounces) instant
    chocolate pudding mix
¾   cup sour cream
½   cup oil
½   cup water
½   cup toasted chopped
    almonds

¼   cup mayonnaise
4   eggs
3   tablespoons almond
    extract
1   cup semisweet chocolate
    chips
Cocoa

In a large bowl add all ingredients except chocolate chips. Mix on low speed until moistened, then beat 2 minutes at medium speed. Batter is quite thick. Stir in chips by hand. Pour batter into a bundt pan that has been greased and dusted with cocoa and bake 50 to 55 minutes at 350°. Serves 12 to 16. *This is a family favorite and is always requested for birthdays. This cake freezes well.*

Mrs. Bob McGoldrick (Fran)

Chocolate Applesauce Cake

2   cups flour
3   tablespoons cocoa
1½ teaspoons baking soda
½   teaspoon salt
¾   cup margarine, softened
1¼ cups sugar
3   eggs

2   teaspoons vanilla extract
2   cups applesauce
1   package (6 ounces)
    semisweet chocolate chips
1   cup chopped walnuts
1   cup sifted powdered sugar

Combine flour, cocoa, baking soda and salt. Set aside. In a large bowl cream the margarine and sugar until light and fluffy. Add eggs one at a time, beating well after each addition. Stir in vanilla. Add flour mixture alternately with applesauce; beat well on low speed after each addition. Pour into greased and floured 9x13 inch baking pan. Sprinkle top with chocolate chips, walnuts and powdered sugar. Bake at 350° for 35 minutes. Do not overbake. Serves 20 to 24.

Mrs. Bob West (Linda)

Eggs can absorb strong odors in your refrigerator. Do not put them next to garlic or other highly flavored items.

Smyth Family Devil's Food Cake

Cake:

2 cups sugar
3 tablespoons cocoa
1 cup butter, softened
5 eggs, beaten

2½ cups cake flour
1 rounded teaspoon baking soda
1 cup buttermilk
1 teaspoon vanilla extract

In a large bowl combine sugar and cocoa. Add butter and cream well. Mix in eggs. Sift together flour and soda and add to mixture alternately with buttermilk; beat well between each addition. Mix in vanilla. Pour into either a 9x13 inch pan or three 9 inch round cake pans which have been greased and floured. Bake at 350° for 25 to 30 minutes. Cool slightly, then remove from pans and pour icing over top and sides of layers as quickly as possible.

Icing:

1 cup butter
1½ cups milk
1 tablespoon corn syrup

3 cups sugar
1 teaspoon vanilla extract
1 cup chopped pecans

Melt butter in large saucepan. Add milk, corn syrup and sugar, and cook over medium heat, stirring frequently, to 234° on a candy thermometer. When icing reaches 234°, remove from heat and beat until thickened slightly. Serves 24. *This recipe has been handed down through my family for generations.*

Ada Smyth

Fresh Apple Cake

½ cup shortening
1 cup sugar
1 egg, beaten
2 cups chopped fresh apples, unpeeled
¼ cup chopped maraschino cherries

1 cup chopped pecans
2 cups flour
1 teaspoon baking soda
½ teaspoon salt
1 teaspoon cinnamon
1 teaspoon nutmeg

Cream shortening and sugar; add egg. Beat until fluffy. Add apples, cherries and pecans. Sift dry ingredients together and add to sugar mixture. Blend well. Pour into greased and floured 7½x11½ inch glass baking dish. Bake at 350° for 40 to 45 minutes. Serves 10 to 12.

Mrs. Ron Bruney (Carol)

Country Apple Cake

Cake:

1 cup sugar	½ cup shortening
1½ cups flour	½ cup milk
¼ teaspoon salt	1 egg
½ teaspoon baking powder	3 cups chopped tart apples
1 teaspoon baking soda	

Sift together sugar, flour, salt, baking powder and baking soda. Cut in shortening. Add milk, egg and apples and blend well. Spread into a greased 9x13 inch baking dish.

Topping:

½ cup brown sugar	2 teaspoons cinnamon
2 tablespoons butter	¾ cup chopped pecans
2 teaspoons flour	

Cream all topping ingredients together and crumble over cake batter. Bake at 350° for 40 to 45 minutes. Serve with vanilla ice cream. Serves 16.

Mrs. Rick Denbow (Susan)

Choco-Cherry Cake

Cake:

1 box (18 ounces) chocolate fudge cake mix	1 can (21 ounces) cherry pie filling
2 eggs, beaten	1 teaspoon almond extract

Combine cake ingredients; mix well by hand. Pour into a greased and floured 10x15 inch jelly roll pan. Bake at 350° for 20 to 25 minutes. Cool.

Frosting:

1 cup sugar	1 cup semisweet chocolate chips
5 tablespoons margarine	
⅓ cup milk	

Boil sugar, margarine and milk for 1 minute, stirring constantly. Add chocolate chips and stir until melted. Frost cake. Serves 18 to 20.

Mrs. Jim Schultz (Mary Kay)

Cooking apples are tarter and firmer in texture than eating apples; thus they taste and look better in baked preparations.

Japanese Fruit Cake

Cake:

3½ cups flour	1 tablespoon baking powder
1⅓ cups shortening	1 cup chopped pecans
2 cups sugar	2 cups raisins
4 eggs	1 teaspoon allspice
1 cup buttermilk	1 teaspoon ground cinnamon
1 teaspoon baking soda	1 teaspoon ground cloves

Blend flour, shortening, sugar, eggs, buttermilk, soda and baking powder. Divide in half. To one half add nuts and to the other half, raisins and spices. Stir well. Pour each half into 2 greased 9 inch cake pans. There should be four layers. Bake at 325° for 30 minutes.

Filling:

1 fresh coconut	4 tablespoons flour
2 lemons, divided	2 cups sugar

Take the milk from the coconut; add juice from 1 lemon and add enough water to make 1½ cups. Grate 1 lemon rind. Add 4 tablespoons flour, 2 cups sugar, and 1 cup grated coconut. Combine with coconut milk and boil until thick, stirring constantly. Cool and spread between layers of cake.

Powdered Sugar Frosting:

1 box (16 ounces) powdered sugar	2 teaspoons vanilla extract
½ cup butter, softened	4 to 6 tablespoons of milk

Mix sugar, butter and vanilla together and beat well. Add enough milk to achieve spreading consistency. Frost top and sides of cake. Must be stored, covered, at least two days prior to serving. Serves 14 to 16.

Cindy Morris Weldon

Hummingbird Cake

3 cups flour	1 teaspoon butter flavoring
1 teaspoon baking soda	3 eggs
1 teaspoon salt	1 can (8 ounces) crushed
1 teaspoon cinnamon	pineapple, undrained
2 cups sugar	2 medium bananas, chopped
1½ cups oil	1 cup chopped pecans

Mix all ingredients by hand, stirring well before each new ingredient is added. Bake in a greased and floured bundt pan at 350° for 60 to 70 minutes. Serves 10 to 12. Cool 1 hour before removing from pan. *This is so easy, only one bowl and it is a delicious, moist cake.*

Mrs. Jim Schultz (Mary Kay)

Fresh Coconut Cake

Fresh Coconut Cake:

1 yellow cake baked in 2 round layers
1 recipe Lemon Jelly Filling

1 package (7.2 ounces) white fluffy icing
Fresh grated coconut, generous amount

Split layers and fill with lemon jelly. Also put lemon jelly between cake layers. Frost with white fluffy icing and cover generously with fresh grated coconut so that it looks like a giant snowball. Serves 14 to 16. *This is an old recipe and a marvelous Southern treat.*

Lemon Jelly Filling:

¼ cup butter
½ cup water
1¼ cups sugar
1 egg

2 egg yolks
1 heaping tablespoon flour
Juice and grated rind of 1 lemon

Put butter and water into a pan and heat until melted. Mix together remaining ingredients and add to butter and cook until thick.

Mrs. Dudley Baker (Kathy)

Simply Scrumptious Sherry Cake

1 package (18.5 ounces) yellow cake mix
1 package (3 ounces) instant vanilla pudding
4 eggs

1 cup oil
1 cup sherry
1 teaspoon nutmeg
Powdered sugar for garnish

Combine all ingredients except powdered sugar and mix well. Pour into a greased bundt pan or an angel food cake pan. Bake at 350° for 45 minutes. Cool 20 to 30 minutes. After removing from pan, sprinkle with powdered sugar. Let stand 15 minutes before slicing or serving. Serves 16. *This moist and rich cake seems like it would take much more effort to make than it does. It is a nice dessert for brunches or buffets.*

Mrs. Jette Campbell (Sally)

Except when separating the yolk from the white of an egg, always let it come to room temperature before using it in your recipe. An egg separates easier if it is straight from the refrigerator.

Rum Cake

Cake:

1 cup margarine	2 cups flour
1¾ cups sugar	1 teaspoon rum extract
5 eggs	1 teaspoon vanilla extract

Cream margarine, sugar and eggs. Add flour and flavorings and blend well. Pour into a greased, floured tube pan and bake at 375° for 1 hour.

Icing:

1 cup sugar	1 teaspoon rum extract
½ cup water	

Bring all icing ingredients to a boil, stirring to dissolve sugar. While cake is still hot, pour icing on top. Serves 16 to 18.

Mrs. Jim Smith (Jare)

Coconut Macaroon Cake

Cake:

5 tablespoons shortening	¼ teaspoon salt
10 tablespoons sugar	6 tablespoons milk
3 egg yolks	½ teaspoon lemon extract
1 cup flour	½ teaspoon vanilla extract
1¼ teaspoons baking powder	

Blend shortening, sugar and egg yolks together. Add remaining ingredients and pour into a greased and floured tube pan. Add topping.

Topping:

3 egg whites, beaten	1 cup coconut
1 cup powdered sugar	

Combine all topping ingredients together and place on top of cake. Bake at 300° for 45 minutes. Invert and then turn again so macaroons will be on top. Serves 18 to 20.

Mrs. Leo Mueller (Nancy)

 Always listen for liquid in a fresh coconut before buying it. The sloshing sound means the coconut is fresh.

Tropic Delight

Cake:

2 cups flour
1½ cups sugar
½ cup brown sugar
2 teaspoons baking soda
2 eggs

1 can (20 ounces) crushed pineapple, undrained
1 teaspoon vanilla extract
1 teaspoon butter flavoring

Sift flour, sugars and soda together. Blend together eggs, pineapple, vanilla and butter flavoring and fold into flour mixture. Bake in a 9x12 inch pan at 350° for 45 minutes.

Frosting:

1 box (16 ounces) powdered sugar
8 ounces cream cheese
6 tablespoons butter, softened

2 teaspoons vanilla extract
1 cup shredded coconut
1 cup chopped pecans

Blend together powdered sugar, cream cheese, butter and vanilla in mixer. Fold in coconut and pecans. Ice cake while still hot. Serves 16 to 20.

Mrs. James C. Doss (Charlene)

Orange Date Nut Cake

Cake:

1 cup shortening
2 cups sugar
4 eggs
4 cups flour
½ teaspoon salt
1 teaspoon baking soda

1⅓ cups buttermilk
1 teaspoon vanilla extract
1½ tablespoons grated orange rind
1 cup dates
1 cup pecans

Cream shortening and sugar. Add eggs and blend well. Add dry ingredients alternately with buttermilk. Stir in dates and pecans. Pour batter into a greased bundt pan and bake at 325° for 1½ hours.

Glaze:

2 cups sugar
1½ cups orange juice

1½ tablespoons orange rind

Mix sugar, orange juice and orange rind together and blend well. Bring to a boil and pour glaze over cake while hot. Do not try to pour all the glaze on at once; it will take a few minutes for the cake to absorb it all. Then let cool. Serves 20.

Mrs. Charles Perry (Carolyn)

Mama's Banana Nut Cake

2 cups flour	½ cup, less 2 tablespoons,
1 teaspoon baking powder	buttermilk, divided
1 teaspoon baking soda	1 cup mashed bananas
¾ teaspoon salt	1 teaspoon vanilla extract
1⅓ cups sugar	2 eggs
½ cup butter, softened	½ cup chopped pecans

Mix flour, baking powder, soda, salt, and sugar. Cut in butter. Add ¼ cup buttermilk and bananas. Mix until flour is damp. Continue beating at low speed for 2 minutes. Add remaining buttermilk, vanilla, eggs and pecans and beat at low speed for 1 minute. Turn batter into 2 nine inch greased and floured cake pans. Bake at 375° for 20 to 25 minutes. When cool, frost with Creamy Nut Icing. Serves 12 to 15. *This is an old recipe that called for beating 300 strokes by hand. Although I have changed it to a mixer and do not sift the flour twice, it is still the best banana nut cake. It has to be my all time favorite.*

Florence Batey

Creamy Nut Icing

½ cup butter	½ cup brown sugar
2½ tablespoons flour	2 cups powdered sugar
¼ teaspoon salt	1 teaspoon vanilla extract
½ cup milk	½ cup chopped pecans

Melt butter in a saucepan and remove from heat. Blend in flour and salt. Slowly stir in milk. Bring to a boil, stirring constantly and boil for 1 minute. Stir in brown sugar. Remove from heat and add powdered sugar. Set saucepan in a bowl of ice cubes and water and beat until spreading consistency. Stir in vanilla and pecans. Spread on cake. Yields icing for 2 layer (9 inch) cake or 1 sheet cake. *This icing is wonderful on Mama's Banana Nut Cake.*

Florence Batey

The name pineapple is derived from the fact that the fruit resembles a pinecone.

Mandarin Orange Cake

Cake:

1 cup sugar	1 egg
1 cup flour	1 can (11 ounces) mandarin
1 teaspoon baking soda	oranges, drained
½ teaspoon salt	1 teaspoon vanilla extract

Mix all ingredients except vanilla in a bowl and beat 3 minutes on medium speed. Add vanilla. Pour into an 8 inch square pan and bake at 350° for 30 to 35 minutes. While cake is still warm, pierce holes in top with fork.

Topping:

¾ cup brown sugar	3 tablespoons milk
3 tablespoons butter	

Bring topping ingredients to a boil and pour over hot cake. Serve warm or cold. Serves 16.

Mrs. Bill Wittenbrook (Linda)

Peach Preserves Cake

1 cup butter, softened	1 teaspoon baking soda
2 cups sugar	1 cup buttermilk
4 eggs	1 cup chopped pecans
3 cups flour	1 jar (12 ounces) peach
1 teaspoon cinnamon	preserves
½ teaspoon ground cloves	

Cream butter and sugar. Add eggs, one at a time, mixing well after each addition. Sift flour, cinnamon, cloves and baking soda together. Add dry ingredients to butter mixture gradually with buttermilk, chopped pecans and peach preserves. When mixed, pour into a greased angel food or bundt pan. Bake at 350° for 1 hour. You may also use 3 small pans and bake at 350° for 45 minutes. Serves 16. *This cake freezes well and stays moist a long time.*

Barbara Beall Stanley

Unlike pears, peaches and plums do not ripen much after they are picked.

Carrot Cake

Cake:

2 cups sugar	1¼ cups oil
2 cups flour	4 eggs, beaten
2 teaspoons baking soda	3 cups coarsely grated
2 teaspoons cinnamon	carrots
1 teaspoon salt	

Sift dry ingredients together into a large mixing bowl. Add oil and eggs, beating well. Stir in carrots and mix well on medium speed. Pour into 2 greased and floured 9 inch pans. Bake at 350° for 35 to 45 minutes or until done. Cool completely before frosting.

Frosting:

8 ounces cream cheese	1 teaspoon vanilla extract
¾ cup butter	1 cup chopped pecans
1 box (16 ounces) powdered sugar	

Blend cream cheese and butter. Beat in powdered sugar, a little at a time, mixing well. Add vanilla and stir in pecans. Frost cake and refrigerate. Serves 16.

Mrs. Bill Wittenbrook (Linda)

Carrot Yogurt Cake

1 cup butter	¾ cup plain yogurt
1⅔ cups sugar	2¼ cups flour
4 eggs	1 teaspoon baking soda
1 teaspoon grated lemon peel	1½ teaspoons baking powder
1 teaspoon cinnamon	½ teaspoon salt
1 teaspoon vanilla extract	¾ cup chopped pecans
	2½ cups finely grated carrots

Beat butter until creamy. Beat in sugar and eggs. Mix in lemon peel, cinnamon, vanilla and yogurt. Stir together the flour, baking soda, baking powder and salt, and add to the creamed mixture, beating until smooth. Mix in pecans and carrots. Turn into a greased and floured 10 inch bundt or tube pan. Bake at 350° for 70 minutes, or until golden brown. Let cool on a rack 10 minutes, then remove from pan. Serves 24.

Mrs. Ernest Butler (Sarah)

Surprise Cupcakes

1 package (18.5 ounces) chocolate cake mix	1 egg
	⅛ teaspoon salt
8 ounces cream cheese, softened	1 package (6 ounces) semisweet chocolate chips
⅓ cup sugar	

Prepare cake mix according to directions on package. Place paper baking cups in muffin pans and fill ⅔ full with cake mix. Cream the cheese with sugar and beat in egg and salt. Stir in chocolate pieces, then drop one rounded teaspoon of mixture into each cupcake. Bake at 350° for 25 to 30 minutes. Refrigerate until served. Yields 18 cupcakes.

Mrs. Ed Fomby (Beaty)

Chocolate Chip Cupcakes

Cupcakes:

½ cup margarine	1 cup plus 2 tablespoons sifted flour
6 tablespoons sugar	
6 tablespoons brown sugar	½ teaspoon baking soda
½ teaspoon vanilla extract	½ teaspoon salt
1 egg	

Cream together margarine, sugar, brown sugar and vanilla. Add the egg and mix well. Sift the flour, baking soda and salt together. Stir into creamed mixture and blend well. Place cupcake papers into muffin tins. Spoon 1 rounded tablespoon of this mixture into cupcake paper. Bake at 375° for 10 minutes.

Topping:

½ cup firmly packed brown sugar	1 package (6 ounces) semisweet chocolate chips
1 egg	½ cup chopped pecans
⅛ teaspoon salt	½ teaspoon vanilla extract

Combine the brown sugar, egg and salt. Gradually add the chocolate chips, pecans and vanilla. Remove cupcakes from oven and place 1 tablespoon topping on each cupcake. Bake at 375° for 15 additional minutes. Yields 16.

Mrs. Greg Gordon (Kathy)

Mocha Pie

Crust:

1 cup sugar
1 teaspoon instant coffee powder
2 teaspoons cocoa
4 egg whites
½ teaspoon cream of tartar
12 round rich crackers, crushed
¾ cup finely chopped walnuts

Mix sugar, coffee powder and cocoa. Beat egg whites with cream of tartar until soft peaks form. Gradually add sugar mixture, beating until stiff; fold in cracker crumbs and walnuts. Pour into lightly buttered 9 inch pie pan, and bake at 300° for 30 minutes. Cool.

Topping:

1 tablespoon sugar
½ teaspoon instant coffee powder
1 teaspoon cocoa
1 cup whipping cream

Mix sugar, coffee powder and cocoa. Whip cream until soft peaks form. Gradually add sugar mixture and continue to beat until stiff. Add topping immediately before serving. Serves 6.

Mrs. Denman Smith (Sandra)

Brownie Pie

½ cup margarine
¼ cup cocoa
2 eggs, beaten
1 cup sugar
¼ cup flour
½ teaspoon vanilla extract
1 cup chopped pecans
1 unbaked 9 inch pastry shell
Ice cream

Melt margarine and stir in cocoa. Add remaining ingredients and mix well. Pour into pie shell and bake at 350° for 25 minutes. Cool and refrigerate. Serve topped with ice cream or whipped topping. Serves 8.

Mrs. Terry Steigelman (Kathleen)

Pennsylvania Dutch Pie Crust

3 cups sifted flour
1 teaspoon salt
1¼ cups shortening
1 egg
5 tablespoons water
1 teaspoon vinegar

Combine flour and salt and cut in shortening. Beat egg, adding water and vinegar. Stir into dry ingredients. Chill for approximately two hours, or 30 minutes in the freezer. Roll out on waxed paper. Makes two 9 inch crusts. *Easiest ever and never fails!*

Gail Hunt

Bavarian Chocolate Pie

¾ cup sugar
½ cup flour
¼ teaspoon salt
2 cups milk, divided
1 bar (4 ounces) sweet baking chocolate
3 egg yolks

2 tablespoons butter
1 teaspoon vanilla extract
½ teaspoon butter flavoring
1 cup flaked coconut
¾ cup chopped pecans
1 baked 9 inch pastry shell
Whipped cream for garnish

Combine sugar, flour, salt and ½ cup cold milk. Mix well. Scald remaining 1½ cups milk and add chocolate. Stir until chocolate is melted. Add scalded milk and chocolate to the first mixture and cook until thickened. Beat egg yolks slightly and add slowly to hot mixture, stirring constantly. Continue to cook over low heat for 2 to 3 minutes. Remove from heat and add remaining ingredients. Cool and pour into baked pie shell. Chill and top with whipped cream. Serves 6. *This is the very best chocolate pie you will ever eat.*

Mrs. Terry Jackson (Joyce)

Bless You Yogurt Pie

Crust:
½ cup chopped raw almonds
½ cup chopped pitted dates

1 to 2 tablespoons butter, melted
Dash of cinnamon

Combine almonds and dates in food processor. Dribble in the melted butter, mixing thoroughly. Press into a 9 inch pie pan. Dust on a little cinnamon and chill.

Filling:
1 cup plain lowfat yogurt
8 ounces cream cheese, softened
1 tablespoon honey

1 tablespoon vanilla extract
½ cup sliced fresh strawberries
1 teaspoon honey

In a large bowl mix yogurt, cream cheese, 1 tablespoon honey and vanilla until very smooth. Meanwhile, slice strawberries and sweeten lightly with 1 teaspoon honey. Pour yogurt filling into chilled crust and arrange strawberries on top. Chill at least 3 hours, until set. Serves 6. *This pie is absolutely divine. It's light, very good for you and best of all, less than 250 calories per serving!*

Mrs. Dan Steakley (Susan)

In many recipes yogurt or buttermilk can be substituted for sour cream thus saving precious calories.

Dude's Pecan Pie

1 cup white corn syrup
1 cup dark corn syrup
⅓ cup butter, melted
1 teaspoon salt
1 teaspoon vanilla extract

3 eggs, slightly beaten
1 cup pecans
1 unbaked 9 inch pastry
   shell

Combine corn syrups, butter, salt, vanilla, eggs and pecans. Mix well.
Pour into pie shell and bake at 350° for 45 to 50 minutes or until set.
Serves 6 to 8. *This pie is a Christmas tradition for my family.*

Mrs. Steve McMillon (Mary Beth)

Cashew Pie

2 cups dark corn syrup
⅓ cup brown sugar
4 eggs
½ cup butter
Dash of salt

1 teaspoon vanilla extract
1⅓ cups chopped cashew nuts
1 unbaked 9 inch pastry
   shell

Cook corn syrup and sugar together for 5 minutes, stirring constantly.
Remove from heat. Beat eggs and add syrup gradually, mixing well.
Add butter, salt, vanilla and nuts. Pour into chilled unbaked shell and
bake at 375° for 40 to 45 minutes. Serves 6.

Mrs. Roger Borgelt (Cindy)

Banana Split Pie

8 ounces cream cheese,
   softened
1 cup powdered sugar
5 tablespoons milk
1 graham cracker crust, 9
   inch
2 bananas, sliced

1 can (8 ounces) crushed
   pineapple, drained
1 carton (8 ounces) whipped
   topping
1 bottle (6 ounces)
   maraschino cherries,
   drained

Mix cream cheese, powdered sugar and milk together and put into
graham cracker crust. Slice the bananas and place on top of mixture.
Top with crushed pineapple, followed by the whipped topping. Add
the cherries for decoration. Refrigerate for several hours or overnight
before serving. Serves 6.

Claire Shavers Hayden

Praline Pie

⅓ cup brown sugar
⅓ cup margarine
½ cup pecan pieces
1 baked 9 inch graham
   cracker crust

1 package (3½ ounces)
   instant chocolate pudding
Whipped cream for garnish

Boil sugar, margarine and pecans until sugar is dissolved, about 3 minutes. Place this mixture in the pie shell. Prepare chocolate pudding according to directions; layer on pecan mixture. Refrigerate; top with whipped cream before serving. Serves 6 to 8.

Mary Campbell

Buttermilk Pie

½ cup butter, room
   temperature
2 cups sugar
3 eggs
3 tablespoons flour

1 cup buttermilk
1 teaspoon vanilla extract
1 unbaked 9 inch pastry
   shell

Cream butter and sugar. Add eggs and beat well. Add flour, buttermilk and vanilla, mixing well after each addition. Pour into pastry shell and bake at 350° for 50 to 60 minutes or until set. Serves 6. *This pie freezes well.*

Mrs. B. Lynn Turlington (Jill)

My Favorite Chess Pie

3 eggs, beaten
6 tablespoons butter, melted
1½ cups sugar
1 teaspoon vanilla extract

1 tablespoon cornmeal
1 tablespoon white vinegar
1 unbaked 9 inch pastry
   shell

Mix filling ingredients together and pour into pie shell. Bake at 350° for 35 minutes or until set. Serves 6.

Mrs. Larry Nau (Rose)

Adding cream of tartar when beating egg whites will increase the volume.

Strawberry Satin Pie

Pastry Shell:

1 baked 9 inch pastry shell	½ cup sliced toasted almonds

Bake your favorite crust; cool and cover bottom of the pastry shell with almonds.

Creamy Satin Filling:

½ cup sugar	2 cups milk
3 tablespoons cornstarch	1 egg, slightly beaten
3 tablespoons flour	½ cup whipping cream
½ teaspoon salt	1 teaspoon vanilla extract

Combine sugar, cornstarch, flour and salt. Gradually stir in milk. Bring to a boil, stirring constantly. Lower heat and cook, stirring until thick. Stir a little of the hot mixture into egg and return to hot mixture. Bring just to a boil, stirring constantly. Cool, then chill. Whip cream and vanilla until stiff, then fold into chilled mixture. Pour carefully into pie shell and top with glaze.

Glaze:

3 to 4 cups fresh strawberries	2 teaspoons cornstarch
½ cup water	Dash of red food coloring
¼ cup sugar	Whipped cream for garnish
	Almonds for garnish

Reserve a few whole perfect berries for garnish. Slice 2½ cups strawberries in half. Crush the rest of the berries, at least ½ cup. Add water and cook a couple of minutes. Mix sugar and cornstarch, gradually stirring in berry mixture. Cook and stir until thick and clear. Add food coloring and cool slightly. Place strawberry halves on the filling in a pretty pattern and decorate center with whole berries. Pour glaze over top. Refrigerate until serving time. Serves 8. *To garnish, place rosettes of whipped cream around the edges with a sprinkle of almonds.*

Mrs. Dudley Baker (Kathy)

Crispy Fruit Cobbler Topping

1 cup flour	1 tablespoon shortening
½ cup sugar	1 egg
1 teaspoon baking powder	Fruit pie filling
Dash of salt	Cinnamon, optional

Mix flour, sugar, baking powder, salt, shortening and egg together until crumbly and spread over any pie filling. Sprinkle top with cinnamon, if desired. Bake at 350° for 30 minutes. Serves 6.

Mrs. Eldon Price (Thelma)

MaMaw's Lemon Meringue Pie

Pie:

1 cup sugar	1 lemon rind, grated
3 tablespoons cornstarch	½ cup lemon juice
½ teaspoon salt	2 tablespoons butter
1 cup boiling water	1 baked 9 inch pastry shell
3 egg yolks	

Mix sugar, cornstarch, salt and water in a double boiler. Stir constantly until the mixture boils. Reduce heat. Add a small amount of hot mixture to egg yolks; stir in lemon rind, lemon juice and butter and return to double boiler. Boil for 1 minute, stirring constantly. Cool. Beat lightly before pouring into cool pastry shell.

Meringue:

3 egg whites	Dash of cream of tartar
½ teaspoon baking powder	

Beat the egg whites, baking powder and cream of tarter with electric mixer until stiff peaks form. Place on top of lemon filling and bake at 250° for 15 to 20 minutes, until meringue is lightly browned. Serves 6 to 8.

Mrs. Tom Hollis (Doris)

Dutch Apple Pie

2 tablespoons flour	6 tart apples, peeled, cored and sliced
1 cup sugar	
Pinch of salt	1 cup half and half cream
1 unbaked 9 inch pastry shell	Vanilla ice cream, optional

Mix flour with sugar and salt. Spread evenly into an unbaked pastry shell. Arrange apples over sugar mixture, and pour cream over apples. Sprinkle with cinnamon. Bake at 350° for 1½ hours, or until apples are tender. Serve with vanilla ice cream. Serves 8.

Mrs. Ron Bruney (Carol)

 For measuring purposes, usually 3 medium apples are equal to a pound.

Nutmeg Logs

Logs:

1 cup butter, softened	1 egg
2 teaspoons vanilla extract	3 cups flour
1 teaspoon brandy extract	1½ teaspoons nutmeg
¾ cup sugar	¼ teaspoon salt

Cream butter with vanilla and brandy extracts. Gradually beat in sugar, mixing well. Add egg; sift flour, nutmeg and salt into butter mixture and mix well. Divide into 4 equal portions on a sugared board. Shape each piece into roll 12 inches long and ½ inch in diameter. Cut into 2 inch lengths and place on greased and floured cookie sheets. Bake at 350° for 12 minutes. Cool on racks.

Frosting:

⅓ cup butter	2 cups powdered sugar
1 teaspoon vanilla extract	2 tablespoons light cream
2 teaspoons brandy extract	Colored sugar, optional

Cream butter with vanilla and brandy extracts. Blend in powdered sugar and cream. Beat until smooth and creamy. Frost each log and sprinkle with colored sugar if desired. Yields 48.

Mrs. Dudley Baker (Kathy)

Java Sticks

1 cup unsalted butter, softened	2 cups flour
¾ cup powdered sugar	¼ cup finely ground pecans
2 teaspoons coffee powder	3 ounces semisweet chocolate, melted

Cream together unsalted butter and powdered sugar. Beat in coffee powder, flour and pecans. Roll into finger shapes and place on greased sheet. Bake at 350° for 8 to 10 minutes. Let the sticks cool on racks. Dip in melted chocolate. Yields 6 dozen sticks.

Mrs. Thomas Schwartz (Ellana)

If you need soft margarine or butter in a hurry, grate the sticks in the food processor.

Walnut Frosties

Cookie:
1 cup firmly packed brown sugar
½ cup butter
1 egg

1 teaspoon vanilla extract
1¾ cups flour
½ teaspoon baking soda
¼ teaspoon salt

Cream brown sugar and butter until light and fluffy. Blend in the egg and vanilla. Gradually add flour, baking soda and salt to creamed mixture and mix well. Chill dough about 1 hour.

Topping:
1 cup chopped walnuts
¼ cup sour cream

½ cup firmly packed brown sugar

Preheat oven to 350°. Combine all topping ingredients. Roll chilled dough into 1 inch balls. Place on ungreased cookie sheet about 2 inches apart. With thumb or thimble make an imprint in the center of each cookie and fill with 1 teaspoon of topping. Bake for 10 to 14 minutes or until delicately browned. Yields 36 cookies. *Always place chilled cookie dough on cool cookie sheet to prevent spreading. When storing, place waxed paper between layers of cookies to prevent sticking.*

Mrs. Sid Mann (Kathi)

Walnut Butter Cookies

1 cup butter, melted
2 tablespoons sugar
1 teaspoon baking powder
2¼ cups flour

½ cup finely chopped walnuts
½ cup sugar

Preheat oven to 350°. Combine the melted butter, 2 tablespoons sugar and baking powder. Sift in the flour, about ¼ cup at a time, beating well after each addition; then stir in walnuts. Using about 2 tablespoons of dough, shape into small round balls and flatten with cookie stamp. Place on ungreased cookie sheet and bake 12 to 15 minutes or until lightly browned. Cool the cookies on a rack. Just before serving, sprinkle the cookies with the remaining ½ cup sugar. Yields 24.

Suzanne Smith

Choco Peanut Pan Cookies

1 cup butter
1 cup peanut butter
1 cup sugar
1 cup firmly packed brown
  sugar
2 eggs

1¼ cups flour
1 teaspoon baking soda
½ teaspoon salt
2¼ cups quick oats
1 cup plain chocolate candy
  coated pieces, divided

Beat together the butter, peanut butter and sugars until light and fluffy. Blend in eggs. Combine flour, soda and salt and add to butter mixture. Mix well. Stir in oats and ⅓ cup candies. Pour onto a greased, foil lined cookie sheet with sides. Sprinkle remaining candies on top. Bake at 325° for 25 to 30 minutes or until done. Yields 24 pieces.

Courtney E. Bone

Mom's Peanut Butter Cookies

1¼ cups smooth peanut butter
1 cup sugar
1 cup brown sugar
1 cup shortening
2 eggs

2 teaspoons vanilla extract
2½ cups flour
1½ teaspoons baking soda
1 teaspoon baking powder

Blend until smooth the peanut butter, sugars, shortening, eggs and vanilla. Measure, then sift together, the remaining ingredients. Add to sugar mixture and blend well. Make into small balls, using about a teaspoon of dough for each. Place on an ungreased baking sheet. Flatten each ball slightly using a fork dipped in sugar, creating a crisscross pattern. Bake at 375° for 9 to 10 minutes. Yields 36.

Mrs. Sid Mann (Kathi)

Crunchy Oatmeal Cookies

1 cup butter
1 cup brown sugar
1 cup sugar
1½ cups flour
1 teaspoon salt

1 teaspoon baking soda
2 eggs
1 teaspoon vanilla extract
3 cups oatmeal
½ cup chopped pecans

Cream butter and sugars. Sift together flour, salt and baking soda and add to creamed mixture. Add eggs, vanilla, oatmeal and pecans. Drop from a teaspoon a couple of inches apart onto a cookie sheet and bake at 375° for 10 minutes. Yields 36.

Mrs. W. H. Heggen III (Maryellen)

Oatmeal Crispies

1 cup butter, softened
½ cup sugar
1 cup flour

1½ cups quick cooking oats
Powdered sugar

Beat butter until creamy; add remaining ingredients. Mix well and chill. Shape into tiny balls, slightly larger than marbles. Flatten on ungreased cookie sheets with floured glass or fingers. Bake at 350° for 10 to 12 minutes. Dust with powdered sugar. Store in a tight container. Yields 4 to 5 dozen. *These cookies are dainty and one would never guess oatmeal is an ingredient.*

Mrs. Larry Nau (Rose)

Famous Oatmeal Cookies

1½ cups butter
2 cups dark brown sugar
1 cup sugar
2 teaspoons baking soda
2 teaspoons salt
2 teaspoons vanilla extract

3 eggs
2¼ cups flour
1 cup raisins and/or
   chopped pecans
6 cups oatmeal

Cream butter and sugars until fluffy. Add baking soda, salt, vanilla and eggs. Blend well. Add flour until well blended. Stir in raisins, nuts and oatmeal. Drop from a tablespoon on lightly greased cookie sheets. Bake at 375° for 9 to 11 minutes or until edges are lightly browned. Yields 6 dozen.

Mrs. Terry Jackson (Joyce)

Mom Calhoun's Tea Cakes

4 eggs
2 cups sugar
1 cup butter
¾ teaspoon baking soda

¼ teaspoon salt
1 teaspoon lemon extract
⅔ teaspoon nutmeg
7 cups flour

Mix all ingredients except flour. Sift flour and work into mixture until it will roll. Roll into a log and chill. Slice thinly and bake at 350° for 10 to 12 minutes. Yields 5 dozen.

Mrs. Kempe Hayes (Stephanie)

The Best Sugar Cookies

1	cup granulated sugar	2	teaspoons vanilla extract
1	cup powdered sugar	5	cups flour
1	cup butter	1	teaspoon cream of tartar
2	eggs	¼	teaspoon salt
1	cup oil	1	teaspoon baking soda

Cream sugars and butter; add eggs. Blend in oil and vanilla. Add the dry ingredients and mix well. Roll into balls and flatten with a glass. Bake at 350° for 10 minutes. Yields 6 dozen. *My mother gave me this recipe for these melt-in-your-mouth cookies. We love it!*

Mrs. Terry Jackson (Joyce)

Cream Wafers

Wafers:

1	cup butter, softened	2	cups flour
⅓	cup whipping cream		Sugar

Mix butter, cream and flour thoroughly. Chill. Heat oven to 375°. Divide dough into thirds, and place two-thirds in the refrigerator until ready to roll. Roll one-third of dough to ⅛ inch thickness on floured cloth. Cut with 1½ inch cookie cutter. Place rounds on heavily sugared waxed paper. Turn each round with spatula so both sides are coated with sugar. Place on ungreased baking sheet; prick each about 4 times with fork. Bake 7 to 9 minutes. Cool.

Filling:

¼	cup butter, softened	1	teaspoon vanilla extract
¾	cup powdered sugar		Red or green food coloring,
1	egg yolk		optional

Mix all ingredients until smooth, tinting with food coloring if desired. When cookies are cool, put 2 cookies together with filling. Yields 5 dozen filled cookies.

Mrs. Marcus Bone (Beverly)

Orange Slice Bar Cookies

4	eggs, beaten	¼	teaspoon salt
1	pound orange slice candy, diced	¼	teaspoon baking powder
2	cups brown sugar	1	teaspoon cinnamon
2	cups flour	2	cups chopped pecans

Mix eggs, orange candy and brown sugar. Mix in remaining ingredients and bake in an oiled jelly roll pan at 375° until brown. Test with toothpick for doneness. Yields 48 bar cookies.

Mrs. M. J. Moore (Jean)

Gingerbread Men Cookies

Dough:

½ cup shortening	3 cups flour
½ cup sugar	¼ teaspoon salt
½ cup molasses	½ teaspoon baking soda
½ tablespoon vinegar	½ teaspoon cinnamon
1 egg, beaten	½ teaspoon ginger

Place shortening, sugar, molasses and vinegar in a saucepan and bring to a boil. Remove from heat and cool. Stir in egg. Sift together dry ingredients and add to molasses mixture. Mix well and chill dough for 30 to 45 minutes. Roll the dough out to ¼ to ½ inch thickness and cut with a gingerbread man cookie cutter. Bake at 375° for 12 to 15 minutes on a greased cookie sheet.

Decorator Icing:

1 box (16 ounces) powdered sugar	¼ cup almost boiling water
½ cup shortening	1 teaspoon vanilla extract
	⅛ teaspoon salt

Cut shortening into powdered sugar, then add very hot water. Mix well; add vanilla and salt. Drizzle over cookies. Yields 30 cookies. *These cookies were sold in the gift shop at Christmas at Caswell House in 1984.*

Mrs. Jim Rado (Vicki)

Ice Box Cookies

1 cup shortening	2 eggs
1 cup brown sugar	3 cups flour
1 cup sugar	½ teaspoon baking soda
½ teaspoon salt	¾ cup chopped pecans

Blend shortening, sugars and salt together. Beat in eggs, one at a time. Stir in flour that has been sifted with soda. Add pecans. Shape into a roll about 2½ inches in diameter. Wrap in waxed paper and chill overnight. Cut into ¼ inch slices and bake at 375° for 8 to 10 minutes. Yields 36.

Mrs. Don Kothmann (Sheila)

When baking cakes or cookies, add the flavoring extracts with the liquids, and they will be more easily distributed.

Carrot Cookies

Cookies:

¾ cup shortening
¾ cup sugar
1 egg
1 cup cooked, mashed
  carrots

2 teaspoons vanilla extract
2 cups sifted flour
2 teaspoons baking powder
½ teaspoon salt
½ cup chopped pecans

Blend shortening and sugar. Add egg and carrots and beat. Add vanilla. Sift flour, baking powder and salt together and mix with shortening mixture. Add pecans and mix well. Drop dough from a teaspoon onto greased baking sheets and bake at 375° for 10 to 12 minutes until light brown. Cool cookies.

Frosting:

1¾ cups powdered sugar
1 tablespoon grated
  orange peel

3 tablespoons margarine
1 teaspoon orange extract
Orange juice

Blend sugar, orange peel, margarine, orange extract and enough orange juice to make a spreading consistency. Frost cooled cookies. Yields 5 dozen.

Mrs. Leo Mueller (Nancy)

Almond Crunch Cookies

1 cup sugar
1 cup powdered sugar
1 cup butter
1 cup oil
1 teaspoon almond extract
2 eggs
3½ cups flour
1 cup whole wheat flour

1 teaspoon baking soda
1 teaspoon salt
1 teaspoon cream of tartar
2 cups chopped almonds
1 package (7 ounces)
  almond brickle baking
  chips

Blend sugars, butter and oil together. Add almond extract and eggs and mix well. Mix flours, soda, salt and cream of tartar together. Add slowly to moist mixture. Stir in almonds by hand. Roll into balls, about walnut size or smaller. Crisscross with fork and bake at 350° for 10 to 12 minutes. Yields 8 dozen cookies.

Mrs. William Heggen III (Maryellen)

 Never add vanilla or other flavoring extracts when a mixture is on direct heat, for most of the flavor will be lost. If possible, add when the mixture cools.

Candy Cane Cookies

½ cup butter
1 cup powdered sugar
1 egg
1½ teaspoons almond extract

1 teaspoon vanilla extract
2½ cups flour
1 teaspoon salt
½ teaspoon red food coloring

Cut butter into powdered sugar. Add egg, almond and vanilla extracts. Slowly add flour and salt. Mix well. Divide into 2 parts. Add red food coloring to 1 part. Roll into strips and twist together to form a rope. Shape into candy canes and bake on a greased cookie sheet at 350° for 9 minutes. Yields 24 candy canes.

Mrs. Jim Rado (Vicki)

Cocoa Crunchies

1 cup shortening
2 cups sugar
2 eggs
3 cups flour
¼ teaspoon salt

1 teaspoon baking soda
1½ teaspoons vanilla extract
4 cups chocolate flavored
rice cereal

Cream shortening and sugar. Add eggs and beat until light and fluffy. Add flour, salt, baking soda and vanilla, mixing well. Add cereal. Roll into balls and place about 2 inches apart on an ungreased baking sheet. Bake at 350° for 13 to 15 minutes. Yields 6 to 7 dozen. *Easy, fast and delicious. Tastes like there are nuts, too!*

Mrs. Charles Smith (Jeannie)

Nanemo Bars

¾ cup butter, divided
¼ cup sugar
5 tablespoons cocoa
2 eggs, divided
2 teaspoons vanilla extract,
divided

1⅔ cups graham cracker
crumbs
1 cup grated coconut
½ cup chopped pecans
2¼ to 2½ cups sifted
powdered sugar

In a saucepan combine ½ cup butter, sugar, cocoa, 1 egg, and 1 teaspoon vanilla. Cook over low heat, stirring constantly until thickened. Stir in graham cracker crumbs. Add grated coconut and pecans. Press into a 9 inch square pan and refrigerate. Cream ¼ cup butter and gradually beat in powdered sugar. Add 1 egg and 1 teaspoon vanilla. Spread filling over crumb mixture and chill 15 minutes. Serves 12.

Mrs. Robert S. Brown (Mary)

Mint Stick Brownies

Cookie:

2 squares baking chocolate
½ cup butter
2 eggs, well beaten
1 cup sugar

¼ teaspoon peppermint flavoring
½ cup sifted flour
⅛ teaspoon salt
½ cup chopped pecans

Melt chocolate and butter together over hot water. Cool. Add remaining ingredients. Pour batter into a well greased 9 inch square pan. Bake at 350° for 20 to 25 minutes. Cool. Frost brownies with the double layer of frosting.

Mint Frosting:

2 tablespoons soft butter
1 cup sifted powdered sugar
1 tablespoon whipping cream

½ teaspoon peppermint flavoring
Few drops green food coloring, optional

Mix all ingredients together until creamy and spread on cooled brownies. Refrigerate while making glaze.

Glaze:

1 square baking chocolate

1 tablespoon butter

Combine chocolate and butter and melt over hot water. Blend well. Dribble glaze over Mint Frosting. Carefully tilt pan back and forth to cover surface. Refrigerate to set chocolate glaze. Cut into fingerlike sticks. Yields 4 dozen brownies. *Attractive party cookies can be made by cutting diagonally across the pan and then cutting diagonally the other way to make small brownies.* **The Cookbook Committee**

Gingersnaps

1½ cups shortening
2 cups sugar
2 eggs
½ cup molasses
4 cups flour

2 teaspoons baking soda
2 teaspoons ground cinnamon
2 teaspoons ground cloves
2 teaspoons ginger
½ cup sugar

Cream together shortening and sugar; beat in eggs. Add molasses and mix well. Sift together flour, baking soda, cinnamon, cloves and ginger; blend into creamed mixture. Chill dough for 1 hour. Roll into 1 inch balls and dip into sugar. Place on lightly greased cookie sheet 2 inches apart. Press each ball to flatten. Bake at 375° for 12 to 15 minutes. Yields 12 dozen.

Mrs. Ron Bruney (Carol)

Chewy Brownies

2 squares (1 ounce each)
unsweetened chocolate
⅓ cup butter
1 cup sugar
2 eggs

1 cup unsifted flour
¼ teaspoon baking powder
¼ teaspoon salt
½ teaspoon vanilla extract
½ cup chopped pecans

Place chocolate squares in medium glass bowl. Microwave on MEDIUM, for 1 minute. Add butter and microwave for 1 minute more, or until melted. Stir in sugar and beat in eggs. Stir in remaining ingredients. Spread batter into a 8x8 glass baking dish and microwave on LOW for 7 minutes. Then increase baking speed to HIGH for 3 to 4 minutes, or until puffed and dry on top. Cool until set; cut into bars. Yields 16 square brownies.

Mrs. Ken Moyer (Bonnie)

Best Ever Brownies

½ cup butter
2 cups dark brown sugar
2 eggs
1 teaspoon vanilla extract
1 cup whole wheat pastry
flour

1 cup unbleached white
flour
¼ teaspoon salt
2 teaspoons baking powder
1 cup shredded coconut

Melt butter and add brown sugar over low heat, until bubbly. Remove from heat and cool. Add eggs one at a time, beating thoroughly after each addition. Add vanilla, dry ingredients and coconut. Mix thoroughly. Spread in a 9x13 inch baking dish and bake at 325° for 30 minutes or until done in center. Cut into squares while warm. Yields 16 squares.

Mrs. Dan S. Steakley (Susan)

St. Nick Cookies

1 cup butter
½ cup sifted powdered sugar
1 teaspoon vanilla extract
2¼ cups flour

¼ teaspoon salt
1 cup finely chopped pecans
Powdered sugar

Cream butter and sugar; add vanilla. Combine flour and salt and stir into sugar mixture. Add pecans. Chill dough. Shape into 1 inch balls and place about 2 inches apart on an ungreased cookie sheet. Bake at 375° until set, but not brown. Roll in powdered sugar while warm and again when cookies have cooled. Yields 48 cookies.

Mrs. Henry Alexander (Roma)

Chocolate Chip Squares

1 cup butter	2¼ cups flour
¾ cup sugar	1 teaspoon baking soda
¾ cup brown sugar	1 teaspoon salt
1 teaspoon vanilla extract	1 package (12 ounces)
½ teaspoon water	semisweet chocolate chips
2 eggs	1 cup chopped pecans

Cream butter, sugars, vanilla and water. Add eggs, blending well. Add flour, ½ cup at a time, mixing after each addition; add soda and salt. Stir in chocolate chips and pecans with a spoon. Pour into a greased 15x10 inch jelly roll pan and bake at 350° for 15 to 20 minutes. Cut into squares when cool. Yields 48 squares.

Cyndee McBee

Cream Cheese Brownies

1 package (4 ounces) sweet baking chocolate	1½ teaspoons vanilla extract, divided
5 tablespoons butter, divided	½ cup unsifted flour
3 ounces cream cheese, softened	½ teaspoon baking powder
	¼ teaspoon salt
1 cup sugar	½ cup coarsely chopped pecans
3 eggs, divided	¼ teaspoon almond extract
1 tablespoon flour	

Melt chocolate and 3 tablespoons butter over very low heat, stirring constantly. Cool. Cream remaining butter with cream cheese until softened. Gradually add sugar, beating until light and fluffy. Blend in 1 egg, 1 tablespoon flour and ½ teaspoon vanilla. Set aside. Beat remaining eggs until thick and light in color. Gradually add remaining ½ cup flour, baking powder and salt. Blend in cooled chocolate mixture, pecans, almond extract and remaining 1 teaspoon vanilla. Measure 1 cup chocolate batter and set aside. Spread remaining chocolate batter into a greased 9 inch square pan. Top with cheese mixture. Drop measured chocolate batter by tablespoon onto cheese mixture, and swirl with spatula to marble. Bake at 350° for 35 minutes. Cool before cutting into squares. Cover and store in refrigerator. Yields 16 brownies.

Mrs. Ron Bruney (Carol)

Always store eggs with the large end up.

Brownie Mix

4 cups flour
1 tablespoon plus 1
  teaspoon baking powder
1 tablespoon salt

8 cups sugar
2½ cups cocoa
2 cups shortening

Combine dry ingredients. Mix well. Cut in shortening with pastry blender until the mixture resembles coarse meal. Place in an airtight container. Store in a cool place or in the refrigerator for up to 6 weeks. Yields 16 cups.

Mildred Bradford

Quick and Easy Brownies

3 cups Brownie Mix
3 eggs, beaten

1½ teaspoons vanilla extract
½ cup chopped pecans

Combine all ingredients, stirring until well mixed. Spoon into a greased and floured 8 inch square pan and bake at 350° for 35 to 40 minutes. Cut into squares. Yields 16.

Mildred Bradford

Cherry Coconut Bars

Pastry:
2 cups sifted flour
1 cup butter, room
  temperature

4 tablespoons powdered
  sugar

Heat oven to 350°. Coat a 9x13 inch pan with nonstick spray or grease lightly. Mix flour, butter and powdered sugar until smooth. Moisten fingers and spread into pan. Bake at 350° for 25 minutes, until lightly browned.

Filling:
4 egg whites
2 cups sugar
½ cup flour
½ teaspoon salt
2 teaspoons vanilla
  extract

1½ cups chopped pecans
1 cup coconut
½ cup quartered maraschino
  cherries, well drained

Beat egg whites until frothy. Stir the rest of the ingredients into egg whites. Spread over top of hot pastry. Bake at 350° for 25 minutes. Cool. Cut into bars. Yields 24. *This has been a Mann family favorite recipe for 25 years.*

Mrs. Sid Mann (Kathi)

Chewy Peanut Butter Bars

⅓ cup shortening
½ cup peanut butter
¼ cup brown sugar
1 cup sugar
1 teaspoon vanilla extract
2 eggs

1 cup flour
¼ teaspoon salt
1 teaspoon baking powder
1 can (3½ ounces) flaked
   coconut

Cream shortening, peanut butter and sugars together. Add vanilla and eggs. Mix in flour, salt and baking powder. Stir in coconut. Spread evenly in a greased 9x12 inch pan. Bake at 350° for 25 minutes. Cool and cut into squares. Yields 24.

Mrs. Roger Borgelt (Cindy)

Cookies and Cream Ice Cream

6 eggs
1 cup sugar
1 can (14 ounces) sweetened
   condensed milk
3 tablespoons vanilla extract
Dash of salt

1 package (3 ounces) instant
   vanilla pudding
2 cups half and half cream
1 package (1 pound 4
   ounces) chocolate fudge
   sandwich cookies, crushed
Milk to fill gallon container

Beat eggs until frothy. Add sugar until well mixed. Add remaining ingredients, except cookies. Mix well and pour into freezer container. Stir in cookies, add enough milk to fill container, and freeze in ice cream freezer until firm. Yields 1 gallon.

Dudley Duggan Baker, IV

Frozen Pumpkin Pie

1½ pints butter pecan ice
   cream, softened
1 cup canned pumpkin
1 cup sugar
1 teaspoon cinnamon

¼ teaspoon ginger
¼ teaspoon nutmeg
Pinch of salt
1 cup whipping cream

Line a 9 inch pie pan with ice cream to resemble a crust. Freeze. Combine pumpkin, sugar, cinnamon, ginger, nutmeg and salt. Place in a saucepan and cook for 3 minutes over low heat until the sugar is melted. Remove from heat and cool. Whip cream and fold into cooled filling. Pour into pie crust and freeze until firm. Remove from freezer about 15 minutes before serving. Serves 6 to 8.

Mrs. Bob Edgecomb (Mary)

Peanut Butter Ice Cream Pie

1 quart vanilla ice cream
1 cup creamy peanut butter

1 graham cracker crust, 9 inch
Chocolate sauce, optional

Soften ice cream in a mixing bowl, add peanut butter and mix thoroughly. Fill crust with mixture and freeze. Drizzle with chocolate sauce if desired. Serves 6.

Mrs. Roger Borgelt (Cindy)

Avocado Ice Cream

4 eggs, beaten
2½ cups sugar, divided
4 cups milk
1 teaspoon vanilla extract
1 teaspoon almond extract

2 cups half and half cream
5 ripe avocados, peeled and seeded
2 cups whipping cream

Beat together eggs and 2 cups sugar. Combine with milk in a saucepan and cook, stirring constantly, over medium heat until smooth and custard is formed. Remove from heat and stir in vanilla and almond extracts and chill. Process half and half cream and avocados in blender until smooth. Add to chilled custard. Whip remaining cream with ½ cup sugar until soft peaks form and fold into custard mixture. Freeze according to freezer directions. Yields ½ gallon.

Mrs. Denman Smith (Sandra)

Creme de Menthe Freeze

2 boxes (8½ ounces each) chocolate wafers
½ cup margarine, melted
1 cup powdered sugar

½ gallon vanilla ice cream, softened
3 ounces creme de menthe

Crush wafers. Reserve ½ cup crumbs. Combine remaining crumbs, margarine and sugar. Press into the bottom of a 9x13 inch pan. Place in freezer. Whip together ice cream and creme de menthe and pour over crust. Garnish with remaining wafer crumbs. Freeze until ready to serve. Serves 12.

Mrs. Greg Gordon (Kathy)

Elsie's Old Fashioned Homemade Ice Cream

5 eggs, beaten	3 cups fresh fruit of your
1 tablespoon vanilla extract	choice, peeled and
1 can (12 ounces)	mashed
evaporated milk	Milk

Beat eggs; add vanilla, evaporated milk and fruit. Pour milk into ice cream freezer to fill line. Freeze until stiff. Pack with ice and cover with newspaper and let set 30 minutes. Yields 1 gallon.

Mrs. Steve McMillon (Mary Beth)

Cognac Ice Cream

8 cups milk	4 tablespoons vanilla extract
4 cups sugar, divided	16 egg yolks
1 cup cognac	4 cups whipping cream

Combine milk, 2 cups sugar, cognac and vanilla in a large saucepan. Bring to a simmer over medium heat. Remove from heat and cool 10 minutes. Combine remaining 2 cups sugar with egg yolks in a large mixing bowl and beat at medium speed until mixture is thick and falls from beaters in ribbons. With mixer running, add warm milk to yolk mixture in a slow, steady stream, blending well. Return to saucepan. Cook over medium low heat until thickened. *Do not boil.* Cool at room temperature. Blend in cream and transfer to a chilled freezer canister and freeze according to manufacturer's directions. Yields 1 gallon.

Mrs. Jim Rado (Vicki)

Grapefruit Sorbet

8 large Texas Ruby Red	2 cups sugar
grapefruit	32 ounces water

Remove all peel and section the grapefruit. Place the sections in a ceramic or stainless steel pan. Mix sugar and water and simmer on low heat until all sugar is dissolved. Cool. Pour the light syrup over grapefruit sections and freeze. Before serving, place sorbet in food processor with steel blade; blend quickly. Scoop mixture into balls for serving and return to the freezer to firm and hold shape until serving. Yields 2 quarts, 16 (4 ounce) scoops.

Mrs. Mark White (Linda Gayle)

Our Texas Ruby Red grapefruits are richer in Vitamin A than their yellow-fleshed counterparts.

Champagne Ice

½ cup sugar
1⅓ cups spring water
1½ cups champagne
1⅓ cups lemon lime soda

2 teaspoons lime juice
Mint leaves to garnish
Kiwi slices to garnish

Mix all ingredients and freeze. When frozen, blend mixture into a slush and pour into serving bowls and refreeze. Remove from freezer just before serving and garnish with fresh mint and kiwi slices. Yields 4 cups. *This can be used as a dessert or to cleanse the palate between courses.*

Mrs. O. B. Carlson (Marie)

Orange Sherbet

½ cup orange liqueur
3 jars (6 ounces each)
   cocktail cherry juice

5 cans (11 ounces each)
   orange segments, drained
Lemon sherbet

Mix orange liqueur with juice from cherries. Add orange segments and let soak overnight. Arrange oranges on a scoop of sherbet and drizzle with 1 tablespoon orange liqueur/cherry syrup. Serves 16. *This is an elegant and cool dessert!*

Mrs. Ron Bruney (Carol)

Apricot Ice Cream Freeze

2½ cups crushed vanilla
   wafers
½ cup butter, melted
1 teaspoon slivered almonds

3 pints vanilla ice cream,
   softened
1 jar (16 ounces) apricot
   preserves

Mix vanilla wafers, butter and almonds together and line an 8x8 inch pan with one-third of the crumb mixture. Cover with half the softened vanilla ice cream, then spread with half of the apricot preserves. Repeat, finishing with crumbs as the top layer. Cover with foil and place in the freezer for 3 to 4 hours. Slice and serve. Serves 16.

Mrs. D. D. Baker, Jr. (Agnes)

Manhattan Pudding

Orange Ice:

2 cups water	1 teaspoon grated orange
1 cup sugar	rind
¼ teaspoon salt	1 cup orange juice

Boil water and sugar for 5 minutes. Add salt and rind; let cool. Add orange juice and pour into a loaf pan or an ice cube tray with sections removed and partially freeze. Do not stir.

Topping:

2 cups whipping cream	1 teaspoon vanilla extract
1 cup chopped pecans	½ cup sugar

Whip cream and add pecans, vanilla and sugar. Mix well and pour over sherbet. Freeze and slice. Serves 6.

Mrs. Charlie W. Ford (Ruth)

Frozen Chocolate Peanut Squares

¾ cup butter, divided	1½ cups salted peanuts,
2 cups vanilla wafer crumbs	coarsely chopped, divided
2 cups powdered sugar	½ gallon vanilla ice cream,
3 eggs	slightly softened
1 package (6 ounces) semisweet chocolate chips, melted	

Melt ¼ cup of butter and mix with crumbs. Press evenly into the bottom of a 9x13 inch dish. In a large bowl, beat remaining ½ cup butter and powdered sugar until creamy. Beat in eggs, one at a time; then beat in chocolate until well blended. Fold in 1 cup of peanuts. Spread mixture evenly over the crust. Freeze until chocolate mixture is firm, at least 30 minutes. Spread vanilla ice cream evenly over top. Sprinkle with remaining ½ cup peanuts. Cover and freeze until firm, at least 12 hours. Let stand at room temperature 5 to 10 minutes before cutting into squares to serve. Yields 16 squares.

Mrs. Craig Smith (Sherrie)

 Pecans are native to the United States. Pecans do not keep for long periods of time, so it is best to store shelled nuts in the freezer.

Frozen Chocolate Dessert

Crust:
1½ cups finely crushed
  chocolate wafers

⅔ cup melted butter

Mix and press into a 9 inch pie pan. Bake at 325° for 10 minutes.

Filling:
8 ounces cream cheese,
  softened
½ cup sugar, divided
1 teaspoon vanilla extract
2 eggs, divided

1 package (6 ounces)
  semisweet chocolate
  chips, melted
1 cup whipping cream,
  whipped
¾ cup chopped pecans

Combine cream cheese, ¼ cup sugar and vanilla, mixing until well blended. Beat egg yolks and stir in along with melted chocolate. Beat egg whites until soft peaks form, gradually adding ¼ cup sugar. Fold egg whites into chocolate mixture. Then fold in whipped cream and gently stir in pecans. Pour over crumbs and freeze. Remove about ½ hour before serving. Serves 8.

Mrs. Dudley Baker (Kathy)

Peaches and almonds are members of the same family.

Butter Peach Crisp

5 cups peeled sliced fresh
  peaches
1¼ cups flour, divided
⅓ cup brown sugar
½ teaspoon cinnamon
½ teaspoon nutmeg, divided

½ cup water
1 cup sugar
1 teaspoon baking powder
½ teaspoon salt
1 egg, beaten
½ cup butter, melted

Put peaches in an oblong glass baking dish. Combine ¼ cup flour with brown sugar, cinnamon, ¼ teaspoon nutmeg and water. Blend well and stir into peaches. Combine remaining flour, nutmeg, sugar, baking powder and salt. Add egg and stir with fork until crumbly. Sprinkle over peaches. Drizzle butter over topping and bake at 350° for 70 to 80 minutes. Serves 8.

Mrs. Jim Schultz (Mary Kay)

Pan Chocolate Eclairs

Cake:

1   package (16 ounces)
    graham crackers, divided
2   packages (3 ounces each)
    instant vanilla pudding

3⅓ cups milk
1   carton (8 ounces) whipped
    topping

Butter the bottom of a 9x13 inch cake pan and line with graham crackers, trying to fit right to the edges. Mix the pudding with milk and beat at medium speed for 2 minutes. Fold in whipped topping and pour half the pudding mixture over the crackers. Place a second layer of whole graham crackers over the pudding and pour the remaining pudding on top. Place a third and final layer of graham crackers on top and cover with plastic wrap. Refrigerate for 2 hours.

Frosting:

¼   cup cocoa or 1 square (1
    ounce) unsweetened
    chocolate, melted
2   teaspoons white corn
    syrup

2   teaspoons vanilla extract
2   tablespoons margarine,
    softened
1½ cups powdered sugar
3   tablespoons milk

Beat all frosting ingredients together until smooth and spread over cooled cake. Cover and refrigerate for 24 hours. Serves 16.

Mrs. Chris Reed

Butternut Apple Crisp

¾   cup packed brown sugar,
    divided
2   tablespoons lemon juice
1   teaspoon ground cinnamon
½   teaspoon salt
1   small butternut squash

1   can (20 ounces) sliced
    apples, undrained
½   cup flour
½   cup quick rolled oats
6   tablespoons butter
Whipped cream

Combine ½ cup brown sugar, lemon juice, cinnamon and salt. Pare, quarter, seed and slice the butternut squash. Mix squash, apple slices and brown sugar mixture, tossing gently to coat. Turn mixture into a 10x6x2 inch baking dish. Bake covered at 375° for 30 minutes. Combine flour, oats and the remaining ¼ cup brown sugar; cut in butter until mixture resembles coarse crumbs. Sprinkle over mixture. Bake uncovered 45 minutes until squash is tender and topping is browned. Serve with whipped cream. Serves 6. *This is a vitamin-packed squash that sneaks into a fun and flavorful dessert.*

Mrs. Joe Bowles (Mary)

Pumpkin Roll

Roll:

3   eggs
1   cup sugar
¾   cup canned pumpkin
1   teaspoon lemon juice
¾   cup flour
1   teaspoon baking powder

2   teaspoons cinnamon
½   teaspoon ground cloves
¼   teaspoon salt
¼   teaspoon ginger
1   cup pecans
Powdered sugar

Beat eggs with mixer on high for 5 minutes. Add sugar and beat 5 minutes more. Add pumpkin and lemon juice and mix well. Combine dry ingredients, then add to pumpkin mixture. Line a 15x10x2 inch jelly roll pan with waxed paper. Pour into pan and top with pecans. Bake at 375° for 12 to 15 minutes. Sprinkle powdered sugar on a 15x10 inch linen towel. Loosen roll from pan and turn out onto towel. Peel off waxed paper and roll. Cool on rack. Unroll and spread with filling. Reroll and refrigerate.

Filling:

¼   cup butter, softened
4   ounces cream cheese,
    softened
1   cup powdered sugar

½   teaspoon vanilla extract
½   teaspoon butter flavoring
Pinch of salt

Cream butter and cream cheese together; add powdered sugar and mix well. Add vanilla, butter flavoring and salt. Spread on roll. Serves 15 to 20.

Mrs. Rick Denbow (Susan)

Strawberry Dessert

1   box (12 ounces) vanilla
    wafers, crushed, divided
¾   cup butter
1   cup sugar
2   eggs

½   cup chopped pecans
2   boxes (10 ounces each)
    frozen sliced strawberries
1   cup whipping cream,
    whipped

Place three-fourths of the crushed vanilla wafers on the bottom of a 9x13 inch pan. Cream butter and sugar and add the eggs, one at a time. Put this as a layer over the vanilla wafers. Spread the pecans as the next layer. Spoon thawed strawberries with juice on top of the pecans. Cover with whipping cream and sprinkle the remaining vanilla wafer crumbs on top. Refrigerate until ready to serve. Serves 12 to 15. *This is a very good light dessert for a hot summer day. You can substitute 1 cup crushed, drained pineapple for strawberries.*

Mrs. David Armour (Betsy)

Apple Betty

1 cup sugar
¾ cup flour
½ teaspoon cinnamon
¼ teaspoon nutmeg

½ cup margarine
4 cups peeled and sliced
apples

Combine sugar, flour, cinnamon and nutmeg. Cut margarine into dry ingredients and set aside. Place peeled and sliced apples in a buttered 9 inch pie pan. Sprinkle dry ingredients over apples and spread evenly. Bake at 375° for 45 minutes. Cool slightly before serving. Serves 6. *Serve warm with vanilla ice cream.*

Mrs. Jerry Holder (Pat)

Cannoli

Shells:
1¾ cups flour
½ teaspoon salt
2 tablespoons sugar
1 egg, slightly beaten

2 tablespoons butter
¼ cup dry white vermouth
Egg white
Oil

Sift flour with salt and sugar. Make a well in the center and add egg and butter. Cut into small pieces and stir with a fork, working from center out. To moisten flour mixture, add vermouth, 1 tablespoon at a time, until dough begins to cling together. Form dough into a ball. Cover and let stand for 15 minutes. Roll dough out on floured board until very thin. Cut into 3½ inch circles. Roll circles into ovals. Wrap around cannoli forms; seal edge with egg white. Fry 2 or 3 at a time in deep hot oil about 1 minute until lightly golden. Remove with tongs to paper towels to drain; let cool about 15 seconds then slip out of form carefully. Cool shells completely before filling.

Filling:
2 pounds Ricotta cheese
1½ cups powdered sugar
4 teaspoons vanilla
extract
¼ cup chopped citron

Chopped orange peel
Powdered sugar for garnish
Chocolate shavings for
garnish

Beat Ricotta cheese with mixer until very smooth. Fold in remaining ingredients. Chill several hours. Fill shells before serving. If filled more than an hour before serving, shells may become soft. Sprinkle powdered sugar over shells, then garnish with chocolate shavings. Serves 10. *This is a traditional Italian dessert.*

Mrs. Art DeFelice (Connie)

Baklava

1½ cups sugar, divided
1½ cups water
1 cup honey
Whole peel of 1 lemon, not grated
1 cinnamon stick
4 whole cloves

1 pound pecans, finely chopped
2 teaspoons ground cinnamon
1 teaspoon allspice
1 pound frozen phyllo strudel dough leaves
1 pound melted butter

Combine 1 cup sugar, water, honey, lemon peel, cinnamon stick and whole cloves in a saucepan and bring to a boil. Lower heat and simmer for 15 minutes. Remove lemon peel and spices and cool. In a large bowl combine the pecans, remaining ½ cup sugar, ground cinnamon and allspice. Set aside. Lay the phyllo sheets flat; cover with a slightly damp, clean towel and keep covered except when removing to assemble the baklava. Count 8 sheets for bottom layer. Brush melted butter on the bottom of a 17x11x1 baking sheet. Lay a phyllo sheet on the bottom of the pan, brush with warm butter and repeat, using 8 sheets. Sprinkle ⅓ of the nut mixture evenly over the 8th layer. Add 3 more phyllo sheets, brushing each with butter. Sprinkle again with ⅓ of nut mixture. Add 3 more buttered phyllo sheets. Then, using a long, very sharp knife, cut baklava from top to bottom into diamond shapes. Be sure the knife touches the bottom of the pan as you cut. Heat remaining butter to sizzling and pour over top. Bake at 300° for 40 to 60 minutes or until flaky and golden in color. Remove from oven to a rack and spoon the cooled syrup over the entire pastry. Cool in pan and serve each piece in a cupcake baking cup. This avoids handling each delicate piece too much. Yields 50. *Store in airtight container for up to 4 days. Freezes well.*

Mrs. Don Bradford (Melinda)

Flaming Bourbon Apples

1 large tart apple, cored, peeled and cut into ⅛ inch slices
1 tablespoon fresh lemon juice

2 tablespoons butter
2 tablespoons brown sugar
2 tablespoons warmed bourbon
Topping of your choice

Combine apple slices and lemon juice in a bowl and toss gently. Melt butter in a medium skillet; and add apples and cook, turning frequently, until crisp-tender, about 10 minutes. Stir in brown sugar. Add bourbon and flame, shaking skillet gently until flame subsides. Serve warm with desired topping. Serves 2. *This is a versatile dessert and is delicious served with a dollop of sour cream, yogurt or vanilla ice cream.*

Mrs. Cecil Smith (Diana)

Butterscotch Cheesecake Bars

1 package (12 ounces)
butterscotch chips
⅓ cup margarine, melted
2 cups graham cracker
crumbs
1 cup chopped pecans

8 ounces cream cheese,
softened
1 can (14 ounces) sweetened
condensed milk
1 teaspoon vanilla extract
1 egg

In a medium saucepan melt butterscotch chips and margarine over medium heat. Remove from heat and stir in crumbs and pecans. Press half the mixture firmly into bottom of a greased 9x13 inch baking pan. Beat cream cheese until fluffy. Add condensed milk, vanilla and egg and mix well. Pour on top of crumbs, and top with remaining crumb mixture. Bake at 325° for 25 to 30 minutes. Cool to room temperature, then chill before cutting into bars. Refrigerate leftovers. Yields 48 bars.

Mrs. Tommy Gardner (Peggy)

Bread Pudding with Rum Sauce

Pudding:
3 tablespoons butter
1 loaf (1 pound) French
bread
1 quart milk
2 cups sugar

3 eggs
2 tablespoons vanilla
extract
1 cup raisins

Preheat oven to 350°. Melt butter in a 4 quart baking dish over low heat. Cool. Tear bread into large pieces and place in a very large bowl. Pour milk over. Let stand several minutes, then lightly stir bread until soaked through. Beat sugar, eggs and vanilla in a medium bowl to blend. Add to bread mixture. Stir in raisins. Pour into prepared dish. Bake at 350° for about 2 hours or until firm. Let cool.

Rum Sauce:
1 egg, room temperature
1 cup sugar

½ cup butter, melted and hot
2 to 4 tablespoons rum

Beat egg in a small bowl until thick and lemon colored. Gradually, add sugar, beating constantly until thick, 2 to 3 minutes. Add hot, melted butter and stir until smooth. Blend in rum. If sauce is too thick, thin with water to desired consistency. Pour sauce over pudding. Serves 6.

Mrs. Marcus Bone (Beverly)

Candied Marmalog

1½ cups butter
1 package (16 ounces)
   marshmallows
2 tablespoons brown sugar
1 tablespoon vanilla extract
1 box (16 ounces) vanilla
   wafers, finely crushed

4 ounces candied pineapple,
   chopped
4 ounces candied cherries,
   chopped
1 can (3½ ounces) flaked
   coconut
16 ounces whole pecans,
   chopped

In a large saucepan melt butter and marshmallows. When melted, add brown sugar and vanilla. In a large mixing bowl combine cookie crumbs, fruit, coconut and pecans. Pour hot mixture over fruit and stir well. Form into rolls and wrap with waxed paper. Refrigerate or freeze. Slice to serve. Yields 2 rolls. *This is a wonderful accompaniment to a tray of holiday sweets.*

Mrs. B. Lynn Turlington (Jill)

Strawberry Shortcake Royal

Shortcake:
⅓ cup shortening
2½ cups biscuit mix
3 tablespoons sugar
1 teaspoon vanilla extract

¾ cup milk
1 to 1½ quarts strawberries,
   sliced
⅓ cup sugar

Cut shortening into biscuit mix until crumbly. Combine 3 tablespoons sugar with vanilla and milk. Stir into biscuit mix. Pat into 2 well greased 8 inch cake pans. Bake at 425° for 12 to 15 minutes. Cool. Sprinkle berries with ⅓ cup sugar and let stand 30 minutes. Spread half the sweetened berries on a shortcake layer. Top with the second layer and add remaining berries. Spoon Triple Cream Sauce over shortcake.

Triple Cream Sauce:
1 cup vanilla ice cream,
   softened
½ cup sour cream

¼ cup sugar
1 teaspoon vanilla extract
1 cup whipping cream

Combine softened ice cream, sour cream, sugar and vanilla. Whip cream until quite stiff. Thoroughly fold into ice cream mixture. Serves 6 to 8.

Mrs. Bill Hayes (Ginger)

Fruit Pizza

Crust:

1 cup margarine, softened	1½ cups flour
½ cup sugar	¾ cup finely chopped pecans

Mix all ingredients and pat into a greased pizza pan. Bake at 350° for 18 to 20 minutes. Cool.

Filling:

8 ounces cream cheese, softened	½ cup sugar

Beat cream cheese with sugar and spread over the cooled pie crust. Select 2 or 3 of the following toppings:

Toppings:

Pineapple	Kiwi fruit
Mandarin oranges	Strawberries
Peaches	Blueberries
Bananas	Cherries

Arrange fruit pieces over cream cheese layer.

Glaze:

1 cup apricot, peach, plum or currant jam or jelly	6 tablespoons water

Choose your favorite jam or jelly for the glaze and thin with water. Cook until melted and drizzle over fruit. Serves 16.

Mrs. Cary Petri (Sherry)

Old Fashioned Egg Custard

6 cups milk	¾ teaspoon salt
6 eggs	1 tablespoon vanilla extract
1 cup sugar	12 to 16 tablespoons brown sugar

Scald milk. Beat eggs and add sugar gradually. Add to milk. Add salt and vanilla. Put 1 tablespoon brown sugar in the bottom of each of 12 to 16 custard cups. Pour milk mixture into each. Set custard cups in a pan containing enough water to come about one inch up the sides of the cups. Bake at 350° for 45 minutes or until set. Serves 12 to 16.

Mrs. Al Myers (Jan)

Plan to let eggs come to room temperature before using them in a recipe.

Irish Coffee Cream

½ cup milk
¼ cup Irish whiskey
1 teaspoon instant coffee powder

1 quart vanilla ice cream, slightly softened
Whipped cream, optional

Pour milk, whiskey, instant coffee and ice cream into blender and mix well. Pour into 4 goblets and top with whipped cream. Serves 4. *This is a fast and easy dessert.*

Mrs. David King (Priscilla)

Almond Dessert

6 eggs, separated, at room temperature
1 cup butter, room temperature
3 cups powdered sugar, divided

1 cup chopped almonds, toasted in butter
½ pound vanilla wafers, crushed

Beat egg whites very stiff. In a separate bowl beat egg yolks until thick. Cream butter and 1½ cups sugar. Add egg yolks. Beat and add remaining sugar. Add toasted almonds to mixture, saving a few almonds for top. Fold in egg whites. Pour crumbs into an 8x12 inch dish, reserving some for top. Add mixture. Garnish with almonds and crumbs. Refrigerate 48 hours before serving. Serves 12. *It is very important to have butter and eggs at room temperature or mixture will curdle.*

Mrs. Jim Schultz (Mary Kay)

Brandied Strawberries

1 quart fresh strawberries, stems removed
½ cup sugar
½ cup orange juice concentrate

½ cup brandy
1 cup whipping cream
1 tablespoon sugar

Gently stir strawberries into a mixture of sugar, orange juice concentrate and brandy. Let stand 30 minutes. Meanwhile whip cream with 1 tablespoon sugar. Serve in individual dishes topped with whipped cream. Yields 1 quart.

Mrs. Terry Arndt (Barbara)

Easy Chocolate Mousse

1   package (12 ounces)
    semisweet chocolate chips
¾ cups boiling water
8   eggs, separated
½ tablespoon almond extract
1   tablespoon coffee flavored
    liqueur

½ teaspoon instant coffee
    powder, dissolved
1   carton (8 ounces) whipped
    topping
Cherries

Combine chocolate chips in blender with boiling water and egg yolks. Add almond extract, liqueur and coffee and blend. Beat egg whites. Fold egg whites into chocolate mixture. Place in freezer until serving time. Remove 5 to 8 minutes before serving. Serve in parfait, sundae or pilsner glasses. Top with whipped topping and a cherry. Serves 8. *Best made 2 to 3 hours before serving. Should not be put in freezer overnight.*

Mrs. James Albrecht (Donne)

Chocolate Fondue

3   bars (3 ounces each) milk
    chocolate
3   tablespoons whipping
    cream

2   tablespoons brandy
½ tablespoon instant coffee
Pinch of cinnamon

Dissolve chocolate in a fondue pot over low heat. Add cream, brandy, coffee and cinnamon, stirring well. Place the pot on a candle warmer or very low sterno flame. Serves 4. *If fondue gets too thick, stir in a little more brandy. Place goodies such as cherries, strawberries, banana slices, apple slices or pound cake cubes on a skewer to dip fondue. Make sure fruit is dry.*

Mrs. Bob McGoldrick (Fran)

Almond Snow Jell

2   packages unflavored
    gelatin
½ cup water

1   quart whole milk
½ cup sugar
1   tablespoon almond extract

Soften gelatin in water. Scald milk. Add sugar, gelatin and almond extract to milk. Pour into individual bowls or 1 quart mold. Refrigerate until firm. Serve with Mandarin oranges, strawberries or kiwi fruit. Serves 6. *A light refreshing, easy dessert. A typical end to a Chinese meal.*

Mrs. William Dufour (Vera)

Cherry-Berry Cobbler

1 package (10 ounces) frozen raspberries, thawed	1 can (16 ounces) tart cherries, pitted and drained
¼ cup sugar	¼ cup margarine, softened
1½ tablespoons cornstarch	¼ cup sugar
⅛ teaspoon salt	½ cup flour
1 teaspoon lemon juice	⅛ teaspoon salt

Squeeze thawed raspberries through a strainer, reserving juice. Discard seeds. Combine juice with sugar, cornstarch and salt; add lemon juice. Cook 1 minute, stirring constantly. Stir drained cherries into raspberry mixture and spoon into a lightly greased 1 quart baking dish. Cream margarine and sugar. Stir in flour and salt, blending just until mixture resembles coarse meal. Sprinkle mixture over top and bake at 375° for 30 minutes. Serves 6. *This is really good when topped with vanilla ice cream.*

Mrs. Andrew Tewell (Judy)

Any Fruit Cobbler

1 quart fresh peaches, cherries or other fruit in juice	1 cup flour
	3 teaspoons baking powder
2 cups sugar, divided	Dash of salt
½ cup butter	1 cup milk

Put fruit and 1 cup sugar in a saucepan; heat to boiling. Melt butter in shallow 8x11 inch baking pan. Mix remaining sugar with remainder of ingredients. Pour batter over melted butter. Spoon hot fruit over top. *Do not stir.* Bake at 350° for 30 minutes. Serves 8.

Mrs. Larry Hanners (Sally)

Coffee Praline Cream

2 envelopes unflavored gelatin	4 cups pecan praline ice cream
½ cup sugar	½ cup bourbon
1 cup coffee	Whipped cream
	Chocolate shavings

Mix gelatin, sugar and coffee in saucepan and heat, stirring until all gelatin is dissolved. Add ice cream and bourbon and pour into a mold. Chill overnight. Unmold and garnish with whipped cream and chocolate shavings. Serves 8 to 10.

Mrs. Denman Smith (Sandra)

Peach Cobbler

Pastry:

5 cups flour	1½ cups shortening
5 teaspoons sugar, divided	2 egg yolks
½ teaspoon baking powder	Cold water
½ teaspoon salt	

Sift all dry ingredients together, reserving 1 teaspoon sugar. Cut in shortening. Beat egg yolks together and add enough cold water to make one cup and mix with dry mixture. Blend pastry until soft. Divide pastry in half. Roll out half of pastry until ¼ inch thick. Place in a deep dish and sprinkle with remaining teaspoon of sugar. Pierce crust with fork. Bake at 350° for 3 to 5 minutes to seal bottom crust.

Peach Filling:

6 cups peeled and sliced peaches	2 teaspoons cornstarch
1 cup sugar	½ cup butter, divided
4 teaspoons cinnamon, divided	2 tablespoons sugar

Sprinkle peaches with 1 cup sugar, 2 teaspoons cinnamon and cornstarch. Cut butter into pieces and layer throughout filling. Roll out remaining pastry into 1 inch strips. Lay strips on top of pie and sprinkle with 2 teaspoons cinnamon and 2 tablespoons sugar. Dot with butter. Bake at 350° for 25 to 35 minutes. Serves 8.

Mrs. David Stallings (Sheila)

Pineapple Cream

½ cup butter	¾ cup crushed pineapple, well drained
1½ cups sifted powdered sugar	1 cup sour cream
2 eggs, separated	8 ladyfinger cookies, split in half
½ teaspoon lemon extract	Whipped cream, optional

Cream butter and sugar until fluffy. Add the egg yolks one at a time, beating well after each. Stir in lemon extract and pineapple. Mix in sour cream and gently fold in stiffly beaten egg whites. Line the bottom of a 9x5 inch loaf pan with half the ladyfingers. Top with half the filling. Repeat with a second layer. Refrigerate overnight. Serve with whipped cream. Serves 8 to 10.

Mrs. D. D. Baker, Jr. (Agnes)

Crepes

4   eggs
2   cups milk
1½ cups sifted flour

2   tablespoons sugar
½   teaspoon salt

Place all ingredients in a blender container, cover and blend on high until smooth. Chill 1 hour. Lightly butter a 6 to 8 inch crepe pan and set over medium heat. For each crepe, pour 2 tablespoons batter onto pan. Bake until golden brown on both sides, turning once. Cool. Serves 12.

The Cookbook Committee

Mincemeat Crepes with Bourbon Sauce

Mincemeat Filling:
1   jar (18 ounces) prepared
    mincemeat
1   cup chunky style
    applesauce

1   tablespoon lemon juice
1   teaspoon vanilla extract
½   teaspoon grated lemon
    peel

Combine all ingredients and heat until boiling. Set aside to cool. Fill crepes and when ready to serve, put into a 250° oven covered with a damp tea towel until warm through. Serve 2 crepes per person, with warm Bourbon Sauce. Yields filling for 12 crepes.

Bourbon Sauce:
½   cup butter
1   cup sugar
½   cup water

1   egg, beaten
½   cup bourbon

On low heat melt butter in a heavy saucepan. Stir in sugar and water, dissolving sugar. Remove from heat and let stand for 10 minutes. Beat in the egg and add bourbon. Yields sauce for 12 servings of crepes.

Mrs. Stephen Scheffe (Betsy)

Big Tex, the four story talking cowboy statue, greets the more than 3 million visitors who attend the State Fair of Texas, held annually during October in Dallas. It is the largest permanent fair in the United States.

Apple Cheese Dumplings

Apples:

6   Jonathon apples   ½   cup sugar
1   tablespoon butter   1½ teaspoons cinnamon

Wash, peel and core apples. Mix butter, sugar and cinnamon. Sprinkle evenly into the cavity of the six apples.

Cheese Pastry:

2   cups flour   ⅔   cup plus 2 tablespoons
1   teaspoon salt   shortening
1   cup grated Cheddar   4   tablespoons water
    cheese

Mix together flour, salt and cheese. Cut in shortening thoroughly. Sprinkle with water, a tablespoon at a time, mixing with fork until flour is moistened. Gather into a ball. Roll pastry and cut in squares large enough to cover apples. Wrap apples and seal.

Syrup:

1   cup sugar   4   tablespoons butter
2   cups water   ½   cup rum
½   teaspoon cinnamon

Combine all syrup ingredients in a saucepan and boil for 3 minutes. Arrange apples in a shallow pan, pour syrup over all and place in preheated 500° oven for 5 to 7 minutes. Reduce heat to 325° and bake 35 to 40 minutes. Serves 6.

Mrs. Roger Borgelt (Cindy)

Cherries Jubilee

½   cup slivered almonds   ¼   teaspoon almond extract
2   tablespoons butter   2   tablespoons kirsch or
1   can (16 ounces) bing   brandy
    cherries, pitted   1   quart vanilla ice cream
1½ teaspoons cornstarch

Sauté almonds in butter until golden. Set aside. Drain juice from cherries into a chafing dish or saucepan and stir in cornstarch; bring to a boil and cook until sauce thickens. Add cherries and almonds and heat. Stir in almond extract. Pour on kirsch or brandy and flame. Let flame burn out, then spoon cherries over vanilla ice cream. Serves 6.

Mrs. Marcus Bone (Beverly)

K-K's English Trifle

Sponge Cake:
3 eggs, separated
1 cup sugar
¼ cup cold water
1 teaspoon vanilla extract

1 cup plus 3 tablespoons cake flour
1½ teaspoons baking powder
¼ teaspoon salt

Beat egg yolks until light, adding sugar gradually. Add water and vanilla. Sift flour and resift with baking powder. Add sifted ingredients gradually to yolk mixture. Beat until blended. Whip the egg whites and salt until stiff, but not dry. Fold whites lightly into batter. Bake the cake in an ungreased 9 inch tube pan at 325° for 50 minutes. Invert to cool. Remove from pan when completely cool.

Custard Sauce:
3 eggs
⅜ cup sugar
⅛ teaspoon salt

3 cups milk
1 teaspoon vanilla extract

Beat eggs well and add sugar and salt. Scald the milk and stir it slowly into the eggs. Place the custard over a very low fire. Stir it constantly being careful that it does not boil, until it begins to thicken. You may wish to cook the custard in a double boiler. Chill thoroughly.

Filling and Frosting:
¾ cup dry sherry
1 jar (8 ounces) raspberry jam

1 cup whipping cream, whipped
1 package (8 ounces) whole almonds

To assemble trifle, arrange in layers; cake, sprinkle with sherry, jam, custard. Repeat layers three times. Cover the top with whipped cream and stand almonds on end in whipped cream. Serves 12 to 16.

Mrs. Bob Edgecomb (Mary)

Austin was chosen as the capital city of Texas in 1839. When scouts came upon the small settlement of Waterloo on the north bank of the Colorado River, they knew they had found the central site they were seeking, a community with rich farmland to the north and scenic hills to the west. Waterloo became Austin, named for the "Father of Texas," Stephen F. Austin.

Irish Trifle

2 packages (5⅝ ounces each) instant vanilla pudding
4 cups milk
2 containers (16 ounces each) frozen pound cake
¼ cup sherry

2 bags (1¼ pounds each) whole frozen strawberries
1 pint fresh strawberries
1 carton (8 ounces) whipped topping
½ cup toasted slivered almonds

Prepare vanilla pudding with milk according to directions on the package. Slice pound cake and cover the bottom of a large glass bowl. Sprinkle with part of the sherry and cover with a portion of the pudding and frozen strawberries. Top with more pound cake and continue the same layering procedure until you reach the top of the bowl. Refrigerate. Minutes before serving, decorate with fresh strawberries, whipped topping and toasted almonds. Serves 24.

Mrs. Richard Dorrell (Marianna)

Butterscotch Crunch

1 cup packed brown sugar, divided
3 tablespoons cornstarch
¼ teaspoon salt
3 cups milk
3 egg yolks, beaten

3 tablespoons butter
1½ teaspoons vanilla extract
3 bars (1½ ounces each) chocolate toffee candy, crushed
⅓ cup toasted coconut

In a large saucepan, combine ½ cup brown sugar, cornstarch and salt. Stir in milk. Cook and stir over medium heat until thick and bubbly. Gradually stir about 1 cup of the hot mixture into beaten egg yolks. Return to saucepan and bring to a boil; cook and stir 2 minutes more. Remove from heat. Add remaining ½ cup brown sugar, butter and vanilla, stirring gently just until combined. Cover surface of pudding with waxed paper and cool. Combine crushed candy bars and coconut. In 4 to 6 sherbet dishes alternate layers of pudding and candy mixture, starting and ending with pudding mixture. Chill. Serves 4 to 6.

Mrs. Jim Carpenter (Holly)

The test for ripeness in many fruits — peaches, pineapples, pears, to name a few — is whether they smell good. If the fruit has a pleasing aroma, then it is ripe.

Kiwi Cheese Cake

3 to 4 kiwi, peeled, puréed and strained
16 ounces cream cheese, cubed at room temperature
1 pound Ricotta cheese
2 cups sour cream
5 eggs
2 cups sugar
½ cup flour
½ cup butter
2 tablespoons fresh lime juice
1 teaspoon vanilla extract
Pinch salt
3 kiwi, peeled and sliced
½ cup apricot preserves
1 tablespoon fresh lemon juice

Butter bottom and sides of a 10 inch springform pan. Cook puréed kiwi in a small saucepan over medium heat until reduced to ¼ cup. In a mixing bowl combine kiwi, cheeses, sour cream, eggs, sugar, flour, butter, lime juice, vanilla extract and salt. Blending well at low speed, increase speed to medium and beat 20 minutes. Pour batter into prepared pan. Set pan on a baking sheet in the middle of the oven. Bake at 250° for 2¼ hours. Turn off heat and let cake remain in oven with door closed 1 hour longer. Transfer cake to rack and let cool in pan. Arrange sliced kiwi in overlapping pattern around outer edge of cake. Melt apricot preserves in a small saucepan over low heat. Press through sieve set over a small bowl. Stir in lemon juice. Brush apricot mixture over kiwi slices and top of cake. Cover and refrigerate overnight. To serve, bring cheese cake to room temperature. Remove springform pan and cut. Serves 10 to 12

Mrs. Marcus Bone (Beverly)

Souffle de Chocolat au Creme de Cacao

2 envelopes unflavored gelatin
½ cup water
⅔ cup creme de cacao
1¼ cups brown sugar, divided
1 package (12 ounces) semisweet chocolate chips
8 eggs, separated
½ teaspoon salt
2 cups whipping cream, whipped
½ cup chopped pecans

Mix gelatin, water, creme de cacao and ½ cup brown sugar in a saucepan. Heat and stir until dissolved. Add chocolate and stir until melted. Remove from heat and beat in egg yolks 1 at a time. Cool. Add salt to egg whites and beat until stiff, but not dry. Gradually beat in remaining sugar. Continue beating until very stiff. Fold egg whites into chocolate mixture. Then fold in whipped cream. Turn into a 2 quart souffle dish with a 2 inch collar. Chill for several hours. Sprinkle with pecans. Serves 12 to 14.

Mrs. Clark Rector (Sue)

California Fudge

1 package (12 ounces)
  semisweet chocolate chips
1 teaspoon vanilla extract
½ cup butter, melted
1 cup coarsely chopped
  walnuts

10 large marshmallows
1 can (5.33 ounces)
  evaporated milk
2 cups sugar

In a large bowl mix chocolate chips, vanilla, melted butter and nuts. Set aside. In a heavy pan bring marshmallows, milk and sugar to a boil; lower heat, but continue to boil for *exactly* 6 minutes, stirring constantly. Pour this mixture over the chocolate mixture in the bowl and stir constantly until chips are melted and butter is well incorporated. Pour into waxed paper-lined 9x9 inch pan. Cool overnight. Yields 81 one inch squares.

Mrs. Sid Mann (Kathi)

Microwave Fudge Delight

1 box (16 ounces) powdered
  sugar
½ cup cocoa
¼ cup plus 3 tablespoons
  milk

½ cup butter, softened
1 tablespoon vanilla extract
½ cup chopped pecans or
  crunchy peanut butter

Blend sugar and cocoa in a 2 quart mixing bowl. Add milk and butter. *Do not stir.* Microwave on HIGH for 2 minutes. Remove bowl from microwave and mix well with hand mixer for 1 to 2 minutes. Add vanilla and pecans or peanut butter. Pour into a greased 8 inch square dish. Place in refrigerator for at least 1 hour. Yields 64 one inch squares.

Mrs. Jerry Holder (Pat)

Peanut Butter Fudge

¾ cup evaporated milk
2 cups sugar
½ square baking chocolate
⅛ teaspoon salt
2 tablespoons dark corn
  syrup

2 tablespoons margarine
2 teaspoons vanilla extract
½ cup peanut butter
Pecans to taste

Heat evaporated milk, sugar, baking chocolate, salt and corn syrup in a saucepan over low to medium heat to soft ball stage, or 238°. Stir often. Add margarine, vanilla, peanut butter and pecans. Pour into a greased pan to cool. Yields 24 squares.

Mrs. Charlie Carpenter (Judy)

Date Loaf Candy

2 cups sugar	1 cup chopped dates
1 cup milk	2 cups chopped pecans
1 teaspoon butter	

Boil sugar and milk until the mixture forms the soft ball stage in water or 236° with a candy thermometer. Add dates and pecans and cook until a firm ball forms in water, or 240°. Remove from heat. Let stand until lukewarm, then beat as fudge. When mixture begins to thicken, pour onto a damp cloth and roll. Place in the refrigerator until cold and firm, then slice. Yields 24. *This is a family favorite. My grandmother always had this candy at her house during Christmas time.*

Mrs. Bill Hayes (Ginger)

Peanut Brittle

½ cup water	2 cups raw peanuts
3 cups sugar	3 teaspoons butter
1 cup white corn syrup	2 teaspoons baking soda

Combine water, sugar and corn syrup and cook to a hard crack stage. Add peanuts and cook until brown. Add butter and stir. Add soda and fold together. Pour immediately onto greased cookie sheet lined with foil. When set, break up into pieces. Yields about 30 pieces.

Mrs. Jim Rado (Vicki)

Meja

1 cup butter	1 tablespoon white corn syrup
1 cup blanched, slivered almonds	4 plain chocolate bars
1 cup sugar	⅓ cup finely chopped pecans
1 tablespoon water	

Melt butter in a heavy skillet. Add almonds, sugar, water and corn syrup. Cook on high flame, stirring constantly. Have some dark brown sugar sitting on the stove. Cook candy until one shade darker than brown sugar. Immediately pour and spread on a cookie sheet. Break chocolate bars on top of hot candy. Spread melted chocolate and sprinkle with pecans. Cool and break into pieces and enjoy. Yields 16 to 18.

Mrs. Jerry Dow (Annette)

Pecan Nut Caramels

¾ cup chopped pecans, divided
2 cups sugar
½ cup margarine

¾ cup white corn syrup
2 cups evaporated milk, divided

Butter an 8x8 inch pan. Sprinkle with ½ of the pecans. Combine sugar, margarine and corn syrup in a heavy saucepan. Stir in 1 cup evaporated milk. Bring to a boil over medium heat, stirring constantly. Add remaining milk slowly so mixture continues to boil. Cook, stirring frequently, until candy thermometer measures 244°, about 1½ hours. Pour into pan; sprinkle with remaining pecans. Cool and cut into squares. Wrap individually in plastic wrap. Yields 36 squares.

Mrs. Jim Schultz (Mary Kay)

Chewy Pralines

¾ cup sugar
¾ cup brown sugar
1 cup dark corn syrup
Pinch salt
⅓ cup water

⅓ cup butter plus 1 tablespoon
1 can (13 ounces) evaporated milk
3 cups chopped pecans
1 teaspoon vanilla extract

Combine sugars, syrup, salt, water and 1 tablespoon butter in a large saucepan and bring to a boil. Add remaining butter. Boil to 230° on a candy thermometer. Warm the milk and add 1 tablespoon at a time, to the sugar mixture, stirring constantly and keeping temperature at 230°. Leave 3 to 5 minutes. Remove from heat and stir in pecans and vanilla. Beat a little, then drop by teaspoonsful onto a buttered brown paper bag. Yields approximately 28 to 32.

Mrs. Ken McConchie (Paulette)

Caramel Pecan Chews

1 package (14 ounces) caramels
2 teaspoons water
2 teaspoons butter

2½ cups broken pecans
1 (8 ounces) milk chocolate bar
⅓ block paraffin

Heat caramels, water and butter in double boiler until melted. Add pecans and stir until well mixed. Drop by teaspoonsful onto waxed paper. Melt milk chocolate and paraffin in double boiler. Dip caramel pieces into chocolate and return to waxed paper. Yields 36.

Mrs. Jack Seiders (Peggy)

Chocolate Covered Cherries

30 to 40 maraschino cherries
with stems
1 box (16 ounces) powdered
sugar
⅓ cup butter
⅓ cup white corn syrup

Dash of salt
½ teaspoon vanilla extract
1 package (16 ounces)
dipping chocolate with
paraffin

Place cherries in a sieve and drain for 2 hours; pat very dry. Combine sugar, butter, corn syrup, salt and vanilla and mix well. Make a 1 inch ball of sugar mixture and flatten with your hand. Press and mold around cherry. Place on waxed paper-covered cookie sheet and freeze for 30 minutes. Melt chocolate in double boiler. Dip, holding cherries by stem. Let set at least 1 week to cordialize. Wrap in candy wrappers. Store in airtight container in single layers. Yields 48.

Mrs. Tommy Love (Sherry)

Harriette's Winter Strawberries

1 package (16 ounces) dates,
chopped
1 cup flaked coconut
1 cup sugar
½ cup butter
2 eggs, slightly beaten

⅛ teaspoon salt
3 cups crisp rice cereal
1 cup chopped walnuts
2 teaspoons vanilla extract
4 jars red sugar
2 cans green decorator icing

Combine dates, coconut, sugar, butter, eggs, and salt. Cook and stir over medium heat until thick and bubbly, 5 to 10 minutes. Remove from heat. Stir in cereal, walnuts and vanilla. Cool 10 minutes. Use 1 tablespoon for each strawberry. Shape and keeping fingers moist, roll in red sugar. Set and make leaves from the decorator icing to put on top. Yields 26.

Mrs. Dan O'Donnell (Sharon)

Chocolate Strawberries

1 pint strawberries

1 package (6 ounces)
semisweet chocolate chips

Wash and thoroughly dry strawberries, leaving stems attached. Melt chocolate chips and dip strawberries into chocolate. Place on waxed paper to cool and harden. Yields 18 to 24.

Mrs. John Perkins (Sandy)

White Chocolate Crunchies

2 pounds white chocolate
1 jar (13 ounces) dry roasted
peanuts

2 cups crisp rice cereal

Melt white chocolate slowly. Add nuts and cereal. Drop by spoonsful on waxed paper. Refrigerate for fast hardening. Yields 48.

Marsha Hynes

Wild Strawberry Divinity

3 cups sugar
¾ cup light corn syrup
¾ cup water
2 eggs, separated

1 package (3 ounces) wild
strawberry gelatin
½ cup flaked coconut
1 cup chopped pecans

Combine sugar, corn syrup and water in a 2 quart saucepan. Heat to boiling point, stirring constantly. Continue cooking without stirring to hard ball stage, 260°. Beat egg whites until foamy; add gelatin, beating until mixture forms peaks. Pour hot syrup slowly into beaten egg whites, beating constantly, on high setting, until candy holds its shape. Fold in coconut and pecans. Quickly drop from a greased teaspoon onto waxed paper or spread into a greased 9 inch square pan. Cool and cut into squares. Yields 4 dozen.

Mrs. Jim Schultz (Mary Kay)

Candied Orange Peel

2 large oranges
6 tablespoons sugar

¼ cup water

Using vegetable peeler, remove colored part of peel from oranges in pieces as wide as possible. Cut into thin stips, discarding ragged edges. Blanch peel in small saucepan of boiling water 5 minutes; drain and pat dry. Combine sugar and water in same saucepan and cook over low heat until sugar is melted, swirling pan occasionally. Stir in peel; increase heat to medium and cook until peel is glazed and candied, about 30 minutes. Remove from syrup using slotted spoon and arrange on rack to dry, separating pieces. Store in an airtight container. Yields ½ cup. *This may also be used for grapefruit which may be tinted red or green for the holiday season.*

Mrs. Steve McMillon (Mary Beth)

In the spring these delicately-tinted blossoms announce the promise of an ambrosial delight. Early summer brings the juicy, sweet peach to plump ripeness. Then, an assortment of wooden stands, pickup trucks and temporary lean-tos magically appear beside fruit-laden orchards throughout the Hill Country, and one can almost smell the delicious aroma of freshly baked pies and cobblers.

Serendipity pictured: Pork Roast, Peach Cake, Peach Pork Chops, Bellini, Peach Marmalade, Peach Chutney, Peach Cobbler, Peach Soup, Spiced Peaches, Peach Preserves, Peach Brandy and Peach Ice Cream.

Serendipity

Manifold Cooking

Cooking while driving, or manifold cooking, had its beginning with resourceful G. I.'s faced with the dreary prospect of cold beans. G.I.'s found they could heat their beans on the manifolds of their jeeps! This grew into the idea of wrapping packages of food in foil to place on the manifold of cars to cook while driving. Whatever you are cooking must be securely wrapped in several layers of extra heavy duty foil using the drugstore wrap and reversing the seam side with each wrapping. Try to wrap the packages to more or less conform to the shape of the manifold. The foil packages should be 'tied' onto the manifold with coated wire to prevent the wire from cutting the foil. Of course, no steam escapes during the cooking, so the food is literally cooked in its own juices. Meat does not brown; however, the meat may be quickly browned before packaging it. This also improves the flavor — just as it does when cooking in your kitchen. As with camp cooking, the exact cooking times are variable. As a general guideline, you can figure that 100 miles of manifold cooking, based on an average speed of 50 to 55 miles per hour, is equal to an hour in your home oven at 300° to 325°. In most cases, you should turn the package about halfway through the cooking period, but be careful not to puncture the foil! There are unlimited possibilities to manifold cooking — use your imagination! So, fill up the tank and let's go cooking! And may you never lose your pot roast.

Mrs. Jim Albrecht (Donne)

100 Mile Chicken

Broiling chickens, split in half
Butter mixed with garlic
powder

Salt and pepper to taste
Paprika, optional

Brush chicken halves liberally with melted butter and garlic powder. Season with salt and pepper. *You might also sprinkle with paprika for added color if you don't choose to brown the chickens before packaging.* Carefully pad with wads of foil any areas where bones might puncture the foil covering. Wrap as directed. Turn after 50 miles. Serves 4.

Mrs. Jim Albrecht (Donne)

200 Mile Pot Roast

3   pound boneless roast
1   envelope (2 ounces) onion
     soup mix

Canned potatoes, optional
Canned carrots, optional

Sprinkle half the soup mix in the center of a large piece of heavy duty foil. Place roast on the mix. *Browning the roast before packaging gives a good flavor, but this is not necessary.* Sprinkle the remaining soup mix on the meat. If adding vegetables, place them around the meat, making the package in the general shape of the manifold. Wrap as in general directions. Tie packet to manifold carefully with coated wire. After 100 miles, turn the package. If you have calculated correctly, another 100 miles will take you to your destination where you can enjoy, enjoy! Serves 6.

Mrs. Jim Albrecht (Donne)

Orange Liqueur

1   quart pure grain alcohol
1   orange

12 ounces sugar
16 ounces water

Pour a quart or liter of 180 proof alcohol in a wide mouth jar. Suspend an unblemished orange from a string, about ¼ inch above the alcohol and cap tightly. Let stand quietly in a dark place unopened for 14 days. Oils from the orange peel will drip into the alcohol, flavoring and turning it yellow. Mix the sugar and water, slowly boiling the solution until the syrup will almost thread when poured from a spoon. Pour this hot mixture into the jar after removing the orange. Stir slowly until mixed. Pour liqueur into an appropriate bottle. Yields 1½ quarts.

Mrs. Daniel O'Donnell (Sharon)

Scotch Liqueur

1½ cups pure grain alcohol,
     190 proof
2   jiggers Scotch whiskey
1½ cups sugar

1½ cups water
2   drops red food coloring
2   drops yellow food coloring
1   drop green food coloring

Mix alcohol and Scotch and set aside. In a saucepan heat the sugar and water until all sugar is dissolved; then cool. Add food colorings, then add alcohol. Pour into a jar and shake well. Let stand 2 weeks. Yields 8 (4 ounce) servings.

Mrs. Daniel O'Donnell (Sharon)

Irish Cream Liqueur

1¾ cups Irish whiskey
1 can (14 ounces) sweetened
    condensed milk
1 cup whipping cream
4 eggs

2 tablespoons chocolate
    syrup
2 teaspoons instant coffee
1 teaspoon vanilla extract
½ teaspoon almond extract

Place all ingredients in a blender and blend until smooth. If desired, serve over ice. Keeps up to 1 month in the refrigerator. Stir before serving. Yields 4 cups.

Mrs. Charles Smith (Jeannie)

Caswell House Mulling Spices

1 pound cinnamon bark
1 pound whole cloves
1 pound whole allspice
1 pound orange peel

½ ounce cinnamon oil
2 ounces orange oil
4 ounces lemon peel
1 ounce whole coriander

Mix all ingredients together well to coat spices with oils. Store in airtight container 7 to 10 days to allow flavors and scents to mix. After 10 days remove and package in 2 ounce plastic bags. Tie with ribbon for Christmas gifts. Makes 34 (2 ounce) packages.

Austin Junior Forum

Hot Spiced Cider

½ gallon apple juice,
    cranapple juice or apple
    cider

2 ounces Mulling Spices

Bring juice to simmer stage. Place spices in a tea ball or tie in a cheese cloth square. Add spices and cover; turn off heat and steep 15 to 30 minutes. Serves 8. *You can make another delicious drink for a cold winter night by substituting ½ gallon of Burgundy wine for the juice.*

Austin Junior Forum

 Most of the Vitamin C in Americans' diets comes from the orange.

Holiday Coffee

1   pound ground coffee
¾ to 1 ounce ground orange
    peel

4 to 6 tablespoons ground
    cinnamon

Combine all ingredients. Store in an airtight container until ready to use or to give as a gift. Yields 1 pound coffee.

Mrs. Denman Smith (Sandra)

Walking Pudding

Any flavor instant pudding
Milk

Ice cream cones

Mix instant pudding with milk in a bowl according to package directions. Pour into flat bottom ice cream cones. Refrigerate until set. Serves 8 to 10. *These are wonderful for children's parties or refreshments for Scout meetings. They are a lot of fun if several flavors are used.*

Mrs. James Albrecht (Donne)

Strawberry Jam

1   package (10 ounces)
    frozen strawberries
3   tablespoons powdered
    fruit pectin

1½ cups sugar
1   tablespoon lemon juice

Place frozen strawberries in a 2 quart glass bowl. Microwave on HIGH 2 minutes. Stir in pectin and microwave on HIGH 2 minutes. Stir in sugar and lemon juice. Microwave on HIGH 6 minutes, stirring midway through cooking. Pour into glass jars; cover and refrigerate when cooled to room temperature. Yields 2 cups.

Mrs. Stephen Scheffe (Betsy)

 Do not wash strawberries until ready to use. Do not take the stems off until after they are washed.

Plum Jam

5 pounds plums
5¾ cups sugar

Juice of 1 lemon
Finely grated peel of 1 lemon

Make a slit in side of the plums with a sharp knife. Remove and discard pits, leaving plums whole. Arrange plums in bottom of a heavy medium sized saucepan. Add sugar, lemon juice and peel. Set aside in cool area overnight. Bring plum mixture to a boil over medium high heat. Remove from heat and stir. Set aside in cool area 1 day. Bring plum mixture to a boil over medium high heat, skimming frequently. Remove fruit from saucepan using slotted spoon . Boil liquid until syrup registers 230° on a candy thermometer. Add fruit and return mixture to boil stage. Cool completely. Pour into sterlized jars and seal. Yields 4 pints.

Mrs. Don Bradford (Melinda)

Orange Nut Butter

½ cup chopped pecans
1 cup margarine, softened
2 tablespoons orange juice

2 tablespoons powdered sugar
1 tablespoon grated orange rind

Roast pecans in microwave on HIGH for 3 minutes. Combine margarine, orange juice, powdered sugar, orange rind and pecans and beat until fluffy. Yields about 1 cup. *This butter is great when used on muffins, fruit breads, waffles or pancakes.*

Mrs. Jim Schultz (Mary Kay)

No Salt Seasoning

1 teaspoon chili powder
2 teaspoons ground oregano
2 teaspoons pepper
1 tablespoon garlic powder
2 tablespoons dry mustard

6 tablespoons onion powder
3 tablespoons paprika
3 tablespoons poultry seasoning

Mix all ingredients together and use to season. Yields ½ cup.

Mrs. Tom Hollis (Doris)

Bread and Butter Pickles

16 cups (5 pounds) sliced
   cucumbers, about ¼ inch
6 cups (2½ pounds) thinly
   sliced boiling onions
½ cup salt
Water
3 trays ice cubes

5 cups sugar
5 cups cider vinegar
1½ teaspoons celery seed
1½ teaspoons mustard seed
1½ teaspoons turmeric
6 jars (1 pint) and lids

In a large bowl mix well the cucumbers, onions and salt. Cover mixture with cold water and ice cubes. Let stand 3 hours. Drain, rinse well and drain again. Let set about 30 minutes more. In large pot mix sugar, vinegar and seasonings. Heat mixture to boiling, stirring well. Reduce heat and simmer 30 minutes or until syrup is formed. Prepare jars and lids and leave in hot water. Over high heat add cucumbers and onion to syrup. Heat until almost boiling. Ladle hot mixture into hot jars, leaving ¼ inch head space. Use a spatula and release air bubbles. Wipe jar and close. Place jars on a rack in canner full of boiling water and cover with 1 to 2 inches of water. Reduce heat after bringing to a gentle boil and boil for 15 minutes. Remove jars; cool on rubber racks for 12 hours. Test seal and store. Use within the next year. Yields 6 pints.

Mrs. David Hart (Sue)

Dill Pickles

6 cups water
1 cup white vinegar
½ cup salt
Cucumbers
5 dill leaves

10 cloves garlic
10 hot red peppers
10 green grapes
5 grape leaves
Alum

Put water and vinegar into a saucepan and bring to a boil. Pack 5 to 6 quart jars tightly with fresh whole cucumbers. Add 1 dill leaf, 2 garlic cloves; 2 peppers; 2 grapes, 1 grape leaf and a pinch of alum to each jar. Fill jars with hot liquid and seal well. Pickles will be ready to eat in six weeks. Yields 5 to 6 quarts.

Mrs. Charlie Tupa (Sidney)

In 1836 the population of the Republic of Texas was no more than 50,000 and land sold for 50 cents an acre.

Ten Day Pickles

Use country well water or water without chlorine. One cup 100% grain vinegar per 1 gallon of water or 2 cups of 45% grain vinegar. One cup pickling salt per 1 gallon of water. Mix salt, vinegar and water in a container. In a large mouthed crock layer whole cucumbers mixed with dill and some chopped garlic, about 1 pod per 5 gallons of water, and grape leaves until crock is ¾ full ending with the grape leaves. Pour liquid solution in crock until top layer of grape leaves is covered. Place weight of some sort, I use a plate with a brick, on top so cucumbers and grape leaves will not float to top. Leave at 80 degrees F., more or less, for 10 days. After 10 days, leaves can be removed and pickles can be left in crock, if consumed in a reasonable amount of time or placed in containers with liquid mixture and stored. Refrigerate if desired.

The Honorable W. T. McDonald, Jr.

Pickled Vegetables

½ pound green beans, trimmed and halved	2 dried red chilies, seeded
¼ pound snow peas, trimmed and strings removed	1 piece (1 inch) fresh ginger, thinly sliced
1¼ cups rice vinegar	½ teaspoon salt
1¼ cups water	¼ pound small oranges, thinly sliced and seeded
½ cup sugar	

Bring a large amount of salted water to a rapid boil over high heat. Add beans and cook until crisp-tender, about 5 to 6 minutes. Remove with a slotted spoon and drain well. Rinse in cold water and drain again. Repeat with snow peas and dry. Combine vinegar, water, sugar, chilies, ginger and salt in a large saucepan over low heat and cook until sugar dissolves, swirling mixture occasionally. Increase heat and bring to a boil. Let boil 5 minutes. Add orange slices and let marinate until completely cool. Pack beans, peas, ginger and orange slices evenly into 1 quart jar with tight fitting lids. Pour in marinade. Refrigerate for at least 1 day or up to 3 days. Yields 1 quart.

Mrs. Don Bradford (Melinda)

Better to buy any fruit individually than from a bag. One rotten apple can spoil the whole bag!

Dilly Beans

2	pounds trimmed fresh green beans	4	heads fresh dill
1	teaspoon cayenne pepper, divided	¼	cup salt
		2½	cups white vinegar
4	cloves garlic	2½	cups water

Pack the beans lengthwise into hot, sterile canning jars, leaving a ¼ inch headspace. To each pint, add ¼ teaspoon cayenne pepper, 1 clove garlic and 1 head dill; set aside. Combine salt, vinegar and water in a saucepan and bring to boil. Pour over beans leaving ¼ inch headspace. Remove air bubbles with a non-metallic spatula. Adjust caps. Process 10 minutes in boiling water bath. Yields 4 pints.

Nancy Young Chandler

Pickled Okra

2	pounds okra, 3 inch pods	2½	cups white vinegar
8	sprigs dill	2½	cups water
4	small hot red peppers	¼	cup salt
4	cloves garlic	1	tablespoon mustard seed

Wash and sterilize 4 pint jars. Prick each okra pod with fork. Pack okra lengthwise, with points alternating up and down in hot jars. Place 2 sprigs dill, 1 pepper, and 1 clove garlic in each jar. Heat vinegar, water, salt and mustard seed to boiling. Pour boiling brine to within ½ inch of top of jars; seal. Process in boiling water bath 20 minutes. Yields 4 pints.

Mrs. Marcus Bone (Beverly)

Pickled Mushrooms

2	cans (4 ounces each) mushroom caps	1	sprig parsley
		1	bay leaf
⅔	cup mild cider or wine vinegar	3	ribs of celery with leaves, sliced
6	peppercorns	¼	cup olive oil
1	slice onion		

Drain mushrooms and set aside. Mix vinegar, peppercorns, onion, parsley, bay leaf and celery in a saucepan and boil for 10 minutes. Pour over mushrooms. Cool. Add olive oil. Put into a tightly covered jar. Shake well. Refrigerate at least one day before serving. Serves 6.

Susan Hutchison

Marinated Mushrooms

⅔ cup olive oil
½ cup water
Juice of 2 lemons
1 bay leaf
2 cloves garlic, coarsely
   chopped

6 peppercorns
½ teaspoon salt
1 pound small whole
   mushrooms

Combine all ingredients except mushrooms in a stainless steel skillet and bring to a boil over moderate heat. Reduce heat; cover and simmer for 15 minutes. Strain marinade and return to skillet. Bring to simmer over low heat. Drop in mushrooms and simmer for 5 minutes, turning the mushrooms several times. Let mushrooms cool in marinade. Serve at room temperature, or after mushrooms have cooled, refrigerate and serve cold. In either case, before serving, lift mushrooms out of the marinade with a slotted spoon, drain and arrange on a platter as part of an antipasto or in a bowl by themselves. Yields 2 cups.

Mrs. Don Bradford (Melinda)

Texas Caviar

5 cups water
2 cups dried blackeyed peas
3 teaspoons salt, divided
¾ cup red wine vinegar
½ teaspoon black pepper

2 cups oil
1 medium onion
2 cloves garlic
1 tablespoon minced parsley

Bring water to boil over high heat. Add peas and cook 2 minutes. Turn off heat and let peas soak for 1 hour. Add 1 teaspoon salt and boil again. Simmer 40 to 50 minutes. Drain. Combine vinegar, 2 teaspoons salt and pepper in a bowl. Pour oil into mix, beating constantly until thick and smooth. Peel onion and slice into separate rings. Peel garlic and bruise with a knife handle. Add to marinade, along with peas and parsley. Cover and refrigerate for 3 days. Remove garlic and serve. Serves 8 to 12. *Texans like to have blackeyed peas on New Year's Day to bring good luck and wealth during the coming year. This is a delicious way to fulfill this tradition.*

Mrs. Ed Fomby (Beaty)

Spiced Cantaloupe

4 medium cantaloupes
12 cups water
2 teaspoons powdered alum
4 cinnamon sticks, 3 inches long

1 tablespoon whole cloves
1 tablespoon whole allspice
4 cups sugar
2 cups white vinegar
1 cup water

Quarter melons, remove seeds and rind. Cut melons crosswise into ¼ inch pieces and place in a large container. Combine 12 cups water and alum; pour over melon. Cover and let stand overnight. Drain, rinse and set aside. Tie cinnamon sticks, cloves and allspice in a cheesecloth bag. Add to sugar, vinegar and 1 cup water in a large saucepan and simmer 5 minutes. Add melon and simmer 20 minutes, stirring occasionally. Remove spice bag and continue to simmer while packing melon into hot canning jars. Cover melon with vinegar solution leaving ½ inch headspace. Remove air bubbles with a non-metallic spatula. Adjust caps and process 5 minutes in boiling water bath. Yields 6 to 7 pints.

Nancy Young Chandler

Spiced Peaches

Wash peaches and peel. Remove any bad spots and leave peaches whole. Place peaches in a large pan; cover with water and bring to a boil. Continue boiling for 30 minutes. Strain liquid and put 3 cups of liquid in another pan with 2 cups sugar. Bring to a boil and add a healthy handful of whole mixed spices. Cinnamon and cloves may be used. Bring to a boil and add enough whole peaches to fill two quart jars. Allow peaches to get slightly soft; place in jars and fill with liquid from peaches. Add 3 cups water and 2 cups sugar. Add spices as needed for flavor. Continue cooking peaches in same manner but only 2 quarts at a time so peaches don't get too soft. Can be eaten immediately but will last in jars indefinitely. Yields 2 quarts.

Mrs. Charlie Tupa (Sidney)

Spiked Watermelon

1 watermelon
1 cup orange juice

¼ cup rum, or more to taste
⅓ cup sugar

Cut the melon lengthwise close to the top. Remove all the meat with a melon-baller and discard the seeds. Purée enough meat to make 1 cup liquid. Add the orange juice, rum and sugar to the purée. Mix until the sugar is dissolved. Return melon balls to cavity and cover with liquid. Chill and serve. Serves 10.

Mrs. Jim Smith (Jare)

Spiced Grapes

1 pound tokay grapes, cut in half and seeded
1½ cups sugar
½ cup cider vinegar
¼ cup maraschino cherry juice
3 sticks cinnamon

Place grapes in a 1 quart jar or glass container. Heat remaining ingredients to boiling in small saucepan, stirring constantly until sugar is dissolved. Reduce heat. Simmer uncovered 5 minutes. Pour hot syrup on grapes; cool. Cover and refrigerate at least 2 hours. Serves 6. *These grapes are very good served with a glazed ham.*
Mrs. Marcus Bone (Beverly)

Peach Chutney

4 quarts peeled, chopped peaches
1 cup chopped onion
1 clove garlic, chopped
1 hot pepper pod
1 cup raisins
1 quart white vinegar
2 tablespoons ground ginger
¼ cup mustard seeds
3 cups brown sugar
2 teaspoons salt

Mix all ingredients together and cook until thick, stirring frequently. Pour into hot sterilized jars. Seal immediately. Yields 4 quarts.
Mrs. Charles R. Smith (Jeannie)

Fresh Mint Chutney

2 ounces fresh mint leaves
2 to 3 tablespoons chopped onion
1 tablespoon chopped green chilies
1 teaspoon chopped fresh ginger
1 teaspoon sugar
Salt
1 tablespoon cider vinegar

Combine all ingredients except vinegar in processor or blender and mix to a paste. With machine running, gradually add vinegar. Transfer to a small container with tight-fitting lid and refrigerate up to 2 days. Yields ¾ cup.

Nikki Kincaid Keller

Peaches do not keep well and should be used soon after buying. They keep best in the refrigerator.

Cranberry Apple Relish

2	cups sugar	2	tablespoons grated orange peel
1	cup water	1	tablespoon grated lemon peel
1	pound cranberries, washed and drained	2	sticks cinnamon
2	large apples, cored, peeled and sliced		

Dissolve sugar in water and bring to a boil; add cranberries, apple, lemon and orange peel and cinnamon sticks. Bring back to a boil and then simmer for about 10 minutes, or until the skin of the berries bursts and apples are tender. Chill. Yields 5 cups. *This can be made ahead and will keep for 6 to 8 weeks. Very good served with pork or fowl.*

Mrs. Bernard Vise (Marion)

Tomato Relish

3	medium tomatoes, peeled and diced	¼	cup white vinegar
1	green bell pepper, seeded and diced	¼	cup sugar
1	onion, chopped	1½	teaspoons salt
½	cup finely chopped celery	¼	teaspoon pepper
		¾ to 1	cup cold water

Combine tomatoes, pepper, onion and celery in a large bowl. Mix vinegar, sugar, salt and pepper in a small bowl. Add water to vinegar mixture as desired. Pour over vegetables. Cover and refrigerate at least 8 hours. Drain mixture thoroughly before serving. Yields 4 cups.

Mrs. Greg Gordon (Kathy)

Hot Pepper Relish

15 to 20	hot peppers or banana jalapeño peppers, chopped	1	clove garlic, minced
6	medium onions, chopped	1	can (8 ounces) tomato sauce
			Salt to taste

Put all ingredients into a saucepan and bring to a boil. Boil for 5 minutes, then pour into sterilized half pint jars. Seal. Yields 10 half pints.

Bill Aston

Jean's Vegetable Relish

6 large green tomatoes, chopped	2 tablespoons salt
6 medium onions, chopped	4 cups sugar
1 head cabbage, shredded	2 quarts white vinegar
6 green bell peppers, finely chopped	2 teaspoons cloves
6 red bell peppers, finely chopped	2 teaspoons allspice
3 small hot peppers, finely chopped	2 teaspoons ginger
	2 teaspoons dry mustard
	2 teaspoons cinnamon
	2 teaspoons turmeric

Mix all vegetables together and sprinkle with salt and sugar. Set aside. Mix vinegar and spices into two quart pans, halving the batch into two pans. Bring to a boil . Add vegetables and return to a boil until vegetables look clear. Pour into pint jars and seal. Yields 6 jars.

Mrs. M.J. Moore (Jean)

Never Fail Hollandaise Sauce

3 egg yolks	½ cup butter, room temperature
1 tablespoon lemon juice	¼ cup boiling water
½ teaspoon salt	
⅛ teaspoon white pepper	

Put all ingredients except water in a blender. Blend about 10 seconds or until smooth. Add boiling water gradually as blending continues. Pour into top of double boiler and cook over hot water, stirring constantly until sauce thickens. Keep warm until serving time or refrigerate in a covered jar. Yields 1 cup.

Mrs. Terry Arndt (Barbara)

Microwave Hollandaise Sauce

¼ cup butter	1 tablespoon lemon juice
2 egg yolks	¼ teaspoon salt
1 tablespoon half and half cream	¼ teaspoon dry mustard

Put butter in a 2 cup glass measuring cup. Microwave 30 seconds to melt. Add egg yolks and whip with a wire whisk. Add the remaining ingredients and whip until well mixed. Microwave 1 minute, stirring about every 15 seconds. Do not overcook or it will curdle. Serve warm over vegetables or fish. Yields ⅔ cup.

Mrs. Greg Gordon (Kathy)

Ham Glaze

½ cup red cinnamon jelly   ⅛ teaspoon dry mustard
¼ cup corn syrup   Whole cloves, optional

Heat all ingredients over low heat, stirring constantly until jelly is melted. About 30 minutes before ham is done, remove from oven and cut surface ¼ inch deep in diamond pattern. If desired, insert whole clove in each diamond. Spoon ham glaze onto ham every 10 minutes for the remaining cooking time. Yields ¾ cup.

Mrs. Marcus Bone (Beverly)

Raisin Sauce for Ham

1 cup brown sugar   ¼ cup sherry
2 tablespoons cornstarch   ½ cup raisins
1 cup water

Mix sugar and cornstarch. Add water and sherry. Cook until thickened. Add raisins. Baste ham. Yields 1 cup.

Mrs. Stephen Scheffe (Betsy)

Frying Batter

1 cup flour   1 egg, slightly beaten
½ teaspoon salt   ½ cup ice water
½ teaspoon sugar   ½ cup beer

Combine flour, salt and sugar. Add egg, water and beer, and mix thoroughly. This makes a very light batter to use with shrimp, onion, okra, etc. Yields 2 cups.

Mrs. Jerry Holder (Pat)

Shrimp Batter

1 cup flour   ¼ teaspoon baking powder
¼ cup cornstarch   1½ cups water
⅛ cup cornmeal   ¼ cup milk

Mix all ingredients together and beat well. Use to coat shrimp, vegetables or fish before frying. Yields 3 cups.

Mrs. Charlie Tupa (Sidney)

Cherry Sauce for Ham

1 jar (10 ounces) apple jelly
2 tablespoons prepared
  mustard
⅓ cup unsweetened
  pineapple juice

¼ cup white wine
1 can (21 ounces) cherry pie
  filling
1 cup golden raisins

Combine apple jelly, mustard, pineapple juice and white wine in saucepan and heat to boiling. Just before the ham is finished baking, approximately 30 to 40 minutes, put one-third of the sauce on ham and continue baking and basting occasionally. Before serving, add cherry pie filling, raisins and some ham juice to the rest of the sauce and bring to a boil. Serve in a side dish with the ham. Serves 10 to 12

Mrs. Dudley Baker (Kathy)

Mustard Sauce

1½ tablespoons Dijon mustard
¾ cup plain yogurt
1 cup beef broth
1 tablespoon cornstarch

1 tablespoon dry vermouth
Salt and pepper to taste
1 tablespoon minced parsley

Blend mustard with yogurt and set aside. In a small pan heat the broth and beat in the yogurt mixture. Cook over low heat; do not allow to boil. Mix the cornstarch and vermouth together and add to mixture, stirring to blend well. Cook over low heat, stirring constantly. Add salt, pepper and parsley just before serving. Yields 2 cups sauce.

Mrs. Ernest Butler (Sarah)

Bing Cherry Sauce

1 can (16 ounces) pitted
  bing cherries
1 tablespoon sugar

1 tablespoon cornstarch
½ cup reserved cherry syrup
1½ teaspoons rum flavoring

Drain cherries and reserve ½ cup syrup. In a saucepan combine sugar and cornstarch. Add reserved cherry syrup and cook, stirring constantly, until mixture thickens and boils. Cool. Stir in rum flavoring and cherries. Yields 2 cups. *This sauce is very good spooned over ice cream pies or ice cream.*

Mrs. Marvin Sentell (Julie)

Otelia's Bar-B-Que Sauce

1 cup cooking oil	⅓ cup chili powder
⅔ cup flour	½ cup paprika
2 large onions, chopped	1 teaspoon red pepper
4 cloves garlic, minced	½ cup sugar
½ bunch parsley, chopped	1 cup white vinegar
3 ribs celery, chopped	½ cup margarine
2 green bell peppers, chopped	Juice of 2 lemons
8 cups water	1 tablespoon black pepper
2 cans (6 ounces each) tomato paste	Salt to taste

Heat oil and add flour to brown while stirring constantly to make a roux. Cook until dark brown. Add onion, garlic, parsley, celery and bell peppers. Cook 15 to 20 minutes until vegetables are soft. Add this mixture to a 6 quart pan. Add water, tomato paste, chili powder, paprika, red pepper, sugar, vinegar, margarine and lemon juice. Cook mixture over low heat until all of the vegetables have disappeared, about 2 hours. Add water as necessary; the sauce should not be too thick. It should be slightly thinner than catsup. Yields 1 gallon of sauce. *This recipe was obtained from Mrs. Otelia Collins of Galveston, Texas, who operated a very popular Bar-B-Que establishment for many years in Galveston. This sauce may also be frozen or refrigerated for a prolonged period of time.*

Dr. Gerald A. Beathard

Barney's Barbeque Sauce

1 cup margarine	2 cloves garlic, chopped
¼ to ½ cup water	Salt and pepper to taste
2 onions, chopped	1 teaspoon imitation smoke flavor
2 ribs celery with leaves, chopped	1½ cups white vinegar

Melt margarine with water. Add onions, celery, garlic, salt and pepper and simmer for 20 minutes. Add more water if needed. Remove from stove and add imitation smoke flavor and vinegar. When cool, process in a blender. Yields 4 cups.

Mrs. Robert Brown (Mary)

Spices were used in ancient times to retard food spoilage.

Nani's Barbeque Sauce

1 onion, finely chopped
2 tablespoons oil
3 tablespoons vinegar
2 tablespoons brown sugar
¼ cup lemon juice
1 cup catsup
3 tablespoons Worcestershire sauce
½ teaspoon prepared mustard
1 teaspoon salt
1½ teaspoons chili powder
2 tablespoons parsley flakes
1 cup water

Sauté onion in oil; drain. Add remaining ingredients and simmer for 30 to 45 minutes. Yields 2 cups. *This is wonderful barbeque sauce for chicken.*

Mrs. Bryan Wooten (Sherri)

Basting Sauce for Barbecued Chicken

2 cups margarine
1 cup lemon juice
1 cup water
5 tablespoons salt
3 tablespoons paprika
1 tablespoon garlic powder
1 tablespoon curry
3 tablespoons black pepper

Melt margarine in a 2 quart saucepan. Add remaining ingredients; stir to mix well. Place halved chickens on grill. Turn frequently. Baste chickens liberally with a basting brush each time they are turned. Cook until leg bone is loose. Yields basting sauce for 4 chickens. *This sauce is not edible; however, it makes a fantastic barbecued chicken. The use of barbecue sauce when chicken is served is generally unnecessary.*

Dr. Gerald A. Beathard

Baked Potato Chips

3½ pounds red or white boiling potatoes
6 tablespoons butter, melted
Salt and pepper

Position oven racks in upper and lower third of oven and preheat to 500°. Cut potatoes crosswise into ⅛ inch thick slices. Lightly grease 2 baking sheets. Arrange potato slices in a single layer on prepared sheets. Brush generously with butter. Bake 7 minutes; switch pan positions and continue baking until potatoes are crisp and browned about edges, about 7 to 9 minutes. Sprinkle with salt and pepper and serve immediately. Serves 6 to 8.

Mrs. Don Bradford (Melinda)

Granola

4 cups rolled oats	1 cup coconut flakes,
4 cups wheat flakes	optional
2 cups sunflower seeds	½ to ¾ cup safflower oil
2 cups raw wheat germ	1 to 1½ cups honey
1 cup pecans, optional	1 teaspoon cinnamon
	2 cups dried fruit, optional

Combine all dry ingredients, except fruit and cinnamon. Combine oil, honey and cinnamon; mix well. Pour over dry ingredients, blending well. Pour into 2 or 3 large cake pans; spread thinly and toast at 300° until light golden brown, about 30 to 45 minutes. Stir every 10 minutes to toast evenly. Remove from oven and cool. Add fruit. Store in refrigerator in tightly sealed containers. This will keep for months. Yields 16 cups. *You may use any combination of fruits and/or nuts; for example pears and almonds, cinnamon and apricots, pineapple and cashews. This makes a nice gift. It is a delicious topping for ice cream and a great after school snack.*

Dr. Rose Ann Shorey

Maple Almond Granola

⅔ cup maple syrup	4 cups rolled oats
2 tablespoons oil	1 cup unblanched almonds
½ teaspoon vanilla extract	

Mix all ingredients together. Place on two lightly oiled 15½x10½x1 inch baking pans. Bake at 300° for 15 minutes. Yields 6½ cups. *Most prepared granolas are full of salt; this one is salt free.*

Mrs. Ernest Butler (Sarah)

Cereal Crunch

½ cup dark corn syrup	½ teaspoon salt
½ cup brown sugar	6 cups round oat cereal
¼ cup margarine	

Combine corn syrup, brown sugar, margarine and salt. Heat in a small saucepan until sugar dissolves. Pour over cereal and coat evenly. Bake in ovenproof dish at 325° for 15 minutes. Yields 7 cups.

Mrs. Charles Cantwell (Winn)

Equivalents

Ingredient	Equivalents
3 medium apples	3 cups sliced apples
3 medium bananas	2½ cups sliced, 2 cups mashed banana
1 medium lemon	2 to 3 tablespoons juice and 2 teaspoons grated rind
1 medium lime	1½ to 2 tablespoons juice
1 medium orange	⅓ cup juice and 2 tablespoons grated rind
4 medium peaches	2 cups sliced peaches
4 medium pears	2 cups sliced pears
1 quart strawberries	4 cups sliced strawberries
1 pound head cabbage	4½ cups shredded cabbage
1 pound carrots	3 cups shredded carrots
2 medium corn ears	1 cup whole kernel corn
1 large green pepper	1 cup diced green pepper
1 pound head lettuce	6¼ cups torn lettuce
8 ounces raw mushrooms	1 cup sliced cooked mushrooms
1 medium onion	½ cup chopped onion
3 medium white potatoes	2 cups cubed cooked or 1¾ cups mashed white potatoes
3 medium sweet potatoes	3 cups sliced sweet potatoes
8 slices cooked bacon	½ cup crumbled bacon
1 pound American or Cheddar cheese	4 to 5 cups shredded cheese
4 ounces cheese	1 cup shredded cheese
5 large whole eggs	1 cup eggs
6 to 7 large eggs	1 cup egg whites
11 to 12 large eggs	1 cup egg yolks
1 cup quick-cooking oats	1¾ cups cooked oats
1 cup uncooked long grain rice	3 to 4 cups cooked rice
1 cup pre-cooked rice	2 cups cooked rice
1 pound coffee	40 cups perked coffee
1 pound pitted dates	2 to 3 cups chopped dates
1 pound all-purpose flour	4 cups flour
1 pound granulated sugar	2 cups sugar
1 pound powdered sugar	3½ cups powdered sugar
1 pound brown sugar	2¼ cups firmly packed brown sugar
1 cup (4 ounces) uncooked macaroni	2¼ cups cooked macaroni
4 ounces uncooked noodles	2 cups cooked noodles
7 ounces uncooked spaghetti	4 cups cooked spaghetti
1 pound shelled nuts	4 cups chopped nuts

1 cup whipping cream	2 cups whipped cream
1 cup soft bread crumbs	2 slices fresh bread
1 pound crab in shell	¾ to 1 cup flaked crab
1½ pounds fresh, unpeeled shrimp	2 cups cooked, peeled, deveined shrimp
1 pound fresh small shrimp . . .	35 or more shrimp
1 pound fresh medium shrimp .	26 to 35 shrimp
1 pound fresh large shrimp	21 to 25 shrimp
1 pound fresh jumbo shrimp . .	less than 20 shrimp

Crackers

19 chocolate wafers	1 cup crumbs
14 graham cracker squares	1 cup fine crumbs
28 saltines	1 cup finely crushed crumbs
22 vanilla wafers	1 cup finely crushed crumbs

Substitutions

Recipe Ingredients	Substitutions
1 cup sour or buttermilk	1 tablespoon vinegar or lemon juice plus sweet milk to make 1 cup
1 cup commercial sour cream .	1 tablespoon lemon juice plus evaporated milk to equal 1 cup
1 cup yogurt	1 cup sour or buttermilk
1 whole egg	2 egg yolks plus 1 tablespoon water
1 tablespoon cornstarch	2 tablespoons all-purpose flour
1 teaspoon baking powder	½ teaspoon cream of tartar plus ¼ teaspoon baking soda
1 cup cake flour	1 cup all-purpose flour minus 2 tablespoons
1 cup self-rising flour	1 cup all-purpose flour plus 1 teaspoon baking powder and ½ teaspoon salt
1 cup honey	1¼ cups sugar plus ¼ cup liquid
1 ounce unsweetened chocolate	3 tablespoons cocoa plus 1 tablespoon butter or margarine
1 pound fresh mushrooms	6 ounces canned mushrooms
1 tablespoon fresh herbs	1 teaspoon ground or crushed dry herbs
1 teaspoon onion powder	2 teaspoons minced onion
1 clove fresh garlic	1 teaspoon garlic salt or ⅛ teaspoon garlic powder

Measurements to Remember

3 teaspoons	=	1 tablespoon
4 tablespoons	=	¼ cup
8 tablespoons	=	½ cup
16 tablespoons	=	1 cup
5 tablespoons plus 1 teaspoon	=	⅓ cup
4 ounces	=	½ cup
8 ounces	=	1 cup
16 ounces	=	1 pound
1 ounce	=	2 tablespoons fat or liquid
2 cups fat	=	1 pound
2 cups	=	1 pint
1 pound butter	=	2 cups or 4 sticks
2 pints	=	1 quart
4 cups	=	1 quart

The Metric System

2 cups	=	473 milliliters
1 cup	=	237 milliliters
¾ cup	=	177 milliliters
⅔ cup	=	157 milliliters
½ cup	=	118 milliliters
⅓ cup	=	79 milliliters
¼ cup	=	59 milliliters
1 tablespoon	=	15 milliliters
1 teaspoon	=	5 milliliters
1 fluid ounce	=	30 milliliters

How to Convert:

liters	x 2.1 = pints		kilograms	x 2.2	= pounds
liters	x 1.06 = quarts		grams	x .035	= ounces
cups	x .24 = liters		pounds	x .45	= kilograms
gallons	x 3.8 = liters		ounces	x 28	= grams

Temperatures:

250 degrees Fahrenheit = 121 degrees Celsius
300 degrees Fahrenheit = 149 degrees Celsius
350 degrees Fahrenheit = 177 degrees Celsius
400 degrees Fahrenheit = 205 degrees Celsius
450 degrees Fahrenheit = 232 degrees Celsius

Index

G

P

PASTA

W

Austin Junior Forum Publications
P.O. Box 26628
Austin, Texas 78755-0628

Please send _____ copies of *Lone Star Legacy II*   @ $14.95 each_____
Please send _____ copies of *Lone Star Legacy*
 (Bluebonnet Edition)   @ $14.95 each_____
Texas residents add 5⅛% sales tax   @   .77 each_____
Postage and handling   @ 2.00 each_____
Gift wrap   @ 2.00 each_____
    Total Enclosed_____

Name _____

Address _____

City _____State _____Zip _____

Make checks payable to *Lone Star Legacy.*

Austin Junior Forum Publications
P.O. Box 26628
Austin, Texas 78755-0628

Please send _____ copies of *Lone Star Legacy II*   @ $14.95 each_____
Please send _____ copies of *Lone Star Legacy*
 (Bluebonnet Edition)   @ $14.95 each_____
Texas residents add 5⅛% sales tax   @   .77 each_____
Postage and handling   @ 2.00 each_____
Gift wrap   @ 2.00 each_____
    Total Enclosed_____

Name _____

Address _____

City _____State _____Zip _____

Make checks payable to *Lone Star Legacy.*

Austin Junior Forum Publications
P.O. Box 26628
Austin, Texas 78755-0628

Please send _____ copies of *Lone Star Legacy II*   @ $14.95 each _____
Please send _____ copies of *Lone Star Legacy*
 (Bluebonnet Edition)   @ $14.95 each_____
Texas residents add 5⅛% sales tax   @   .77 each_____
Postage and handling   @ 2.00 each_____
Gift wrap   @ 2.00 each_____
    Total Enclosed_____

Name _____

Address _____

City _____State _____Zip _____

Make checks payable to *Lone Star Legacy.*

If you would like to see *Lone Star Legacy* or *Lone Star Legacy II* in your area, please send the names and addresses of your local gift or book stores.

If you would like to see *Lone Star Legacy* or *Lone Star Legacy II* in your area, please send the names and addresses of your local gift or book stores.

If you would like to see *Lone Star Legacy* or *Lone Star Legacy II* in your area, please send the names and addresses of your local gift or book stores.

Austin Junior Forum Publications
P.O. Box 26628
Austin, Texas 78755-0628

Please send _____ copies of *Lone Star Legacy II*   @ $14.95 each_____
Please send _____ copies of *Lone Star Legacy*
  (Bluebonnet Edition)   @ $14.95 each_____
Texas residents add 5⅛% sales tax   @   .77 each_____
Postage and handling   @   2.00 each_____
Gift wrap   @   2.00 each_____
                                                       Total Enclosed_____

Name _____

Address _____

City _____State _____Zip _____

Make checks payable to *Lone Star Legacy*.

Austin Junior Forum Publications
P.O. Box 26628
Austin, Texas 78755-0628

Please send _____ copies of *Lone Star Legacy II*   @ $14.95 each_____
Please send _____ copies of *Lone Star Legacy*
  (Bluebonnet Edition)   @ $14.95 each_____
Texas residents add 5⅛% sales tax   @   .77 each_____
Postage and handling   @   2.00 each_____
Gift wrap   @   2.00 each_____
                                                       Total Enclosed_____

Name _____

Address _____

City _____State _____Zip _____

Make checks payable to *Lone Star Legacy*.

Austin Junior Forum Publications
P.O. Box 26628
Austin, Texas 78755-0628

Please send _____ copies of *Lone Star Legacy II*   @ $14.95 each_____
Please send _____ copies of *Lone Star Legacy*
  (Bluebonnet Edition)   @ $14.95 each_____
Texas residents add 5⅛% sales tax   @   .77 each_____
Postage and handling   @   2.00 each_____
Gift wrap   @   2.00 each_____
                                                       Total Enclosed_____

Name _____

Address _____

City _____State _____Zip _____

Make checks payable to *Lone Star Legacy*.

If you would like to see *Lone Star Legacy* or *Lone Star Legacy II* in your area, please send the names and addresses of your local gift or book stores.

If you would like to see *Lone Star Legacy* or *Lone Star Legacy II* in your area, please send the names and addresses of your local gift or book stores.

If you would like to see *Lone Star Legacy* or *Lone Star Legacy II* in your area, please send the names and addresses of your local gift or book stores.